Industrial Economics

ROGER CLARKE

Industrial Economics

Basil Blackwell

© Roger Clarke 1985

First published 1985

Basil Blackwell Ltd
108 Cowley Road, Oxford OX4 1JF, UK

Basil Blackwell Inc.
432 Park Avenue South, Suite 1505,
New York, NY 10016, USA

British Library Cataloguing in Publication Data
Clarke, Roger
   Industrial economics.
   1. Industrial organization (Economic theory)
   I. Title
   338   HD2326
   ISBN 0–631–12958–8
   ISBN 0–631–14305–X Pbk

Library of Congress Cataloging in Publication Data
Clarke, Roger.
   Industrial economics.
   Includes index.
   1. Industrial organization (Economic theory)
   I. Title.
   HD2326.C5 1985   338.8   85–4023
   ISBN 0–631–12958–8
   ISBN 0–631–14305–X (pbk.)

Typeset by Advanced Filmsetters (Glasgow) Ltd
Printed in Great Britain by Bell and Bain Ltd, Glasgow

For Janet, Robin and Richard

Contents

Preface

This book has grown out of a course in industrial economics which I have given to third-year undergraduate students at Sheffield University for a number of years. In writing it, I have sought to provide a balanced coverage of the core material in the field including more recent theoretical (and empirical) developments. This, in my view, fills an important gap in the existing market in that, while a number of useful textbooks are available, they tend either to present material at too elementary a level or, alternatively, to offer treatments which are too comprehensive and/or advanced for textbook undergraduate teaching. A need, therefore, exists for a reasonably concise and up-to-date treatment, which is also accessible to undergraduate students, and this has been my main aim in writing this book.

Since the material covered in an industrial economics course ranges from advanced theoretical analysis, through econometric and descriptive empirical studies, to policy analysis, problems arise as to the focus and level at which to pitch such a book. I have tried here to concentrate on the development of analytical principles in the subject, also considering available statistical and descriptive evidence as appropriate. I have not given extensive consideration to case study evidence in the field, despite the insight that this can give into the analysis; to include such material on a systematic basis would have led to a much longer and more unwieldy book than the present one. While, therefore, it may be desirable to supplement the material included here with reference to case study work, it seemed best not to make such work an integral part of the book.

I have tried to use a non-mathematical approach as far as possible. As undergraduate economics courses develop, undergraduate student training in analytical and statistical methods improves. Consequently, students today can handle much more advanced techniques than their counterparts of even a decade ago. Nevertheless, not all students taking industrial economics courses are specialist economists, and so it seemed appropriate to limit the mathematical content of the book. Verbal and diagrammatic exposition have been used where possible; in places where it has been necessary to use more formal mathematics, the discussion for the most part does not go beyond elementary manipulation and differentiation. (The material in the appendices to chapter 3 and at one or two other points is slightly more demanding, however.) Nothing more than an introductory knowledge of calculus and statistics, and the ability to read a regression equation, is therefore assumed.

To a certain extent, selection of topics is a matter of personal preference in a book such as this, although I have tried to include those topics which form the core of most industrial economics courses. One notable exception is the theory of the firm, which is a major topic in its own right and has been excluded for reasons of balance (and space). At Sheffield the theory of the firm is taught as a separate course, and this is also the case in many other institutions. Most other topics, however, are covered, including market concentration, oligopoly theory, technical progress, advertising and so on, as well as two topics which are less often treated fully: vertical integration and conglomerate diversification. I have also attempted to include enough material to allow some choice of topics within the book. In my own course, for example, I have taught a standard course on structure, conduct and performance using the core material selected from chapters 1–7 and chapters 10–12. As a variation on this, I have included material on product differentiation and monopolistic competition within such a course. Alternatively, I have slanted the material more towards integration and diversification (chapters 8 and 9), together with a discussion of merger policy (in chapter 12), in place of the (full) chapters 10–12 material. Finally, in more recent years I have given increased emphasis to major new theoretical developments in the field, notably in entry theory (chapter 4) but also in profitability and market structure (chapter 5) and vertical integration (chapter 8). Some selection of material both within and between chapters should, therefore, be possible within the book as a whole.

In writing this book I have received advice and encouragement from a number of friends and colleagues. Thanks go to John Cubbin, Steve Davies, Simon Domberger, Peter Else, Paul Geroski, Peter Hart, Martin Howe, Bruce Lyons, Tony McGuinness, Sig Prais, Gavin Reid and Mike Utton, all of whom offered useful comments on some part or parts of the manuscript. Particular thanks go to Steve Davies and Paul Geroski for reading large chunks of the first draft, and for offering extensive comments. Thanks also go to René Olivieri and Tony Sweeney of Basil Blackwell for their helpful advice and encouragement over a period of years. None of these individuals can, however, bear any responsibility for the final product.

Finally, I would like to thank Wendy Rogerson, Pat Fall and Rebecca Jackson for typing the first draft, and Ruth Barker, Mary Green and Steve Mathias for their work on the final draft. Last but not least, special thanks go to my wife, Jan, and children, Robin and Richard, for their support and patience during my often long absences while writing this book.

1 Introduction

This book is concerned with the analysis of industries and markets, and with the behaviour of firms within those markets. More specifically, it deals with the interdependence between (mainly private) firms within markets and the links that exist between market conditions, firm behaviour and economic performance.

In contrast to standard microeconomic analysis, industrial economics takes as its starting point the view that (in industrial markets at least)[1] competition is less than perfect. In some markets, a single monopolist may operate protected by high barriers to entry, so that standard monopoly analysis can be applied. In most industrial markets, however, barriers to entry are insufficient to exclude all new competition, and/or a number of firms operate in the market. In these cases some degree of competition (actual or potential) will exist so that intermediate imperfect competition outcomes are most likely. Industrial economics seeks to analyse the mixture of competition and monopoly that results. Moreover, in contrast to the standard focus of analysis on industry pricing, industrial economics recognizes the wider nature of competition in real-world markets in which product and process development, product design, advertising, investment strategies and so on all play a role. In some markets these wider areas of competition may well be more important than price competition itself, and therefore we consider various dimensions of competition in this book.

While the origins of industrial economics can be traced back to the beginning of this century (and before), it is only more recently, and most notably since the 1950s, that it has developed as a separate economic discipline. Since that time, however, a growing interest in the subject has been accompanied by important developments within the field. Some of these, as we shall see, have taken place in theoretical analysis, as more economic theorists have become interested in industrial economic problems. In addition, developments in policy and empirical analysis have also been made, with more widespread use of statistical and econometric techniques being particularly important in the latter context. Not surprisingly, given its relatively recent origins, much remains to be discovered within the subject and some issues are still hotly contested (see section 1.2 below). Nevertheless, a body of knowledge has been collected, and it is this which we are concerned with in this book.

The rest of this chapter sets the scene for the subsequent analysis. Section 1.1 outlines the standard framework of industrial economic analysis (the so-called structure–conduct–performance paradigm) and considers one or two reservations one should bear in mind in its use. Section 1.2 briefly considers some of the alternative schools of thought in the field. Finally, section 1.3 provides a plan of the rest of the book.

1.1 Framework of Analysis

The basic approach or paradigm of industrial economics emphasizes links between market *structure* and business *conduct* in determining market *performance*. In its simplest form it suggests that a causal link exists running from market structure to conduct and hence to performance. Such a one-way relationship was emphasized by early writers on industrial economics, notably the American economists E. S. Mason (working in the 1930s and 1940s) and later his student, J. S. Bain (working in the 1950s and 1960s).[2] More recent work in the field, however, has emphasized the complexity of relationships between structure, conduct and performance. For example, current work stresses the possibility that conduct and performance may in turn affect structure, or more generally that structure, conduct and performance may be jointly determined in a given market situation. These matters are further discussed after a brief outline of the basic paradigm.

Some key elements in the structure–conduct–performance analysis are given in table 1.1. *Performance* in particular industries or markets is indicated by such factors as profitability, efficiency and market growth. Such performance is assumed to depend on the *conduct* of firms in the market, where conduct affects factors such as pricing, advertising and product development, research and development, etc. In each of these areas, one considers the goals of firms, the degree of collusion or competition between firms and other aspects of business practice. Market conduct, in turn, depends on market *structure*, including such things as the degree to which production is concentrated in the hands of a few firms (market concentration), the degree of product differentiation and barriers to new competition.

Several features of table 1.1 are worthy of note. First, in contrast to some treatments of structure–conduct–performance analysis, the extent of vertical integration and conglomerate diversification are included as elements of market structure in this book. The rationale for doing this is that we are interested in how these factors affect conduct and performance, in much the same way as how market concentration may affect conduct and performance. In particular, this approach enables us to focus attention on public policy issues relating to vertical integration and diversification, and these matters are discussed in some detail in the relevant chapters below. Second, table 1.1 also indicates that the basic economic conditions of cost, demand and technology underlie the structure–conduct–performance paradigm. Standard economic theory, of course, tells us that these factors are important in any market or industry, and this point should always be borne in mind.

Table 1.1 Outline of the structure–conduct–performance paradigm

Basic conditions
   Costs
   Demand
   Technology
      ↓
Market structure
   Market concentration
   Product differentiation
   Barriers to entry
   Vertical integration
   Conglomerate diversification
      ↓
Conduct
   Business goals
   Business strategy
   Competitive practices
      ↓
Performance
   Efficiency
   Profitability
   Technical progress
   Growth

Some of the key relationships in industrial economics are implicit within the table. For example, in the case of pricing, the conventional argument suggests that high profitability in a market is associated with collusive behaviour induced by high market concentration. Again, if one considers research and development, greater research activity may be encouraged where firms are protected (to some extent at least) from actual or potential competition. Hence, again, market structure may influence conduct and performance. Finally, advertising competition too may be linked to market structure if, for example, moderate concentration leads to increases in mutually offsetting advertising expenditure. These hypotheses each fall within the structure–conduct–performance paradigm, and represent some of the core hypotheses considered in this book.

It is important to recognize, however, that simple one-way causations running from structure to conduct to performance are by no means the only relationships that may exist between variables. It is easy to think of examples in which reverse or two-way causations may operate. For example, technical developments induced by research and development activity have feedback effects on cost and demand conditions and may affect market structure in the long run. More immediately, successful advertising campaigns affect market shares and hence concentration, so that, not only may concentration affect advertising intensity in an industry, but a reverse effect may also apply. On a slightly different track, underlying efficiency differences between firms may lead to high profitability and high concentration in an industry as leading firms have both high profits and high market shares. This possibility suggests a chain of causation from basic cost conditions to structure and to performance rather than a causation running from structure to conduct to performance.

These and other possibilities suggest that one should be cautious in treating structure–conduct–performance relationships as simply one-way causations. On the theoretical front, it is obviously important to investigate all the ramifications of any particular piece of analysis in order to determine the exact nature of possible effects. Perhaps even more so on the empirical front, one should watch for possible spurious correlations between variables. In the past this has been a rather neglected area of empirical work such that a fair amount of questionable empirical evidence has been presented. Some attempt has been made in recent years, however, to tackle these problems using more sophisticated econometric techniques. While such studies are currently in their infancy, they nevertheless represent a step in the right direction, and some account of their findings is given at the appropriate points below.

1.2 Alternative Schools of Thought

While structure–conduct–performance analysis provides a basic framework for industrial economics, there remain a number of schools of thought within the field. This is true to some extent in the UK as well as in the USA. Increasingly, however, industrial economics is adopting a standard form of analysis, and we choose to emphasize this unity in this book. Nevertheless, many of the debates and disagreements that do take place involve separate schools of thought, so it is worthwhile briefly distinguishing them. For simplicity, in what follows we mention only three schools of thought: an important division in the USA between the Harvard and Chicago schools, and, more briefly, the so-called 'new Austrian' school of economic thought.

We begin with the Harvard school, which to some extent now merges with the mainstream approach adopted in this text. This school's work dates back to the traditional structure–conduct–performance paradigm developed by Mason at Harvard University in the interwar period.[3] This approach in turn developed from mainly institutional and case study work on firms and industries carried out at Harvard in the 1930s and before, linked to an interest in Edward H. Chamberlin's work on monopolistic competition theory published in 1933. As conceived by Mason, industrial organization, while relying heavily on empirical and institutional studies, should at the same time operate with a more general framework of analysis as outlined in the previous section. In particular, Mason stressed the importance of market structure and other objective market conditions as the key to identifying more general patterns of behaviour in markets. Thus, emphasis was placed firmly on the study of market structure as a unifying basis for industrial economic analysis.

Subsequent writers in the Harvard school, the most notable of whom has been Joe S. Bain, have continued to stress the importance of market structure. In particular, important work has been done by Bain on barriers to entry into an industry, which, together with market concentration and product differentiation, represent key elements of market structure. As their work has become part of mainstream industrial economics, and as techniques of economic and econometric analysis have been developed and applied in the field, the Harvard school have moved further from institutional, case study work. Nevertheless, their approach is still distinguished for its emphasis on empirical work and also for its emphasis on market structure. Moreover, a general belief within the school stresses the importance of monopoly power linked to certain market structures as a general issue in industrial economic analysis.

The Chicago school differs from the Harvard school in several important respects.[4] First, on the methodological front, Chicago writers rely much more heavily in their analysis on standard (often competitive) economic theory, which contrasts with the sometimes crude theoretical analysis employed by early Harvard writers. Second, and related to this, Chicago writers have often been sceptical of hypotheses and arguments employed by mainstream industrial economists, particularly in so far as they relate to policy matters. Chicago writers have attempted to use traditional price theory to analyse and criticize various hypotheses that have been advanced, pointing out, in particular, where such hypotheses fail to conform with basic neoclassical profit-maximizing assumptions. And third, and again related, Chicago writers have often been sceptical of arguments advanced for policy intervention in private industry, frequently arguing that elements of conduct and structure viewed with concern by some economists in fact offer no real case for government intervention.

We will refrain at this stage from looking in detail at Chicago arguments. Suffice it to say that a distinct Chicago view can be found on a number of topics discussed in this book. In some areas, such as the profitability–concentration debate of chapter 5 or the discussion of vertical integration in chapter 8, Chicago views have been incorporated into mainstream industrial economics, albeit in sometimes modified or qualified form. However, other Chicago arguments, leading to the view that there may be very little scope for government anti-trust policy (even in the area of horizontal monopoly policy), are less readily accepted. Such views stem from a rather conservative attitude on government intervention, and are much less clear-cut theoretically. Nevertheless, Chicago criticisms serve a useful purpose in sharpening ideas in industrial economics, and some attention will be given to them at various points in this book.

Finally, we may deal more briefly with the 'new Austrian' school.[5] This school claims allegiance to older Austrian economists: von Mises and von Hayek in this century, but going back to Menger in the mid-nineteenth century. They believe that competition is essentially a process which cannot be analysed using conventional, static economic models. In particular, they argue that profit, rather than being an indicator of possible monopoly power, is in fact an integral feature of the competitive process, providing essential signals on resource allocation to entrepreneurs. As such, it plays a key role in the dynamic process of competition, guiding ever-ready entrepreneurs to reallocate resources constantly in order to satisfy consumer demands. Since the operation of this process is looked upon as benign, many Austrian economists strongly oppose all but minimal government intervention in industry.

Austrian economists, in particular, look sceptically on the structure–conduct–performance approach to industrial economics, and indeed look sceptically on much of neoclassical (i.e. standard) microeconomic analysis. The alternative process analysis they offer is, however, somewhat thin on substantive concepts and theories, and often offers little more than political support for a free market economy. Since we are concerned more with basic economic analysis than with the political views of economists, we do not pursue the Austrian line in this book except in passing.

1.3 Plan of the Book

The remainder of the book is divided as follows. Chapters 2–5 deal with the basic analysis of market structure, conduct and performance as it relates in particular to pricing and profitability. Chapters 6–9 then expand the discussion, introducing other non-price variables into the analysis in chapters 6 and 7 and expanding ideas towards multi-market operations in chapters 8 and 9. Finally, chapters 10–12 consider social welfare and public policy issues in industrial economics, dealing with both the social costs of monopoly and actual competition policy in the UK.

Chapter 2 examines the notion of market concentration, and reviews the evidence on concentration in practice as well as looking at several alternative theoretical approaches to market concentration. This chapter provides a basis for the analysis in succeeding chapters and indeed throughout the book.

Chapter 3 then examines the theory of oligopolistic pricing. A discussion of traditional models is followed by a consideration of oligopolistic coordination and its possible links to market concentration. Some more recent work, in particular relating to so-called consistent conjectures models, is also discussed in this chapter.

Market concentration is one factor which might affect the exercise of monopoly power in a market, but another factor is potential competition from new entrants. Chapter 4 considers possible barriers to such new competition, and how these may affect pricing behaviour. More recent developments suggesting that firms erect entry barriers strategically to prevent new competition are also discussed.

Chapter 5 draws this part of the book together by considering empirical evidence on profitability and market structure. Various theoretical and practical problems in this area are discussed and particular attention is given to the effects of market concentration on profitability.

Chapter 6 examines theories of advertising, including the possible effects of market concentration on the extent of advertising. It also considers more general aspects of advertising and its possible effects on competition.

Chapter 7 switches attention to technical progress. New products and processes are developed in a continuing process of invention, innovation and diffusion, and each of these aspects is discussed in this chapter. Particular attention is given to the special problems encountered in the research and development process, and the role of government intervention and competition is also discussed.

Chapters 8 and 9 round out the picture by examining vertical integration and conglomerate diversification. In each case reasons why these developments occur are discussed and their possible competitive effects are examined.

Finally, chapters 10–12 deal more explicitly with problems of economic welfare and public policy. Chapter 10 examines attempts which have been made to measure the aggregate social costs of monopoly in an economy. This chapter, in particular, enables us to draw together some of the ideas of earlier chapters.

Chapters 11 and 12 then discuss competition policy as it currently operates in the UK. Chapter 11 deals with restrictive trade practices policy and considers both older policies on restrictive trading agreements and the comparatively recent legislation on single firm practices. Finally, chapter 12 looks at monopolies and mergers policies and in particular examines the question of whether the UK needs to take a new line on such policies.

Notes

1 By tradition, industrial economics deals mainly with manufacturing and mining industries, although some of its ideas can also be applied to the service sectors. Sectors such as agriculture, financial markets and so on are usually treated in other specialist economics courses and are therefore not specifically dealt with in this book.

2 See, in particular, Mason (1939, 1957) and Bain (1956, 1968).

3 For some historical background on the work of Mason and others see Grether (1970).
4 For a recent review of the Chicago school's work see Posner (1979).
5 More extensive discussion of 'new Austrian' economics may be found, for example, in Littlechild (1978) or Reekie (1979).

2 Market Concentration

In this chapter we consider the concept of market concentration, which has traditionally played a central role in the industrial economics literature. We proceed under three headings. Section 2.1 examines the nature and measurement of concentration and in particular asks the question, What is a good measure of market concentration? In section 2.2 we examine the descriptive evidence on market concentration in the UK. Finally, in section 2.3 we examine theories of concentration and in particular the contrasting arguments that technology on the one hand and chance factors on the other are crucial to an understanding of the determinants of market concentration.

2.1 Nature and Measurement of Market Concentration

As noted in chapter 1, market concentration refers to the degree to which production for or in a particular market or industry is *concentrated in the hands of a few large firms*. Thus, in measuring market concentration we are concerned with individual markets or industries, and with the number and relative sizes of firms in each industry. Other things equal, a market is said to be more concentrated the fewer the number of firms in production or the more unequal the distribution of market shares. Several general distinctions follow from these ideas.

First, we should distinguish between *market concentration* and *aggregate concentration*. The latter relates to the degree to which a few large firms control the production of the economy as a whole or at least broad sectors of it, such as the financial sector or the manufacturing sector. Thus, for example, using the share of the largest 100 firms in manufacturing net output, Prais (1976) has estimated that in 1970 these firms controlled about 40 per cent of net output compared with an estimated 22 per cent in 1949. Such levels and changes in aggregate concentration may have important consequences for the distribution of political, social and economic power in a democratic society. These wider issues associated with aggregate concentration are examined further in chapter 9 below, while in this chapter we focus our attention more narrowly on market concentration.

Second, we should distinguish *absolute* concentration measures from *inequality* measures. The former relate to both dimensions of market concentration, namely firm numbers and relative market shares, while the latter are adapted from standard statistical theory and measure the dispersion of market shares only. We shall argue below that the neglect of firm numbers by inequality measures is often a weakness in their use as market concentration indices. Nevertheless, some important work has been done using such measures, not least in the field of the dynamics of concentration change (see section 2.3.2), and for this reason a brief review of such measures is included in section 2.1.3 below.

A third and final distinction we should make is between *buyer* and *seller* concentration. Our discussion so far, and indeed throughout this chapter, implicitly assumes that it is the latter which is under consideration. It is important to remember, however, that in practice many products are intermediate products being sold between firms, and that even consumer goods are sold by manufacturers to wholesalers and distributors. Hence, it may be relevant in some situations to consider the number and relative sizes of buyers in a market as well as the concentration of sellers. To avoid unnecessary complexity, however, we restrict our attention to seller concentration in this chapter, leaving the reader to consider the parallel arguments relating to buyer concentration.

2.1.1 Measurement Criteria

For present purposes we ignore all practical problems of concentration measurement, and direct our attention to general principles. If one asks the question, What is the best index of market concentration? the answer will depend on the use to which the index is to be put. For example, if one is interested in oligopoly pricing, it can be shown that certain concentration measures are appropriate to the analysis of particular oligopolistic conditions (see chapter 3). Again, certain statistical theories of proportionate firm growth (discussed in section 2.3.2 below) support the use of inequality measures of concentration. Finally, in descriptive studies of trends in market concentration (see section 2.2), where factors such as ease of comprehension are important, yet other measures may be appropriate. In each case one must assess the problem under investigation and ideally select that measure of concentration which is most appropriate.

Abstracting from particular requirements, however, it is possible to consider certain general criteria against which to assess concentration indices, while stressing that an index which fails to satisfy any or all criteria still may be useful in some circumstances. These criteria can be divided into elementary and more general criteria. Among the elementary criteria, we may suggest that an index be easy to understand and to calculate; that it be independent of market size; and that it range from zero (or close to zero) in the competitive case of many equally sized firms to one in the case of monopoly. These criteria are straightforward and, with the exception of the second, mainly of convenience value. The requirement that an index be independent of market size is more important, however, and is equivalent to requiring that it depend on firm market share rather than firm size. Thus, for example, the variance of firm size would not, but the variance of firm market share would, satisfy this criterion, the former being an unsatisfactory concentration measure because it varies with the units of measurement.[1]

In order to develop more general criteria for a concentration index it is useful to proceed with reference to the so-called *concentration curve*. This plots the cumulative percentage of output (taken in this section as the measure of firm size) against the cumulative number of firms ranked from the largest to the smallest. It should be clearly distinguished from the Lorenz curve, which is discussed in section 2.1.3 below.

Concentration curves for three hypothetical industries A, B and C are plotted in figure 2.1. Since firms are cumulated from the largest, the curves are concave from below, being in the limit straight lines when all firms within an industry are of equal size. Thus, firm size inequality is reflected in the concavity of the curves, while firm numbers are indicated by the intersection of the curves with the 100 per cent output level.

Given the definition of market concentration, it is reasonable to suggest that concentration is higher in an industry whose concentration curve lies

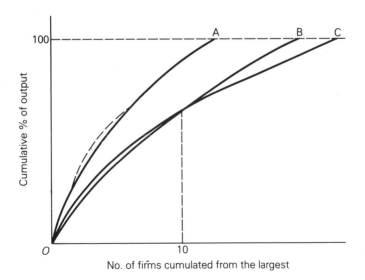

Figure 2.1

everywhere above that of another industry. If this is the case, then for any number, r, of large firms considered, such firms control a larger proportion of market output. This is illustrated in figure 2.1 by comparison of industry A with industry B or C.

When concentration curves cross, however, as for industries B and C, no such simple rule applies. In this case it is not possible to rank industries unambiguously by concentration in general, since such a ranking implies a particular weighting to different parts of the concentration curve. We shall see below that different concentration indices give different weights to different parts of the concentration curve, and hence can rank industries such as B and C differently. This is a general problem with all concentration indices, which is overcome only when, for example, theoretical considerations dictate that a particular index and hence a particular weighting be used.

Hannah and Kay (1977) have suggested a number of criteria as being intrinsic to the notion of market concentration. Among these we may note the following.[2]

(1) *Concentration curve ranking criterion*   A concentration index should rank an industry as more concentrated than another if its concentration curve lies everywhere above the concentration curve of the other. As noted above, this is an intuitively appealing condition for a concentration index.

(2) *Sales transfer principle*   A transfer of sales from a small to a large firm should increase measured concentration. In terms of concentration curve A in figure 2.1, such a transfer will cause the concentration curve to 'bulge' upwards over part of its length as exemplified by the dashed section of the curve. Again, the criterion is intuitively appealing.

(3) *Entry condition*   The addition of a small firm to the industry, the relative market shares of existing firms remaining unchanged, should decrease market concentration; and conversely for the exit of a small firm. Note that this condition is deliberately restricted in that it is conceivable that a new entrant would be so large that concentration would actually increase after entry. Hannah and Kay (1977, p. 49) suggest that the entry of the Xerox Corporation into the copying machine industry might represent a practical example of such an effect.

(4) *Merger condition*   The merger of two or more firms should increase measured concentration. This criterion, in fact, follows from the preceding two, since a merger can be regarded as a sales transfer from a small to a large firm combined with the exit of an arbitrarily small firm from the market. In terms of curve A in figure 2.1, the effect of a merger is to cause the dashed 'bulge' to extend up to the 100 per cent line.

While each of these criteria has intuitive appeal, it should be stressed that not all writers would accept them as appropriate in all circumstances.[3] Moreover, these criteria are insufficient to rank industries unambiguously when concentration curves cross. Nevertheless, they provide a useful reference point for further discussion, and we consider the performance of some of the more common concentration indices against them in the next section.

2.1.2 Some Concentration Indices [4]

A concentration index is a summary representation of a concentration curve. In what follows, we assume an industry with n firms with outputs x_i ($i = 1, \ldots, n$) ranked from largest to smallest. We define industry output $x = \Sigma_{i=1}^{n} x_i$, and hence the market share of the ith firm is $s_i = x_i/x$. Attention in this section is devoted to simpler types of concentration index and an assessment of their merits.

Reciprocal of firm numbers   The simplest possible concentration index is the reciprocal of the number of firms, $1/n$. As can be easily verified, this satisfies each of the criteria referred to above, although a sales transfer will leave this index unchanged. In terms of the concentration curves of figure 2.1, it ranks industries in the order A, B, C from high to low concentration, and attaches a zero weight to the relative sizes of firms. Indeed, this latter point explains its limited practical use, since in reality it is usually desirable to take some account of the relative sizes of firms as well as their number. In certain theoretical models, however, where firms are assumed to be of equal size for simplicity (so-called 'symmetrical' models), it becomes the theoretically appropriate concentration measure and has been mentioned here accordingly.

Concentration ratio   The most widely used concentration index is the concentration ratio. It is defined as the proportion of industry output accounted for by the r largest firms, where r is an arbitrary number. Thus,

$$C_r = \sum_{i=1}^{r} x_i/x = \sum_{i=1}^{r} s_i. \tag{2.1}$$

With $r = 5$, for example, we have the five-firm concentration ratio, C_5, which shows the share of industry output accounted for by the largest five firms. If these shares in a certain industry are, say, 0.15, 0.12, 0.06, 0.04 and 0.03, then the five-firm concentration ratio for this industry is 40 per cent. The measure is particularly favoured in descriptive empirical work (see section 2.2 below) because it is both easy to calculate and easy to understand intuitively. In certain circumstances, as noted in chapter 3, it may also be applicable to oligopolistic pricing problems.

   Criticisms of the concentration ratio as a measure of concentration centre on the arbitrary selection of r (the number of large firms to be considered) and on the fact that only a single point on the concentration curve is taken. When concentration curves intersect, the measure will give different rankings of industries by concentration for different values of r. In figure 2.1, industries

B and C are judged to be equally concentrated with $r = 10$, but for $r < 10$ industry C appears more concentrated, while for $r > 10$ industry B appears more concentrated by this measure. Also, by choosing just a single point on the concentration curve, the measure suppresses a great deal of information which might be of relevance to the problem at hand, such as the relative sizes of the leading r firms and the remaining $n - r$ firms. This suppression of information accounts for the ambiguous nature of the concentration ratio's response to Hannah and Kay's criteria for a good concentration measure. A sales transfer or a merger may produce the appropriate change in the concentration ratio *ceteris paribus*, but C_r may be unaffected by such a change if the largest r firms are unaffected. While all summary measures of concentration inevitably suppress information about the concentration curve, the concentration ratio is particularly subject to this criticism and the insensitivity it implies.

Hirschman–Herfindahl index   This index, which was proposed first by Hirschman and later by Herfindahl, has become increasingly popular among industrial economists in the last few years.[5] In particular, it has importance for the analysis of oligopolistic pricing models as discussed in chapter 3. Unlike the concentration ratio, it takes account of all points on the concentration curve, being the sum of squared market shares of the firms in the industry:

$$H = \sum_{i=1}^{n} (x_i/x)^2 = \sum_{i=1}^{n} s_i^2. \tag{2.2}$$

The index, by squaring market shares (effectively, weighting market shares by themselves in the sum (2.2)), gives most weight to the larger firms in the industry. This can be easily verified by considering a market of four firms with market shares 0.4, 0.3, 0.2 and 0.1. The squared market shares are thus 0.16, 0.09, 0.04 and 0.01, giving $H = 0.3$, and it is clear that the largest firm contributes disproportionately to this sum.

The H index can be written in slightly different form to bring out its properties more clearly. Denoting average firm size as

$$\bar{x} = \frac{1}{n} \sum_{i=1}^{n} x_i$$

and the variance of firm size as

$$\sigma^2 = \frac{1}{n} \sum_{i=1}^{n} x_i^2 - \bar{x}^2,$$

we can define a unit-free measure of the inequality in firm market shares as

$c = \sigma/\bar{x}$ (which is known as the *coefficient of variation* (of firm size)). Since

$$c^2 = \frac{1}{n}\sum_{i=1}^{n} x_i^2/\bar{x}^2 - 1,$$

it is easily seen on rearrangement that

$$H = \frac{c^2 + 1}{n}. \tag{2.3}$$

Thus the H index depends both on market share inequality (as measured by c^2) and on firm numbers, n. It takes a maximum value of 1 for monopoly ($c^2 = 0$, $n = 1$) and a minimum value of $1/n \to 0$ for the case of many small equally sized firms ($c^2 = 0$, $n \to \infty$). Moreover, by taking the reciprocal of the index we can partially overcome the weakness it possesses from the viewpoint of intuitive understanding. This is because the reciprocal of H is a *numbers equivalent*, being the unique number of equally sized firms which would give the corresponding H value. Thus an H value of 0.018, say, for a particular industry is equivalent to approximately 56 firms of equal size operating in that industry and producing that H value. If there are 200 firms actually operating in that industry, then it is easy to work out that 0.013 of the observed H value is attributable to the inequality in firm size component, c^2.

The Hirschman–Herfindahl index, as with the more general Hannah and Kay index discussed below, satisfies each of Hannah and Kay's criteria. Referring again to figure 2.1, the concentration curve ranking criterion is satisfied since a concentration curve which lies everywhere above another involves bigger market shares in the hands of fewer firms, a factor which on squaring market shares must involve higher measured concentration. Similarly, a sales transfer must increase H since the contribution of the increased market share of the larger firm to increasing H must outweigh the decreased contribution of the smaller firm. This applies *a fortiori* to the merger condition, which in addition involves a reduction in firm numbers. The entry condition is a little more difficult to deal with intuitively, not least because the entry of a very large firm could conceivably raise H (see Hannah and Kay, 1977, pp. 57–8). It is clear, however, that some small firm entry will lower the concentration curve at all points so that criterion (1) is operative. Larger entry will cause the concentration curves to intersect (twice), and in this case a trade-off between greater firm numbers and market share inequality will decide whether or not new entry decreases H. Suffice it to say that new entry will not raise H unless a very large firm relative to existing market participants comes into the market.

Hannah and Kay's indices   The H index, like any other index of concentration, implies a specific weighting of market share inequality and firm numbers, which is particularly relevant to cases where concentration curves cross. That is, the H index, by weighting market shares by themselves according to equation (2.3), will give a particular concentration value to industries B and C in figure 2.1 which will define a cardinal relationship between concentration in these industries. (Indeed, the measure will imply a cardinal relationship between concentration in all industries even when concentration curves don't cross.) This weighting may not be appropriate in all circumstances.

Consequently, Hannah and Kay (1977, pp. 55–8) have suggested a more general class of concentration indices, similar to the H index but varying in the weight they give to large firms. These indices are based on the generalization

$$R = \sum_{i=1}^{n} s_i^{\alpha} \quad \alpha > 0 \tag{2.4}$$

where α is an arbitrary elasticity parameter. Clearly, the H index corresponds to the case of $\alpha = 2$ in equation (2.4). The numbers equivalent of R can be shown to be $R^{1/(1-\alpha)}$, and we have Hannah and Kay's indices defined in this form:[6]

$$HK = \left(\sum_{i=1}^{n} s_i^{\alpha} \right)^{1/(1-\alpha)} \quad \alpha > 0, \alpha \neq 1. \tag{2.5}$$

It can be shown that these indices satisfy the criteria (1)–(4) laid down by Hannah and Kay. Their chief merit arises from the flexibility they introduce into the measurement of concentration, in that they allow greater weight to be attached to large firms by increasing the value of α.[7]

Entropy index   Finally, we may briefly mention the entropy index, which is an inverse measure of concentration.[8] This index weights market shares by $\ln(1/s_i)$ and then sums them as follows:

$$E = \sum_{i=1}^{n} s_i \ln(1/s_i). \tag{2.6}$$

It takes values of zero in the monopoly case and $\ln(n)$ in the case of n firms of equal size. (This latter problem can be overcome, however, by forming a relative entropy measure $E/\ln(n)$ which varies from zero to one.) A useful transformation of E (Marfels, 1971) is to take the reciprocal of its antilogarithm

$$e^{-E} = \prod_{i=1}^{n} s_i^{s_i}. \tag{2.7}$$

This measure varies positively with concentration and has been shown by Hannah and Kay (1977, pp. 56–7) to conform in the limit to the case of $\alpha \to 1$

in equation (2.5) above. Thus the entropy index gives less weight to larger firms than the H index of concentration.

2.1.3 Inequality Measures

We complete the discussion of concentration indices by briefly mentioning inequality measures of concentration. Such measures ignore firm numbers and can be regarded as summary representations of the Lorenz curve, in the same way as absolute measures summarize the concentration curve. The Lorenz curve plots the cumulative percentage of market output against the cumulative percentage of (rather than number of) firms. Firms are also typically cumulated from the smallest to the largest in constructing a Lorenz curve, in contrast to the cumulation from the largest firm for the concentration curve.

In figure 2.2 a single Lorenz curve for industry A is drawn. This curve is concave to the diagonal from below, reflecting cumulation from the smallest firm. The diagonal line OT represents the situation in which firms are of equal size such that y per cent of firms account for y per cent of market output for any y ($0 < y < 1$). Greater inequality in firm size is broadly shown by Lorenz curves being further from the diagonal (although, as with concentration curves, no unambiguous ranking of industries according to firm size inequality

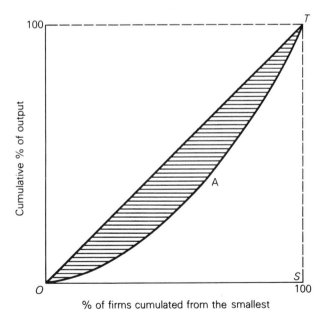

Figure 2.2

can be obtained when Lorenz curves intersect). Finally, the fact that firm numbers are irrelevant in the Lorenz diagram is easily seen in an industry of equally sized firms, where the Lorenz curve coincides with the diagonal OT for any number of firms operating in that industry.

Several measures of inequality may be mentioned here.

(1) *Gini coefficient*   This measure has a direct interpretation in terms of the Lorenz diagram, as it is the ratio of the shaded area in figure 2.2 to the area of the triangle OST. The greater is inequality in firm size, the greater is the shaded area in the diagram and hence the larger is the Gini coefficient, G, on a scale from zero to one.

(2) *Coefficient of variation*   As noted above, the coefficient of variation, c, which is the ratio of the standard deviation of firm size to mean firm size, is a unit-free measure of dispersion and hence of firm size inequality.

(3) *Variance of the logarithms of firm size*   This measure is introduced here finally as it is of some importance to our discussion of section 2.3 below. It is defined as

$$v^2 = \frac{1}{n} \sum_{i=1}^{n} [\log(x_i/\bar{x}_g)]^2 \qquad (2.8)$$

where $\bar{x}_g$ is geometric mean firm size. This measure is particularly useful in cases where the distribution of firms by size is lognormal, i.e. is such that the logarithms of firm size are normally distributed. In this case Lorenz curves are non-intersecting and v^2 gives an unambiguous ranking of firm size inequality.

Figure 2.3 shows the particular positive skew shape of the lognormal distribution as applied to firm size. In this diagram most firms are small or

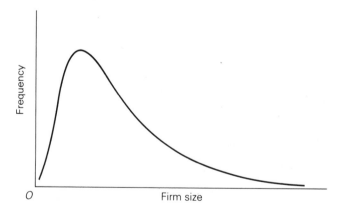

Figure 2.3

moderately sized, while a relatively few large firms dominate the market. In many (if not all) industrial markets, the distribution of firms by size conforms quite closely to this general picture. Hence, the lognormal (and related) distributions are often used in theoretical work in industrial economics to represent firm size distributions (see section 2.3 below). In this context, therefore, v^2 is often used to measure firm size inequality.

Hannah and Kay (1977, pp. 50–2) have stressed the unsatisfactory nature of the above inequality indices when judged against their criteria. Since none of them takes specific account of firm numbers, they are all subject to the limitation of not necessarily satisfying the entry and merger criteria. In addition, as Hannah and Kay imply, sales transfers from smaller to larger firms among the very largest firms can lead v^2 to fall rather than rise. For these reasons, it would not be desirable to rely on inequality measures in dealing with all circumstances of concentration measurement. As stressed initially, however, these measures may be useful in some circumstances, and especially when focusing attention (as we do in section 2.3.2) on issues of relative firm growth.

2.2 Evidence on Market Concentration

In this section we review the descriptive evidence on market concentration in UK manufacturing industry. As can be seen from table 2.1, the manufacturing sector remains a key if somewhat declining sector of the UK economy. It should be remembered that many of the principles discussed in this book have application to other sectors also. Traditionally, however, industrial economists have paid particular attention to manufacturing, and indeed most of the evidence available on concentration relates to this sector. Likewise, descriptive studies have traditionally used the concentration ratio to measure concentration, and we shall uphold both of these traditions in this section.

2.2.1 Measurement Problems

Most data on UK market concentration are obtained from the UK Censuses of Production, and we confine our discussion to these data here. For Census of Production purposes a firm (or enterprise) is defined as one or more plants (or establishments) in an industry 'under common ownership or control'. Thus, only that part of a firm producing in an industry is counted, and this seems to be an appropriate practice. Firm size is typically measured in terms of employment, net output or sales. This can create some discrepancies; for example, larger firms in an industry often have above-average capital/labour ratios so that employment concentration ratios tend to be lower than sales or net output concentration ratios. Again, the size of some firms essentially involved in trading products will tend to be overstated by using sales as a measure of size. These problems give rise to discrepancies with respect to

Table 2.1 Share of manufacturing in UK national output, 1972–82

	1972	1973	1974	1975	1976	1977	1978	1979	1980	1981	1982
Value added (£m)	17,876	20,760	22,651	27,404	31,511	37,813	43,648	47,762	52,635	53,783	56,492
Share of GDP (%)	32.1	32.0	30.1	28.8	28.0	29.5	29.6	28.2	26.8	25.2	24.3

Source: Annual Abstract of Statistics, 1984, table 14.7.

individual concentration ratios, although in aggregate concentration ratios using different measures of size tend to be highly correlated in practice.

In a world of differentiated products we can loosely describe a market as consisting of a collection of products which are highly substitutable in demand. The main weakness of Census concentration data is that official industries do not tally closely with this notion. In the first place, since Census of Production data relate to *production* in the UK, they take no account of foreign trade in manufactures. Manufacturing imports and exports, however, have shown dramatic increases in recent years, with imports as a proportion of home demand and exports as a proportion of manufacturers' sales both reaching approximately 25 per cent for total manufacturing by the end of the 1970s.[9] This growth in foreign trade is likely to have had important effects on competition in manufacturing, particularly in recent years, and some discussion of the (so far limited) evidence available on it is given in section 2.2.2.

Even within the domestic framework, however, Census industries are not always closely linked to the economist's notion of a market. Most Census concentration data relate to so-called Minimum List Heading (MLH) industries,[10] which consist of groups of products typically using similar materials and/or processes in production. Following US terminology, such industries are often called *three-digit* industries, while principal products within them are called *four-digit* industries. Thus, for example, within the three-digit industry of grain milling, the 1968 Census of Production identified the three four-digit industries: white flour, other flour and breakfast cereals. As is apparent in this example, Census three-digit industries are often too aggregated to provide data on a single market. Moreover, the supply-side basis for their definition can imply that competing products which use alternative materials or processes are classified to different industries: a classic example is paper bags and plastic bags. These problems should be borne in mind when interpreting the evidence in section 2.2.2. Four-digit industry data are preferable in that they offer a more satisfactory level of disaggregation from the viewpoint of economic analysis, although only limited concentration data at this level of aggregation are in fact available.

2.2.2 The Evidence

As might be expected, the level of concentration in UK manufacturing industry varies considerably between industries. Data on three-digit industries for 1980, for example, shows that competition was very strong in such industries as leather goods, furniture and clothing, all of which had five-firm employment concentration ratios below 15 per cent. On the other hand, five-firm employment concentration exceeded 90 per cent in such industries as tobacco products, man-made fibres, sugar and motor vehicles. Of course, most industries were arrayed between these extremes.

Some idea of the broad breakdown of concentration between industries is given in table 2.2. This shows arithmetic mean (hereafter, average) five-firm

Table 2.2 Market concentration by UK manufacturing sector, 1980

Class (two-digit)		No. of industries	Average C_5	Class (two-digit)		No. of industries	Average C_5
21/2/3	Extraction, metal manufacture[a]	4	59	37	Instrument engineering	4	41
24	Non-metallic mineral products	8	54	41/2	Food, drink, tobacco[d]	15	58
25/6	Chemicals[b]	8	53	43	Textiles	9	42
31	Metal goods	5	22	44/5	Leather, footwear, clothing	6	23
32/3	Mechanical engineering	11	36	46	Timber, wooden furniture	7	21
34	Electrical and electronic engineering	7	57	47	Paper, printing	3	30
35/6	Vehicles, transport, equipment[c]	7	65	48/9	Other	6	30
					Total	100	44

Source: Census of Production, Summary Tables, 1980.

Notes

[a] Excludes Iron and steel (221); Steel tubes (222) and Drawing, etc., of Steel (233) because of the likely influence of nationalized British Steel in these cases.
[b] Includes Mineral oil processing (140).
[c] Excludes Railway and tram vehicles (362) because of the likely influence of British Rail workshops in this case.
[d] Excludes Sugar (420) because information was suppressed to avoid disclosure of activities of individual firms.

employment concentration ratios of three-digit industries within each two-digit manufacturing sector (or class) in 1980. As can be seen, capital-intensive/high technology sectors such as vehicles, extraction and metal manufacture, and electrical and electronic engineering tend to be highly concentrated, while more traditional labour-intensive sectors such as timber products,

Table 2.3 Highly concentrated (four-digit) industries in UK manufacturing, 1975[a]

	Concentration ratio	Total no. of producers
Division 1 ($C_5 \geqslant 95\%$)		
Sugar	99.9	9
Margarine	100.0(7)	7
Gin	—	9
Cigarettes	100.0(7)	7
Other manufactured tobacco	98.8	8
Petroleum feedstocks	100.0(7)	7
Halogenated derivatives of hydrocarbons	99.9	9
Allphatic	100.0(7)	7
Additives for liquid fuels and oils	95.1	28
Cables for telecommunications	95.3	14
Telegraph and telephone installations	98.9	13
Tractors	95.7	11
Cars	98.2	20
Aircraft and airframes	100.0(7)	7
Precious metals refined	—	—
Man-made fibres	95.4	14
Tyres and tubes	96.4	8
Division 2 ($C_5 \geqslant 90\%$)		
Breakfast cereals	91.4	16
Ice creams	90.9	29
Potato crisps	94.7	10
Dog and cat food	94.4	39
Coffee	90.6	20
Synthetic rubber	91.9	12
Ball and roller bearings	92.4	15
Batteries and accumulators	90.8	19
Internal combustion engines	91.4	20
Cans and metal boxes	91.5	57
Cement	93.0	10

Source: Census of Production, Summary Tables, 1975.

Note
[a] Based on turnover of £100 million-plus in 1975, excluding certain steel products mainly produced by the British Steel Corporation. Concentration ratios are five-firm sales ratios (although in five indicated cases seven-firm ratios are given). '—' means figure not available.

metal goods, and leather, footwear and clothing are less highly concentrated. Links clearly exist between the nature of technology and market concentration, and these are more fully discussed in section 2.3.1 below.

As noted, three-digit industry data are often too aggregated to give a clear picture of the state of competition in particular industries. In identifying the most highly concentrated industries, therefore, it is convenient to use more suitable four-digit industry data. Table 2.3 shows those major products which in 1975 (according to the Census of Production) were both highly concentrated and had a turnover in excess of £100 million. It is these products which, prima facie, offer the greatest scope for economic welfare loss through the abuse of market power, although there are, of course, many more smaller four-digit industries with similarly high levels of concentration.

Table 2.3 divides them into two: division 1, with five-firm sales concentration over 95 per cent, and division 2, the 90–5 per cent class. Many of the major industries in which monopoly is thought to be a problem appear in this table. Two groups stand out. First there are the motor-vehicle-related products, such as motor cars and tractors, and also tyres and tubes, fuel additives, engines and batteries. Motor vehicle production is, of course, a key UK industry, and while foreign competition is important in car production itself, in several components industries concentration stands at very high levels. A second group, of very highly concentrated food and related industries, is also notable (see also table 2.2); this comprises staple products such as tobacco, sugar and margarine as well as convenience or snack products like cornflakes, ice creams and potato crisps. It is often argued that the susceptibility of consumers to mass advertising is an important bolster to monopoly in such industries, and this matter is returned to in chapter 6 below.

Turning to the evidence on concentration trends, we may note first that, contrary to some suggestions, there is little evidence that very high concentration is a transitory phenomenon. For example, for the 28 industries listed in table 2.3, C_5 exceeded 90 per cent 17 years earlier (in 1958) in all but four cases (allphatic, bearings, batteries and cement). More generally, we can look at trends in concentration by comparing average concentration ratios in constant samples of industries over time. This is done in table 2.4 for the period 1935–70 following the work of Hart and Clarke (1980). The period was one in which a general tendency for rising concentration in UK industry was observed. This is most clearly shown in column (3), where it is seen that average three-firm employment concentration at the three-digit industry level increased from an estimated 26 per cent in 1935 to 41 per cent in 1968. Prior to 1958 concentration appears to have increased at a relatively slow to moderate rate over the years 1935–51 (on average, at about 0.2 percentage points per annum) and at about twice this rate (0.4 percentage points per annum) in the years 1951–8. After 1958 an acceleration in the rate of concentration increase occurred, with an average annual increase approaching 0.9 percentage points. Evidence for this latter period for larger samples of

Table 2.4 The growth of industrial concentration in the UK and USA, 1935–70

Year	(1) %	(2) %	(3) %	(4) %	(5) %
1935			26.3	24	
1947					40.9
1949				22	
1951			29.3		
1953				27	
1954					40.6
1958	55.4	36.9	32.4	32	40.3
1963	58.6	41.6	37.4	37	41.3
1967					41.4
1968	63.4	45.6	41.0	41	
1970				41	42.7

Sources: Hart and Clarke (1980); Prais (1976) (col. 4); and Mueller and Hamm (1974) (col. 5).

Note: column headings are as follows:
(1) Average five-firm sales concentration for four-digit UK industries ($n = 144$).
(2) Average five-firm employment concentration for three-digit UK industries ($n = 79$).
(3) Average three-firm employment concentration for three-digit UK industries ($n = 42$).
(4) Share of the largest 100 firms in UK manufacturing net output.
(5) Average four-firm shipments concentration for four-digit US industries ($n = 166$).

four-digit industries (column (1)) and three-digit industries (column (2)) confirm this dramatic concentration increase in the years 1958–68. Column (1) in particular shows that average five-firm sales concentration of four-digit products at 63.4 per cent in 1968 was 8 percentage points higher than a decade earlier. Comparison of columns (2) and (3) reveals that, on average, the fourth and fifth largest firms in an industry accounted for only 4.5 per cent of industry employment compared with the 41 per cent accounted for by the three largest firms in 1968, while comparison of columns (1) and (2) reveals that concentration levels but not trends differ according to the level of aggregation employed (and to a limited extent because of the measure of firm size used).

A perspective on trends in UK market concentration up to 1968 is given by columns (4) and (5) of table 2.4. Column (4) (based on Prais, 1976) shows that aggregate UK concentration increased at a similar rate to average market concentration in the 1950s and 1960s but that there was a slight fall in aggregate concentration in the period 1935–49. This latter discrepancy can perhaps be explained by the slight difference in time period, although it is possible that wartime and postwar controls on the very largest firms may have affected the aggregate concentration measure. The limitations of the data available for this period should make us careful not to place too much emphasis on this apparent discrepancy. Column (5) shows the trend in average four-firm US market concentration at the four-digit level for the period 1947–70 as found by Mueller and Hamm (1974). These data reveal a slight fall in US concentration prior to 1958 followed by a modest rise of 0.2 percentage points per annum on average up to 1970. While underlying this trend a more substantial rise in concentration was observed in consumer goods industries compared with a slight concentration fall in producer goods industries, overall it is clear that the USA has experienced relatively stable concentration levels in the postwar period, with a rise of only 2 percentage points over 1947–70, compared with a 12-percentage-point increase in the UK for 1951–68. It seems likely that the much stronger competition policy in the USA compared with the UK was a contributory factor in explaining these dramatic differences in concentration trends (see chapter 12 below).

Looking at the evidence in table 2.4, one might well expect that UK manufacturing concentration was rising on an exponential trend, auguring substantial concentration increases in the 1970s. This view would tend to be reinforced, moreover, in that substantial merger activity was observed in the early 1970s, continuing on the considerable merger activity of the later 1960s. In fact, however, it seems that market concentration was actually stable or falling in the 1970s in marked contrast to the experience of the 1960s.

Table 2.5 sets out the available evidence. Part (a) shows average employment, sales and net output concentration ratios for a comparable sample of 93 three-digit industries in 1970, 1975 and 1979. The data show that average concentration was relatively stable in the 1970s, increasing only marginally over the decade as a whole. This apparent stability in concentration levels, however, takes no account of the impact of foreign trade on domestic concentration. Part (b), therefore, reports results obtained by Utton (1982) for a sample of 121 four-digit industries in 1968, 1975 and 1977 which make adjustments for foreign trade. These results show that, while unadjusted four-digit average concentration ratios were fairly stable in 1968–77, in line with the three-digit results reported in part (a), adjustment for imports both lowers the level of average concentration and leads to a 4-percentage-point fall in concentration in this period. These results, therefore, suggest that the growth in import competition in the 1970s led to a substantial increase in competitiveness in UK manufacturing in contrast to the trends observed in the 1960s and before.[11]

Utton's results are subject to a number of reservations, however. First, he assumes that imports are competitive in UK markets, so concentration ratios are simply adjusted downwards by adding imports to the denominators of domestic concentration ratios.[12] As noted in particular by Cowling (1978), however, leading UK producers have themselves been associated with imports of manufactured products, and this factor was of increasing importance in a number of industries (e.g. motor cars, electrical goods, cutlery) in the 1970s. At least some of the growth in imports is attributable to this factor, so that Utton's results overstate the fall in concentration in 1968–77.[13] Second, Utton assumes that no foreign importer was a major supplier of the

Table 2.5 Concentration trends in UK manufacturing in the 1970s

(a) Sample of 93 three-digit industries, five-firm concentration[a]

	1970 (%)	1975 (%)	1979 (%)	Change, 1970–9 (%)
Employment	44.8	45.5	45.6	+0.8
Sales	45.5	47.2	46.4	+0.9
Net output	45.7	47.3	47.2	+1.5

(b) Sample of 121 four-digit industries, five-firm concentration

	1968 (%)	1975 (%)	1977 (%)	Change, 1968–77 (%)
Unadjusted	64.8	65.0	64.8	0.0
Adjusted	58.8	56.4	54.8	−4.0

Sources: (a) Census of Production, Summary Tables, 1970, 1975, 1979; (b) Utton (1982).

Note
[a] Figures relate to largest five firms by employment, so some underestimation of the levels of sales and net output concentration may arise, and this may affect the reported changes in sales and net output concentration.

UK market. This is obviously not the case in all industries, and moreover the growing dominance of imports in some markets, notably by Japanese firms, again suggests that Utton overstates the fall in concentration. Finally, Utton assumes that leading domestic firms export in proportion to their sales so that no special adjustment for exports is necessary. As he notes, however, leading firms tend to export more than in proportion to their sales, and he shows that this may lead to an additional reduction of about 3 percentage points to the adjusted concentration average. The effect on changes in concentration is more difficult to predict, however, although a best guess might be that it is not of major significance.

The results of table 2.5 suggest several tentative conclusions. In the first place, looking at the unadjusted figures, we see an apparent slowing down in the increase in concentration from that observed in the 1960s and before. This may be due in part to foreign trade factors in so far as leading producers increasingly switched production abroad in the 1970s. However, it may also reflect some rationalization of production by leading firms after the 1960s merger boom, and this is consistent with the fact that sectors with large concentration increases in the 1960s (such as food and drink industries, vehicles and electrical engineering) experienced stable or falling concentration on average in the 1970s.

Second, while Utton's calculations of foreign trade adjustments are not definitive, increased import competition was a growing force in the 1970s, and this probably had some effect in reducing UK market concentration after 1968. It is possible that a proper adjustment of concentration ratios for imports and exports, taking account of the points noted above, would reveal a much smaller effect than suggested by Utton. Nevertheless, it seems likely that foreign trade is having increasing effects on competition in UK manufacturing industry, and hence is likely to play an important role in future structure–conduct–performance analysis.

2.3 Theories of Concentration

Examination of the evidence on concentration raises a number of interesting questions. From the policy point of view, of course, the question of the links between high (and/or increasing) levels of concentration and economic welfare is paramount, and this will occupy our attention a good deal in later chapters. In this section, however, we focus on the more immediate questions of why concentration is high in some industries but not others, and why it may increase or decline. There is no general agreement on the answers to these questions, and I have chosen here to contrast two very different approaches to the concentration problem: the scale economies and stochastic explanations. As will become clear, however, these approaches can be regarded as tackling rather different aspects of the same problem, so a synthetic approach is not ruled out of court. This matter is touched on again at the end of this section.

2.3.1 Scale Economies and Market Concentration

We begin by examining the hypothesis that technological opportunities or scale economies are a primary determinant of market concentration. This hypothesis can be regarded as part of a wider approach to the explanation of market concentration, which may be called the *deterministic approach* in contrast to the *stochastic approach* examined in the next section. According to the deterministic approach, there will be a determinant equilibrium level of concentration in a market at a point in time, determined by given demand and cost conditions (and the behaviour of the market participants) and towards which the market will be continuously adjusting. In particular, it is argued that technological factors will play a central role in determining efficient levels of plant operation and hence this equilibrium concentration level. An implication of this particular hypothesis is that high or increasing levels of market concentration can be explained by underlying, mainly technological, changes – an argument which has been used by some authors

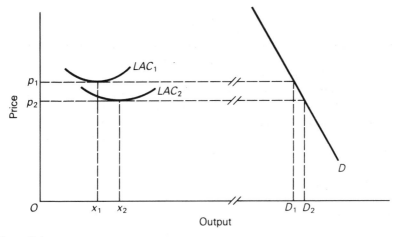

Figure 2.4

as a justification for such high levels of, or increases in, market concentration.

The basic argument for this hypothesis comes from standard micro-economic theory. Consider figure 2.4, which depicts a conventional U-shaped long-run average cost curve, LAC_1, for a firm in a competitive industry. Scale economies operate up to the least cost or optimal scale of production, x_1, and then scale diseconomies immediately set in. In long-run competitive equilibrium price will be p_1 (such that $p_1 = LAC_1 = LMC_1$ (not drawn)) and there is a corresponding market demand $D_1 = f(p_1)$. Each firm will be of optimal size, x_1, and the level of concentration in the market, as measured by $1/n$, is x_1/D_1. It follows that a rise in the ratio of optimal scale to market size owing to a technological change will reduce the number of market participants, thereby increasing market concentration. This is illustrated in figure 2.4 by a downward shift in long-run average costs to LAC_2, which increases optimal scale to x_2 and reduces the competitive price to p_2. Concentration will increase in competitive equilibrium if the growth in market size (D_2/D_1) is less than the increase in optimal scale (x_2/x_1).

Several points should be noted about this analysis. First, the scale economies hypothesis concerns the number of firms which can operate in a market given cost and demand conditions; it does not specifically address aspects of the market share inequality of market concentration. This point is important, and we shall see in the next section that a converse argument applies to the stochastic approach. Second, the hypothesis emphasizes the importance of scale economies relative to market size, rather than scale economies *per se*. The existence of substantial scale economies implies large firms, but if the market is also very large then it may not necessarily be the case that the number of market participants will be low. Finally, it should be noted that the theory is a long-run equilibrium theory and in particular that a change of the type envisaged in the shift from LAC_1 to LAC_2 might take many years to establish a new equilibrium. Technical developments, for example, may permit the bulk handling of chemical products, thereby enabling firms to gain economies of increased dimensions; but plant capacities cannot be increased overnight, and a long period of investment and adaption to the new opportunity may be necessary. The theory suggests that eventually a new equilibrium with fewer firms will arise (given appropriate demand conditions), but the prediction is a long-run one. This point is of some relevance in interpreting the evidence and implications of this hypothesis.

The theory outlined above is a simplification in at least two respects. First, it assumes that long-run average cost curves are U-shaped when a great deal of evidence suggests that they are in fact L-shaped.[14] Figure 2.5 introduces this modification wherein scale economies operate to scale x_1, the *minimum efficient scale* (MES), and constant costs prevail thereafter. (Scale diseconomies may set in at a very large scale.) This modification suggests only that scale economies set a lower bound to concentration in competitive conditions in that $1/n \geqslant x_1/D_1$. Indeed, in this case firms may be of unequal size (x_1 or above), so that without some specification of the distribution of firm size we no longer have a completely specified theory of concentration. Second, this problem is complicated if equilibrium price is greater than p_1, as it may be in oligopolistic or monopolistic circumstances. If the equilibrium price is p_2, say, in figure 2.5, then firms of less than minimum efficient scale may operate, so that x_2/D_2 sets the minimum concentration level, $1/n$. Clearly, the distance x_2x_1, which measures the extent to which production at less than MES is possible, depends upon the steepness of LAC, i.e. the cost disadvantage of operation at suboptimal scale.

The above provisos weaken the scale economies theory of market concentration, in that it is necessary to introduce arbitrary hypotheses to take account of firm size inequality and suboptimal production. The simplest

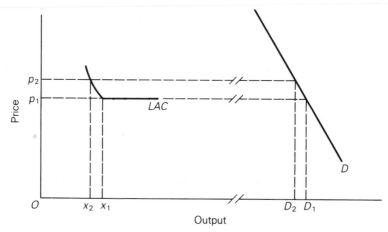

Figure 2.5

hypothesis is that equilibrium is such that the distribution of market shares is fixed about the ratio of MES to market size. This hypothesis is unlikely to be true, as we shall discuss in more detail in the next section. Nevertheless, it underlies much of the empirical work in this area, and we shall pass over this issue here in order to examine the evidence briefly. It should be borne in mind, however, that this problem represents a further weakness (to be added to those discussed below) with empirical work in this field.

A central problem with empirical studies of the scale economies hypothesis centres on the measurement of scale economies. Broadly speaking, estimates of scale economies are obtained either in limited quantity by painstaking research or in greater numbers by more arbitrary procedures. In the former category, Pratten (1971) (see also Silberston, 1972) provides estimates of economies of scale available in 25 manufacturing industries in the 1960s based on questionnaire evidence. His sample was, however, intentionally biased towards capital intensive/technological industries, so that it may not be representative of the links between market concentration and scale economies in general. Nevertheless, Pratten finds that in these industries a positive association exists between MES relative to market size and concentration, as might be expected, with such industries as oil, beer, cement and steel having considerable further scope for reducing costs by increasing concentration. Furthermore, evidence from industries such as beer, cement, turbo-generators and domestic appliances suggests that increasing concentration was often a response to technological opportunities to gain scale economies from rationalization of production. In Pratten's view, there is (in the long run, at least) 'a widespread and sharp conflict between the achievement of economies of scale and the maintenance of competition' (1971, p. 314). As noted above, while this may be true for (some of) the industries in his sample, one cannot infer to what extent it is more generally so.

Several studies have attempted a more quantitative test of the scale economies hypothesis. Weiss (1963), for example, has regressed the proportionate change in the four-firm concentration ratio, Y, for a sample of 85 US industries over 1947–54, on the proportionate change in ratio of plant MES to market size, X, over the same period. In simple linear regression, he finds that

$$Y = 70.2 + 0.295X \qquad r^2 = 0.26. \qquad (2.9)$$
$$(3.14)$$

(t ratio in parentheses). Thus these variables are positively correlated at the 1 per cent level with 26 per cent of the variation in Y explained. For the UK, Hart and Clarke (1980, chapter 4) estimate a log-linear regression for 76 industries in 1958–68 with Y being the proportionate change in the five-firm concentration ratio, X_1 and X_2 being the proportionate change in plant MES and market size treated separately, and X_3 the proportionate change in the plant/firm ratio (a proxy for multi-plant economies of scale). They find that

$$\log Y = 0.18 + 0.32 \log X_1 - 0.36 \log X_2 + 0.35 \log X_3 \qquad (2.10)$$
$$\quad\quad\quad\quad (2.29) \quad\quad\quad (-2.77) \quad\quad (1.00)$$
$$\bar{R}^2 = 0.13.$$

As can be seen, $\log X_1$ and $\log X_2$ with similarly sized coefficients significantly affect $\log Y$ at the 1 per cent level (one tail), although the effect of $\log X_3$ cannot be distinguished from zero. Comparison of equations (2.9) and (2.10) implies that the effect of scale economies in increasing UK concentration in the period 1958–68 was less strong as measured by $\bar{R}^2$ than the corresponding US effect in 1947–54.

Both the above studies are open to the criticism that they employ a proxy measure for MES, referred to by Weiss as the 'mid-point' plant size. This proxy is the plant size such that half of output (or employment) is produced in larger plants and half in smaller plants. It has been shown by Davies (1980b), however, that such a measure may itself be regarded as a measure of *plant* concentration.[15] Hence, it may be that definitional links between plant and firm size mean that part of the correlation reported above would occur independently of our hypothesis. Possible correlations between errors of measurement in this proxy and market concentration may also lead to an overstatement of the relationship, although errors in measurement in themselves can lead to an underestimate of the scale economies effect in the above regressions. These factors may in part explain why Hart and Clarke, for example, found that, in 141 industries in 1968, the levels of the variables in equation (2.10) explained 78 per cent of the variation in five-firm concentration across industries (Hart and Clarke, 1980, p. 45). It is difficult to assess how much weight to attach to these arguments in the absence of 'true' MES figures, however, and hence the degree to which the results given above are affected.

Given these reservations, conclusions at this stage must be tentative. It does not seem unreasonable to suggest that the evidence is consistent with a technological effect in changing concentration which is, however, only part of the story. Given that the scale economies hypothesis is a very long-run one, we expect and find that the broad pattern of concentration across industries conforms to the hypothesis. Changes in actual concentration in a ten-year period or less, however, are due partly to technological changes but predominantly to other unspecified forces. In discussing concentration changes, therefore, it is of interest to examine these other factors. Rather than consider what these factors might be here, however, we turn to examine an alternative general approach to their analysis.[16]

2.3.2 The Stochastic Approach

In contrast to the determinate emphasis on *equilibrium* concentration levels, the stochastic approach focuses attention squarely on the problem of *actual* concentration change. Fundamental to this approach is the idea that the actual process of concentration change reflects the net effect of a multitude of uncertain influences affecting the decisions and growth rates of individual firms. Among these influences we might list such things as days lost through strikes, exchange rate movements, the success of an advertising campaign or a new product launch, the success of a merger, a change in a competitor's price policy and many others. The important point from the stochastic point of view, however, is not what these factors are but rather that each firm's performance in a particular period is likely to be uncertain because of the multitude of influences at work. Given this view, the appropriate thing to do is not to look in detail at these influences but rather to make general assumptions about the process of concentration change. The approach thus argues that chance plays a crucial role in explaining concentration change, but that such change is not random but is subject to general rules.

Stochastic models of various degrees of sophistication can be constructed, but for present purpose we stick to the simplest case in order to bring out general principles.[17] Consequently, we abstract from the possibilities of entry, exit and merger and assume a given number of firms in an industry. Our central hypothesis, called *the law of proportionate effect*, is that each of these firms faces a given probability distribution of proportionate growth which is independent of its size. Thus, according to this assumption, the chance that each firm will grow by p per cent in a certain period does not depend on its current size. A process which supports this assumption is called a *Gibrat process* (Gibrat, 1931). The law is thus of *equiproportionate* growth in the probability sense, although of course the actual outcome growth rates for each firm will not be equal.

Several points should be noted before we look at a simple example of the law in action. First, the law is one of proportionate rather than absolute growth, and this may seem intuitively reasonable *a priori*. We shall see below that it is this factor which imparts the empirically desirable property of positive skewness to the firm size distribution. Second, as shown below, the Gibrat process gives rise to a tendency for concentration to increase persistently over time by increasing the inequality in firm sizes in the process. Thus, the process emphasizes the firm size inequality aspect of market concentration in contrast to the emphasis on firm numbers in the previous section. It should also be noted that this feature of the process is not dependent on proportionate rather than absolute growth effects, but rather arises if there is any dispersion in firm growth rates at all as long as probabilities of such growth rates are independent of size.[18]

In order to understand the process at work, consider the following simple example constructed by Prais (1976, chapter 2). Assume a fixed population of 128 firms, initially of equal size of 100 employees each. Let each firm in each period face the prospect of staying the same size with probability 0.5, of growing by a factor 11/10 with a probability 0.25, and of declining by a factor 10/11 with a probability 0.25. On these assumptions the distribution of firms by size (to the nearest whole number) for several states of the process is given as follows:

	No. of employees				
	83	91	100	110	121
Year 0			128		
Year 1		32	64	32	
Year 2	8	32	48	32	8

In year 1, half the firms stay the same size, a quarter reduce to 91 employees (10/11 of 100) and a quarter increase to 110 employees. In year 2 the same probabilities hold, so independently of size in year 1 we see the same growth process. Thus, for example, firms of size 91 in year 1 divide so that 16 stay the same size, 8 reduce to 83 employees ($10/11 \times 91$) and 8 increase back to 100 employees. A similar argument applies for firms of size 100 and of size 110 in year 1. Looking at the distribution in year 2, it is clear that, since firms, whatever their size, have the same chances of *proportionate* growth or decline, there is a tendency for large firms to grow by larger absolute amounts than small firms. In other words, the distribution becomes positively skew as noted above. It can be shown that as time proceeds the distribution of firms by size will asymptotically approach a *lognormal distribution*.

Whilst the example is simple, it does indicate the central features of the argument. Stated a little more generally, we can say that, for the ith firm,

$$\frac{x_t - x_{t-1}}{x_{t-1}} = \varepsilon_t \tag{2.11}$$

where x_t is firm size at time t (and so the left-hand side is the firm's proportionate growth rate in the period) and ε_t is a random variable with mean m and variance s^2. If (2.11) holds at all points in time and the εs are independent of each other and of the xs, then (by the Central Limit Theorem) in the limited $\log x_{t(t \to \infty)}$ will be normally distributed with mean mt and variance s^2t (Aitchison and Brown, 1966, chapter 3). If all firms in an industry are subject to (2.11), therefore, the firm size distribution will take on a lognormal distribution with these parameters (see section 2.1.3 above). In particular, since the variance of the logarithms of firm size increases with time, so does market concentration (given firm numbers). This is clear from the numerical example above, where firm size inequality (and the market share of the leading firms) increases with each step in the process, and it forms the basis for the prediction that the operation of chance factors alone can give rise to persistently increasing concentration.

While the above discussion does little more than reveal the tip of the iceberg of the stochastic approach, we shall restrict ourselves here to three further comments. First, while more complicated models than that outlined above may be developed, in so far as they embody a Gibrat-type process of proportionate growth, they typically give rise to firm size distributions with positive variance and skewness similar if not identical to a lognormal distribution. It is this factor more than any other which supports the use of the stochastic approach in the theory of concentration because it is just these features which characterize many empirical firm size distributions. Typically, industries consist of a large number of small firms and small number of large firms giving a characteristic positive skew to the distribution of firms by size (see figure 2.3 above). The statistical regularity with which such distributions arise represents strong *a priori* grounds for believing that a Gibrat-type process is at work, although of course it may not represent the whole story.

Second, it is important to note the neutrality of the process with respect to firm size. In postulating that the probabilities of proportionate growth are independent of firm size, the theory in no way derives the prediction of increasing concentration by assuming large firm advantage. This contrasts with the scale economies theory which gives larger firms the advantage of having lower unit costs. According to the present theory, however, concentration will increase stochastically even when unit costs are similar for all sizes of firm. If important scale economies exist favouring the growth of larger firms relative to small, then this offers an additional reason for expecting concentration to increase.

Finally, while additional effects may retard or speed the concentration process, the theory suggests that *laissez-faire* policies may not be sufficient to protect the competitiveness of the economy. It will, of course, be true that the tendency for concentration to increase owing to the Gibrat process can be offset if sufficient new firms enter the market and/or if small firms grow faster than large firms on average. Against these influences, however, we have firm 'deaths' arising from bankruptcy or merger, plus the fact that often large firms do have significant advantages over small firms. The overwhelming predominance of mergers over the divestment of companies, in particular, acts as a force favouring concentration, by simultaneously leading to large increases in firm size and reducing firm numbers, and this factor has been important, particularly in the 1960s in the UK (Curry and George, 1983). Underlying the mergers phenomenon, however, differential internal growth rates of firms can also persistently increase concentration. This suggests that, in the long run at least, a commitment to maintain a competitive economy may require a policy not only to control mergers but also to support small businesses in a positive way (e.g. through the tax system) (see Prais, 1976, *passim*).

2.3.3 Conclusions

It should be clear from the preceding two sections that both the scale economies and the stochastic explanations of market concentration are one-sided. The scale economies approach scores in the explanation of the long-run pattern of concentration across industries, while the stochastic approach emphasizes the multitude of factors which determine actual concentration change and rationalizes the typically observed distribution of firms by size within an industry. On the other hand, the scale economies approach, in itself, is vague over firm size inequality and the exact link between MES and firm size, while the stochastic approach, at least as outlined in section 2.3.2, seems to deny that systematic factors affect concentration at all.

These distinctions are, of course, overdrawn. Each theory tells a part of the story but is not of itself a sufficient general explanation. We can imagine, for example, a more general approach in terms of figure 2.5, whereby scale economies as reflected in the downward slope of the LAC curve have systematic effects on firm growth below output x_1 but not above.[19] Further complications might include special assumptions concerning new entry and mergers (Ijiri and Simon, 1977). The discussion in the present section should make it clear, however, that technology (or any other factor) is unlikely to be a sole determinant of market concentration, and that in the long run systematic forces may exist tending to increase concentration independently of any technological effect.

2.4 Summary and Conclusions

This chapter has examined the measurement of market concentration, descriptive evidence on levels and trends in concentration and some theories of market concentration. As far as measurement is concerned, we found that a number of measures of concentration exist, and some of their properties and interrelationships were discussed. Then, using the concentration ratio to measure market concentration, we examined levels and trends in concentration in UK manufacturing industry. This showed, in particular, that there have been substantial rises in market concentration in the postwar period, and particularly in 1958–68, although concentration appears to have remained stable or even fallen in the decade of the 1970s. Many factors account for these changes, but rather than list a number of separate factors, we examined some broad theoretical approaches to the explanation of concentration change in section 2.3. This suggested that, while technological factors probably account for the broad spread of concentration levels between industries, stochastic factors were also likely to be important in concentration change. It was also suggested that this may mean that active government intervention is desirable in order to protect the long-run competitiveness of the UK economy.

It seems likely that, in the 1960s at least, market concentration increases were associated in particular with merger activity as well as with differential internal growth rates of firms (Hart and Clarke, 1980). In the 1970s, the general decline in tariff barriers, the entry of the UK into the EEC and the rise in UK unit labour costs all tended to increase imports of manufactures, and hence to increase competition in at least some UK industries (Utton,

1982). Whether these effects dominated concentration increasing forces in the 1970s (and also the early 1980s), is at present uncertain (see section 2.2.2), and we must await further research before we can be clearer on the trends in market concentration in these more recent times.

Notes

1 For an excellent discussion of this and other issues pertaining to this section, see Cowell (1977).
2 In fact, Hannah and Kay develop a mathematically advanced treatment of the problem (1977, pp. 52–5) which involves seven conditions in all. We consider only their first four conditions here. An alternative set of conditions is given in Hall and Tideman (1967).
3 Hart (1975) argues, for example, that a merger of two medium-sized firms in a market may offset the market power of a large firm implying an increase in market competition. In this case, therefore, concentration as an indicator of market power should clearly fall.
4 For a fuller discussion of concentration measures and some other material in this chapter, see Curry and George (1983).
5 For the historical background to the index see Hirschman (1964).
6 From the definition of a *numbers equivalent*, there is some number of equal sized firms, m, such that

$$\sum_{i=1}^{m} (1/m)^{\alpha} = R_0$$

is the value of R obtained. Hence

$$HK = R_0^{1/(1-\alpha)} = [m(1/m)^{\alpha}]^{1/(1-\alpha)} = m.$$

Note that in this form HK is an *inverse* measure of concentration.
7 An interesting alternative approach, which also introduces flexibility into the measurement of concentration, has recently been suggested by Davies (1980a) (see also Davies, 1979b). Davies's U index explicitly weights firm size inequalities relative to firm numbers, and this approach provides a way of directly estimating the effects of numbers and relative firm size in empirical structure–conduct–performance studies. Hence it may well have use in determining the relative weighting of these factors in particular circumstances.
8 Entropy indices have been developed in particular in the context of information theory, and in their general form they incorporate other indices such as the H index as special cases. We consider only the first-order entropy of Shannon here (see Hart, 1971, 1975, for more details). This measure has certain desirable mathematical decomposition properties which make it useful in some theoretical analyses. A brief discussion of this is given in Jacquemin and de Jong (1977a).
9 See Hewer (1980). Total manufacturing imports rose from 16.6 per cent of home demand in 1970 to 25.8 per cent in 1979. Over the same period, exports as a proportion of manufacturers' sales rose from 18.1 to 24.3 per cent.

10 Under the revised Standard Industrial Classification (1980), new terminology has been introduced to replace older designations including 'MLH industry'. To avoid complications, we use the two-, three-, etc., digit terminology noted below in what follows.

11 Utton also reports adjustments for his industry sample in 1958 and 1963. These also lead to lower concentration levels in these years, but the impact on concentration trends is less dramatic than for the 1970s. For 1958–68, adjusted concentration rises by 6.5 percentage points compared with 8.3 percentage points without adjustment (Utton, 1982, table 3). This suggests that foreign trade adjustments were of more marginal importance on average prior to 1968. A similar conclusion can be reached from the work of Cannon (1978).

12 That is, Utton calculates the adjusted concentration ratio as $C_A = Q_5/(Q + M)$ where Q_5 is domestic production by the five largest domestic producers, Q is total domestic production and M is total imports. As a technical point, it should be noted that this formula is not correct (on Utton's assumptions) when exports, X, are positive for an industry. The correct formula is

$$C'_A = Q_5 \bigg/ \left(Q + \frac{MQ}{Q - X} \right)$$

which lies below C_A with X and M positive. Adjusted average concentration levels should thus be lower than those reported by Utton (on his assumptions).

13 Utton recognizes this point but suggests, on the basis of some sensitivity analysis (1982, table 4), that concentration continues to fall in 1968–75 even with allowance for some importing by leading producers.

14 For a discussion of this point and wider issues relating to scale economies see Scherer (1980, chapter 4).

15 A similar argument also applies to a proxy suggested by Comanor and Wilson (1967) involving the average size of plants above the mid-point plant size: see Davies (1980b). A recent measure suggested by Lyons (1980) is likely to be less subject to this particular criticism.

16 A number of other factors have been investigated. For details, see the survey by Curry and George (1983).

17 Some useful references on the stochastic approach are Hart and Prais (1956), Simon and Bonini (1958), Prais (1976) and Ijiri and Simon (1977).

18 These and other points are discussed at greater length in Prais (1976, chapter 2). I am grateful to Professor Prais for his advice in the writing of this section, and in particular for allowing me to use his numerical example in the next paragraph.

19 For a recent contribution which develops a model along these lines see Davies and Lyons (1982).

3 Oligopoly Price Theory

This chapter examines the problem of price determination in an oligopolistic market. In section 3.1 we examine a selection of theories of oligopolistic pricing ranging from the earliest theory of Cournot up to more modern game-theoretic approaches. We consider a number of possible solutions to the problem, ranging from the competitive solution to the monopoly (or industry profit-maximizing) solution. In section 3.2, in contrast, we take the monopoly solution as a base and consider the issue of why firms which seek to maximize profits may not coordinate their actions to obtain joint profit maximization. This raises much more practical issues of price determination relating to questions of uncertainty and complexity in the market, of which structural and institutional matters form an integral part.

3.1 Theoretical Approaches

We begin by considering some alternative theoretical approaches to the oligopoly problem. In order to bring out the basic principles underlying the problem we consider mainly simple models of two firms (duopoly) making interdependent decisions in a market. This case highlights the essential characteristic of an oligopolistic market; namely, that each firm knows that its fortunes depend on its rival's actions as well as its own. Hence, a duopolist's pricing problem is the strategic one of determining a policy to ensure a high profit given the policy of its rival. As with most strategic problems (e.g. in politics or war), a multiplicity of 'solutions' will exist, depending on the strategies adopted by the participants and the way the 'game' is played.

In section 3.1.1 we consider some traditional theories of oligopoly which serve to illustrate this multiplicity. Although none of these theories can be taken as *the* theory of oligopoly, it is often useful to use one or other of them as a convenient simplification in further theoretical work in industrial economics. Hence it is desirable to be familiar with these theories in order to understand some other work referred to later in this book. Second, in section 3.1.2, we consider the kinked demand curve oligopoly model which, as will be seen, attacks a rather different issue to the previously discussed models. And finally, in section 3.1.3, we briefly discuss some concepts derived from the mathematical theory of games.

3.1.1 Traditional Theories

Cournot's model   The pioneering work on oligopoly pricing was done as early as 1838 by a French economist, Augustin Cournot (see Cournot, 1960). He assumed that each firm seeks to maximize profit, taking rivals' outputs as given.

Cournot's model can be illustrated by assuming a market with two firms (1 and 2) producing a homogeneous product. Assume that each firm has identical constant costs, c, and that market demand is linear with $p = \alpha - \beta x$ (where p is market price, x is market output, and α and β are positive constants). Then, firm 1, say, seeks to maximize profits.

$$\pi_1 = px_1 - cx_1 \tag{3.1}$$

and a necessary condition for profit maximization is[1]

$$p + x_1 \frac{dp}{dx}\left(1 + \frac{dx_2}{dx_1}\right) - c = 0. \tag{3.2}$$

Crucial to the solution of this equation is the value of dx_2/dx_1, which is known as firm 1's *conjectural variation*. This measures firm 1's expectation as to firm 2's output reaction to a marginal change in its own output. Cournot's assumption is that $dx_2/dx_1 = 0$ (and correspondingly that $dx_1/dx_2 = 0$ for firm 2), such that each firm does not expect its rival to react to a change in its output. It should be stressed that this is an *expectation* on the part of each firm which, as discussed below, need not correspond with the actual reaction of a rival.

Firm 2 also has an equilibrium condition for the maximization of its profits given by

$$p + x_2 \frac{dp}{dx}\left(1 + \frac{dx_1}{dx_2}\right) - c = 0. \tag{3.3}$$

Setting the conjectural variations equal to zero and noting that $dp/dx = -\beta$ with a linear market demand, we can sum equations (3.2) and (3.3) to give

$$2(p - c) - \beta x = 0. \tag{3.4}$$

On substitution for p and rearrangement, we have market output as

$$x = \frac{2(\alpha - c)}{3\beta} \tag{3.5}$$

and market price as

$$p = \frac{\alpha + 2c}{3}. \tag{3.6}$$

These equations represent the market equilibrium solution of the Cournot model assuming profit maximization *and* zero output conjectures by both firms.

The output and price set in (3.5) and (3.6) lie between those set in perfect competition and monopoly. It is easily shown that a monopolist would set output $x_m = (\alpha - c)/2\beta$ with price $p_m = (\alpha + c)/2$, while in perfect competition $x_c = (\alpha - c)/\beta$ and $p_c = c$.[2] Hence, while a monopolist produces half of competitive output in order to maximize industry profits, Cournot duopolists produce two-thirds of that output (one-third each). Hence, they fail to exert as great a price-raising effect as a monopolist (with consequently lower joint profits). Also, it can be shown that, with n Cournot firms, market output and price will respectively be

$$x = \frac{n(\alpha - c)}{(n + 1)\beta} \tag{3.7}$$

and

$$p = \frac{\alpha + nc}{n + 1}. \tag{3.8}$$

Hence, as n rises above 2, market output increases and market price falls. In the limit, of course, price approaches competitive levels as n increases, with much of the price reduction arising as firms are initially added to the market. In this model, therefore, price reductions can be gained particularly by weakening tight oligopoly positions (with two, three, etc., firms) rather than when more firms operate in the market.

Figure 3.1 illustrates these results for the case of Cournot equilibrium for 2, 3, 5 and 10 firms. As can be seen, one-half of the difference between the monopoly price, p_m and the competitive price, p_c, is made up with just three firms in Cournot equilibrium, and further firms make successively smaller contributions to price reductions. As firm numbers increase towards infinity, price approaches competitive levels. This is an attractive property of the Cournot model in that it accords with our intuitive ideas that increased competition as firm numbers rise should lead to lower prices.[3]

Cournot's model rests on rather unsure foundations, however. Apart from the fact that the assumption of zero output conjectural variations is arbitrary,

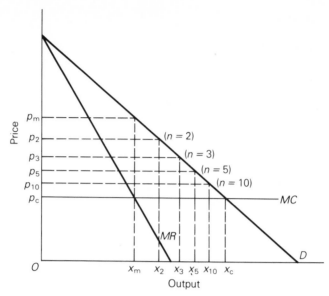

Figure 3.1

it is also frequently noted that such an assumption is inconsistent with actual reactions in the model. Thus, for example, while each firm sets output to maximize profit assuming that its rival's output is given, in disequilibrium situations rivals will in fact respond by changing output, thus nullifying this assumption. Hence, it would seem that firms would learn from this and attempt to incorporate this knowledge into their behaviour.[4]

The point can be usefully illustrated in terms of so-called Cournot *reaction functions*. These express the optimal output of firm 1 as a function of firm 2's output and vice versa. Thus from equations (3.2) and (3.3) we can explicitly write the respective firms' reaction functions as

$$x_1 = \frac{\alpha - c}{2\beta} - \frac{x_2}{2} \tag{3.9}$$

$$x_2 = \frac{\alpha - c}{2\beta} - \frac{x_1}{2}. \tag{3.10}$$

These functions are drawn in figure 3.2. Cournot equilibrium is at point E where the curves intersect, implying that each firm's output at E is its best response to its rival's output.

While the model under consideration is static, it nevertheless implicitly suggests a dynamic adjustment process.[5] Suppose initially that firm 2's output is zero and firm 1's output is x_1' in figure 3.2. Then firm 2, expecting 1's

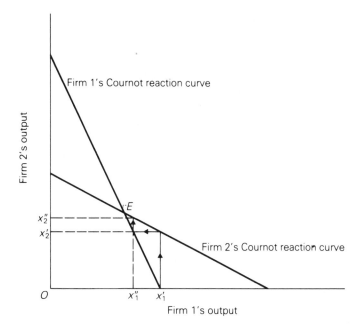

Figure 3.2

output to remain at x'_1, will set output at x'_2, as shown by its reaction function. Firm 1 will respond, however, according to the Cournot model, by taking x'_2 as given and reducing output to x''_1. Firm 2 then responds by raising output to x''_2 and the process continues until the Cournot equilibrium at E is attained. In each step of the process, each firm sets output to maximize profit assuming the other firm's output is given, but at each stage until equilibrium is reached this assumption is shown to be false. Apparently neither firm has the capacity to learn from experience to take advantage of information generated in the adjustment process.

Cournot's model can be defended to a limited extent, however. First, it can be argued that, if the adjustment process does take place in time, then, if firms move rather quickly to a position in the neighbourhood of E, they may not have time to modify their behaviour before an equilibrium is reached (Friedman, 1977, p. 37). In such circumstances, once an equilibrium is established firms may prefer to stick to it rather than promote further competition. Second, the equilibrium may be regarded as simply representative of a wider class of equilibria and hence useful as a benchmark for analysis (see the discussion of generalized oligopoly below). Both arguments are plausible to some extent, although by no means cast-iron. In particular, they fail to deal completely with the consistency issue. Since this issue has been addressed in recent work on consistent conjectures equilibria, we defer further discussion of it to later on in this section.

Bertrand's model   An early critique of Cournot's model was made by Bertrand (1883). He argued that firms might alternatively take rivals' prices rather than outputs as given.

This apparently innocuous change in the analysis has radical implications for equilibrium in the homogeneous product case. Consider a market where all firms initially set a given high price. If one firm adopts Bertrand conjectures, it thinks that by marginally cutting its price (with other prices given) it can capture the whole of market sales. If all firms think this then all will seek marginally to undercut their rivals and a price-cutting war will result. Moreover, firms will stop cutting prices only when competitive cost levels are reached. Hence (at least in the case of constant costs) the Bertrand equilibrium is at the competitive price such that no further price-cutting occurs. This result applies, moreover, for any number of firms in the market so that two firms are sufficient to produce the competitive price in the Bertrand model.[6]

In Bertrand's view, faced with this prospect, firms would merge or at least coordinate their actions to maximize joint profits. This suggestion is discussed more fully below. For the moment, however, we may simply note that Bertrand's conclusion that price competition leads to the competitive solution is sensitive to the assumption of homogeneous goods. When firms produce differentiated products such that all market sales do not disappear for a slightly higher-priced firm, then equilibrium at above competitive price is

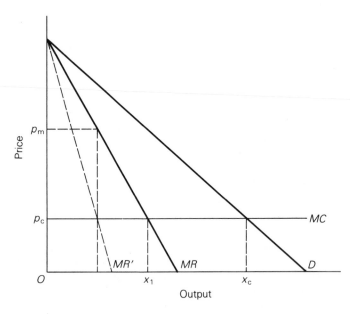

Figure 3.3

possible.[7] Indeed, in such differentiated product price models results much closer in spirit to Cournot's model than to Bertrand's may be obtained.

Edgeworth's model   A variant on the Bertrand model was suggested by Edgeworth (1925). Like Bertrand he assumed that firms adopt zero price conjectural variations, but unlike him he assumed that neither firm had sufficient capacity to supply the whole market at the competitive price.

Suppose for simplicity that each firm has sufficient capacity to supply one-half of the market at the competitive price. Thus a Bertrand solution is feasible (see figure 3.3). However, firm 1 (say) realizes that, with firm 2 producing output x_1x_c at full capacity, it will be unable to supply extra demand should it (firm 1) raise price above p_c. Given an equal distribution of customers between firms, firm 1 then finds itself a monopolist confronted by a demand curve MR in figure 3.3. It therefore maximizes profit by setting the curve marginal to this demand curve, MR', equal to MC and raises price to p_m. Under the assumptions made here of linear market demand and constant marginal costs, p_m is the full monopoly price for the market. Firm 2 then responds by raising its price to just less than p_m, capturing the whole market (of which it will be able to supply all but a small part on our capacity assumption). A Bertrand-type price war then ensues until, at some point between p_m and p_c, it becomes profitable for a firm to raise price to p_m again rather than continue underbidding. There is no equilibrium solution in the Edgeworth model; rather, price oscillates between the monopoly price and some lower price for an indefinite period.

Stackelberg's model   The German economist, Heinrich von Stackelberg, developed a leader–follower analysis of duopoly in 1934 (Stackelberg, 1952). In this model each firm has the option of acting as a Stackelberg leader or follower. A Stackelberg follower is a Cournot firm with a zero output conjectural variation; i.e., it simply sets output to maximize profits taking its rival's output as given. A leader, in contrast, assumes that its rival will adopt the followership pattern, and maximizes its profit given this assumption. Stackelberg assumed that each firm would calculate its profit as a leader or follower in a leader–follower situation and opt for the role which gave the greatest profit.

Assuming that market demand is linear and costs are constant as before, Stackelberg's model can be analysed diagrammatically using *isoprofit curves* (figure 3.4). An isoprofit curve for firm 1, say, shows combinations of outputs x_1 and x_2 which correspond to a given level of profit for firm 1. One such curve is π_1'. It is concave to the horizontal axis as drawn and has a maximum located on firm 1's Cournot reaction function. Further curves may be drawn, and lower curves correspond to higher levels of firm 1's profit. Thus, curve π_1'' is one such curve and firm 1's profit is higher on curve π_1'' than on curve π_1'. One can also construct isoprofit curves for firm 2 with analogous properties relative to the vertical axis; π_2' is one such curve.[8]

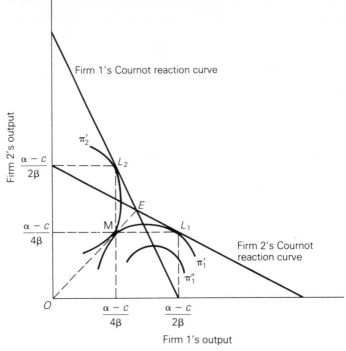

Figure 3.4

In figure 3.4 point E is the Cournot equilibrium point and point M is the industry joint profit-maximizing position. Suppose firm 1 adopts the role of leader and assumes that firm 2 will act as a follower. Then it assumes that firm 2 will set its output x_2 according to firm 2's Cournot reaction function. Firm 1, therefore, maximizes profit given this assumption. Diagrammatically, this implies moving to isoprofit curve π_1' such that π_1' is just tangential to firm 2's reaction function. By doing this, firm 1 attains the highest profit consistent with firm 2's assumed behaviour. L_1 is called the Stackelberg leadership point when firm 1 acts as a leader and firm 2 as a follower. By a similar argument, L_2 is the Stackelberg leadership point when firm 2 acts as the leader with firm 1 as the follower. At these points in our example the leader produces an output $(\alpha - c)/2\beta$ which is one-half the competitive output (i.e. equal to the monopoly output), and the follower produces one-half of this amount. In total, therefore, the firms would produce three-quarters of the competitive output, which is more than the two-thirds of competitive output implied by the Cournot solution.

However, the Stackelberg points are equilibria only where one firm opts to be the leader and the other opts to be the follower. In the present case, since a follower has half the output and hence half the profits of a leader at the

Stackelberg points, each firm will opt to be the leader with the other as follower. Hence there will be a *Stackelberg disequilibrium* such that no specific outcome can be predicted. Initially, both firms will produce half the competitive output so that the competitive price will prevail. However, since their expectations as to their rival's behaviour are not fulfilled, this will not be an equilibrium in general: one or both firms will have to revise its expectations before an equilibrium can be attained.

Dominant firm model   In contrast to the Stackelberg model in which the follower firm adopts a Cournot conjectural variation, followers in the dominant firm model act as perfect competitors. In this model it is assumed that followers take market price as given, setting price equal to marginal cost in order to maximize profits. The dominant firm, in contrast, sets price to maximize its profits given the supply curve of the competitive firms. Therefore the dominant firm acts as a partial monopolist and is constrained by the supply of competitive producers from extracting maximum monopoly profits from the industry.[9]

The analysis is illustrated in figure 3.5. In this diagram, D is the market demand curve, MC is the dominant firm's marginal cost curve and S is the supply curve for the competitive firms. Curve $NN'D$ is then the *net* demand curve for the dominant firm, found by horizontally subtracting S from D. In order to maximize profits, the dominant firm sets the marginal revenue curve,

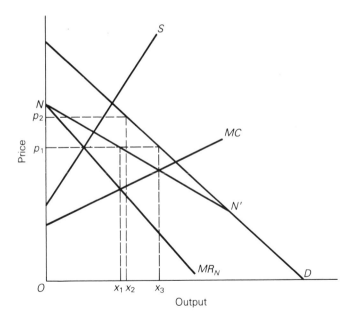

Figure 3.5

MR_N, corresponding to this demand curve equal to marginal cost. The result is output Ox_1 for the dominant firm with price Op_1. Since the competitive fringe also supplies output equal to distance x_1x_3 at this price, market output is Ox_3.

For convenience, we have also marked the monopoly price, Op_2, and monopoly output, Ox_2, on the figure. As one would expect, the introduction of a competitive supply weakens the monopoly power of the dominant firm as shown by the reduction in the price–cost margin, $(p-MC)/p$. Moreover, an expansion of supply tends to reduce market price further. It can be shown, in fact, that increases in market share by the competitive firms (or, alternatively, decreases in market share by the dominant firm) can act as a useful indicator of the extent to which price exceeds marginal cost in this model. This analysis is sketched in appendix 3.1 (following Saving, 1970) for the case of a dominant cartel of k firms whose joint market share is given as the k-firm concentration ratio. This analysis, therefore, points to links between prices and leading firm concentration ratios in models of this kind. The analysis is, however, slightly complex and hence has been consigned to an appendix.

Coordinated behaviour   Assuming that firms in an oligopolistic industry seek to maximize profits, an obvious incentive exists for cooperation rather than competition between them. Such cooperation could take the form of cartels or less binding arrangements between firms on prices, outputs, etc. In addition, however, Chamberlin (1966) has suggested that oligopolistic firms may tacitly coordinate their actions to this end. Specifically, he suggested that oligopoly groups would recognize their mutual interdependence and hence refrain from costly competition. In Chamberlin's view, even with two or more producers in a market and no formal collusion, one may still observe approximate monopoly pricing. More generally, however, oligopolistic coordination may vary systematically with firm numbers or market concentration, with higher concentration leading to more coordinated behaviour. Hence one can imagine a spectrum of behavioural possibilities ranging from competition to collusion and depending on the degree of concentration in the market.

One way of showing this formally is as follows. Following Cowling and Waterson (1976), we can consider a market with n firms producing a homogeneous product. Also assume that each firm maximizes profits adopting arbitrary output conjectural variations, say $\lambda_i = d\Sigma_{j \neq i}x_j/dx_i$ for firm i. Under these conditions, Cowling and Waterson show that market equilibrium implies that

$$\frac{p-\Sigma_i MC_i(x_i/x)}{p} = \frac{H}{\eta}(1+\mu) \tag{3.11}$$

where H is the Hirschman–Herfindahl index of market concentration, η is the market price elasticity of demand and μ is a weighted average of the $\lambda_i s$.[10] Hence, in this generalized model, different conjectures over rivals' output responses (as reflected in μ) influence the weighted average price–cost margin in the industry.

Now let us be more specific about these conjectures. In particular, following Clarke and Davies (1982), assume that each firm adopts a constant proportionate output conjectural variation, α, with respect to each rival such that $\alpha = (dx_j/dx_i)(x_i/x_j)$. The parameter α, therefore, represents the degree of implicit collusion in the market, with higher values of α corresponding to greater anticipated (proportionate) output responses from rivals. As outlined in appendix 3.2 below, Clarke and Davies show that, with this parameterization, equation (3.11) becomes

$$\frac{p - \Sigma_i MC_i(x_i/x)}{p} = \frac{H(1-\alpha)}{\eta} + \frac{\alpha}{\eta}. \tag{3.12}$$

Hence, α now summarizes the behavioural content in the model. Moreover, it can be shown that as α rises (with η held constant), weighted average price–cost margins in the market increase.[11]

Several cases of (3.12) may be noted. First, with $\alpha = 1$, each firm expects its rivals to match proportionately any change in output that it makes. Such expectations induce firms to restrict output rather than compete, and as shown in (3.12) lead to the monopoly solution where the price–cost margin equals $1/\eta$. More generally, with α between zero and one, only partial output matching is expected of rivals so that, as α is reduced, more scope for competitive expansion is envisaged, and the weighted average price–cost margin reduces. Clearly, if α depends on firm numbers or market concentration, then Chamberlin's hypothesis is consistent with $\alpha = 1$, while, more generally, lower concentration may give rise to lower values of α.

A simpler version of this argument can be made in the linear duopoly model considered elsewhere in this section. For this purpose, we need only assume constant conjectural variations, say $r = dx_2/dx_1 = dx_1/dx_2$. From equations (3.2) and (3.3) above, it can be readily shown that market output and market price will be

$$x = \frac{2(\alpha - c)}{(3+r)\beta} \tag{3.13}$$

and

$$p = \frac{\alpha(1+r) + 2c}{(3+r)}. \tag{3.14}$$

Hence, by equation (3.14) market price depends directly on r, rising as r rises. At one extreme, with $r = 1$, complete output matching is expected so that price rises to monopoly levels (i.e. $p = (\alpha + c)/2$). At the other extreme, with

$r = -1$, each rival expects complete accommodation of its output change, and the competitive or Bertrand solution (i.e. $p = c$) emerges.[12] At intermediate values of r, the greater is anticipated output matching, the higher is price.

Similar constructions to this can be made in the case where products are differentiated rather than homogeneous. In this case, firms which anticipate greater price matching by rivals tend to raise price and extract greater monopoly profits. The essential logic of the argument is the same. It is, therefore, possible to incorporate ideas of oligopolistic coordination fairly easily within models of this sort by adopting appropriate characterizations of firms' conjectural variations. A broader review of factors which may affect oligopolistic coordination is given in section 3.2 below.

Consistent conjectures equilibrium   Finally, we shall consider briefly some recent work on so-called consistent conjectures equilibrium (CCE) as developed by Bresnahan (1981) and others.[13] This work emphasizes the inconsistency of many oligopoly models, such as the Cournot model, which adopt conjectural variation assumptions for oligopolists which are not consistent with actual reactions of firms in the model. In the Cournot case, firms assume that rivals maintain their output levels when (with constant costs at least) such an assumption implies that actual reaction functions are not constant. Hence, the model lacks internal consistency, and this might be manifested by non-constant rival reactions in a dynamic version of the model.

Proponents of consistent conjectures models have suggested that, if firms are rational, one must expect them to adopt consistent conjectural variations. Hence, this requirement can be used to define admissible oligopoly solutions which ensure that firms do not (apparently) behave misguidedly. The idea is analogous to some extent to the idea of a rational expectations solution in macroeconomic theory. As developed so far, however, it has been applied only in a static context, and it is not clear in general how it would work under dynamic conditions. Moreover, as we shall see, the idea can give rise to undesirable market solutions from the point of view of market participants and hence may be regarded as less than rational from this wider viewpoint.

This point, and indeed the approach, can be illustrated for the homogeneous product duopoly case we have considered elsewhere, where demand is linear and costs are constant (see Bresnahan, 1981). As in the previous section, we assume that each firm adopts an identical constant output conjectural variation, r (equal to dx_2/dx_1 for firm 1 and dx_1/dx_2 for firm 2). From equations (3.2) and (3.3), therefore, we can write general reaction functions for each firm as

$$x_1 = \frac{\alpha - c}{\beta(2+r)} - \frac{1}{(2+r)} x_2 \tag{3.15}$$

and

$$x_2 = \frac{\alpha - c}{\beta(2+r)} - \frac{1}{(2+r)}x_1. \tag{3.16}$$

These equations show the actual reactions of each firm as a function of the output of the other firm and as a function of the anticipated reactions, r. For a consistent conjectures equilibrium, anticipated and actual reactions should coincide. In this simple case, therefore, the actual response of each firm to a unit change in its rival's output (i.e. $-1/(2+r)$) must equal the anticipated response, r.[14] In the Cournot case $r = 0$ and the actual rival response is $-1/2$, so that conjectures are not consistent. Moreover, any value of r other than -1 also produces inconsistent conjectures. Hence in this model a consistent conjectures equilibrium exists with $r = -1$.[15] As noted in the previous section, however, this conjectural variation corresponds to the competitive or Bertrand solution in this model. Hence, by behaving consistently the firms end up by making only normal profits.

Paradoxically, therefore, firms can increase their profitability in this case by adopting more coordinated conjectures, even though this implies that their conjectural variations thereby become inconsistent.[16] While one should not read too much into a particular example, this case does seem to raise question marks over consistency as a general oligopoly solution concept. In other circumstances, however, the concept may provide a useful way of approaching the oligopoly problem. Since work in this field is continuing and we have no more than touched the surface here, we conclude only that it is too early to draw any strong conclusions on the likely value of the consistent conjectures concept.

3.1.2 Kinked Demand Curve Theory

The kinked demand curve theory of oligopoly was introduced almost simultaneously by Paul Sweezy (1939) in the USA and by R. L. Hall and C. J. Hitch (1939) in the UK. As in section 3.1.1, the theory is concerned to model the conjectural variations of oligopolists (in this case with respect to price). In contrast to the last section, however, the primary focus of the analysis is not on the equilibrium price but rather on movements in oligopolistic prices. Specifically, the theory suggests that oligopolistic prices may tend to be rigid, not responding to changes in cost and demand conditions to the extent that one would expect in normal profit-maximizing theory.

We assume an oligopolistic market with differentiated products. Figure 3.6 depicts the situation for a typical oligopolist with current price, p_0. Curve DD' represents the oligopolist's demand curve on the assumption that rivals match its price changes, while the more elastic demand curve dd' would apply if rivals held price constant as the firm changed price. The kinked demand curve theory assumes that oligopolistic firms expect rivals to match price cuts but not price increases. Hence, the typical firm's perceived demand curve is

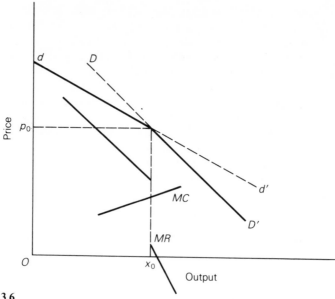

Figure 3.6

DD' below current price, p_0, and dd' above p_0, implying a kinked demand curve at the current price. This in turn implies that the firm's marginal revenue curve (MR) (made up of the appropriate sections of the marginal revenue curves corresponding to DD' and dd') is discontinuous over a range at current output, x_0. Given these conjectural variations, if marginal cost (MC) cuts marginal revenue at some point in the latter's discontinuous range, then the current price and output are perceived to be at profit-maximizing levels.

The novelty of the theory is that it predicts that oligopolistic prices will tend to be rigid to changes in cost and demand conditions. As drawn, large rises or falls in marginal cost can occur with marginal revenue remaining equal to marginal cost at output x_0, thus giving no incentive for the firm to change price. Similarly, lateral shifts (inwards or outwards) of market demand, while they will induce corresponding output changes, need not induce firms to raise or lower price if marginal cost continues to intersect marginal revenue in the latter's discontinuous range.[17] In both cases the firm's perceived notion of rivals' responses militates against the making of price changes which would seemingly make it worse off. Hence, it tends to stick to its current price, and this will be the more so the larger is the difference in demand elasticity between DD' and dd' at p_0 and hence the larger is the discontinuity in MR.

The hypothesis that oligopolistic firms expect to follow price cuts but not price rises is obviously only one possibility. In his original article, Sweezy suggests several alternative possibilities such that no kink would appear.

First, if an oligopolist can make secret price cuts then it may not expect rivals to follow it, such that dd' is also its demand curve below current price. Second, if the oligopolist regards itself as a price leader then it might expect price rises to be followed, and then DD' would be its appropriate demand curve above p_0. Clearly, there is no way of knowing *a priori* which of these hypotheses is important in practice, and it is therefore necessary to examine the empirical evidence.

Some evidence apparently in favour of the kinked demand curve hypothesis was presented by Hall and Hitch. Their study looked at pricing behaviour based on the interpretation of interviews with 38 UK businessmen. They found that these businessmen tended to set prices to cover unit costs according to a 'full-cost' principle and then not to vary these prices for kinked demand curve reasons. As noted by Stigler (1947; see also Stigler, 1978), however, these inferences are not wholly consistent. According to the 'full-cost' principle, price is set equal to average cost at a normal rate of output, with a conventional allowance being made for profit. Such a 'full-cost' price, according to Hall and Hitch, is likely to be revised upward in response to an industry-wide increase in costs, or alternatively to be cut when a sustained decrease in demand is observed. Neither observation squares well with the kinked demand curve idea and the second also conflicts with the 'full-cost' principle. Hence the evidence presented by Hall and Hitch is subject to some reservation.

In his 1947 paper, Stigler examined empirical evidence on the kinked demand curve hypothesis more thoroughly. First, he attempted to test the hypothesis by examining price movements in seven oligopolistic industries. Contrary to expectations engendered by the hypothesis, he found no tendency for rivals to follow price increases less than price decreases. This result was interpreted as implying that there was no formal basis for firms to believe in asymmetric rival responses to price changes so that they would not rationally hold such beliefs. Since, however, actual price changes strongly imply that something has happened to make marginal cost go through the defined part of the marginal revenue curve, this conclusion may not be warranted.[18]

Stigler also looked at the predictions of the theory using US monthly price and output data for 19 oligopolies and two monopolies in 1929–37. Among other things, he found that

(1) prices were much more rigid in his two monopolies (aluminium and nickel) than in his oligopolies in this period and this could not be accounted for by less variation in demand:
(2) prices were more rigid in periods of known collusion than in periods when the kink might have been operative; and
(3) prices were more rigid in industries with more heterogeneous products, although in such markets one would expect a smaller kink (as less product substitutability would make dd' less elastic, *ceteris paribus*, in figure 3.6).

Each of these results is contrary to the view that kinked demand curves are an important feature of oligopolistic markets. And, indeed, Stigler was unable to find any systematic evidence to support the kinked demand curve theory.

Further empirical studies have also cast doubt on the importance of the hypothesis. Simon (1969) looked at the possibility that the theory might apply with respect to magazine advertising rates but found that advertising rates were more rigid where a single magazine served a market area compared with market areas served by several magazines. Primeaux and Bomball (1974) looked at the price behaviour of electric utilities in US cities; they found that more price changes were observed in cities with duopoly supply compared with monopoly supply, and that duopolists more commonly followed rate increases than decreases. Primeaux and Smith (1976) found similar negative results in the application of these tests to prescription drugs.

Despite an abundance of casual empiricism in support of the kinked demand curve hypothesis, therefore, evidence of a systematic kind in its support does not appear to be available.

3.1.3 Game Theory

In this section we shall examine briefly the impact that the mathematical theory of games has had on the theory of oligopolistic pricing, following the pioneering work of von Neumann and Morgenstern (1944). No attempt will be made to deal explicitly with game-theoretic models, which are technically advanced; however, some basic ideas will be reviewed, both because of their increasing use in the general literature and as a basis for access to more advanced work.[19]

We may begin with an example of a game which has particular relevance to the oligopoly problem. This is the so-called Prisoner's Dilemma game. In this game two players (1 and 2) each consider adopting one of two strategies (A and B). The set of strategies adopted by the players determines an outcome which defines payoffs for each of them (measured as expected utilities). A possible payoff matrix is shown in table 3.1. In this table, the first value of an element of the payoff matrix is the payoff to player 1 and the second value is the payoff to player 2. Thus, for example, if player 1 opts for strategy A and player 2 for strategy B, the payoffs are -10 for player 1 and 10 for player 2.

Table 3.1 The Prisoner's Dilemma

	2's strategy A	B
1's strategy A	0, 0	$-10, 10$
B	$10, -10$	$-5, -5$

Now, according to this game, the two players involved are prisoners held on suspicion of having committed a major crime. Each knows that, if he turns state's evidence against his partner, he will receive a pardon if his partner does not also confess. If both confess then they receive a reduced sentence, but if neither confesses then they merely receive a minor sentence for a lesser charge. The strategies in this case are not to confess (A) or to confess (B). Thus, if prisoner 2 confesses but 1 doesn't, say, then 2 goes free (with utility 10) and 1 gets the maximum sentence (with utility -10). If both confess they get the reduced sentence (worth -5 each), but if they both hold out then they simply get prosecuted on a lesser charge (taken as the base with utility of 0 for each). The prisoner's dilemma is whether to confess and risk conviction (with a reduced sentence) should his partner confess, or to hold out and risk being left with the maximum sentence should his partner confess.

In we assume that the prisoners behave *non-cooperatively*, then game theory asks the question, Which strategy will individually rational players choose? Consider player 1. If player 2 chooses to not confess (A), then 1's best policy is to confess (B). If player 2 chooses to confess (B) then 1's best policy is to again confess (B). Hence for player 1, strategy (B) dominates strategy (A) whichever policy 2 chooses, and hence it is individually rational for player 1 to confess. By the same logic, player 2 will also choose to confess (B) and the equilibrium pair involves both players in payoffs of -5. But it is clear that, if both players could have cooperated and established a binding agreement not to confess (A), they both would have had payoffs of 0. This would have been a *Pareto improvement* over the non-cooperative equilibrium pair since both players would have been better off. This illustrates a basic feature of this type of game-theoretic situation: namely, that individually rational actions do not necessarily further group interests.[20]

The prisoner's dilemma game is an archetypal example of a non-zero sum game. The distinction between a *zero sum* and a *non-zero sum* game is crucial. In a zero sum game, with two players for simplicity, the utilities of the players always sum to zero whatever the game's outcome. On certain simplifying assumptions, a zero sum game is equivalent to a zero money sum game. In these circumstances, zero sum games are such that, whatever the outcome, one player's monetary gain is the other's loss. This contrasts with non-zero sum games, where outcomes do not simply involve transfers of money or utility between players. In non-zero sum games the interests of the players are not directly opposed and hence it may be possible for the players to gain from cooperation. Hence the assumption that the game is non-cooperatively played takes on added significance with non-zero sum games.

It should be clear that the Prisoner's Dilemma game illustrated in table 3.1 may well be a useful model for oligopoly theory. Suppose players 1 and 2 are duopolists and we consider the two strategies of producing one-quarter of the competitive output (A) or one-third of the competitive output (B). The payoffs (which might be interpreted simply as profits) are scaled such that, if both firms choose (A) (the joint profit-maximizing solution), payoffs are zero.

Then the non-cooperative solution to this game involves strategies (B, B) as before, which in this case are the Cournot outputs (see section 3.1.1). This solution is in fact an example of a *Nash non-cooperative equilibrium point*, which has the feature that each player maximizes his payoff given the strategy of his opponent. Clearly, Cournot's quantity-setting duopoly equilibrium has this property and as such is actually referred to today as a Cournot–Nash equilibrium. We know, of course, from section 3.1.1 that this is by no means the only non-cooperative equilibrium solution.

The Prisoner's Dilemma game highlights the possibility of firms making gains from cooperation in non-zero sum games. Such gains may be realized if the players can make binding agreements to behave cooperatively. If this is the case then we are concerned with *cooperative games* as opposed to non-cooperative games, and attention shifts from strategies to the payoffs that the players receive. Cooperative games may occur with *no side payments*, in which case players must be satisfied with the payoffs they receive in the cooperative solution, or *with side payments*, such that redistribution of payoffs is possible after the game is played. In general, a cooperative solution is Pareto-optimal for the players in that no opportunities for an improved payoff to one player (which does not reduce the payoff of another player) is forgone. In addition, no player will rationally accept a payoff (with side payments, if permitted) which is below that which he would receive in a non-cooperative equilibrium.

In cooperative games it is assumed that players submit to binding agreements on which there is no reneging. Such games may well be a useful model in situations where competing firms merge or alternatively form a strong cartel. However, they ignore the important possibility that players can often gain from reneging on an agreement, i.e. by behaving non-cooperatively. Thus, as we have seen in the simple example in table 3.1, player 1 may gain by adopting strategy (B) if 2 adopts (A). In addition, while the players may not openly reach an agreement to cooperate, they may nevertheless tacitly seek to coordinate their strategies to mutual advantage. This possibility of tacit but possibly incomplete coordination of policies is of considerable interest in oligopoly theory and forms the subject matter of section 3.2 below.

3.2 Oligopolistic Coordination

Oligopolists have an incentive to cooperate rather than compete. In the limit, if they are able to coordinate their actions completely and if there is no threat of new competition, they may be able to behave as a monopolist and maximize joint industry profits. Such behaviour, subject to the usual provisos, involves economic resource misallocation and is detrimental to consumers.

In this section we examine oligopolistic markets from the point of view of oligopolistic coordination. This does not mean that all oligopolists collude rather than compete. Nevertheless, we identify certain market conditions which may tend to facilitate coordination. This exercise is useful as a basis for empirical work and as a guide for possible public policy action.

3.2.1 Market Conditions and Coordination

The extent of oligopolistic coordination in a market is likely to depend on a variety of factors, including the legal framework within which firms in the market find themselves, market structure including entry conditions, and cost, demand and any other market conditions that may be relevant. In addition, the attitudes of the firms in the market (whether they are competitively or cooperatively inclined) may act as an independent influence, i.e. one which is not wholly determined by objective market conditions. Clearly, it may only be possible to find general tendencies with respect to factors influencing oligopolistic coordination. Moreover, such factors may interact in a complex way such that general principles are hard to find. In this section we review some of the hypotheses that have been put forward in the literature as to factors likely to affect oligopolistic coordination.

We may begin with several general points. First, the ability of firms to coordinate their actions will be influenced by the legal framework within which they operate. In some circumstances legal restrictions on oligopolistic coordination may be so minor that there is no bar to the formulation of *formal cartels*, which may control every aspect of price and production policy, etc. In the UK, for example, prior to the 1956 Restrictive Trade Practices Act, legal restrictions were of this type and restrictive agreements between firms were widespread in much of UK industry (see chapter 11). Since 1956, however, the law has been tightened up and formal cartels (excepting export cartels) are *de facto* illegal. Cartels in the USA are also (*de jure*) illegal, and prosecution of cartels has taken place since the passing of the Sherman Act of 1890.

This does not mean that oligopolistic coordination is severely prescribed, however. The US experience of prosecutions under the Sherman Act, for example, shows that many firms are prepared to act illegally in order to secure the benefits of coordination. Moreover, it may not be necessary to form a formal cartel to attain at least some degree of coordination. Inevitably, there are 'grey areas' in the law which firms are able to utilize. In particular, anti-trust policy in both the USA and the UK has not been able to deal satisfactorily with oligopolistic coordination in the absence of explicit agreement. Such tacit collusion may be effected simply on the understanding of market participants and may or may not involve one of the firms acting as price leader. Tacit collusion is greatly facilitated by the provision of comprehensive and up-to-date information on prices and cost structures of market participants, and such data are frequently provided by trades associations in the relevant markets. Some strengthening of the law on information exchanges was made in the UK in 1968, however (see chapter 11), with apparently some success (see Swann et al., 1974).

Second, the goal of oligopolistic coordination need not be short-run profit maximization. In the USA, for example, there is evidence that levels of anti-trust enforcement efforts and penalties can limit price markups.[21] Also, in many industries the threat of new competition may serve to limit the price that established oligopolists may seek to set. The problem of new competition and associated barriers to entry will be considered in detail in the next chapter. In what follows, we shall implicitly assume that entry is blockaded in an industry, so that joint profit maximization is a possible goal. This represents a convenient simplification which can be modified when one wishes to consider the more general problem of possible new entry.

In his analysis of oligopoly, E. H. Chamberlin (1966) suggested that oligopolistic coordination was more likely to occur with a limited number of sellers in the market. In such a situation, firms would recognize their interdependence and hence the joint advantage in coordinating their actions. If any firm attempted to cut its price to increase market share, it would expect its rivals to do likewise and hence make all firms worse off. Hence each firm would perceive its own advantage as coincident with oligopolistic coordination, and the result would be the maximization of industry profits.

Chamberlin's hypothesis that relatively small firm numbers are conducive to oligopolistic coordination has formed the basis for much subsequent work in industrial economics. At the same time, however, it has been recognized that this is likely to be only one of a number of factors at work. Among other things, the ability of oligopolistic firms to coordinate their actions may be influenced by the heterogeneity of cost and demand conditions, the level of market demand and opportunities for secret price-cutting in the market.

Cost and demand heterogeneity   In the models considered in section 3.1, oligopolistic firms were typically assumed to have identical cost and demand conditions. In real-world markets, however, asymmetries are likely to exist with respect to cost and/or demand. Such asymmetries may have several effects, tending to limit oligopolistic coordination by introducing *complexity* and *implicit bargaining* into the problem of price determination. Particularly where a number of firms are involved, it may be difficult for firms to perceive and adhere to a price and production configuration approaching a cooperative solution. Hence we may expect that, as such complexities increase, oligopolistic firms may deviate further and further from industry profit-maximizing positions.

We can elaborate these points by means of a simple illustration. Assume that there are two firms, 1 and 2, producing a homogeneous product but under differing cost conditions. Let firm 1 be more efficient than firm 2 and assume that each firm has a rising marginal cost curve, shown respectively as MC_1 and MC_2 in figure 3.7. As a reference point, note that industry profit maximization would require each firm to produce to the point where marginal cost equals marginal revenue. Thus, the industry profit-maximizing output is such that the horizontal sum of the marginal cost curves, MC_s,

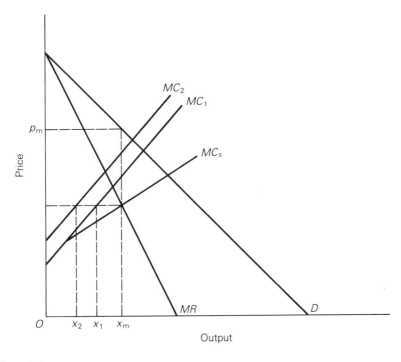

Figure 3.7

equals marginal revenue, MR. With joint output x_m (and price p_m), output would be allocated between firms such that firm 1 has output x_1 and firm 2 output x_2. That is, the more efficient firm 1 would produce a larger output than firm 2 to maximize industry profits.

Now consider the factors working against oligopolistic coordination in this example compared with the case in which both firms have the same costs. In the latter case, firms will soon recognize what the joint profit-maximizing price is and also that, by each producing one-half of monopoly output, they will secure one-half of monopoly profits. In the case depicted in figure 3.7, however, things are not so simple. If firms are operating with incomplete information of cost and demand conditions, cost asymmetries tend to increase the complexity in locating the optimal price–output configuration. Moreover, the scope for implicit bargaining over profits is increased. Firms may attempt to improve their prospects by giving misleading signals as to their relative competitive positions. Also, weaker firms may be less willing to accept the lower profits that are likely to accompany their lower output shares. In some cases, indeed, full joint profit maximization might imply that some weak firms have negative profits (or even negative outputs), which is unlikely to be acceptable to them. Also, large and small firms may have different perspectives on market conditions with, for example, larger firms taking a longer-run view and tending to want to set a lower price (e.g. to stave off new competition) than smaller firms (see Fog, 1956). Finally, firms may have difficulty in monitoring the policies of their rivals in complex situations, and small firms in particular may be able to encroach on implicit output quotas without retaliation.

While such complexities undoubtedly create problems for oligopolistic co-ordination, it should not be thought that they are necessarily insurmountable. In a symmetrical model firms recognize that they are competing on equal terms and so, according to Chamberlin, see the joint advantage of industry profit maximization. In the non-symmetrical world, however, firms may recognize their relative competitive strengths and come to a tacit under-standing not to compete. Price leadership is a relatively simple device whereby oligopolistic firms may cut through the complexities described above. Particularly in situations where one firm is clearly the market leader, price leadership may evolve with neither the weaker firms nor the leader wishing to upset the balance. Hence it is not clear that greater cost and demand asymmetry, and presumably greater firm size inequality, does necessarily lead to less oligopolistic coordination in general.

Level of market demand   A second factor which is likely to influence the ability of oligopolistic firms to coordinate their actions is the level of market demand. When business conditions are depressed, because of either cyclical depression in the economy or secular decline in a particular industry, profits will suffer and prices may tend to fall. In itself, a falling price is not necessarily evidence of the breakdown of oligopolistic coordination, since it may be desirable to reduce price when demand declines in order to maximize industry profits. Pressure on profits is likely, however, to place stress on price discipline; and financially weak oligopolists, in particular, may risk price cuts to gain market share. Once price discipline is broken in depressed conditions, it may be very difficult to restore. Thus, while it remains in the joint interest of firms to 'hold the line', pressures on financially weak firms create additional reasons for price competition to break out.

This is particularly likely to be the case in industries with relatively high fixed costs. The argument is illustrated in figure 3.8, which shows the cost curves for an efficient size of plant in a capital-intensive industry. Marginal operating costs, MC, are relatively low up to, say, 90 per cent of full capacity and then they rise steeply. Average costs, AC, fall sharply more or less to full capacity, reflecting the large capital costs of the plant. We assume initially that demand is high and that oligopolists have coordinated their actions to set price p_1 with 90 per cent capacity working. This is shown by curve D_1, which represents this firm's share of the market curve in normal times. Now suppose demand falls to D_2 and the optimal joint profit-maximizing price falls to p_2. The required capacity working is 60 per cent, and with 40 per cent excess capacity the firm is no longer able to make positive profits. Obviously the problem arises from the high capital charges; and, *ceteris paribus*, the

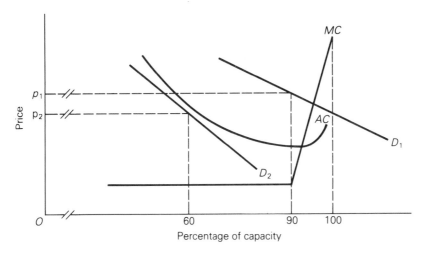

Figure 3.8

higher are these charges, the greater will be the financial problem from operating with a given degree of excess capacity. In industries in which fixed costs are relatively high, the financial pressures for moving closer to full-capacity working are that much greater, and hence the greater is the pressure to risk a price cut. The firm can see that, even at a price slightly below p_2 in figure 3.8, it can make a profit if it can increase its output to say 70 per cent of full capacity. If all firms think the same way, however, they end up sliding down such share of the market curves as D_2 and losses increase.

Clearly, while the financial pressures to cut price may be great when demand is low, the risks of very high losses should industry discipline break down must also be considered. Oligopolists thus have a strong incentive to stick together in times of adversity. Whether they will be able to or not is likely to depend on particular institutional and other factors. UK experience in the depressed interwar years (1918–39) shows that both forces were at work (see Swann et al., 1974). Attempts at maintaining or creating effective cartels in industries such as cotton spinning, coal mining and iron and steel, for example, all broke down in the 1920s as firms attempted to cut prices to survive. As the depression continued, however, increased cartelization and rationalization (often with government support) was observed. Indeed, many of the agreements which survived to the 1950s – in cement, heavy steel, transformers, etc. – were formed in the 1930s. This evidence suggests that, over a long period of depressed demand, when some firms and plants have closed down, surviving oligopolists may be able to restore some degree of coordination. In the shorter run, however, it may well be that more competitive instincts will prevail, leading to open price war and low or possibly negative profits in depressed industries.

Secret price-cutting   The other side of the coin to tacitly or formally agreeing on a price is the problem of policing that agreement once it has been made. As discussed in section 3.1.3, while it is in the joint interests of firms to set a collusive price, it is in the individual interests of each participant to undercut that price, gaining market share at the expense of rivals. According to Chamberlin, such chiselling on agreements will not occur if each firm recognizes that its rivals are likely to retaliate by matching price cuts, leaving all firms worse off. This argument assumes, however, that sellers will have *full information* on the prices charged by rivals, so that retaliation on price might be expected with a minimal lag. If, on the other hand, it is possible for firms to cut price secretly without rivals suspecting, then the ability of firms to keep prices up by tacit or explicit coordination is likely to be severely reduced.

This issue has been addressed, in particular, by Stigler (1964), who postulates that firms may secretly cut price below joint profit-maximizing levels (see also McKinnon, 1966). Many goods are sold to other producers, retailers and even consumers at prices set by negotiation between the parties involved. Such transactions prices (as opposed to list prices) are not readily observable to competing firms and hence offer scope for secret price-cutting. In Stigler's model, the extent of such price-cutting will be set by the ability of firms to avoid detection, which in turn depends on the amount of uncertainty over market demand.

While Stigler's analysis is too complex to treat fully here, several of his conclusions are worthy of mention. First, the fewer the number of firms in the market, the easier it will be for firms to police each other's actions and hence the less secret price-cutting there will be. This idea generalizes to market concentration, moreover, where, interestingly, less price-cutting occurs for larger values of the H index of concentration. Second, the greater the turnover of customers in the market, the greater is the problem of policing rival actions and hence the more price-cutting there will be. Third, the smaller the probability of repeat purchasing by customers, the greater the problem of policing will be. And finally, the more buyers there are, the more difficult it will be to capture a further x per cent of the market without price-cutting being detected. These arguments, therefore, suggest that oligopolistic co-ordination will be most effective where few firms sell to many customers and where those customers form a regular clientele for the firms involved.

Other factors   A number of other factors may influence oligopolistic co-ordination, of which we may mention three.[22] First, oligopolistic coordination is most likely to be successful in stable market conditions, where new competition is not a threat and technology is static. In more dynamic industries, however, where rapid technical change is accompanied by signifi-cant new entry, cost and demand conditions are likely to be changing so fast that oligopolistic coordination is not feasible. Markets for hi-fi equipment, personal computers and other electronic goods readily spring to mind as examples. Second, when heterogeneous products are not standardized but are rather capable of variation in a number of dimensions, then oligopolistic coordination may be difficult. In some cases the nature of the product (e.g. nuts and bolts) is such that long but complete price lists can be produced to facilitate collusion. In other cases, however, (e.g. motor vehicle tyres) firms may compete on product variation itself so that coordination is more difficult. Finally, when demand comes in large lumps (as, for example, with boilerhouse plant, aero-engines, ships, etc.), a problem exists over matching demand to supply. As in the case when demand in an industry is low, firms have the problem of ensuring that they have sufficient work on hand while at the same time avoiding 'cut-throat' competition. In some markets – for example in shipbuilding, where competition takes place on a world scale – there is little scope for oligopolistic coordination. In other cases, however, some degree of stability can be imposed, often with government acquiescence.

3.2.2 Empirical Evidence

In addition to case study analyses of individual industries, three types of systematic evidence have been used to examine oligopolistic coordination. First, cross-section econometric techniques have been used to consider inter-industry variations in profitability and prices. Second, systematic analyses of price-fixing cases caught under anti-trust legislation have been made. And finally, a number of simulation experiments of oligopolistic games under controlled conditions have been reported. We shall examine the econometric evidence in detail in chapter 5; in this section we briefly review some of the results obtained by the latter two methods of approach.

We begin with several studies of price-fixing cases initiated by the US Department of Justice since 1890.[23] Several possible weaknesses of these data should be noted. First, since the data relate to cases instituted by the Department of Justice, they may not be representative of all price-fixing conspiracies in the USA. In particular, cases in which tacit rather than explicit collusion is used tend not to be represented owing to difficulties in obtaining successful prosecutions in such cases. Also, price-fixing conspiracies may differ in their detectability in systematic ways, which may also lead to unrepresentativeness of the sample. Second, in many cases instituted by the Department of Justice, a settlement was made out of court, so that a judgement on price-fixing was not obtained. This is probably not a major weakness of the data, however, since it seems likely that in most, if not all, of such cases settlement was made because a government victory was virtually assured. Most studies have used these data, since not to do so would mean a great reduction in sample size.

The pioneering work in this field was done by Posner (1970). He looked at Department of Justice cases for 1890–1969, of which 989 related to horizontal conspiracies. He found that, in the vast majority of cases for which information was available, 20 or fewer firms were involved in the conspiracy, and in nearly two-thirds of cases 10 or fewer firms were involved. This evidence clearly

points to the importance of small numbers in effecting oligopolistic coordination. He also noted that many conspiracies (47 per cent) were of a local or
regional nature, a factor which is, of course, likely to be of greater importance
in a large country such as the USA. Third, conspiracies often encompassed
much wider policies than simply price-fixing, the most important of which
were division of territories (15 per cent of cases) and collusion on terms and
conditions (14 per cent of cases). In 10 per cent of cases the conspiracy was
associated with patents or copyrights, while 14 per cent of cases involved
bidding for contracts (government or otherwise). Finally, in 44 per cent of
cases the conspiracy was effected via a trade association, and such cases were
particularly prevalent when firm numbers were relatively large.

A number of studies have followed up Posner's work. Hay and Kelley
(1974) looked at a limited sample of 65 cases in 1963–72 which were either
won by the government or settled by *nolo contendere* ('no contest') pleas.
Using confidential Anti-trust Division information, they concluded that the
principle characteristics of price-fixing conspiracies were small firm numbers,
high market concentration and relative product homogeneity. These results
led them to suggest that formal collusion may be necessary for oligopolistic
coordination even under these very favourable conditions. This conclusion
was contested by Fraas and Greer (1977), however, in a sample of 606 price-
fixing cases for 1910–72. They found that the modal class of firm numbers
among price-fixing industries was between four and six firms. When compared
with the distribution of industries by firm numbers in manufacturing as a
whole, they felt that the evidence was consistent with tacit coordination being
prevalent where firm numbers are low, giving way to formal collusion and
then competition as numbers increase. It should be noted that the evidence
they present in favour of this conclusion is only mildly persuasive, however.

Finally, Asch and Seneca (1975), using a slightly different approach,
compared a sample of 51 manufacturing firms found by the courts to have
colluded with a random sample of 50 non-colluders in the period 1958–67.
Among other things, they found that colluders tended to be low-profit-
making but large firms and that they tended to operate in industries with
relatively low advertising intensity. The low profitability result is particularly
striking and may reflect the defensive nature of some collusion.

A rather different line of attack on the problem is the experimental
approach. In this case a hypothetical oligopoly game is played under
controlled conditions in an attempt to see what factors are likely to affect the
oligopolistic outcome. These experiments are normally conducted without
explicit cooperation between participants and so they directly examine the
tendency to oligopolistic coordination via tacit collusion. Factors which may
be varied include the number of players, the information available to them
and the heterogeneity of cost and demand conditions.

A good example of the approach is given by the work of Dolbear *et al.*
(1968). They took a differentiated product market with linear demand curves
and constant marginal costs and examined the influence of firm numbers and

information availability on oligopolistic outcomes. Ninety subjects participated in the study, and each undertook 15 successive trials in a particular 'industry'. In all cases the subject chose a firm's product price in each trial, given a matrix of profits obtainable relating to various prices. In complete-information experiments these profit matrices were also related to rivals' average prices and subjects were told that they all had the same profit matrix. In incomplete-information experiments, however, subjects' profit matrices only showed profits that would be obtainable if various output levels were obtained given the price set by the subject. In this case, each subject was told that he would sell more the lower his price and/or the higher his competitors' prices. In all cases the first seven and the last three trials were ignored in order to avoid possible beginning and end effects in the experiment. The average price in trials 8–12 was then taken as the 'equilibrium' estimate.

The results obtained by Dolbear *et al.* are generally consistent with *a priori* expectations. Comparing markets with two, four or 16 firms (with or without complete information), average prices and profits were significantly lower the greater the number of firms using a 5 per cent test of statistical significance. By construction of the experiment, this was taken as evidence of a behavioural effect of increased firm numbers, i.e. an effect related to the increased complexity of the problem of tacitly colluding. (Structural effects relating to variations in the reward structure as firm numbers varied were excluded by design.) There was also some slight evidence that prices and profits were lower with incomplete information, but this finding was statistically significant only at the 10 per cent level (in the two-firm industry case). In only one out of the 26 markets investigated (a duopoly with complete information) was joint profit maximization attained by tacit collusion. Somewhat surprisingly, competition was so rife in eight of the markets that price was set below the Cournot-type price-setting equilibrium. Dolbear *et al.* suggested that this finding might mean that more than seven trials were needed in such cases before the firms settled down to some degree of oligopolistic coordination.

Several further studies may be mentioned briefly. First, in an early study, Fouraker and Siegel (1963) showed that, in homogeneous product oligopoly with price setting, price tended to closely approximate the Bertrand or competitive solution. Murphy (1966), however, qualified this result by showing that more cooperative behaviour could be induced by introducing the threat of losses into the experiment. Second, Lowes and Pass (1970) examined the influence of cost and demand asymmetries in a duopoly market with product differentiation. They emphasized the learning behaviour of firms in successive trials, showing that in situations with cost or demand asymmetry the variance of prices (in successive groups of four trials) tended to be higher while on average prices were lower compared with a symmetric experiment. This is consistent with subjects having to 'sound out' their rivals more in non-symmetric markets. Lowes and Pass also conducted an experiment in which participants were told that one of them had a competitive advantage. Interestingly, in these cases there was a marked tendency to adopt the joint profit-maximizing solution as participants recognized their relative competitive positions and were prepared to accept cooperation. In three out of ten cases where 'weak' firm exit was allowed, however, the dominant player opted to drive his rival out and then attain monopoly profits to himself thereafter.

Experimental studies suffer from obvious weaknesses in that they employ relatively inexperienced subjects and artificial conditions. They cannot hope to capture the history and complexities of real-world markets, or the structure of competition and cooperation which may take place in real time. On the other hand, by examining particular factors under experimental conditions new insights and hypotheses about the competitive process may and have emerged. This evidence is, therefore, useful as a supplement to direct observation of real-world markets.

3.3 Summary and Conclusions

This chapter has considered oligopolistic pricing and the possibilities for raising price above competitive levels in oligopolistic markets. In section 3.1 we considered a number of alternative theories and theoretical approaches to oligopolistic pricing, pointing to the variety of possible 'solutions' to the oligopoly problem. In section 3.2, in contrast, we considered the particular issue of oligopolistic coordination and the extent to which prices can be raised towards monopoly levels. A number of factors which might affect oligopolistic coordination were discussed, and some limited evidence relating to these factors was also presented.

The material discussed in this chapter suggests that oligopolistic pricing is a complex phenomenon, and that no one theory is likely to apply to all, or indeed most, oligopolistic industries. Nevertheless, as a broad generalization, factors such as high market concentration, stable market conditions, homogeneous demand and cost conditions, full information and so on all tend to facilitate oligopolistic coordination and hence lead to higher prices. Some limited evidence in support of some of these hypotheses was noted, and broader econometric evidence on profitability and concentration will be considered in chapter 5.

Appendix 3.1 The Dominant Cartel Model

Following Saving (1970), we assume a dominant cartel of k firms in a market together with a competitive fringe of $n-k$ firms. Fringe firms act as price-takers in the market with a normal upward-sloping supply curve $S(p)$ (where p is market price). The dominant cartel selects p to maximize its profits given $S(p)$.

If market demand is $D(p)$, then the cartel faces a net demand

$$N(p) = D(p) - S(p). \tag{A3.1}$$

Differentiating this with respect to p, and multiplying both sides by p/N, gives

$$N'(p)(p/N) = D'(p)(p/N) - S'(p)(p/N). \tag{A3.2}$$

If we define elasticities of demand and supply as $\eta_N = -N'(p)(p/N)$; $\eta_D = -D'(p)(p/D)$ and $\eta_S = S'(p)(p/S)$, then (A3.2) can be written as

$$-\eta_N = -\eta_D(D/N) - \eta_S(S/N). \tag{A3.3}$$

The dominant cartel seeks to maximize profits in relation to the net demand curve, $N(p)$ (see figure 3.5). Hence, it sets its price–cost margin equal to $1/\eta_N$. Substituting from (A3.3), therefore, we find that

$$\frac{p - MC_k}{p} = \frac{1}{\eta_D(D/N) + \eta_S(S/N)} \tag{A3.4}$$

where MC_k is dominant cartel marginal cost. Since we can define the k-firm concentration ratio as $C_k = N/D$, we have $D/N = 1/C_k$ and $S/N = (1 - C_k)/C_k$. On substitution and multiplication of numerator and denominator of (A3.4) by C_k, therefore, we find

$$\frac{p - MC_k}{p} = \frac{C_k}{\eta_D + \eta_S(1 - C_k)}. \tag{A3.5}$$

Also, since competitive firms set price equal to marginal cost, MC_{n-k}, the market-share-weighted average price–cost margin for the market as a whole is

$$\frac{p - MC_w}{p} = \frac{C_k^2}{\eta_D + \eta_S(1 - C_k)} \tag{A3.6}$$

where MC_w is the weighted average marginal cost.

Equations (A3.5) and (A3.6) indicate that price–cost margins for the dominant firms and the market as a whole vary positively with C_k and negatively with η_D and η_S. In particular, ceteris paribus, for η_D and η_S, price–cost margins and C_k move in the same direction. Any market changes which tend to increase C_k, therefore (and leave η_S and η_D relatively unchanged) will lead to a rise in price–cost margins. The k-firm concentration ratio, therefore, acts as a useful indicator of the cartel's influence over market price in this model, once allowance is made for possible changes in elasticities of demand and supply.

Appendix 3.2 Generalized (Homogeneous) Oligopoly

Following Cowling and Waterson (1976) (as developed by Clarke and Davies, 1982), we postulate a homogeneous product market with n firms ($i = 1, \dots, n$). Firm i has an output x_i with marginal cost MC_i while market price is $p = p(x)$, where $x = \Sigma_i x_i$ is market output. Firm i also has an output-conjectural variation, which (following Clarke and Davies) we take as $dx_j/dx_i = \alpha x_j/x_i$ for $j \neq i$. This implies that each firm expects a constant proportionate output response, α, from each of its rivals.

Firm i seeks to maximize profits

$$\pi_i = p(x)(x_i) - c_i(x_i) \tag{A3.7}$$

where $c_i(x_i)$ are its total costs. Differentiation with respect to x_i then gives a first-order condition

$$\frac{d\pi_i}{dx_i} = p(x) + (x_i)p'(x)\frac{dx}{dx_i} - MC_i = 0. \tag{A3.8}$$

Since the firm adopts constant (proportionate) conjectural variations we have

$$\frac{dx}{dx_i} = 1 + \sum_{j \neq i}\frac{dx_j}{dx_i} = 1 + \alpha\sum_{j \neq i}\frac{x_j}{x_i} = 1 + \alpha\left(\frac{x}{x_i} - 1\right).$$

Substituting into (A3.8), and multiplying all terms by x_i, gives

$$px_i - x_i^2\left(\frac{1}{\eta}\right)\frac{p}{x}\left[1 + \alpha\left(\frac{x}{x_i} - 1\right)\right] - MC_i x_i = 0 \tag{A3.9}$$

where η is the market price elasticity of demand (taken as positive).

Note, in particular, that $H = \Sigma_i x_i^2/x^2$ is the Hirschman–Herfindahl index of concentration. Hence, on summing (A3.9) over all n firms, we find

$$px - \left(\frac{H}{\eta}px + px\frac{\alpha}{\eta} - \frac{H\alpha}{\eta}px\right) - \sum_i MC_i x_i = 0. \tag{A3.10}$$

This can be rearranged to give

$$\frac{p - \Sigma_i MC_i(x_i/x)}{p} = \frac{H(1 - \alpha) + \alpha}{\eta}. \tag{A3.11}$$

Equation (A3.11) shows that the market-share-weighted price–cost margin in this industry is positively related to H and α, and negatively related to η.

Ceteris paribus, a rise in concentration as measured by the Herfindahl index would be linked to a rise in price–cost margins. Higher values of α (implying greater anticipated rival output matching) also lead to higher average margins. Hence, the parameter α provides a natural indicator of coordinated behaviour of market participants in a model such as this. It can also be shown that, at least where marginal costs are constant, increases in α lead to a rise in market concentration (H) in addition to average price–cost margins (see Clarke and Davies, 1982).

Notes

1 Readers who are not happy with the idea of differentiation may safely skip to the paragraph after next for a diagrammatic illustration of the Cournot solution. At one or two other points in this chapter, however, diagrammatic solutions are not available and some elementary algebra has been used in these cases.

2 The competitive solution follows directly from the condition that price equals marginal cost ($p_c = c$) and demand price is $p = \alpha - \beta x$. The monopoly solution follows because with a linear market demand the marginal revenue curve is twice as steep as the demand curve, so that the monopolist sets one-half of the competitive output, i.e. $x_m = \frac{1}{2}[(\alpha - c)/\beta]$.

3 These ideas can be extended to more general cost and demand conditions; see for example Seade (1980). Also, as discussed below, more general models which permit firm size inequality show that price (or at least price–cost margins) will be linked to the Hirschman–Herfindahl index of concentration in Cournot (and related) models.

4 For a standard discussion of the naivety of Cournot conjectures see Koutsoyiannis (1975). A model which incorporates learning in a dynamic context is developed in Cyert and de Groot (1973).

5 Within the context of the Cournot model as a static model, inconsistency manifests itself (in equation (3.9), say) by an assumption of no output reaction, which in fact implies a reaction for firm 1 of $dx_1/dx_2 = -\frac{1}{2}$. Similarly for firm 2. Inconsistency, therefore, is a feature of Cournot *equilibrium* and not merely of a dynamic adjustment process. This matter is considered further below when we discuss recently developed ideas concerning consistent conjectures equilibria.

6 A similar result also applies when markets are perfectly contestable (see chapter 4). In that case, the market is completely open to new competition and the threat of such competition ensures that only competitive prices can obtain.

7 See, for example, Friedman (1977, pp. 38–9; and chapter 3).

8 The properties of isoprofit curves and the other results in this section all pertain to the case of linear market demand and constant costs. These results can be derived analytically, but for convenience the analysis is omitted here.

9 This model can be viewed as an oligopoly model with a limited number of followers, or, alternatively, as a variant of the monopoly model with a dominant firm and many fringe suppliers. While on this latter interpretation the model is not strictly an oligopoly model, it is nevertheless convenient to consider it here.

10 As pointed out in note 3 above, the H index of concentration comes out fairly naturally in this kind of model. Since the Cournot model is a special case of

Cowling and Waterson's model (with $\mu = 0$), the link between H and average price–cost margins is not associated with the point we wish to make here concerning market coordination.

11 This point is not immediately obvious from equation (3.12), since H varies with α also. For details see Clarke and Davies (1982, p. 281).

12 The case of $r = -1$ is equivalent to the Bertrand price conjecture. To see this note that an expectation that a rival will not change price is equivalent to an expectation that the rival will accommodate any output expansion by a firm.

13 Useful references include Perry (1982), Ulph (1983) and Kamien and Schwartz (1983).

14 In general, consistent conjectures requires that actual and anticipated reactions be matched exactly (i.e. that first and higher-order derivatives be equal). In this case, of course, all higher-order derivatives are zero.

15 Bresnahan (1981) shows that this consistent conjectures equilibrium is unique in the class of polynomial conjectures.

16 See Perry (1982) for further discussion.

17 It should be noted that Sweezy (1939, pp. 407–8) felt that there would be a tendency for price to rise if demand increased, although he argued that prices would tend to alter firms' expectations, causing them to be less pessimistic that price cuts would be followed and price rises not followed. The reverse effect when demand decreases would then strengthen resistance to (open) price cuts in a depression.

18 I'm grateful to Steve Davies for this point.

19 A useful introductory account of game theory is given in Bacharach (1976). For applications to oligopoly theory see Shubik (1980) and (more advanced) Friedman (1977).

20 This point was also seen, of course, in the case of consistent conjectures equilibrium analysed in section 3.1.1 above.

21 See, for example, Block, Nold and Sidak (1981).

22 The list of other factors which have been suggested is very long. A comprehensive discussion is given in Scherer (1980).

23 For work on UK data see Swann et al. (1974) and O'Brien et al. (1979). These studies are concerned mainly with the effects of UK restrictive trade practices policy and are discussed further in chapter 11.

4 Barriers to Entry

We now switch our attention away from actual competition in a market and consider the question of potential competition and barriers to entry. This has been a particularly active area of research in recent years, and a number of important developments have occurred. Much of this work is of a theoretical type, and in what follows we concentrate on theoretical developments. Some reference to empirical evidence is, however, briefly made in section 4.1 and also in subsequent chapters.

Section 4.1 discusses the seminal work of J. S. Bain on entry barriers which provides the basis for much of the subsequent work in this field. This is followed in section 4.2 by a discussion of entry barriers and oligopoly pricing in the theory of the limit price. Section 4.3 then reviews more recent developments, first in respect of the recent literature on strategic entry-deterrence and then (more briefly) on contestable markets.

I shall begin by indicating briefly some alternative definitions of entry barriers which have been used in the literature. For many years, discussion of entry barriers has been considerably enlivened by debates on what is and what is not an entry barrier, and no general resolution of the problem has yet been made.[1] In this chapter (and indeed in chapter 6, where the subject again raises its head) I have adopted the fairly broad approach suggested by Bain (1956), which links entry barriers to the capacity to raise price above unit cost. Other suggestions have been made, however (notably by economics associated with Chicago), and two of these are mentioned in addition to Bain's definition.

First, a number of writers (e.g. Demsetz, 1982; Brozen, 1975) have sought to restrict the idea of entry barriers to government-based restrictions on entry. This approach has its roots in classical economics and in particular in the work of Adam Smith (1970). On this definition a tariff is an obvious example of a barrier to entry in that it limits the ability of foreign producers to operate in the home market. As argued by Demsetz (1982), however, any government restriction which increases costs of production constitutes an entry barrier. He gives the example of taxi operation in a city. Obviously, a requirement that an official medallion be held by taxi operators in a city is a barrier to entry if it restricts the number of taxi operators to less than would otherwise operate. According to Demsetz, however, even if medallions are not restricted in distribution, they still constitute a barrier to entry (although probably not a significant one) if they raise costs of taxi operation and thereby restrict entry artificially. Less fancifully, safety regulations such as vehicle checks or a requirement that taxis be fitted with safety belts are likewise barriers to entry in that they impose additional costs on taxi operation.[2] In Demsetz's view, when such costs arise from government restrictions, rather than occurring naturally in the market, entry will be restricted and an entry barrier will exist.

This somewhat fundamentalist line has its basis in the view that entry barriers can arise only from government intervention because only governments have the (legal) power to prevent entry. In the absence of government-based restrictions, it is argued that the free working of the competitive economy will eradicate monopoly rents in the long run. Hence, only governments ultimately have the power to prevent free competition. Such an argument, however, only represents an expression of faith in the competitive economy and ignores the possibility that market power can exist in the absence of government restrictions. Most industrial economists would argue that non-government-based barriers to entry can exist and hence support a wider definition than this school of thought.

A second definition, suggested by Stigler, focuses on asymmetries in demand and cost conditions between established firms and potential new entrants. Specifically, he defines a barrier to entry as 'a cost of producing (at some or every rate of output) which must be borne by a firm which seeks to enter an industry but is not borne by firms already in the industry' (Stigler, 1968, p. 67). On this definition, any advantages of established firms over potential new entrants are treated as a barrier to entry and a potential source of long-run monopoly rents. However, when established and entrant firms face the same cost and demand conditions in the market, Stigler argues that there is no barrier to entry.

This definition is relatively clear-cut, but as Demsetz notes it is different from his. For example, Stigler's definition would cite international transport costs as a barrier to entry in that foreign firms would operate at a cost disadvantage relative to domestic firms, but he would not make taxi medallions an entry barrier if both established firms and new entrants were required to obtain taxi medallions at market-determined prices. Essentially, these examples point to different conceptions of entry barriers, with Stigler tending to emphasize asymmetrical market conditions as a barrier to the eradication of monopoly rents and Demsetz stressing legal restrictions on freedom of entry.

A third definition of barriers to entry, and that which is most often used in industrial economics, is given by Bain. Bain also refers to the extent to which new entrants may be disadvantaged relative to established firms, but, more specifically, he relates entry barriers to the extent to which, in the long run, established firms can elevate their selling prices above the minimal average costs of production and distribution (those costs associated with operation at optimal scales) without inducing potential entrants to enter an industry. (Bain, 1968, p. 252)

For Bain, therefore, it is the potential effect of barriers to entry (the persistence of prices above minimum unit cost in the long run) which defines their nature. This definition is wider than Stigler's in that Bain regards scale economies as a barrier to entry since they may be conducive to persistent pricing above minimum unit cost (see section 4.1). Stigler, would argue, however, that economies of scale are not an entry barrier if the same cost conditions are available to entrants and established firms at any given output level. Bain's definition is *a fortiori* different from that of Demsetz. Whereas Demsetz would argue that a requirement that taxi operators carry medallions is a barrier to entry even if these are available to all at competitive prices, Bain would not accept this since neither taxi operators nor medallion producers would be making supernormal profits in such a situation.

As we shall see in what follows, Bain's definition can be regarded as the most problematic of the three discussed here. This is because, in defining entry barriers in an effects-based way, Bain implicitly introduces market conduct as well as market conditions into his definition. This is in contrast to the definitions of both Demsetz and Stigler, which in principle are independent of market conduct. On the other hand, as we shall also see, Bain's definition raises important issues of interdependence between structure and conduct which have proved to be the source of much productive research on entry barriers. It is for this reason that I, and indeed most workers in the field, follow his broader definition.

4.1 Bain's "Barriers to New Competition"

Bain's pioneering work on *Barriers to New Competition* was originally published in 1956 (see also Bain, 1954, 1968). In it he considered three basic sources of barriers to entry on his definition: absolute cost advantages, product differentiation advantages and economies of scale. In this section we shall briefly examine his work on each of these categories as the basis for subsequent developments in this and later chapters.

I shall begin by quickly outlining Bain's concepts of the *maximum entry-forestalling price* and the *condition of entry*. Bain assumes that in a given market there is a maximum entry-forestalling price, which is the highest price which established firms can set without inducing entry. He then defines the condition of entry as the percentage markup of the maximum entry-forestalling price over the minimum attainable average costs of established firms.[3] In other words, the condition of entry measures the 'height' of entry barriers in a particular market. As defined by Bain, this is a long-run concept. Specifically, independently of the short-run price set by established firms, the condition of entry gives the maximum markup that could prevail in the industry in the long run. Thus it provides an indicator of the extent to which the free flow of resources between trades may be inhibited in the long run, and (subject to the usual provisos) the extent to which resources are inefficiently allocated.

It should be noted, however, that this markup is not totally objective. As is discussed explicitly in section 4.2 below, the maximum entry-forestalling price is determined by objective market conditions combined with entrant expectations. Particularly in situations where established firms form an oligopoly or where there is an established monopoly, normal strategic considerations enter into the formation of entrant expectations. Put simply, if entrants expect established firms to engage in intense price competition following entry, then they will tend to be less ready to enter than if they expect a more accommodating response. Hence, the maximum entry-forestalling price will tend to be higher, the more pessimistic are entrants' expectations concerning post-entry competition. This insight in fact forms the basis of the theory of limit price discussed in section 4.2 below. Like Bain, however, we set it on one side for the present in order to concentrate on objective market conditions.

4.1.1 Absolute Cost Advantages

Absolute cost barriers to entry relate to the *ability of established firms to produce any given level of output at lower unit costs than potential entrants.* In the simple case of constant long-run unit costs, potential entrants have a cost curve, LAC_2, which lies everywhere above that of the established firms, LAC_1 (figure 4.1).

Suppose, for simplicity, that potential entrants expect established firms to

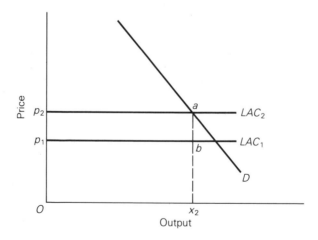

Figure 4.1

maintain the pre-entry price after entry. Then the maximum entry-forestalling price in figure 4.1 is p_2, and long-run supernormal profits in this industry will be equal to area $p_1 p_2 ab$. In this simple case, the condition of entry is given exactly by the proportionate absolute cost advantage of established firms, that is,[4]

$$\frac{p_2 - p_1}{p_1} = \frac{LAC_2 - LAC_1}{LAC_1}.$$

Absolute cost advantages of established firms are also recognized by Stigler as a barrier to entry. They may arise for a variety of reasons. For example, established firms may have control of superior production techniques relative to entrant firms, through control of key patents. Alternatively, established firms may have access to superior resources, including management, relative to new entrants. Third, new entrants may have to pay higher prices for inputs compared with established firms, for example if the latter are able to secure discounts from input suppliers for bulk purchase. A potentially important example of this third possibility, recognized by Bain, is with respect to the cost of funds. Particularly in circumstances where potential entrants to a market are small firms, there may be difficulties in raising capital at competitive rates of interest. Either funds have to be raised at higher effective interest cost relative to established firms, or they are simply not available in the required amounts. This implies that, in markets with large capital requirements, the pool of potential entrants may be substantially reduced. Further, however, even when one considers large diversified entry into a market, established firms may still have a cost-of-funds advantage linked simply to the fact that they have an established position in the market.

It is useful to have some idea of the empirical importance of various barriers to entry, and we can briefly mention the work of Bain (1956) and Mann (1966) in this respect. Bain conducted a case study of 20 US manufacturing industries in the early 1950s and Mann did a follow-up study of a further 13 industries. In both studies the authors used their expertise to gauge the condition of entry in each industry, classifying barriers as 'slight', 'moderate' or 'high'. While the samples are small and tend to consist of industries with above-average market concentration, they nevertheless provide a useful picture of the general importance of barriers to entry. Full details of results and methods are given in tables 4.1 and 4.2.[5]

Setting the capital requirements barrier on one side for the moment, the principal source of absolute cost advantage found by Bain and Mann related to control of raw materials. Not surprisingly, metal manufacture industries were involved here, with Bain recording 'high' entry barriers from this source in the copper and steel industries, and Mann adding the sulphur and nickel industries. Bain also noted that patent protection was important in the gypsum products industry, but in all other cases he found that absolute cost barriers to entry were 'slight'. Mann, on the other hand, found a larger

Table 4.1 Entry barriers in Bain's 20 industries[a]

Aggregate barriers	Entry barriers			
	Scale economies	Product differen- tiation	Absolute costs	Capital require- ments
'Very high'				
Automobiles	III	III	I	III
Cigarettes	I	III	I	III
Fountain pens ('quality' grade)[b]	n/a	III	I	I
Liquor/spirits	I	III	I	II
Tractors	III	III	I	III
Typewriters	III	III	I	n/a
'Substantial'				
Copper	n/a	I	III	n/a
Farm machines (large)[b]	II	III	I	n/a
Petroleum-refining	II	II	I	III
Shoes (high-priced men's)[b]	II	II	I	Ø
Soap	II	II	I	II
Steel	II	I	III	III
'Moderate or low'				
Canned fruits and vegetables	I	I–II	I	I
Cement	II	I	I	II
Flour	I	I–II	I	Ø
Gypsum products[c]	n/a	I	III	I
Meat packing	I	I	I	Ø or I
Metal containers[c]	n/a	II	I	I
Rayon	II	I	I	II
Tyres and tubes	I	II	I	II

Source: Bain (1956, tables XIV and XV, pp. 169–70).

Notes

[a] Each entry barrier is (roughly) categorized as 'high' (III), 'medium' (II) or 'low' (I). For absolute cost barriers there is no 'medium' ranking and I denotes a 'slight' barrier. For capital requirements barriers there are four categories with Ø as the lowest. Data non-availability is denoted 'n/a'.

[b] Sub-industries only. Other parts of these industries are classified as having aggregate 'moderate or low' entry barriers.

[c] Product differentiation rating refers to post-1950. A rating of III is probably indicated for early years, implying substantial aggregate barriers.

proportion of industries in which absolute cost advantages were at least moderately important. In fact, as can be seen in table 4.2, he found that this was true in six out of his additional 13 industries.

These results ignore the capital requirements barrier, however. As noted

Table 4.2 Entry barriers in Mann's 13 industries[a]

Aggregate barriers	Entry barriers			
	Scale economies	Product differen- tiation	Absolute costs	Capital require- ments
'Very high'				
Sulphur	n/a	II	III	II
Nickel	n/a	II	III	n/a
Ethical drugs	I	III	n/a	II
Flat grass	III	I	n/a	II
Chewing gum	n/a	III	II	II
'Substantial'				
Aluminium reduction	II	I	II	II
Shoe machinery	I	I	III	n/a
Biscuits	I	II	n/a	I
'Moderate or low'				
Glass containers	I	I	I	n/a
Baking[b]	I–III	I–III	I	I
Bituminous coal	I	I	II	II
Beer	I	I	n/a	n/a
Textile mill products	I	I	I	I

Source: Mann (1966, table A1, p. 301).

Notes
[a] Specific entry barriers are classified as 'unimportant' (I); 'moderately important' (II) and 'very important' (III); n/a means not available.
[b] Alternative rankings for entry by independent bakers (locally) or grocery store chains.

above, this barrier may have the principal effect of reducing the pool of potential entrants in a market rather than representing a barrier to the entry of all prospective entrants. Nevertheless, Bain noted that, for many of the industries in his sample, substantial amounts of capital were required to enter at an efficient scale, and this forms the basis for his classifications reported in table 4.1. As can be seen, he felt that capital requirements gave rise to at least 'moderate' barriers to entry in one-half of his 20 industries. Mann came to similar conclusions (table 4.2), although, unlike Bain, he was not prepared to categorize any capital requirements barrier as 'very high'.

4.1.2 Economies of Scale

Bain's second type of entry barrier arises from significant scale economies relative to market size. In this case established firms have no cost advantage

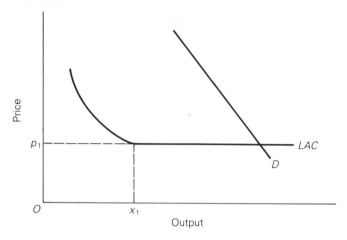

Figure 4.2

over potential entrants in the sense of being able to produce a given output at lower unit cost. Rather, the entry barrier arises from entrants being unable to secure the full advantages of scale without contributing a significant share of industry output (figure 4.2).

In the case as drawn the entrant faces a dilemma. If it enters at minimum efficient scale, x_1, or above, it makes a significant contribution to industry output and is likely to cause a substantial drop in market price, possibly to below its unit costs. Alternatively, if it enters at less than minimum efficient scale, x_1, it will suffer a cost disadvantage, assuming that established firms are operating at x_1 or above, and again it may make a loss. Established firms will then have some leeway to raise price above p_1 in the long run without attracting entry.[6]

While finding that economies of scale were often present in manufacturing industry, Bain was able to attribute 'high' barriers to entry to this source in only three of his 20 industries (see table 4.1). In a further seven industries, however, he found that they gave rise to 'moderate' barriers to entry. Mann found 'very high' scale economy barriers in the flat glass industry and also in baking (if this industry is viewed in regional terms). Also, aluminium reduction had a 'moderately important' scale economy barrier. Both studies, therefore, regarded high scale economy barriers as being of limited importance in a US context. Bain, however, felt that economies of scale were a moderate deterrent to entry in a good proportion of industries, and this might be *a fortiori* the case in a smaller economy such as that of the UK.

4.1.3 Product Differentiation Advantages

Bain's third category of entry barrier arises from product differentiation. In a market characterized by product differentiation, established firms may have advantages over new entrants arising from consumer preferences for their products.[7] Such preferences sometimes arise where established firms have exclusive control of superior product design through patent protection. However, even in situations where practical duplication of product quality and design is possible, established firms may still have an advantage in terms of customer goodwill. This may arise where established brand names (or, more generally, company names) have earned a reputation for supplying good quality and competitively priced products and services. In addition, the cumulative effect of past advertising expenditures may have built up consumer allegiance to established products, an issue which we consider separately in chapter 6.

In such circumstances, established firms may be able to charge above unit cost without attracting entry. Because of consumer preferences for established products, a new entrant may find that it is able to sell its desired output only by offering a price discount relative to established products and/or by incurring greater selling expenditures per unit of output than established firms. Effectively, therefore, the new entrant has an absolute cost disadvantage relative to established firms owing to product differentiation. Note, however, that this disadvantage will be of only limited duration as new entrants establish their products in the market during an initial 'break-in' period, after which, if successful, their products may compete on more equal terms with the initial established products. Nevertheless, since firms are concerned with the present value of their investments, the initial extra costs of entry arising from product differentiation barriers will act to deter entry, the more so the longer the expected 'break-in' period is and the greater the firm's discount rate.

A simple illustration of a product differentiation barrier is given in figure 4.3.

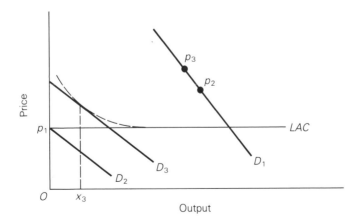

Figure 4.3

Assume that an established firm is a monopolist with demand curve D_1. Both the established firm and a potential new entrant have constant costs of production, LAC, and we ignore sales promotion costs for simplicity. If the established firm has a product differentiation advantage, then it can set price above average cost and leave the entrant with no profitable opportunities for entry. Suppose that the entrant expects no change in price should it enter. Then if the established firm sets price, p_2, the potential entrants' demand curve is, say, D_2; while a higher price, p_3, allows the entrant a higher demand curve, D_3. As drawn, it is clear that the maximum entry-forestalling price is p_2, since the potential entrant with demand curve D_2 can produce no output profitably. (This argument obviously could be modified if the product differentiation advantage were to be of only limited duration.)

As Bain notes, product differentiation barriers may be enhanced in the presence of scale economies. Suppose in figure 4.3 that economies of scale in production exist, as shown by the dashed portion of LAC. Then the established firm can raise price to p_3 without inducing entry owing to the cost disadvantages of small-scale production. Even then, the entrant with demand curve D_3 can barely cover production costs at output x_3. Clearly, in the presence of scale economies and product differentiation, new entrants may face great difficulties in obtaining a sufficient market share to make production economical.[8] This would be the case *a fortiori* if new entrants expected some price competition on their entry.

In his empirical work, Bain found that product differentiation barriers to entry were often very important (see table 4.1). 'High' barriers to entry from this source arose, in Bain's view, in five industries as well as in parts of two further industries. In addition, in seven further industries, or parts thereof, product differentiation gave rise to 'medium' entry barriers. In Mann's sample, on the other hand, while 'very important' product differentiation barriers were observed in three industries, in over half the industries such barriers were judged as 'unimportant'. (Mann's results may reflect a preponderance of producer and/or non-branded goods in his sample, however.) In Bain's view, product differentiation was the most important source of entry barriers, particularly if one took account of interactions with economies of scale. Both sets of results suggest that product differentiation may create a very important barrier to entry, particularly in consumer goods industries.

4.1.4 Aggregate Barriers to Entry

In any particular industry, more than one type of entry barrier may be at work. In order to take account of this and possible interactions between entry barriers, Bain classified his sample in terms of an *aggregate* barrier to entry. His industries were classified into three categories according to the aggregate condition of entry: a 'very high' category, such that established firms might be able to raise price by 10 per cent or more without inducing entry; a 'substantial' category, corresponding to a 5–9 per cent possible price elevation;

and a 'moderate or low' category, involving a potential 1–4 per cent markup. Mann adopted a similar approach for his additional 13 industries.

Full results for both Bain's and Mann's samples are given in tables 4.1 and 4.2. Bain classified six industries or parts thereof as having a 'very high' aggregate entry barrier, with six industries or parts in the 'substantial' category and 11 in the 'moderate or low' group. As can be seen from the table, the product differentiation barrier was a particular feature of the 'very high' aggregate entry barrier cases, with scale economies (and capital requirements) barriers also being important in some industries. Mann's results in table 4.2 are more mixed, with five of the 13 industries having 'very high' aggregate barriers but no one entry barrier having a dominant role in all cases. While we must stress again the somewhat arbitrary nature of the classifications, the combined evidence of tables 4.1 and 4.2 provide some evidence of the empirical importance of Bain's barriers to entry in US manufacturing industry.

4.2 Limit Price Theory

In section 4.1 we considered the *long-run* issue of the condition of entry and the maximum entry-forestalling price in a market. We said nothing, however, about the pricing policy of established firms, and how it might interact with the condition of entry.

When established firms form an oligopoly (and *a fortiori* when there is a single established firm), they may be able to coordinate their actions and establish an agreed-upon market price. If this price is above the maximum entry-forestalling price, it will give rise to new entry and to reductions in established firms' market shares and profits in the long run. On the other hand, if it is less than or equal to the maximum entry-forestalling or *limit price*, then new entry will not be forthcoming and current profits and market shares will continue into the long run. If, as assumed by Bain, established firms seek to maximize long-run profits (i.e. the expected discounted present value of their future profit stream), then they will choose the policy which best suits their aim. In some cases this may cause them to take account of possible entry and to set the limit price to prevent entry taking place.

In fact, Bain distinguished four possible cases arising from such considerations. First, entry conditions may be *easy*, in which case price in the long run could not exceed competitive levels. Second, entry conditions may be such that entry is *ineffectively impeded*, in that established firms have the option to limit prices and prevent entry but choose not to do so. Third, entry may be *effectively impeded*, when established firms opt to forestall entry by limiting price. And finally, entry may be *blockaded*, in that even prices at the monopoly level fail to attract entrants.

In this section we focus attention on Bain's third case: that of effectively impeded entry. First we shall examine the determination of the price which just prevents entry (the *limit price*) under a particular entrant behavioural assumption known as the *Sylos postulate*. Section 4.2.2 then considers some weaknesses of this postulate and more generally of the limit price approach.

4.2.1 Limit Pricing under the Sylos Postulate

In order to employ the notion of entry barriers in a theory of oligopolistic pricing, it is necessary to specify the way in which potential entrants expect existing firms to react to their entry. An entrant is concerned that after entry the post-entry price should exceed its unit cost (including normal profit) at its planned output level. Hence, it needs to conjecture how established firms will react to its entry in order to link the post-entry to the pre-entry price. Most of the work in this field has followed an Italian economist, Sylos-Labini (1962)[9] in making a Cournot-type assumption for this conjecture. Known as the Sylos postulate, this assumption is that *new entrants expect established firms to maintain their current output levels after entry.* Given this assumption, potential entrants can estimate how much their entry is likely to reduce price in the industry and hence whether entry is worthwhile. More important, established firms can work out what current price to set which would just deter entry from taking place, given the Sylos postulate. The reasonableness of this postulate is discussed further in section 4.2.2.

In principle, the Sylos postulate can be employed to analyse limit pricing in any market situation. It is most often used, however, in the context of large-scale entry and scale economy barriers to entry, and we shall confine our attention to this case only. This analysis was dealt with by Sylos-Labini and to some extent by Bain, but was generalized in an important paper by Modigliani (1958) and we follow the latter's analysis here.

We begin with a simplifying assumption that there is a minimum efficient scale of production ($\bar{x}$ in figure 4.4) and that entrants consider entry only at

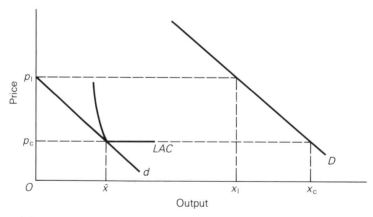

Figure 4.4

this scale or above. In figure 4.4, LAC is the long-run unit cost curve for established firms and new entrants, and D is market demand. Under the Sylos postulate, new entrants expect established firms to maintain their existing output level after entry. Hence with market demand curve D, new entrants expect to meet demand only to the right of the output level established by existing firms. The established firms will therefore fix this output such that, if entrants attempted to enter at scale $O\bar{x}$, price would fall below the competitive price, p_c. As can be seen in the figure, this entails that they set a limit output, Ox_1, such that distance x_1x_c is equal to (just less than) $O\bar{x}$. The limit price is then Op_1. This result is alternatively demonstrated by drawing the potential entrant's demand curve, d, with the axes drawn as coordinates. With limit price OP_1, this demand curve lies everywhere below the long-run unit cost curve, LAC, just failing to touch it at minimum efficient scale. Hence, under the Sylos postulate new entrants will be deterred, and Op_1 is the limit price.

Given the Sylos postulate, the limit price increases directly with the extent of scale economies. This can be illustrated by considering the simple case of a linear market demand curve. Let x be market demand and p market price, and assume

$$x = \alpha - \beta p \qquad (4.1)$$

where α and β are positive constants. The limit output is given by

$$x_1 = x_c - \bar{x} \qquad (4.2)$$

where x_c is the competitive output and $\bar{x}$ is minimum efficient scale. Hence, substituting (4.1) into (4.2), with p_1 and p_c the prices corresponding to x_1 and x_c, rearrangement gives

$$\frac{p_1 - p_c}{p_c} = \frac{\bar{x}/x_c}{\beta p_c/x_c}. \qquad (4.3)$$

We note that $\eta_c = \beta p_c/x_c$ is the market demand elasticity at the competitive price (defined to be positive), so that[10]

$$\frac{p_1 - p_c}{p_c} = \frac{\bar{x}/x_c}{\eta_c}. \qquad (4.4)$$

The proportionate markup over the competitive price thus increases as:

(1) minimum efficient scale, $\bar{x}$, increases *ceteris paribus*; i.e., the new entrant must enter at a larger scale to obtain full economies of scale;
(2) market demand at the competitive price, x_c, falls, *ceteris paribus* (note that, with market demand elasticity held constant, this implies that the demand curve shifts inwards and becomes steeper at p_c);

(3) market demand elasticity at the competitive price, η_c, falls, *ceteris paribus*, again implying a steeper demand curve.

In sum, the limit price increases with the ratio of minimum optimal scale to market demand and decreases as the market elasticity of demand increases.

We can now consider the more general case in which entry at below minimum efficient scale is possible. In this case established firms must set the limit price to ensure that entry at *any* output level will not produce profits given the Sylos postulate (see figure 4.5). As before, D is market demand and LAC is the entrant's unit cost curve. The established firms then pre-empt the limit output Ox_1 such that the entrant cannot supply *any* of the remainder of demand at a profit. This can be shown

(1) by drawing the entrant's demand curve, d, tangential to LAC so that at no point does d exceed LAC, giving limit price Op_1;
(2) alternatively, by shifting LAC right until it is just tangential to market demand, D. The coordinates of LAC, being shifted likewise, give limit output Ox_1 and limit price Op_1.

It can be seen that, in this more general formulation, prevention of entry at minimum efficient scale or above is only a special case. The point at which LAC just touches the entrant's demand curve in figure 4.5 gives the size of firm which represents the *most immediate threat of entry* (Ox_1 as drawn). As a limiting case this may be at the minimum optimal scale (such that $Ox_1 = O\bar{x}$), in which case the simpler model described above applies. When a suboptimal firm size poses the more immediate threat, however, established firms limit output below the competitive level by less than in this simpler model. That is, output was limited by $O\bar{x}$ in the simpler case, but by

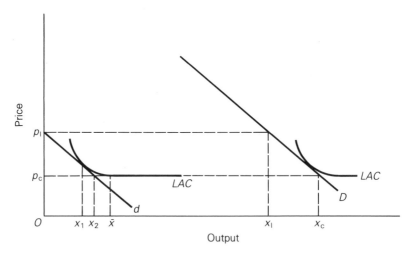

Figure 4.5

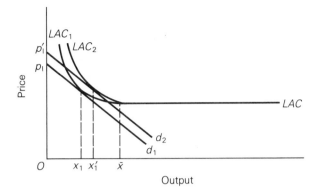

Figure 4.6

$x_1x_c < O\bar{x}$ in the more general case ($x_1x_c = Ox_2$). Thus, the simpler model sets a lower bound to limit output (x_1x_c at a maximum), and when existing firms fear suboptimal size entry the limit output will be higher and hence the limit price lower.

In the more general model, the proportionate markup over the competitive price is more difficult to determine. Intuitively, however, in addition to the results noted for the simpler model, one would expect that the greater the cost disadvantage of suboptimal production, the higher the limit price will be. This is illustrated in figure 4.6, which shows a *ceteris paribus* rise in the cost disadvantage of suboptimal production as a shift from curve LAC_1 to LAC_2. As drawn, this has the effect of increasing the scale which poses the most immediate threat of entry from x_1 to x_1' and raising the limit price from p_1 to p_1'. Hence, given demand conditions, both minimum efficient scale and the cost disadvantage of production at suboptimal scale will influence the limit price in the general case.

4.2.2 Limit Pricing Further Considered

While the theory of limit pricing based on the Sylos postulate is logically consistent and represents a determinate theory of pricing, it also makes a number of assumptions which may not be warranted in practice. We shall briefly consider some of the problems of the theory in this section.

First, the theory assumes that established firms in the industry can coordinate their actions to set the limit price. We have already discussed some of the problems which limit the effectiveness of oligopolistic coordination in chapter 3, so this need not detain us further here.

Second, the theory assumes that established firms deter entry absolutely, and this may not in fact be an optimal policy. More generally, established firms in a dynamic context may prefer to allow entry but regulate the *rate* at which it takes place. On this viewpoint, the problem for established firms is to determine an optimal time path for price which trades off current profits against future market share, and the appropriate tool of analysis is dynamic programming. Bain's classification of outcomes into effectively and ineffectively impeded entry is really just a static approximation to the full dynamic problem, and a complete theory should be framed dynamically.

Such a dynamic approach has been pursued in an important paper by Gaskins (1971) which we may mention for illustrative purposes. Gaskins considers the case of small-scale entry where an established dominant firm has an absolute cost advantage over potential rivals. He assumes that entrants adopt the (non-Sylos) view that current price is a reasonable proxy for future price. The rate at which entry takes place is assumed to be proportional to the difference between current price and the limit price, where the latter is defined as the price where net entry is zero.

The established firm chooses price at each point in time so as to maximize the present value of its profits. Gaskins shows that, in the case where rivals' outputs are relatively low, the optimal policy for the dominant firm will be set a high price initially to permit entry but gradually to lower it towards the limit price. The initial price will always be below the short-run profit-maximizing price, except in the (trivial) case where entry is blockaded, i.e. where net entry is zero or negative at the short-run profit-maximizing price. More generally, however, the established firm chooses neither to maximize short-run profits nor to prevent entry, but rather to regulate the rate at which it takes place. It is only when the structure of the industry has adapted to the long-run steady-state solution that a policy of limiting price to deter further entry becomes optimal.

A third criticism of the limit price model is that the basic Sylos postulate is arbitrary. There is no reason in general why new entrants should expect established firms to maintain their pre-entry output levels after entry. If entrants expect established firms to adopt an accommodating stance on entry, then prices below the limit price on the Sylos postulate will be needed to deter entry. Alternatively, if entrants expect an aggressive policy from established firms after entry, then higher limit prices will prevail. As discussed further in section 4.3, the true state of entrants' expectations may be influenced by current and expected future cost and demand conditions in the market together with certain non-price policy commitments entered into by established firms. For the moment, however, we merely note that the state of entrant expectations, while it affects the height of an entry barrier, need not in itself undermine the limit price theory. As in oligopoly theory, where the Cournot conjecture plays a similar role, the Sylos postulate may represent a useful benchmark for analysis. As long as potential entrants have reasonably stable expectations of established firm responses in a given situation, established firms can use this fact to limit price, and the precise nature of these expectations is not important.

Finally, the limit price theory can be criticized for its assumption that the prospect of negative profits is sufficient to deter new entry. Bhagwati (1970) has argued that, according to the theory, all firms will make losses if entry occurs, and it is not clear that it would necessarily be the new entrant who would be squeezed out.[11] The new entrant may, for example, make smaller losses than established firms if it enters at just minimum efficient scale when they are operating at larger scales. Also, firms may differ in their ability to survive a period of loss-making; and, particularly in the case where a firm established elsewhere diversifies into the industry, the presumption that new entrants may be at a financial disadvantage may not be warranted. Also, in practice, new entrants are likely to produce new products which may eventually find a profitable place in the market. In such circumstances a new entrant will probably be prepared to accept losses in an initial break-in period until the new product is established, and the notion of limit pricing to deter new entry may have limited value.[12]

4.3 More Recent Developments

In the last few years entry theory has undergone substantial development in the industrial economics literature and a number of new ideas have been advanced. First, a considerable literature has developed on oligopolistic aspects of entry theory, and in particular on the use of non-price strategic entry deterrence by established or incumbent firms. Some of this work is reviewed in section 4.3.1. In addition, a number of authors have looked at (in some senses) the opposite extreme to this: the case where no barriers to entry (or exit) in a market exist at all. This is considered in the theory of contestable markets, and a (brief) review of the key ideas here is given in section 4.3.2.

4.3.1 Strategic Entry Deterrence

A major weakness of limit price theory is its presumption that established firms are prepared to meet the threat of new competition by reducing price to entry-deterring levels. This is a bit like cutting off one's nose to spite one's face. Far better, from the established firms' point of view, to use other (non-price) variables to deter entry, leaving price relatively free for the pursuit of profits. While any entry-deterring strategy will involve a cost and hence a potential reduction in profits below short-run profit-maximizing levels, it at least seems likely *a priori* that the cost would be less than with a policy of directly reducing price and hence profits.

Established firms may prevent entry either by raising entry barriers or by influencing entrant expectations towards a more pessimistic outcome of post-entry competition. These goals may be attained in a variety of ways, depending on particular market circumstances. In this section we look at two suggestions, the use of excess capacity and product proliferation; we consider a third, the use of advertising, in chapter 6. Other possibilities might be the use of pre-emptive patenting or the use of predatory pricing tactics should entry take place.[13] In all cases, established firms endeavour to protect themselves from the threat of new competition in order to be able to earn monopoly profits into the long run. It is these active entry-deterring strategies which represent a major potential threat to economic welfare.

Several key ideas have come out of the recent literature on entry deterrence which it may be worthwhile briefly mentioning first. One such idea is the notion of a *first-mover advantage*. Such an advantage typically lies with an incumbent firm *vis-à-vis* an entrant in that an incumbent can adopt a position in the market before entry takes place. An obvious example of this (discussed below) is where an incumbent chooses the number and quality of product brands to produce with a view to restricting the 'space' available in the market for new entrant products. Because the incumbent firm is already in the market, this gives it an advantage in being able to choose its product position, and this may enable it to prevent entry.

Second, an incumbent firm may seek to persuade a new entrant that new entry would not be profitable. Following the work of Schelling (1960) (see also Dixit, 1982), it has been suggested that one way the incumbent can do this is to adopt a policy before entry which commits it to a certain line of action should entry occur. This idea of *commitment* applies, for example in international politics, where countries are committed to use nuclear defence in response to an attack as (hopefully) a deterrent to such an attack. An example of this idea in the entry deterrence field might be the building of production capacity ahead of demand with the threat of its use should entry occur. In both cases, commitment prior to an event is regarded as a deterrent to that event occurring. As we shall see, however, the problem remains that, should the event (war or entry) occur anyway, then the threatened strategy may not look like such a reasonable policy, and to that extent its deterrent effect is reduced.

This brings us to a third idea related to bolstering one's commitment to a strategy. In the political field this may be done by underinvesting in conventional defence such that nuclear defence is the only option should attack occur. In the entry field such binding commitments are less readily available. However, one way for an incumbent to bolster its commitment is to undertake investments which are wholly or partly irreversible should entry take place. Thus, for example, an incumbent can invest in plant with little or no resale or scrap value, thereby incurring a *sunk (i.e. non-recoverable) cost*. Should entry occur, therefore, at the least the incumbent reduces its options for accommodating rather than competing with the entrant. Similarly, an incumbent who selects product positions in the market prior to entry will be committed to those positions, in so far as repositioning after entry is a costly affair. Again, therefore, such costs bolster an incumbent's position in the market.

Much of the recent literature on entry deterrence has centred on the ideas of *first-mover advantages*, *commitment* and *sunk costs*, and these ideas are each implicit in the two examples considered below.

Capacity as a deterrent to entry   The idea of capacity as a deterrent to entry has been explored by Spence (1977). The basic idea behind this is the dynamic observation that established firms frequently build plant capacity ahead of demand in a growing market and may carry excess capacity in a static or declining market. Spence has suggested that such excess capacity may play an entry-deterring role in that it reveals a commitment on the part of established firms to the industry. More specifically, since established firms have made a more or less irreversible investment in capacity prior to entry, it is argued that this is likely to make a threat of price competition, should entry take place, more credible to new entrants. As we shall see, it is the effect of this on *entrant expectations*, rather than the raising of an existing entry barrier, which represents the means of entry deterrence. Indeed, in the model discussed below no entry barriers exist in the market.

Spence considers two models in his paper but we concentrate on his first model here for simplicity. This model is represented in figure 4.7 in the case of a single established firm operating with plant of capacity $\bar{k}$ (measured in units of output). For simplicity, we assume that there are constant capital costs, r, per unit of *capacity installed* and that operating costs, c, are also constant (per unit of output). Hence with full capacity working average costs are $c+r$. When output falls below full capacity, however, unit costs rise along AC as capital costs are spread over fewer units of output. While average costs

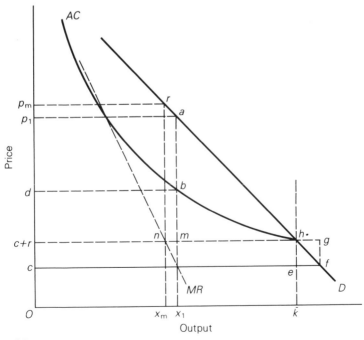

Figure 4.7

of $c+r$ can thus be obtained for any output *de novo* (i.e. by building a plant with the requisite capacity), once built, higher average costs are obtained with excess capacity working for any given plant.

Spence shows that in this model the established firm can set output and capacity *separately* to deter new entry without too much sacrifice of short-run profits. To do this he makes the assumption (analogous to the Sylos postulate) that potential entrants expect the incumbent firm to increase output to full capacity should entry take place.[14] Under the cost conditions here, therefore, the established firm sets capacity at $\bar{k}$ such that no market demand is left to entrants should entry occur. Given this capacity, however, the established firm can operate at output $\bar{k}$ or any lower output. With entry barred by its provision of capacity, $\bar{k}$, it chooses to restrict output to x_1, setting marginal revenue, MR, equal to marginal cost, c. Thus, the established firm earns profits of area $p_1 abd$ by carrying excess capacity as a deterrent to new competition.

In this model, therefore, the established firm takes advantage of its position by building excess capacity to deter entry in the market. This is clearly a superior policy to limit pricing under the Sylos postulate, since (under the cost conditions considered here) the firm must build and operate a plant at capacity $\bar{k}$ in order to deter entry. In this case, therefore, the limit price is simply $c+r$ and there are no monopoly profits to be earned. On the other hand, carrying excess capacity to prevent entry involves some sacrifice of monopoly profits compared with a situation of short-run profit maximization. A pure profit-maximizer would set output and capacity at x_m in figure 4.7 (with corresponding price p_m) such that marginal revenue equals full long-run marginal cost, $c+r$. Hence, while Spence's capacity hypothesis gives the firm some freedom to raise price, it does not completely divorce short-run pricing from entry deterrence.[15]

It is also interesting to consider the issue of economic welfare in this model. If we adopt the conventional simplification that economic welfare is simply the sum of producer and consumer surplus, then on Spence's hypothesis there is a deadweight consumer surplus loss of area amh in figure 4.7 and an efficiency loss of area $dbm(c+r)$. This compares with the deadweight consumer welfare loss of area rnh under pure profit maximization. As Spence notes (with reference to his second more general model), the policy of entry prevention may give rise to greater welfare loss than pure monopoly since, although output is larger under entry prevention, production is also inefficient. In fact, this is quite likely to be the case, particularly when capacity costs are relatively low and excess capacity therefore relatively high.[16] Hence, in so far as excess capacity can be used to deter entry as suggested by Spence, the welfare cost may be high.

Spence's model can be criticized along similar lines to the limit pricing model. First, the model assumes that incumbent firms can coordinate their actions to prevent entry, and this may be reasonable only in monopoly or tight oligopoly situations. Against this, however, it may be easier to coordinate tacitly on capacity rather than price. Second, the model assumes that incumbent firms want to deter entry rather than let some entry take place, and this may not be so.[17] Third, the model assumes that a new entrant would not enter if his entry would be unprofitable, even though incumbent firms might also make a loss should entry take place. Spence's model 1 is particularly weak in this respect because it assumes a simple technology with no economies of scale. Referring to figure 4.7, if a new entrant comes in and price falls to c, say, then the incumbent firm makes losses totalling $(c+r)hec$ while the entrant makes losses $hefg$. While losses will be proportionate to firm size, it is not clear that it would be the entrant who is squeezed out.[18] This argument may be less strong with respect to Spence's second model, however, where the entrant may come in at a cost disadvantage relative to established firms.

A final problem with Spence's model is in its assumption regarding entrant expectations. In figure 4.7, the entrant is assumed to expect incumbent firms to produce at full capacity should entry take place. If entry does occur, however, it will not in general be optimal for established firms to pursue this policy. For example, a chemical processing firm with a monopoly in a particular country may take on extra capacity to deter new entry. If a new firm enters, however, it is not clear in general that it would use this extra capacity and engage in a price war. If the entrant thinks it will not, then the full capacity threat is not credible. Of course, the established firm *may* engage in a price war if it can gain a *reputation* thereby which enables it to deter future entry.[19] On the other hand, it may accept that entry has occurred and compete with the rival firm. Dixit (1980)[20] has analysed this latter case on the assumption that the entrant expects the post-entry game to yield a Cournot equilibrium. Given this assumption, it is still possible for the incumbent firm to deter entry by an appropriate choice of capacity. It turns out, however, that under this assumption the incumbent firm would never hold unused capacity (whether or not it chose to deter entry). Spence's model, therefore, is to some extent sensitive to the assumption one makes with regard to entrant's expectations.

Product proliferation as a deterrent to entry   A second method of deterring entry by non-price means is by product or brand proliferation. Such a policy can be applied in markets with product differentiation, such as breakfast cereals, cigarettes, soaps and detergents, etc. Basically, the policy involves established firms 'packing' the market with a variety of products or brands so that insufficient room exists for a new firm's product to compete profitably. If this can be done, then established firms may be able to have high prices and profits without attracting entry.

A useful analysis of this possibility is provided by Schmalensee (1978) in his discussion of the US ready-to-eat breakfast cereal industry. Schmalensee considers a conceptual framework characterized by three assumptions. First, he assumes that there are increasing returns to the production and marketing of individual brands or products, at least up to some output level. This assumption sets a limit on the number of brands that can be produced by implying that, given market price, there is a minimum market share at which a product can be viably produced. Second, it is assumed that rivalry is localized in the sense that the market can be regarded as more or less segmented with a limited number of competing products in each segment. And third, it is assumed that products are relatively immobile in economic space, reflecting substantial costs of 'repositioning' the product in product space. This assumption lends credibility to the established firms' entry-deterring strategy, since with substantial repositioning costs an entrant would not normally expect an accommodating movement of products should entry take place.

Schmalensee analyses product differentiation by analogy to spatial competition following the initial work of Hotelling (1929).[21] Only simple illustrative models are available concerning the distribution of demand in geographic or product space, but these may be sufficient to indicate general principles. An extremely simple case is where buyers are assumed to be uniformly distributed around a circle of unit circumference. Schmalensee assumes there are N brands, located at distances $1/N$ apart on the circle, and that there is a common price, p. If we take p as given, then there is some finite maximum number of brands, $\bar{N}$, such that profits of a typical brand are zero; i.e. $\pi(p, \bar{N}) = 0$ where π is profit. Now consider a new entrant who locates optimally, given existing brand locations, midway between two existing brands on the circle. Given price, the new brand will capture sales from its rivals on either side, and the symmetrical conditions assumed imply profits of $\pi(p, 2N)$ for the new brand. These will be positive only if $2N < \bar{N}$, and established firms can prevent new entry by proliferating brands such that $N > \bar{N}/2$. Established firms are, however, able to make positive profits, since in this simple model each established brand has twice the market that a new entrant can expect to obtain.

Schmalensee derives two interesting results from his model. First, he shows that, if the established firms collude to maximize profit in such a market, subject to the condition that entry is prevented from a price-matching entrant, then it will be optimal to secure deterrence solely by brand proliferation. While this result is derived using a rather special form of demand function, it nevertheless seems intuitively plausible that brand proliferation rather than price would be the best weapon to use to deter new entry.[22] Second, Schmalensee shows that advertising may also be used effectively alongside product proliferation to deter new entry. He considers, for simplicity, introductory advertising, which is required by each brand to persuade buyers to try it for the first time. If new entrants are assumed to match the introductory spending per brand of established firms, then for each dollar spent their payoff will be less since they will serve a smaller market area with only an equiproportionate effect of advertising on sales. Hence, it pays established firms to advertise more than they otherwise would to take advantage of this effect. Basically, the argument is one of spreading an overhead over fewer sales in the case of the new entrant.

While this analysis is based on a very simplified model, it does suggest that there is a theoretical rationale for the use of product proliferation as a deterrent to entry. This is not to say, however, that such a policy necessarily will be employed successfully. In order to be successful it is necessary for established firms to conduct good enough market and product research to ensure that no profitable gaps arise in the market. Established firms can always be surprised, however, by a new product development or shift in demand. An example of the latter in the US ready-to-eat breakfast cereal market was the rapid growth in demand for so-called 'natural cereals' in the early 1970s (Schmalensee, 1978). The market for such products grew from negligible proportions in 1972 to a peak of 10 per cent in mid-1974, and this apparently was not anticipated by most of the established firms. Consequently, a number of new firms successfully entered the market before the established firms could bring out new products to fill this market segment. However, a decline in the market in 1974–7, together with competition from previously established firms, meant that only one of these new entrants was still in national distribution by late 1977.

A further problem with product proliferation as a deterrent to entry is product imitation. An alternative strategy for a new entrant to that of producing for gaps in product space is to attempt closely to imitate existing brands and to compete on price. Replication of existing brands is, of course, illegal, but in some cases, such as breakfast cereals, it is possible to produce a fairly close substitute for a product under a different brand name. Paradoxically, an established firm will be more at risk from such new competition the more successful is one of its brands, at least to the extent that an imitative product is more likely to compete equally on cost terms the larger is its potential market. Against this, successful established brands often accumulate a large stock of consumer goodwill which may inhibit sales of a cheaper similar product. If a new entrant has to incur heavy advertising expenditures to break down the barrier of perceived inferiority of his product, then entry may not seem worthwhile. The role of advertising as a barrier to entry is further discussed in chapter 6. We may note for the moment, however, that retailer own-brand products may be a way of partially overcoming this problem in that they attach retailers' own reputations for good quality to imitative products.

In some cases one or several firms may come to dominate a market with product proliferation through merger, while in other cases the history of the market may be important with first-comers able to establish and then maintain their dominant positions. In either case, however, the test of high prices and profits will indicate monopoly welfare loss and a potential gain in welfare from the reduction of prices.[23] It is less clear, however, how one might best effect such a change through government policy. In the breakfast cereals case in the USA, the Federal Trade Commission sought structural remedies whereby leading firms would be split into separate companies (divestiture); in addition, compulsory licensing of trademarks to other companies was sought. Such policies are quite radical, however, in that it might be argued that they penalize business success, at least where dominant positions are not due to merger. Alternative policies might be direct controls on prices and profits, or the encouragement of new competition, for example by limiting further product proliferation. The former policy was recommended, for example, by the UK Monopolies Commission in its report on household detergents (Monopolies Commission, 1966), and cuts in excessive advertising expenditures were also suggested in this case. Less attention appears to have been paid to positive policies of encouraging new competition in such markets. The emergence of retailers' own-brand products in recent years has shown that new entry *is* a feasible alternative, although it might be argued that the strength of established firms in many markets implies that such new competition is likely to have only limited effect.[24]

4.3.2 Contestable Markets

In contrast to recent developments in the field of strategic entry deterrence, which emphasize ways in which firms limit new competition, recent work on contestable markets has re-examined conceptual ideas on free entry. This work has focused on the concept of a *perfectly contestable market* in which incumbent firms are not protected in any way from potential entry. The study of this concept is of particular interest from a welfare or public policy point of view and hence deserves brief mention here.[25]

The idea of a perfectly contestable market is relatively straightforward. A market is perfectly contestable if it is *completely* open to potential new competition. This implies two things in particular. First, potential entrants should operate under identical cost (or product quality) conditions to incumbent firms; i.e., there should be no barriers to entry on Stigler's definition of the term. Second, new entrants should be able to enter and leave the industry at no net cost; that is, no entrant should be deterred from entry by the thought that it will lose money if it has to exit again. Hence, on these assumptions there is no risk to entry and incumbent firms find themselves in an openly competitive environment.

Not surprisingly, under these assumptions incumbent firms have very little or no monopoly power. Even when there is one or just a few firms in the market, perfect contestability ensures that no profits are made in long-run equilibrium, since if they were an entrant would come in and undercut price thereby eliminating profits. Even more important, such markets tend to operate with zero price-(marginal) cost margins, thereby fulfilling a basic condition for Pareto optimality. Such a result also applies, of course, in long-run perfectly competitive equilibrium. The novelty of perfect contestability, however, is that this result does not require large numbers of actual firms producing in the market. Rather, as long as a new entrant can come in when price exceeds marginal cost and finance a small price cut by producing slightly more than an incumbent firm, then price cannot exceed marginal cost in long-run equilibrium. It has been shown that a sufficient condition for this is that there be two (or more) incumbent firms in the market (see, for example, Baumol, Panzar and Willig, 1982, chapters 2 and 11). Hence, in strong contrast to perfect competition, duopoly is enough to produce an optimal allocation of resources.[26]

If markets were perfectly contestable, there would be no need to worry about various oligopoly outcomes as discussed in chapter 3. Rather, as long as two firms compete in the market and potential entrants can come in and leave at will, marginal cost pricing will be the rule.[27] In some markets, indeed, perfect contestability may be a reasonable assumption. The key factor is that potential entrants feel that there are no costs specific to entry and exit, i.e. that any investment in plant and other assets required for entry is recoverable on exit (after allowance for depreciation, etc.). This may be a reasonable assumption for many service industries (fast food restaurants, hairdressers, etc.), for example. In other cases, however, entry requires an initial investment which is partly irreversible and hence involves a non-recoverable sunk cost. In these cases, markets are less than perfectly contestable and entry deterrence again rears its head. As noted by Spence (1983), sunk costs are likely to be positively correlated with economies of scale, and we know (chapter 2) that high scale economies relative to market size are linked to high market concentration. Hence, it may be that contestability is of more limited use as a descriptive tool in high concentration markets notwithstanding the conceptual breakthrough that has been made.

As a contribution to welfare and public policy analysis, however, the idea of perfect contestability is clearly very important. In particular, its emphasis on potential rather than actual competition as a mechanism for efficient resource allocation is likely to be important. The theory suggests that greater emphasis should be placed on increasing contestability in markets rather than merely on preventing concentration increases. Obvious policy moves in this direction might include removing government and legal restrictions on entry (or exit); improving the quality of accounting and other information; and improving the efficiency of second-hand asset markets. Such developments should increase the threat of new competition and hence reduce the market power of incumbent firms.

4.4 Summary and Conclusions

This chapter has considered the effects of entry barriers and potential competition on market equilibrium. Section 4.1 considered the pioneering work of Bain on entry barriers and the possible reasons for the persistence of monopoly profits in long-run equilibrium. Section 4.2 considered limit price theory as a theory of oligopolistic pricing in the short run. Finally, section 4.3

looked at some more recent developments in entry theory, in particular dealing with some examples of non-price strategic entry deterrence on the one hand, and with contestable market theory on the other.

As has been stressed, entry theory has undergone substantial development in recent years and work in this area is continuing. These developments are clearly diverse, although each in its own way has made important contributions. Above all these approaches (in their different ways) have emphasized the importance of entry, and it seems likely that subsequent work in this area will highlight still further the crucial role of entry to industrial markets.

Notes

1 See Goldschmid *et al.* (1974) for some general discussion relating to the entry barrier debate. A recent discussion of definitions of entry barriers can be found in Waterson (1981).

2 It is well recognized in practice that legal requirements such as health and safety or quality standard regulations are an alternative to overt barriers to entry. In the international sphere Japan has long used such measures, and they are increasingly being used in the EEC, particularly with respect to farm products.

3 It is assumed for simplicity here that established firms on the one hand and potential entrants on the other are identical with respect to demand and cost conditions. Additional complexities are introduced when this is not the case: see, for example, Bain (1968).

4 It might be thought in this case that the condition of entry is objectively given independently of entrant expectations. A moment's reflection, however, will reveal that prices above p_2 might persist in the long run without entry if entrants think that vigorous price competition to price levels below p_2 would occur if they did enter.

5 It should be stressed that the evidence reported in tables 4.1 and 4.2 is based on judgemental classifications and hence is not objective. Nevertheless, it provides some idea of the likely importance of entry barriers in practice.

6 It is particularly in this case that entrant expectations are important in determining the height of the entry barrier. This matter is discussed extensively in section 4.2. Note also, however, that if entrants take pre-entry price as given and markets are *contestable*, as discussed in section 4.3, then p_1 will be the long-run equilibrium price. See section 4.3 for details.

7 A Bain-type entry barrier does not, in fact, require any asymmetry between entrants and established firms, since an equally well placed entrant may not be able to enter even when price exceeds unit cost. This point is made, for example, in Cubbin (1981) (see chapter 6 for details).

8 This is the basis for the argument that established firms will proliferate products actively to deter new entry in the presence of production differentiation and some scale economies; see section 4.3.1 below.

9 Bain also considers this conjecture, but as one of several possible conjectures by potential entrants.

10 Equation (4.4) is derived by Modigliani. We can alternatively write the result

in terms of the more familiar Lerner (1934) index of monopoly power as $(p_1 - p_c)/p_1 = \bar{x}/[\eta_1(x_c - \bar{x})]$ where η_1 is the market demand elasticity at the limit price.

11 The prospect of negative profits might, however, create capital requirements problems for new as opposed to diversifying firms. I am grateful to Paul Geroski for this point.

12 See, for example, Bevan (1974).

13 For an excellent discussion of pre-emptive patenting see Gilbert and Newbery (1982). Predatory pricing is discussed in chapter 11 below.

14 This is only one possible assumption, of course. For further discussion of this point see below.

15 In his article, Spence considers three possible solutions to his model, the first of which implies that unconstrained profit maximization establishes sufficient capacity to deter entry automatically. In this case, short-run pricing is completely divorced from the problem of deterring entry. Note, however, that, under our assumption of constant unit variable cost with a limit capacity $\bar{k}$, this result cannot apply.

16 It can be shown, for example, that, with a linear demand curve $x = \alpha - \beta p$, where α and β are positive constants, the welfare cost of entry deterrence will exceed that of pure monopoly for unit capacity costs, $r < 0.4(\alpha - c)$. With higher relative capacity costs, the welfare loss is greater under pure monopoly, although it should be noted that at $r = 0.5(\alpha - c)$, capacity costs are so great that the established firm in Spence's model can only set the competitive price and operate at full capacity. Hence, for much of the effective range of relative capacity cost, there is sufficient excess capacity to create greater welfare loss with entry deterrence than under pure monopoly.

17 This issue has been analysed in a static framework by Dixit (1979).

18 If investment in capacity is assumed to be wholly irreversible, say, so that the established firm has incurred associated sunk costs, then it covers its opportunity costs with price equal to c in figure 4.7. This creates an asymmetry before entry when the entrant must consider whether to incur sunk costs. It clearly won't enter if all it expects to get is a loss from doing so, but this does not appear to affect the argument that it may be able to better weather the storm and hence make profits in the long run.

19 The issue of reputation is briefly discussed in Dixit (1982).

20 A slight variant on Dixit's model is given in Schmalensee (1981); see also Spulber (1981).

21 A large literature has developed on spatial competition following Hotelling's work, which we shall not pursue further here. For an alternative conceptual framework employing product characteristics as the basis of analysis, see Lancaster (1979).

22 A similar result is derived in an explicitly spatial framework in Hay (1976).

23 There is also the thorny question of the optimal degree of product differentiation. For recent attempts to deal with this see Lancaster (1979) and Scherer (1979b).

24 This appears to have been the view of the Monopolies Commission in its review of the UK breakfast cereal market: see Monopolies Commission (1973a, para 81).

25 For a useful introduction to contestable markets, see Baumol (1982). A comprehensive treatment is given in Baumol, Panzar and Willig (1982).

26 In the case of an incumbent monopolist, this result does not apply and price may

exceed marginal cost in equilibrium. See Baumol, Panzar and Willig (1982) for details.

27 This is, of course, also the case (at least with constant costs) in the Bertrand model of oligopoly (see chapter 3). The Bertrand result, however, relies on particular behaviour on the part of incumbent firms in contrast to assumptions on entry conditions implied in contestability theory.

5 Profitability and Market Structure

In this chapter we examine the links between profitability and market structure, and in particular market concentration. A great number of empirical studies have been conducted on this issue, particularly in the USA, and some of the results are considered in section 5.3.

The discussion of empirical results is prefaced by an examination of theoretical and more practical issues in sections 5.1 and 5.2. Much controversy exists over the interpretation of empirical results, and some of the central issues are discussed in these sections. These matters are by no means resolved, and this should be borne in mind throughout the chapter.

5.1 Theoretical Issues

The conventional wisdom in the industrial economics literature is that high market concentration leads to high prices and profits, and that this indicates the operation of market power to the detriment of social welfare. This has become known, following Demsetz, as the *market concentration doctrine*.[1]

According to this view, high market concentration, i.e. a small number of firms and/or market share inequality, facilitates collusion in the market, and hence enables firms to approximate the monopoly (joint profit-maximizing) solution: the more so the higher is market concentration. A positive correlation between profitability and concentration is then taken as supporting this hypothesis and appropriate welfare and policy conclusions are drawn. These are that high concentration leads to social welfare losses associated with monopolistic restrictions on output, and that active anti-monopoly policies are required to limit or reduce the amount of market concentration. In the USA in particular it has been suggested that active deconcentration policies be adopted, splitting up companies to ensure that markets become competitive in a structural but implied behavioural and performance sense.

This doctrine has far-reaching political consequences, and it is perhaps not surprising that it has been opposed by liberal/conservative economists. In addition, however, it relies upon a long and possibly oversimplified chain of reasoning which may be open to criticism. We focus here on some of the latter criticisms, leaving aside political and doctrinal issues.

A first criticism of the doctrine is that it oversimplifies links between market concentration and price. Several points are relevant here. First, as we have seen in chapter 3, a great variety of oligopoly theories exist and only some of these suggest that price and concentration will be positively related. While the Cournot and dominant firm models, for example, suggest that prices rise with market concentration, this is not a feature of some other models, e.g. the Bertrand model. Hence it cannot be said that the hypothesis has a firm theoretical base in oligopoly theory. Second, even if we focus on the collusion argument, the link between concentration and collusion may be only one of many factors at work, as discussed again in chapter 3. Hence it might be argued that theory at best suggests only a weak and broad association between profitability, collusion and concentration. Both points would indicate that the theoretical basis for the market concentration doctrine is weak, thereby tending to undermine the doctrine.

A second criticism, made by Demsetz (1974), is that, even if one were to accept a concentration–collusion link in oligopoly theory, there still exists the problem of entry. Standard oligopoly models ignore actual and potential entry, and *assume* that existing firms in concentrated markets have the market power to earn supernormal profits. But firms will not be able to exercise such power if threatened by potential competition from new entrants. This argument might suggest that some interaction between entry barriers and concentration is necessary for high profitability to occur, and indeed a number of studies have allowed such interaction. Thus, we might expect that profitability is higher in industries with high entry barriers, the more so if concentration is also high so that collusion occurs to take advantage of the situation. Note, however, that Demsetz and some other writers do not accept that entry barriers are important empirically (apart from barriers arising from government intervention in the market), and hence argue that potential or actual entry effectively nullifies the market power of oligopolists and with it the market concentration doctrine.

A third criticism, which we shall explore more fully, concerns the interpretation of positive profitability–concentration correlations. The market concentration doctrine interprets them in a causal chain running from concentration to collusion to monopoly profits. Demsetz (1973b) and others have argued, however, that profits are a sign of efficiency rather than monopoly power within a market. The fact that high profits and high concentration go together is not because the latter causes the former, but rather because high efficiency causes both. If some firms in a market possess superior efficiency, they will tend to be large firms and have high profits. In aggregate, in a market where the superior efficiency of large firms is greater, both market concentration and profitability will be higher. Hence, a positive profitability–concentration relationship will result from this superior efficiency argument independently of any market power effects, with consequently radically different implications for social welfare and policy.

Demsetz's argument can be illustrated in terms of absolute cost advantages of successful firms by reference to homogeneous product oligopoly.[2] Consider a market with n firms and assume that firms are ranked from the most to the least efficient in terms of constant marginal costs, c_i ($i = 1, \ldots, n$). Then if $p = p(x)$ is the inverse market demand function and $x = \Sigma_{i=1}^{n} x_i$ is market output, it can be shown that profit maximization implies that

$$\frac{x_i}{x} = \frac{\alpha}{1-\alpha} + \frac{\eta}{1-\alpha}\left(1 - \frac{c_i}{p}\right) \tag{5.1}$$

where $\eta = (-dx/dp)(p/x)$ is the market price elasticity of demand and $\alpha = (dx_j/dx_i)(x_i/x_j)$ ($j \neq i$) is the proportionate conjectured output response of j for i, which is assumed the same for all i and j. Since p is the same for all firms, it follows from (5.1) that, given η and α, lower-cost firms have both higher price–cost margins and market shares. Moreover, by weighting (5.1) by x_i and aggregating over the n firms, it can be shown that

$$\frac{p - \sum_{i=1}^{n} c_i x_i / x}{p} = \frac{H(1-\alpha)}{\eta} + \frac{\alpha}{\eta} \tag{5.2}$$

where $H = \Sigma_{i=1}^{n}(x_i/x)^2$ is the Hirschman–Herfindahl output index of concentration. Thus the weighted average market price–cost margin (with output weights) is positively related to the H index in (5.2) given α and η. This relationship, however, arises in part from the superior efficiency of the largest firms, since it can be shown that

$$H = \frac{1}{n} + \left[1 - \frac{n(\eta - \alpha)}{1-\alpha}\right]^2 \frac{v_c^2}{n} \tag{5.3}$$

where v_c is the coefficient of variation of marginal costs (i.e. the ratio of the standard deviation of the c_i to their mean). It follows that, since $1/n$ is the minimum value for H (which arises when all firms are equally sized), part of the price–cost margin–concentration relationship in (5.2) is by (5.3) associated with the cost efficiency differential between firms (i.e. $v_c^2 > 0$).

It should be pointed out at once that the Demsetz hypothesis of lower cost firms having both higher margins and higher market shares may not extend to all oligopoly models. Nevertheless, it may explain part of any correlation between market concentration and profitability and some empirical evidence on this possibility is discussed in section 5.3. It should also be noted that collusive behaviour associated with higher concentration is not ruled out by Demsetz's hypothesis. In terms of the above model, it can be shown that more collusive outcomes involve higher values of α ($0 \leqslant \alpha \leqslant 1$), implying larger proportionate conjectured output responses from rivals and consequently higher margins. Hence, it would seem likely that collusion and efficiency effects operate together to raise profitability in practice, and this issue is also discussed in section 5.3.

5.2 More Practical Issues

5.2.1 Specification of Econometric Models

Most studies of market structure and profitability use the following general form of econometric model

$$\pi = f(C, B, D) \tag{5.4}$$

where π is an index of profitability, and C, B and D are vectors of explanatory variables (see Martin (1979)). According to this specification, profitability in the market depends on a vector C of variables denoting the ease of collusion; a vector B of variables representing entry conditions; and a vector D of variables representing demand conditions.

Loosely speaking, the rationale for (5.4) draws a distinction between supply-side and demand-side factors as determinants of profitability. On the supply side, profitability is associated with high barriers to entry and collusion. High entry barriers protect established firms from potential competition and hence represent a necessary condition for high profitability. Regardless of the threat of new competition, however, competition between existing firms can erode any supernormal profits. Hence, the effectiveness of collusion in the market determines the degree to which the monopoly situation can be exploited. In so far as existing firms may threaten new competitors more in tight oligopoly situations, moreover, they may also raise the effective barrier to new competition. These considerations suggest that entry barriers and collusion may interact to determine profitability.[3] On the demand side, market growth and price elasticity of demand may also affect profitability as high growth and/or inelastic demand enhance monopoly power given supply conditions.

Consider the factors in equation (5.4) more closely. As noted above, the degree of effective collusion is often proxied by market concentration, measured variously by the reciprocal of firm numbers, the concentration ratio, the Hirschman–Herfindahl index, etc. In addition, in US studies an index of geographic dispersion is often employed to adjust for possible collusion in regional markets. Where foreign trade is thought to be important, adjustment for imports and exports may also be made. This may take the form of simply adjusting the domestic concentration index for foreign trade. Also, it may be hypothesized that foreign competitors have different views on collusion to domestic firms, so that the import share of domestic sales should be separately allowed for. In some studies, countervailing power in the form of buyer concentration is also allowed for as an offset to the collusion of sellers. This argument may sometimes be used to justify a distinction between producer and consumer goods, although continuing increases in concentration in retailing have tended to blur this distinction.

Second, a number of variables have been used as barriers to entry proxies. Following Bain, entry barriers arising from product differentiation, scale economies and capital requirements are allowed for. The product differentiation entry barrier may be proxied by the industry advertising/sales ratio, and may also be allowed for by a consumer–producer good distinction.

Scale economy barriers are usually proxied by an estimate of minimum efficient scale relative to market size, and this is sometimes supplemented by an estimate of the cost disadvantage of operation at less than minimum efficient scale. The capital requirements of a plant of minimum efficient scale may be used to proxy the capital requirements barrier, and some studies also include absolute advertising expenditures from such considerations. Potential competition from abroad is an important factor in open economies, and external tariffs and transport costs per unit of sales value are useful indicators of protection for domestic producers. High transport costs also afford protection from new competition in regional markets. Patents and government patronage protect established firms from new competition, although these factors are often difficult to allow for on a general basis.

On the demand side, both market growth and demand elasticity may affect profitability. Profitability is likely to be higher in growing markets if supply adjustments lag behind increases in demand. Also, perceived inelasticity of demand may give rise to higher prices and profitability. Several writers have suggested that the actual ratio of imports to domestic sales be used as a proxy for the price elasticity of demand, reflecting higher perceived elasticities with a greater threat of foreign competition. High advertising/sales ratios may have a demand-side role if they reduce price elasticities of demand. The division between consumer and producer goods industries is also sometimes justified in terms of reducing heterogeneity in the demand characteristics of industries.

While specific econometric problems are associated with particular studies, several problems of more general interest may briefly be mentioned here. First, a number of variables suggested as determinants of profitability, notably market concentration, import penetration and the advertising/sales ratio, are not strictly exogenous variables. That is, these variables are likely to be determined, along with profitability, by fundamental supply and demand conditions in the market. This implies that the profitability equation is, in fact, only one of a set of simultaneous equations describing industrial economic relationships. Further, if these variables are themselves likely to be affected *by* profitability, or by each other, then this may considerably increase the difficulty of estimating their effect *on* profitability. For example, while advertising intensity may act as a barrier to entry and hence increase profitability, profitability itself may act as an incentive for advertising, so that a two-way relationship between these variables may exist. In these circumstances it may be necessary to use more complicated simultaneous equation estimation techniques to try to separate out the different effects, and the work of several authors using such techniques is considered in section 5.3.

Second, several variables which have been suggested above as determinants of profitability, notably the price elasticity of demand, are often unobservable in practice and hence are simply omitted from the estimated equation. Most particularly, when profitability is measured by the price–cost margin (see next section) it is expected, *ceteris paribus*, to be higher in industries for which demand is less elastic. The omission of the price elasticity of demand as a determinant of profitability in comparing industries can produce biased estimates of the effects of other variables on profitability if these are correlated with the elasticity.

Finally, while in principle there may be good reason for including the variables discussed above as determinants of profitability, in practice it may be extremely difficult to measure their independent effects on profitability if they are highly correlated among themselves. The problem of *multicollinearity* of explanatory variables, while it does not lead to biased estimates of their effects, does tend to lead to unreliable estimates which may be statistically non-significant. Hence, estimated effects on profitability may be inaccurate and/or appear statistically insignificant so that true relationships are not clearly revealed. This is particularly important in the present context, in that high concentration industries often have high capital intensity and/or important scale economies, so that inclusion of such entry barrier variables together with concentration as determinants of profitability can give rise to this problem. Possible multicollinearity of explanatory variables is, therefore, a further econometric problem which must be borne in mind in considering the empirical evidence.

5.2.2 Conceptual and Measurement Problems

US studies of profitability and market structure, particularly prior to the 1970s, have typically examined determinants of rates of return on assets (or equity) across industries. Under competitive conditions, and with proper allowance for depreciation, risk and interest, such rates of return would be zero (in equilibrium). In the presence of monopoly power (or, alternatively, superior efficiency on the part of some firms), above-competitive rates of return would be observed. As frequently noted, this arises because of the use of accounting measures of assets which do not represent the economic value of firms. Since, by definition, anything (including monopoly power) which generates income is an asset to a firm, if one capitalized such assets appropriately then monopoly profits would disappear. The fact that accounting measures of assets deviate from economic values provides the basis for their use in profitability studies. By and large, it is expected that accounting measures of assets will undervalue monopoly power so that reported rates of return will tend to be positively correlated with the degree of monopoly.

There are difficult measurement problems associated with accounting measures of profitability. In so far as they give rise to measurement errors which are uncorrelated with variables used to explain profitability, no problem of bias in estimated effects will arise. This may not be a reasonable assumption, however. For example, asset revaluations are likely to occur particularly in industries affected by merger activity, and if such industries are also those where collusion is prevalent, then monopoly profits will tend to be disguised. Again, some monopoly profits may not be reported as profits, particularly in small firms where the division of income between profits, salaries and expenses may be arbitrary. Stigler (1963) has argued that this factor tends to lead to the understatement of profits in small companies and this effect is greater in unconcentrated industries. Hence, if true, a bias in the direction of a misleadingly strong profitability–concentration relation would be observed. Finally, there is an incentive to disguise high monopoly profits in accounts for tax and public relations purposes, and this may lead to a downwards bias in the estimated profitability–concentration relation. Indeed, as noted above, it is only because accounting conventions do not allow complete accounting adjustments that any evidence of monopoly power is likely to be found.

A major problem with rate-of-return measures of profitability arises from lack of comparable data on assets classified by suitably disaggregated industry. This is particularly the case in the UK. An alternative measure of profitability used in both the UK and the USA is the industry price–cost margin. This variable is often measured from Census of Production sources as value added minus wages and salaries divided by total revenue, and hence is an approximation to the ratio of gross profits and overheads to sales.

Alternatively, it can be viewed not as an index of profitability at all but rather as an approximation to an index of market power. Following Lerner (1934), we may argue that an appropriate index of monopoly power for a firm i is $(p_i - c_i)/p_i$ where p_i is its price and c_i its marginal cost. This index measures the relative deviation of price from (assumed optimal) marginal cost pricing and hence indicates the extent of monopolistic output restriction. Taking a weighted average of such Lerner indices, with revenue weights, we have

$$PCM = \frac{\sum_{i=1}^{n} \frac{(p_i - c_i)}{p_i} p_i x_i}{\sum_{i=1}^{n} p_i x_i} = \frac{\sum_{i=1}^{n} (p_i - c_i) x_i}{\sum_{i=1}^{n} p_i x_i} \tag{5.5}$$

where x_i is firm i's output and PCM is the industry price–cost margin. The measured price–cost margin is only an approximation to (5.5) except in the case where average direct costs are constant and hence equal to marginal costs, c_i. If this approximation can be taken as reasonably accurate, however, then the price–cost margin offers a reasonable direct measure of monopoly power. In other cases, and in particular in the presence of scale economies, the approximation will be more suspect since marginal costs may deviate from average variable costs.

The use of price–cost margin data does not obviate the need to measure capital assets. In a competitive equilibrium the ratio of gross profits and overheads to sales would differ between industries most notably because of differences in capital/sales ratios. Consequently, it is necessary to control for such differences before evaluating possible monopoly power effects. UK studies, in particular, have been bedevilled by this problem, and often very imperfect measures of capital have been employed. Also, some studies attempt to control for advertising and/or research and development expenditure which are both included in the measure of gross profits and overheads. Conceptual problems exist concerning the treatment of these items as current expenses as opposed to investment expenditures, however, and this issue is discussed further (in the case of advertising) in chapter 6. Finally, since sales revenue can be influenced by extraneous factors such as the incidence of excise taxes and internal accounting procedures with vertically integrated firms (see chapter 8), some studies have used the ratio of gross profits plus overheads to value added in place of sales revenue.[4] This measure is effectively the non-wage share in value added, and while it does have these measurement advantages, it is less closely related to the Lerner index of monopoly power than the conventionally measured price–cost margin.

Further problems surround the variables used to explain profitability. As noted in section 5.1, positive correlations between profitability and concen-

Table 5.1 Average profit rates in US manufacturing, by concentration decile, 1936–40

8-firm concentration ratio	No. of industries	Av. profit rate
0–10	1	9.1
10–20	1	17.0
20–30	2	10.4
30–40	5	6.3
40–50	2	8.6
50–60	4	5.8
60–70	5	5.8
70–80	3	16.3
80–90	11	9.8
90–100	8	12.7

Source: Bain (1951, table II, p. 313) (corrected as indicated in the Corrigendum to Bain's paper).

tration may reflect either collusive or efficiency effects leading to problems in interpreting empirical results. There are also problems in measuring concentration (see chapter 2), particularly where imports and exports are an important feature of markets. Second, as noted above, there are conceptual and measurement problems which surround capital and advertising intensity. And, as a final example, scale economy barriers to entry are often proxied rather imperfectly by some average plant size variable used to measure minimum efficient scale of plant in the absence of detailed cost/scale information. In short, there are many conceptual and measurement problems surrounding profitability and market structure studies, and these should be borne in mind in assessing the empirical results considered in the next section.

5.3 Empirical Evidence [5]

5.3.1 US Studies

The pioneering work on profits and concentration was done by J. S. Bain (1951). He looked at a selected sample of 42 US industries in the period 1936–40, and compared average large-firm profit rates (net of income taxes) on net worth for the period with the eight-firm sales concentration ratio for 1935. Bain's data are classified by concentration decile in table 5.1. As can be seen, fairly high average profit rates were observed above the 70 per cent range, and again in the very few industries with concentration below the 30 per cent mark. These data led Bain to conclude that there was at best weak evidence of a positive linear relationship between profitability and concentration but that a sharp break in average profit rates occurred at about the 70 per cent level. More formally, in his sample the simple linear correlation coefficient between profitability and concentration was $r = 0.33$, which is not sufficient to reject the hypothesis of a zero population correlation coefficient at the 5 per cent significance level. On the other hand, the average profit rate in industries with concentration ratios of above 70 per cent was 11.8 per cent compared with 7.5 per cent in the less concentrated industries. This difference was statistically significant at the 1 per cent level, and was consistent with Bain's view that high profit rates were likely to be associated with effective collusion and hence with highly concentrated as opposed to moderate or low concentration industries.

Bain extended his work in his later study (Bain, 1956) to consider the effects of entry barriers in addition to market concentration. As noted in chapter 4, Bain classified a sample of 20 US manufacturing industries according to the categories 'very high', 'substantial' or 'moderate or low' barriers to entry. These industries were also classified as 'high' concentration (with an eight-firm concentration ratio exceeding 70 per cent), 'medium' or 'low' concentration (with a concentration ratio below 70 per cent). Bain found that for 1936–40 and for 1947–51 profit rates were substantially higher in the high concentration as compared to the low concentration industries. In addition, he found that profit rates were substantially higher in 'very high' entry barrier industries, although no distinction in profit rates could be made between 'substantial' and 'moderate or low' entry barrier industries. Finally, while industries with 'very high' entry barriers were also those with very high concentration, some very high concentration industries also fell into the 'substantial' and 'moderate or low' entry barrier categories and profit rates in these cases tended to be higher than average for such entry barrier classes. Broadly similar results were obtained by Mann (1966) in his extended sample of 30 industries in the period 1950–60. Thus, both studies pointed to entry barriers and concentration as two of the major determinants of profitability in US manufacturing industry over a considerable period of time.

The early results of Bain and Mann have not gone unchallenged. Brozen (1971), for example, criticized the sample selection procedures in Bain's original article and, employing a larger sample of industries for 1939 and 1940, argued that there was a negligible difference in average rate of return between high and low concentration industries using the 70 per cent eight-firm concentration ratio cut-off point. Further, a major study by Stigler (1963) (see also Kilpatrick, 1968) examined rates of return and concentration over the period 1938–57. He found that concentrated industries (with four firm value added concentration ratios over 60 per cent) tended to have higher average rates of return in 1938–41 and in 1948–57 compared to unconcentrated industries (with concentration ratios below 50 per cent), but that the reverse was true in 1941–8. The higher profit rates in concentrated industries were only statistically significant at the 5 per cent level in 1951–4 and 1955–7. Also, when adjustments were made for excess withdrawals by officers of small corporations, which play a more prominent role in less concentrated industries, the discrepancies were further reduced. Stigler's work, therefore suggested that there was limited empirical support for the market concentration doctrine.

Collins and Preston (1968, 1969) undertook the first systematic analysis of industry price–cost margins in the USA. Price–cost margin data have the advantage of being more easily accessible in the US Census of Manufactures, permitting the analysis of much larger samples of industries than those considered above. In their 1969 article, for example, Collins and Preston were able to consider a sample of 417 four-digit industries in 1963 and a comparable sample of 243 four-digit industries for 1958 and 1963. Using linear multiple regression techniques, they regressed industry price–cost margins on the four-firm concentration ratio, an index of geographic dispersion (to control for industries serving regional or local markets) and the capital/output ratio (to control for variations in the ratio of fixed to variable costs). They found a significant positive effect of concentration on price–cost margins in both years, a result which was robust to the introduction of the other explanatory variables into the equation. A typical result for all 417 industries in 1963 was

$$PCM = 19.54 + 0.096CR - 0.029GD + 0.092KO \qquad R^2 = 0.19 \qquad (5.6)$$

where the effects of concentration (CR) and capital intensity (KO) on price–cost margins (PCM) were significant at the 1 per cent level, and geographic dispersion (GD) had the expected negative sign and was significant at the 5 per cent level. According to equation (5.6), concentration had a small but significant effect on price–cost margins in 1963, implying a 5 percentage point difference in margins between an industry with a concentration ratio of 20 per cent, say, and one with a concentration ratio of 70 per cent. Note, however, that much of the variation in price–cost margins is unexplained in equation (5.6) as indicated by the low R^2 statistic, so that a great deal of unexplained variability about this average relationship was observed.

Collins and Preston established several other results. First, the price–cost margin–concentration relationship was statistically significant in industries with stable or increasing concentration in 1958–63 but not in industries with declining concentration. Second, the effect of concentration on price–cost margins was much larger in consumer goods industries compared with producer goods industries, a result which they attributed to greater knowledge and bargaining power on the side of buyers of producer goods. A division of consumer goods industries into those with high–moderate product differentiation and those with low product differentiation, however, failed to discriminate further between industry price–cost margins.

Weiss (1974), in a follow-up study, has shown that Collins and Preston's results are not affected by the addition of further explanatory variables. For example, using 399 of Collins and Preston's 1963 industries, Weiss adds variables for advertising intensity (AS) and central office employment (CE) to control for expenses not netted out of the measured price–cost margin, the inventory sales ratio (IS), the growth of output in 1954–63 (G) and the percentage of sales going to consumers entered interactively with the concentration ratio $(CS*CR)$. The results, on a comparable basis to equation (5.6) and with t statistics in parentheses, are:

$$PCM = 16.8 + 0.05CR - 0.03GD + 0.11KO + 1.3AS$$
$$(15.3) \ (2.76) \quad (-3.04) \quad (7.26) \quad (7.23)$$

$$+ 0.20CE - 0.03IS + 0.23G + 0.08CS*CR \qquad R^2 = 0.42.$$
$$(1.46) \quad (-0.69) \quad (2.64) \quad (2.75) \qquad\qquad\qquad (5.7)$$

All variables with the exceptions of CE and IS have the expected signs and are statistically significant at the 5 per cent level. In particular, concentration continues to have a positive and significant effect on price–cost margins, with an additional and increasing effect in more consumer-orientated industries (as indicated by the coefficient on $CS*CR$).

Most studies of profitability or price–cost margins in the USA up to the early 1970s found a significant positive effect of concentration on the dependent variable. This emerges clearly from Weiss's (1974) survey of the evidence, which suggests that, at least for 1953–67, a robust concentration effect was observed. According to Weiss, results for the immediate postwar period were more equivocal, however, and this he attributes to disruptions owing to price inflation in this period.

More recent US work has developed in a number of directions, although we shall consider just two such developments here.[6] First, some work on profitability and market concentration has been done using more detailed business unit data collected under the Profit Impact of Market Strategy (PIMS) programme of the Strategic Planning Institute. These data relate more directly to individual product markets than do Census data and hence offer the potential for more accurate measurement of structure–performance relationships.[7] They have been used, in particular, in a study by Gale and Branch (1982) for US businesses in the late 1970s. While this study has certain statistical weaknesses, the authors find that profitability in their sample is linked mainly to market share and only weakly to market concentration. In particular, in multiple regression analysis, with market share as the other variable, market concentration has a negative (but insignificant) effect on profitability. Gale and Branch suggest that this is evidence for negligible market power effects associated with market concentration, and these results challenge the findings of many earlier US studies. For Gale and Branch, leading firms have lower costs and/or better quality products, so that market shares and profits are positively related. Their results, therefore, are consistent with the efficiency view of high profitability, and further evidence on this view is discussed separately in section 5.3.3 below.

Second, some studies have attempted to employ more sophisticated simultaneous equation estimation techniques to the estimation of links between profitability and market structure. Strickland and Weiss (1976), for example, have estimated a three-equation statistical model in which price–cost margins, advertising intensity and concentration are treated as endogenous variables. This model was estimated using both ordinary least squares (OLS) and two-stage least squares (2SLS) estimation techniques for 408 four-digit US industries in 1963.[8] While, broadly speaking, results are similar between the two estimation techniques used, important discrepancies do emerge in the price–cost margin equation. Specifically, while advertising intensity (as a product differentiation barrier to entry) and concentration have significant positive effects on margins in OLS estimation, once allowance is made for their endogeneity in 2SLS estimation neither effect is statistically significant. One interpretation of these results is that, once allowance is made for the joint determination of variables, the product differentiation barrier to entry and concentration are not important determinants of margins. Strickland and Weiss argue, however, in the case of concentration, that collinearity with another explanatory variable (the scale economy entry barrier) explains the statistically insignificant impact of concentration on margins.[9]

Martin (1979) has criticized Strickland and Weiss's model on technical

Table 5.2 Summary of structure–performance studies for the UK[a]

Study	Profit measure[b]	Concentration measure[b]	Period	Concentration effect[c]	Other significant variables	R^{2d}
Shepherd (1972)	π/R	CR	1958/63	(+)	Market growth; market size	0.114*
Phillips (1972)	π/R	CR	1951	+	Advertising intensity; plant size (perverse sign)	0.260
Holtermann (1973)	π/R	CR	1963	(−)	Capital intensity; advertising intensity; growth; capital expenditure	0.454
Khalilzadeh-Shirazi (1974)	π/R	CR	1963	(+)	Capital intensity; plant size; advertising dummy; exports	0.544
Cowling and Waterson (1976)	$\Delta(\pi/R)$	$\Delta(H)$	1963–8	+	None	0.096*
Hart and Morgan (1977)	π/VA	CR	1968	(+)	Capital/labour ratio; advertising intensity	0.432*
Hitiris (1978)	π/R	CR	1963, 1968	+	Effective protection; capital intensity; growth	0.380
Nickell and Metcalf (1978)	OB/PB	CR	1974, 1976	+	Advertising intensity; minimum efficient size; non-food dummy	0.564
Lyons (1981)	π/R	H	1968	+	Advertising intensity; export intensity; domestic production and intra-industry trade measures	0.312
Geroski (1981)	π/R	CR	1968	nonlinear	Advertising intensity; exports; imports; growth	0.394
Clarke (1984)	π/VA	CR	1970–6	(−)	Advertising intensity; capital intensity; growth; sector dummies	0.655

Notes

[a] Only selected results are referred to. The reader should consult the text and original papers for fuller details.

[b] The measures are: π/R, profit/revenue ratio; π/VA, profit/value added ratio; OB/PB, ratio of own brand to proprietary brand price; CR, concentration ratio; H, Hirschman–Herfindahl index. Δ denotes change.

[c] Sign of concentration effect reported. ( ) denotes not significant on 5 per cent one-tail test.

[d] Figures for R^2 relate to one equation only and hence are only representative; * denotes R^2.

grounds, and suggested a slightly enhanced model which has more attractive properties from an estimation viewpoint. He estimated this model for a sample of 209 US industries in 1967 using a three-stage least squares (3SLS) technique and dividing the sample into producer and consumer goods industries. Again, concentration (measured by the four-firm concentration ratio) had a positive but insignificant effect on industry price–cost margins. Pagoulatos and Sorenson (1980/1) also employ a 3SLS estimation technique for a sample of 47 US food processing industries in 1967; they find that concentration has a positive effect on margins which is statistically significant (at the 10 per cent significance level). They also find that the price elasticity of demand has an expected negative effect on margins which is significant at the 5 per cent level.[10]

5.3.2 UK Studies

In contrast to the generally positive links between rates of return or margins and concentration observed in the USA, UK results have been more mixed. While most studies have found a positive concentration effect (as shown in table 5.2), this effect has not always been statistically significant or robust to alternative specifications. Also, most recent evidence for the 1970s has suggested, if anything, that a negative relationship existed between profitability and concentration in these years. The available evidence, therefore, does not show a clear pattern in the concentration–profitability relationship, and hence gives no general support for the market concentration doctrine.

Some qualifications to this conclusion are noted below. It is useful first, however, to consider one or two of the studies listed in table 5.2 in order to illustrate the diversity of results obtained.[11] Some of the strongest positive results for a profitability–concentration link have been reported by Hitiris (1978) for 1963 and 1968. In this study, Hitiris considered determinants of price–cost margins for (two-and-a-half-digit) input–output industries, paying particular attention to the degree of effective protection from foreign imports available to these industries. He found that price–cost margins were positively related to both concentration and effective protection in his sample, and that market growth and capital intensity also had a positive impact on margins. Hitiris's approach, however, has been criticized by Lyons and Kitchen (Lyons, Kitchen and Hitiris, 1979) who point out that Hitiris used a misleading measure of concentration in his original study. In his revised estimates, however, concentration continued to play an important role in determining margins in 1963, although not in 1968 (see Lyons, Kitchen and Hitiris, 1979, *passim*). Hitiris put this latter result down to the disruptive influence of the merger boom of the 1960s, while Lyons and Kitchen argued that increased import competition may have upset the results.

Several other studies for 1963 and 1968 have reported mixed results. Holtermann (1973) and Khalilzadeh-Shirazi (1974), for example, found insignificant negative and insignificant positive results, respectively (for 1963) using three-digit industry data. Cowling and Waterson (1976) found a positive effect of concentration (as measured by the Hirschman–Herfindahl index) on price–cost margins by examining changes in such margins in 1963–8. This result is interesting since, by using changes in variables, Cowling and Waterson were able partly to justify the omission of unavailable variables (such as the market price elasticity of demand) on the grounds that such variables are relatively constant in time. Unfortunately, their positive results could not be replicated by Hart and Morgan (1977), who found no significant positive concentration effect on profitability in a more appropriate comparable sample of industries in 1963–8.

More recently, Lyons (1981) has reported a positive effect of concentration on price–cost margins at the three-digit industry level in 1968 (compare Hitiris above). A notable feature of Lyons's study is the emphasis he places on foreign trade variables. In particular, he finds that import penetration has a significant dampening effect on margins in 1968 while the degree of intra-industry trade (taken as an indicator of product heterogeneity) was also important. For his sample, price–cost margins were positively related to export intensity, suggesting that higher profits are typically earned on export as opposed to domestic sales.

Geroski (1981) has also examined determinants of price–cost margins in 1968. His results suggest that a highly nonlinear relationship existed between margins and concentration in his sample. Using advanced techniques, he found that the best fit to his data was obtained in a model in which concentration had alternatively positive and negative effects on price–cost margins over several ranges of concentration. These results imply that no monotonic profitability–concentration relationship exists and hence that no simple rules for detecting market power effects can be found. Rather, market power may form a very complex relationship with concentration.

In my own study for 1970–6 (Clarke, 1984) I also found no evidence of simple positive links between profitability and concentration. Using data on profit margins on value added, I found that profitability was particularly high in the food and chemicals sectors, although part of this was attributable to high capital and/or advertising intensity in these sectors. As far as levels of profit margins were concerned, concentration had a *negative* impact on margins which was quite strong but probably not statistically significant. With regard to trends in margins, concentration tended to have a positive sign but was not statistically significant. Somewhat surprisingly, the strongest effect of concentration was on the variability in profit margins, with high concentration tending to be *positively* and significantly correlated with variation in margins in 1970–6. This result would be consistent with greater (not less) competition in concentrated industries in this period, although further work is needed before any such strong conclusions can be drawn.

These and other studies listed in table 5.2 clearly offer no strong support for a positive concentration–profitability relationship. This may mean *either* that such a relationship exists but has not been detected, *or* that no such relationship exists. Several arguments can be made for the former possibility. First, the quality of data available to researchers in the UK is quite poor (even relative to US data), and this may have affected results. Data available on variables such as advertising and capital intensity are particularly poor, and this may be important given the role of these variables in the analysis. Also, as noted in chapter 2, the Census definitions of industries are somewhat crude, while Census data also ignore imports and make no separate allowance for exports. Each of these factors may contribute to a masking of the concentration–profitability relation. Second, the models tested may fail adequately to capture the simultaneity of structure–performance relationships and thereby give misleading results.

Third, problems may have arisen from the time period considered. Over the last 20 years, UK industry has been subject to a series of disturbances which have had important influences on the prospects of different industries. Industry has been under increasing pressure from foreign competition, and at the same time has been subject to increasingly severe downturns in the business cycle. In this period also a number of shocks to the system have occurred (e.g. the 1967 devaluation, entry to the EEC and the GATT tariff reductions of the early 1970s, the world oil price rise of 1973–4 and so on). These factors had a disruptive influence on industry and may therefore have upset more longstanding structure–conduct–performance relationships.

Clearly, each of these arguments may be important. Equally, however, it may be that no general profitability–concentration relationship does exist. Market power is obviously important in some concentrated industries, but relationships between profitability and concentration may be so complex that no simple overall relationship can be found. Such a conclusion certainly cannot be refuted from the available evidence. Whether in fact this turns out to be the case, however, can only await further empirical testing.

5.3.3 Efficiency or Collusion?

As noted in section 5.1, Demsetz and others have argued that positive correlations between profitability and concentration may reflect efficiency advantages of large firms rather than collusion. If this is the case, then conventional public policy concern with concentration may be unwarranted, since profits will reflect superior economic performance rather than the exercise of monopoly power.

Demsetz (1973b) proposed to test the competing hypotheses by considering the *intra-industry* relationships between profitability and firm size. According to the collusion hypothesis, high concentration leads to collusion, so that both small and large firms in high concentration industries should benefit from high concentration. In contrast, according to the efficiency hypothesis, superior efficiency of large firms leads to high concentration and high profits, so that large firms should benefit more than small firms in high concentration industries. Hence, argued Demsetz, on the first hypothesis small-firm profitability should be higher in more concentrated industries, while on the second, profitability differences between large and small firms should be greater the higher is concentration. Using a sample of 95 three-digit US industries for 1963, Demsetz found similar rates of return for small firms (with assets less than $0.5 million) for all levels of concentration, but greater differential rates of return between large and small firms as concentration increased. This last result can be shown by regressing the difference in rate of return between large and small firms, $R_4 - R_1$ (where a large firm has assets over $50 million), on concentration, C_{63}, which, with t ratio in parenthesis, gives

$$R_4 - R_1 = -1.4 + 0.21 C_{63} \qquad r^2 = 0.09. \qquad (5.8)$$
$$(3.00)$$

Equation (5.8) reveals a highly statistically significant positive correlation between $(R_4 - R_1)$ and C_{63}, and this is consistent with the efficiency hypothesis. Note, however, that Demsetz was forced by data availability to use absolute size categories for firms, rather than more appropriate relative size categories, and this may have affected his results.

Demsetz's work has given rise to several further attempts to examine the efficiency hypothesis empirically.[12] One such study, by Carter (1978), looks at data on the top four firms in US four-digit industries compared with the next four firms, i.e. firms ranked 5–8. Carter fits a conventional price–cost margin equation to data in 1963, 1967 and 1972, but using alternately top-four-firm or next-four-firm price–cost margins as the dependent variable. According to the collusion hypothesis, high concentration should raise margins to a similar extent for both groups of firms, but on the efficiency argument, argues Carter, the smaller firms would experience no marginal concentration effect on margins, while the largest firms would do so to the extent of their cost advantage. The latter hypotheses are broadly confirmed in his samples. For example, for 1963 he finds

$$PCM = 16.61 + 2.03 AS + 0.11 KS + 0.07 CR \qquad (5.9a)$$
$$(9.44) \quad (5.17) \quad (3.28)$$

$$PCM = 18.22 + 1.183 AS + 0.09 KS + 0.01 CR \qquad (5.9b)$$
$$(8.48) \quad (4.61) \quad (0.45)$$

where equation (5.9a) relates to the largest firms and (5.9b) to the secondary firms, and t ratios are in parentheses. These results suggest that large firms but not secondary firms benefit from increased concentration, and this would be consistent with those large firms having efficiency advantages which raise concentration and their margins. Note, however, that equation (5.9) does not provide a direct test of this hypothesis which requires that both PCM and CR be determined by superior efficiency.

In the UK, Demsetz's hypothesis has been considered by Clarke, Davies and Waterson (1984). They develop a theoretical framework capable of incorporating both efficiency and market power effects, and attempt to assess the importance of both factors in raising price–cost margins.

Not surprisingly, given the weakness of general UK profitability–concentration relationships (as discussed in section 5.3.2), they find no general evidence for efficiency effects in UK industry in 1971 and 1977. If anything, larger firms (the top five) in each industry tend to have lower margins on average than small firms (the rest). They did, however, find evidence for a positive linear relationship between margins and market shares in a minority of 29 industries.[13] For these industries, therefore, the evidence is consistent with an efficiency–market share relationship. In a generalization of Demsetz's work, however, they also argue that variations in this relationship would signal the presence of market power effects. Specifically, in industries in which market power was important, less pronounced (i.e. flatter) relationships between margins and market shares should be observed, *ceteris paribus* (reflecting the greater importance of the 'price' factor in measured price–cost margins). This hypothesis was confirmed for their sub-sample, in which such 'flatter' relationships were strongly correlated with market concentration. This evidence is therefore consistent with market power effects also operating in concentrated industries.

While these results and others are suggestive, no firm conclusions on the efficiency or collusion debate have yet been reached. In particular, Clarke, Davies and Waterson point out that complications arise in the analysis of efficiency effects when product differentiation or scale economies are important. In the case of product differentiation especially, it appears that no simple relationship between market shares and margins need exist in a market, although under certain special demand conditions such a relationship may be found. Also, Demsetz's original suggestion that demand advantages are similar to cost advantages in their effect on market shares and margins remains speculative at this stage. Clearly, more theoretical and empirical work needs to be done. Nevertheless, the issues raised by Demsetz are important and have led (and are likely to lead in the future) to important revisions in our views on profitability and market structure.

5.4 Summary and Conclusions

This chapter has considered currently available econometric evidence on determinants of profitability in UK and US industries, with particular reference to the effects of market concentration. Sections 5.1 and 5.2 set the scene for the analysis by briefly discussing theoretical and more practical problems respectively. These sections showed, *inter alia*, that important issues relating to the measurement and interpretation of the evidence exist, which gives some grounds for treating results with care. Nevertheless, a fair amount of evidence has been collected and a review of such evidence for the UK and USA was given in section 5.3.

This review showed that, broadly speaking, results for the USA have tended to support a positive (if modest) relationship between profitability and concentration across industries, but that UK results have been more mixed. Recent research, however, has considered the interpretation of any positive relationships that might exist, and in particular has examined the possibility that such relationships might reflect differential efficiency of firms rather than market power effects. Some evidence in support of this has been presented, although on a wider view one suspects that *both* efficiency and market power effects will operate in particular markets. Nevertheless, the introduction of differential efficiency considerations has sparked off a substantial reconsideration of profitability and market structure relationships, and research on these important matters is continuing.[14]

Notes

1 See Demsetz (1973a). A useful reference for the material in this section and more generally is Demsetz (1974). See also Weiss (1974).
2 The analysis of this paragraph is taken from Clarke and Davies (1982). See also appendix 3.2 above. Less technically inclined readers should skip this paragraph.
3 In a recent paper, Sawyer (1982) has argued that either entry barriers or collusion will affect profitability, but not both. A rationale for this argument is in the separate treatment of entry and collusion in available theories of oligopoly pricing (see chapters 3 and 4 above). There seems no reason *a priori* why such theories cannot be integrated, however, so that Sawyer's argument seems unfounded. For discussion of this and other matters raised by Sawyer see Clarke (1983), Sawyer (1983) and Martin (1984).
4 See, for example, Hart and Morgan (1977) and Clarke (1984).
5 A useful survey of the available evidence is Weiss (1974). See also Weiss (1971) and, more recently, Weiss (1979).
6 For a useful survey of recent work see Pautler (1983).
7 The data are collected direct from participating companies at a 'line of business' level of aggregation. In principle, therefore, they should relate directly to identifiable economic markets. Contributing firms, however, appear to have some latitude in deciding how they provide data, and this may affect their quality. For further details see Gale and Branch (1982) and the references cited therein.
8 Two-stage least squares estimation of simultaneous equation models has the advantage of giving consistent estimates of underlying model parameters. See, for example, Maddala (1977), p. 232. For further discussion of simultaneous equation estimation of structure–performance models, see Geroski (1982).
9 When explanatory variables are collinear (i.e. highly correlated), estimates of their individual effects in a regression equation become imprecise; see Wonnacott and Wonnacott (1972), pp. 292–7. This need not mean that no effect operates, however.
10 A recent major study for Canada (Caves et al., 1980) also uses a simultaneous equation approach. This finds significant positive effects of concentration on

profitability in OLS and 2SLS estimation, notably when concentration data are adjusted for imports. These results apply for two of three profitability measures, but not for the price–cost margin (where insignificant negative coefficients were observed). In this latter case, however, a variable measuring the interaction of concentration and entry barriers has a strong and significant positive effect.

11 For a more extensive review of earlier work cited in table 5.2 see Hart and Morgan (1977) and Clarke (1984).

12 See, for example, Bond and Greenberg (1976), Peltzman (1977), Lustgarten (1979), Scherer (1979a) and Peltzman (1979). See also Pautler (1983).

13 Some evidence of a quadratic relationship was found which could also be consistent with their theoretical framework. See Clarke, Davies and Waterson (1984) for details.

14 For more detail on recent revisions of ideas see Pautler (1983).

6 Advertising

Up to now, the discussion in this book has been concerned mainly with pricing and profitability in industrial markets, with limited attention to other dimensions of market competition. We shall remedy this to some extent in this and the next chapter by considering advertising and research and development as alternative features of the competitive process. Chapter 7 looks at the various stages of technical progress (invention, innovation and diffusion) and considers, in particular, the interdependencies which exist between technological change and market structure. In this chapter we focus attention on advertising in mainly differentiated product markets, and consider possible pro- and anti-competitive effects of such advertising.

The chapter is divided into two main sections. Section 6.1 examines theories of the determinants of advertising intensity, focusing on the general 'elasticities' formulation of the problem and then considering more specific hypotheses that have been suggested. One of these (that advertising intensity has an important nonlinear relationship with market concentration) is also considered separately. Section 6.2 then considers possible links between advertising and market competition, focusing in particular on possible anti-competitive effects of advertising. Current theoretical thinking on these issues is discussed, and this is followed by a consideration of the empirical evidence.

6.1 Theories of Advertising

We can begin our discussion of advertising by briefly considering some details of advertising expenditure. In 1981 total UK expenditure on advertising was £2.8 billion or 1.3 per cent of GNP, of which £2.4 billion (1.1 per cent of GNP) was spent by private firms.[1] The bulk of this advertising (55 per cent) was undertaken by manufacturers and directed at consumers (manufacturers' consumer advertising), with other advertising being undertaken by retailers (23 per cent), financial institutions (7 per cent) and by industry for trade purposes (15 per cent). Focusing on manufacturers' consumer advertising, we

Table 6.1 Industries with high advertising/sales ratios in UK manufacturing, 1968

Industry	Advertising/sales (%)
Toilet preparations	14.2
Soap and detergents	9.8
Pharmaceutical chemicals	7.8
Cocoa, chocolate and sugar confectionery	4.9
Soft drinks, British wines, cider and perry	4.5
Fruit and vegetable products	3.8
Domestic electric appliances	3.2
Polishes, adhesives, etc.	3.1
Paint	3.0
Spirit distilling and compounding	2.7
Milk products, margarine, starch, misc.	2.6
Toys, brushes, stationery, misc.	2.3
Rainwear, shirts, corsets, misc.	2.1
Grain milling, animal and poultry foods	2.1

Source: Census of Production, Summary Tables, 1968.

find that in 1981 over half of this advertising was on television (53 per cent) with a further 36 per cent in magazines and newspapers. The main categories of expenditure in manufacturers' consumer advertising were household and leisure goods (£302 million), food (£256 million) and drink and tobacco (£204 million).

These figures, however, fail to indicate the particular industries which advertise most in proportionate terms, and, moreover, the highly skewed nature of the distribution of advertising expenditures by industry. Many industries, in fact, spend very little on advertising when measured against their total sales revenue. For example, in 77 industries (or industry groups) for which data are available in 1968, advertising expenditure as a proportion of sales was less than 1 per cent in 48 cases, and between 1 and 2 per cent in a further 15 cases. Table 6.1 lists the remaining 14 industries for which advertising/sales ratios exceeded 2 per cent in 1968. As can be seen, these industries fall mainly in the categories of chemists' goods, food and household products. Despite the aggregate nature of some of the industry definitions in the table (which tends to mask very high advertising expenditures for some narrowly defined products), it is clear that chemists' goods in particular were heavily advertised. These and some of the other products included in the table are frequently singled out as being of major public concern for 'excess' advertising.

In this section, we are concerned to ask why some industries advertise very heavily and, more generally, why advertising intensity varies between firms and industries. Clearly, the effectiveness of advertising will be a major factor in its use, and indeed this is an important implication of the so-called elasticities approach to advertising which we consider first below. Underlying this are more basic considerations concerning the nature of the product and the market, however, and these matters are dealt with in sections 6.1.2 and 6.1.3.

6.1.1 The Elasticities Approach

The elasticities approach to advertising derives from a classic paper by Dorfman and Steiner (1954). They considered a firm choosing an optimal level of advertising in order to maximize profits. In a slight generalization of the Dorfman–Steiner analysis (see Schmalensee, 1972; Hay and Morris, 1979), we assume that the firm faces a demand function

$$Q = Q(P, A) \tag{6.1}$$

where Q is output, P is price and A is the number of advertising messages purchased by the firm. For simplicity, we ignore the fact that advertising can take place *through* different media, and we also assume that advertising messages are purchased at a constant cost of T per unit. Thus, with television advertising a message might be a one minute ad seen by one viewer, and we assume that it always costs T per unit to get one more message across. (Dorfman and Steiner in fact ignored the distinction between messages and their cost, treating A in (6.1) simply as advertising expenditure.) We assume that more advertising raises demand ($\partial Q/\partial A > 0$) and a higher price reduces demand ($\partial Q/\partial P < 0$).

The problem for the firm is to choose P and A to maximize profit, given as

$$\pi = PQ(P, A) - C[Q(P, A)] - AT \tag{6.2}$$

where C is production cost. The first-order conditions are

$$\frac{\partial \pi}{\partial P} = Q + PQ_P - C_Q Q_P = 0 \tag{6.3}$$

$$\frac{\partial \pi}{\partial A} = PQ_A - C_Q Q_A - T = 0 \tag{6.4}$$

where $Q_P \equiv \partial Q/\partial P$, $Q_A \equiv \partial Q/\partial A$ and $C_Q \equiv dC/dQ$ is marginal production cost. The first condition (6.3) is equivalent to the normal condition that, for any given level of A, the firm should set price to equate marginal cost and marginal revenue. Rearranging (6.3) gives the familiar condition

$$\frac{P - C_Q}{P} = \frac{1}{\eta} \tag{6.5}$$

where η is the price elasticity of demand (defined as positive). Condition (6.4) gives us the optimal level of advertising for any price. It says that advertising should be such that the marginal revenue from advertising $(P(\partial Q/\partial A))$ should equal the marginal cost of advertising, given as the cost of a unit more advertising T and the extra cost of production involved in raising demand by a unit of advertising (given price); i.e. $(dC/dQ)(\partial Q/\partial A)$. Defining the elasticity of demand with respect to advertising messages as

$$a = \frac{\partial Q}{\partial A}\frac{A}{Q} \tag{6.6}$$

and multiplying (6.4) by A/PQ gives

$$\left(\frac{P-C_Q}{P}\right)Q_A\frac{A}{Q} = \frac{AT}{PQ}. \tag{6.7}$$

Given the optimal price by (6.5), we can then write

$$\frac{AT}{PQ} = \frac{a}{\eta}. \tag{6.8}$$

This is the basic Dorfman–Steiner result that the ratio of advertising expenditure to sales should be equal to the ratio of the advertising elasticity of demand to the price elasticity of demand.

Several points should be noted about this result. First, as stressed by Schmalensee (1972), equation (6.8) provides an explanation of the commonly observed business practice of using a constant advertising/sales ratio. Such a policy would be consistent with profit maximization as long as the ratio of the advertising and price elasticities of demand are relatively constant over time. This is particularly likely to be the case for stable, established products, so that for such products (at least) one would expect to find advertising expenditures set as a constant fraction of actual or anticipated sales revenue. A number of surveys (cited by Schmalensee) have shown that such a rule of thumb is a standard business practice. Second, equation (6.8) indicates that ratios of advertising expenditure to sales revenue will be higher the greater the proportionate effect of advertising messages on demand relative to the price elasticity of demand. Thus, for example, products for which image is an important factor, such as perfume or cosmetics, where demand is much less sensitive to price than advertising, would be expected to have higher advertising expenditure to sales revenue ratios. In fact, a large number of different considerations are likely to affect these elasticities, and discussion of some of these is taken up in the next section.

The model as presented above is obviously a simplification. For present purposes, however, we consider only one modification to it, which is of some interest for our discussion in section 6.1.3 below. This concerns its generalization to allow competition between several oligopolistic firms.[2]

Consider a market with n firms in competition, producing slightly differentiated products. In this case we must assume, in general, that the demand for a single firm's product depends on its own price and advertising policies plus those of each of its rivals. For simplicity, however, we assume that all prices are given, and thereby concentrate on advertising effects. Also we assume that advertising effects are identical between firms, so that we can write the demand function for a typical firm as

$$Q = Q(A, \bar{A}) \tag{6.9}$$

where $\bar{A}$ are aggregate advertising messages of rivals. We assume that increased advertising by rivals reduces demand for the firm, i.e. $\partial Q/\partial \bar{A} < 0$.

The typical firm in an industry now has a profit function

$$\pi = PQ(A, \bar{A}) - C[Q(A, \bar{A})] - AT \tag{6.10}$$

and it sets A to maximize profits. In doing this, however, it must consider how it expects its rivals to respond to a change in its advertising policy. Specifically, the first-order condition for profit maximization is

$$\frac{d\pi}{dA} = (P - C_Q) \left[\frac{\partial Q}{\partial A} + \left(\frac{\partial Q}{\partial \bar{A}} \frac{d\bar{A}}{dA} \right) \right] - T = 0 \tag{6.11}$$

where $d\bar{A}/dA$ represents the firm's expectation as to its rivals' response to a change in its advertising policy (i.e. its advertising conjectural variation). Defining the cross-elasticity of demand with respect to $\bar{A}$ as

$$\bar{a} = \frac{\partial Q}{\partial \bar{A}} \frac{\bar{A}}{Q} \tag{6.12}$$

and the advertising conjectural variation elasticity as

$$\alpha = \frac{d\bar{A}}{dA} \frac{A}{\bar{A}} \tag{6.13}$$

we can write equation (6.11) (on multiplying by A/PQ) as

$$\frac{AT}{PQ} = \left(\frac{P - C_Q}{P} \right) \left[\left(\frac{\partial Q}{\partial A} \frac{A}{Q} \right) + \left(\frac{\partial Q}{\partial \bar{A}} \frac{\bar{A}}{Q} \right) \left(\frac{A}{\bar{A}} \frac{d\bar{A}}{dA} \right) \right].$$

Therefore

$$\frac{AT}{PQ} = \left(\frac{P - C_Q}{P} \right) (a + \alpha \bar{a}). \tag{6.14}$$

Comparing (6.14) with (6.8) shows that the oligopolistic firm must also consider the possible proportionate effect of retaliatory rival advertising on its demand (i.e. $\alpha\bar{a}$) in setting its advertising/sales ratio.

Equation (6.14) is not a complete solution to the oligopoly advertising problem since we have not specified how the various terms in it (notably $(P - C_Q)/P$, α and $\bar{a}$) vary with the number of rivals. Several hypotheses, however, might briefly be mentioned here. First, in so far as increased numbers of rivals are associated with greater price competition, we would expect $(P - C_Q)/P$ to fall as the number of firms rises. Hence, this effect will imply increased advertising intensity by firms as the number of firms falls (or, more generally, as market concentration increases). Second, as the number of firms falls (concentration increases), the recognized interdependence of firms should increase. Hence, firms will take more account of possible rival responses in advertising (i.e. larger α) with increased concentration, which, combined with the negative effect of rivals' advertising on their demand (i.e. negative $\bar{a}$), will cause them to advertise less. These two offsetting effects provide the basis for a possible nonlinear relationship between advertising intensity and market concentration, with advertising intensity increasing to moderate or high levels of concentration but declining thereafter. Of course, there is no reason why such a relationship should necessarily be observed. Nevertheless, this hypothesis has formed the basis of some empirical work that has been done, and we examine this work further in section 6.1.3 below.

According to the above analysis, the amount of advertising in an industry (as measured by the advertising/sales ratio) will be influenced by the responsiveness of demand to price and advertising changes and by the extent of competition in advertising between firms. Elasticities of demand will be influenced by both demand and supply factors, while competition of firms represents a supply influence on advertising intensity. The elasticities approach does not specify what these influences may be as they operate through the various elasticities, and we therefore turn to more specific hypotheses on demand and supply in what follows.

6.1.2 Nature of the Product

Firms advertise in order to increase sales of their products or services. The type and extent of advertising will depend on the characteristics of the product: such things as the number and type of buyers, the frequency of purchase, the unit price, the qualities and attributes of the products and so on. Each of these factors is likely to affect the advertising and price elasticities of demand, and hence the advertising intensity in an industry. Since each product is basically unique, one can distinguish a large number of characteristics to 'explain' the advertising intensity in a particular industry. It is more useful, however, to specify a limited number of broader hypotheses to account for variations in advertising intensity, and some of these hypotheses are discussed briefly in this section.

A first and basic hypothesis is that advertising intensity will vary with the type of buyer, tending to be higher in particular for consumer as opposed to producer goods industries. The evidence strongly supports this hypothesis,[3] and indeed many empirical studies confine their attention solely to consumer goods industries as being of most interest in the context of advertising. Several reasons can be given for this distinction. First, buyers of producer goods are likely to be relatively better informed as to products available for sale and hence will require less prompting and reminding over the existence of products than consumers. Second, buyers of producer goods may be less open to *persuasion* than consumers because they spend more time and effort on their purchasing decisions. And third, buyers of producer goods may be more amenable to direct selling methods (e.g. sales representatives) than to advertising as such, and hence promotional efforts in such cases may not be captured adequately in advertising data. Each of these factors suggests that an important division between producer and consumer goods exists and therefore that one should allow for this distinction in analysing determinants of advertising.

If we confine our attention to consumer goods industries for simplicity, several other hypotheses may be noted. First, Nelson (1974) (see also Nelson, 1970) has argued that consumer products can be divided between those with *search* and those with *experience* qualities. Products with search qualities can be evaluated prior to purchase (e.g. a woman's dress), and advertising for such products is mainly to inform consumers of the qualities available. Products with experience qualities, on the other hand, must be purchased before one can assess them (e.g. a tin of tuna fish), and advertising in this case is mainly to signal the existence and reputation of the product. In the former case, therefore, advertising is mainly 'truthful' and informative, while in the latter case it seeks to influence consumer decisions. This led Nelson to suggest that advertising intensity would be higher for goods with experience as opposed to search qualities and he confirmed this hypothesis in a sample of 40 products in 1957.

Several interpretations of this result can be made. According to Nelson, since consumers ultimately experience the goods that are advertised and hence cannot be misled in the long run, the amount of advertising undertaken is a good signal of the 'better buys' available. That is, products which are better buys are advertised more since their ultimate level of sales justifies a high level of advertising. In this case, advertising acts as a positive signal to consumers for experience goods and, as such, is to some extent socially desirable. Against this, however, if heavy advertising *persuades* consumers to buy products, and in the process influences consumers' perceptions of product quality, then it may not be desirable. The ability of consumers to assess product qualities *after* purchase is clearly important here, with reductions in that ability increasing the scope for persuasive advertising. While Nelson would argue that one cannot sell an inferior product by advertising in the long run, this argument postulates a high degree of consumer discrimination which may not be appropriate for all types of goods.

Second, Porter (1974) (see also Porter, 1976) has suggested a distinction between *convenience* goods and *shopping* (or *non-convenience*) goods. This distinction makes use of a classification of goods long used in the marketing field. 'Convenience goods' are characterized by a low unit price, high frequency of purchase and easily accessible retail outlets, e.g. cornflakes, toothpaste or socks. 'Shopping goods', on the other hand, have a higher unit price, are purchased less frequently, and may be purchased after some shopping around by consumers, e.g. furniture, cameras or motor cars. The essential analytical distinction between these types of goods is that consumers spend less time and effort purchasing convenience goods so that they are more susceptible to manufacturers' advertising on these goods. On the other hand, for shopping goods advertising may have less influence on the consumers' purchasing decision than retail sales assistance and the actual characteristics of the product. Therefore we expect that manufacturers' consumer advertising would be considerably higher for convenience goods, and this was confirmed by Porter in a sample of 42 US consumer goods industries. Porter also shows that advertising/sales ratios are a very much more important (positive) determinant of profitability for convenience goods industries.

Various other hypotheses can be suggested. For example, product areas in which there is a high degree of product innovation may be subject to a high level of advertising as the need arises to continually inform consumers of new products available. Product areas such as hi-fi equipment, motor cars or personal computers readily spring to mind in this context. Second, products with a high image or fashion content may be particularly advertising-intensive as the advertising image is an important characteristic of the purchased commodity. Examples of this might relate to perfumes or cosmetics, or again to fashion clothes. Third, the turnover of customers in the market may be important, with a greater turnover implying more advertising to keep current customers informed (Stigler, 1961). In this case, however, too much customer turnover would reduce the incentive to advertise, since too much advertising would then be wasted on customers who will be leaving the market. Clearly, a host of possible hypotheses can be put forward, each of which can be viewed as operating through the elasticities considered in section 6.1.1.

6.1.3 Advertising and Market Concentration

As noted in section 6.1.1, several authors have suggested that advertising intensity will be related to the degree of concentration in a market. The most popular hypothesis has been that a quadratic (inverted U-shaped) relationship will exist, as shown in figure 6.1, with medium concentrated industries experiencing greater advertising intensity than either high or low concentration industries. A simple rationalization for such a relationship was

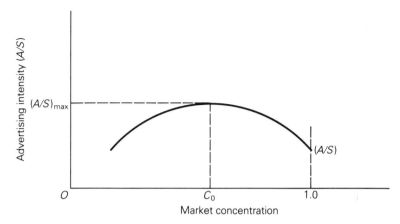

Figure 6.1

suggested in section 6.1.1, whereby advertising increases at first owing to increasing price–cost margins as concentration increases, but falls as increased recognized interdependence between firms leads to less mutually offsetting advertising. This rationalization is, however, by no means the only possibility, and in what follows we briefly note some other suggestions that have been made before turning to the empirical evidence.

One argument, suggested by Cable (1975), is that oligopolists (in contrast to a monopolist) have the opportunity to attract sales from rivals and this will lead them to advertise more. This hypothesis, therefore, suggests a second rationalization for a fall in advertising intensity at very high concentration levels, where opportunities for sales diversion diminish. A similar argument has been made by Sutton (1974), who also argues that scale economies in advertising favour sales diversion for moderate as opposed to low concentration industries.

Sutton also argues that firms have greater incentives to engage in market-expanding advertising in more (as opposed to less) concentrated markets since they are then able to internalize more of the benefits of advertising. Such an effect, therefore, would lead to a positive relationship between advertising and concentration. Finally, Sutton argues that advertising to raise entry barriers and/or increase market concentration is also strongest at moderate concentration levels, again giving an incentive for more advertising at these levels. While many of these hypotheses merely suggest that offsetting effects may be at work in the relationship between advertising and concentration, they do provide a basis for a possible quadratic effect. Ultimately it is a question of empirical evidence, however, which we now briefly consider.

For simplicity we focus mainly on the UK results in what follows. Sutton (1974) tested the hypothesis using a sample of 25 UK Minimum List Heading (MLH) industries in 1963 and found strong support for a quadratic relationship. Defining A as advertising expenditure to gross sales and C as five-firm sales concentration, he found that (with t ratios in parentheses)

$$A = 0.99 + 0.013C \qquad\qquad \bar{R}^2 = 0.01 \qquad\qquad\qquad (6.15)$$
$$(1.29)\ \ (1.13)$$

$$A = -3.15 + 0.19C - 0.0015C^2 \qquad \bar{R}^2 = 0.34. \qquad\qquad (6.16)$$
$$(2.36)\ \ \ (3.71)\ \ \ \ \ (3.51)$$

These results show a dramatic improvement in the fit as a term in C^2 is introduced, supporting the quadratic specification. Equation (6.16) suggests that advertising intensity rises from low to medium concentration industries, reaches a maximum with $C = 64$ per cent and then falls for more concentrated sectors. From this Sutton suggested tentatively that high advertising in medium concentration industries may reflect anti-competitive tendencies and that controls on advertising may give rise to a stimulus to competition in such industries.

However, Sutton's work has not gone unchallenged. Rees (1975) has shown that Sutton's results are sensitive to the measurement of the variables. The basic problem is that Census of Production data do not allow one to test the hypothesis in a clear-cut experiment. Rees employs a number of alternative tests, which are themselves open to criticism, and gets mixed results. Advertising intensity tends to rise with concentration in Rees's equations, but the evidence for a decline in advertising intensity at high concentration levels is not strong.

Reekie (1975) criticized Sutton's evidence on the grounds that his sample consisted of rather broadly defined industries which, moreover, were hetero-geneous in supply and demand characteristics. As only the concentration variable was employed to explain inter-industry variation in advertising intensity, and as such differences were not controlled for, Sutton's estimates must be treated with care. Reekie gets round this problem by employing non-Census information on 63 highly specific consumer non-durable products, which, moreover, he analysed separately in four relatively homogeneous groups: foodstuffs, medicaments, kitchen and household supplies, and toiletries. These data reveal neither a linear association between advertising intensity and market structure nor a quadratic relationship. Reekie, however, was forced to measure market structure by so-called 'density ratios' which rely on data collected in a survey questionnaire where consumers report which brand of each product they use most often. These density ratios for three and five brands are by no means the same as concentration ratios, and this factor necessarily casts some doubt on Reekie's findings in turn.

In his study, Cable (1975) examined evidence for 26 narrowly defined non-durable products, mainly in the food sector but including some household and chemists' goods. His results suggest that a strong quadratic relationship exists between advertising intensity and market concentration when the latter is measured by the Hirschman–Herfindahl index of concentration and multiple regression techniques are used. This was particularly the case when lagged values of advertising (appropriately depreciated) were used to measure the dependent variable as goodwill rather than current advertising intensity. This variable attained a maximum at $H = 0.4$, which Cable characterized as a duopoly situation with a tail of very small sellers (numbers equivalent $= 2.5$). This result suggests that advertising intensity reaches a peak at very high concentration levels, in contrast to Sutton's results; however, the much more narrowly defined nature of Cable's products may explain this discrepancy. Cable found a linear association of advertising intensity and the three-firm concentration ratio but no quadratic effect. On balance, however, Cable's results support the quadratic hypothesis, and his use of multiple regression techniques and narrowly defined products goes some way towards meeting the criticisms raised against Sutton's work.

In a more recent study, Buxton, Davies and Lyons (1984) have examined the quadratic hypothesis in a sample of 51 UK MLH industries in 1968. They argue that explicit allowance should be made for proportions of sales going to producers and consumers in testing the relationship. With no allowance for this factor they find no statistically significant relationship between advertising intensity and concentration in their sample. Allowing for it, however, a significant quadratic relationship is observed for consumer goods industries, and this relationship is quite strong and statistically robust. Their preferred ordinary least squares equation (with t ratios in parentheses) is

$$A = -1.90 + 7.66P + 0.12\pi/S + 0.18(S_c/S)C - 0.0014(S_c/S)C^2$$
$$\quad\ (-2.35)\ (6.31)\quad (3.01)\qquad (5.21)\qquad\quad (-3.53)$$
$$\bar{R}^2 = 0.746 \tag{6.17}$$

where A is advertising intensity, C is the five-firm concentration ratio, P is a dummy variable for 'personal goods', π/S is the rate of return on sales, and (S_c/S) is the proportion of sales made to consumers. All variables are statistically significant at better than the 1 per cent level and the explanatory power of the equation is quite good (although this is, to a large extent, attributable to the allowance for two outlying observations – pharmaceutical chemicals and toilet preparations – in P). Advertising intensity peaks at a five-firm concentration ratio of 64 per cent, which accords with Sutton's results for 1963 using a simple quadratic specification.

Buxton, Davies and Lyons also estimated this model using two-stage least squares (2SLS) techniques to account for reverse causation between advertising intensity and concentration.[4] Their results are very similar to equation (6.17), suggesting that simultaneity problems do not account for the observed relationship. A similar finding has been obtained by Strickland and Weiss (1976) (see also Martin, 1979) using US data on 408 four-digit industries in 1963. They find a statistically significant quadratic relationship between advertising intensity and market concentration in their full sample and in consumer goods industries, but not in producer goods industries. Again, these results are not sensitive to allowance for simultaneous relationships, although they do observe a reduced effect of price–cost margins on advertising intensity in 2SLS estimates (price–cost margins being treated as an endogenous variable in their model). According to their estimates, advertising intensity peaks in consumer goods industries at a four-firm concentration ratio of 46 per cent (or 57 per cent for the full sample). Both sets of results appear, therefore, to give strong support to the view that advertising intensity is particularly high in moderately concentrated industries.[5]

These results may have important consequences for public policy. First, in so far as excess advertising in oligopolistic industries is mutually offsetting, it can be regarded as a socially wasteful expenditure in itself. In addition, however, as discussed in section 6.2 below, excess advertising in oligopolistic markets may raise barriers to new entry and increase market concentration, thereby raising prices and profits. From both points of view, therefore, the association of high advertising intensity with oligopolistic markets (for consumer goods) gives cause for public concern. Possible policy measures to deal with this problem are discussed briefly in section 6.3 below.

6.2 Advertising and Competition

6.2.1 Theory

Some of the major criticisms of advertising from a public policy point of view centre on its role in differentiating products, raising entry barriers and increasing market concentration. These are regarded by some as possible major problems in oligopolistic, consumer goods markets. This view, however, is not universal, with some economists pointing to advantages of advertising in increasing competition and facilitating entry by new firms. Whether, and in what circumstances, advertising is an anti- or pro-competitive force is hotly contested, and we review the principle issues in what follows.[6]

We begin with the relationship between advertising, concentration and price. As noted in section 6.1.3, market concentration may affect the level of advertising intensity in a market, with, in particular, high advertising intensity at medium concentration levels. Here we consider the reverse possibility, that high advertising may increase market concentration, and thereby raise prices. In this scenario, advertising is seen as a means by which some firms can monopolize a market and earn socially disadvantageous monopoly profits.

Consider a market with high entry barriers (e.g. an airline passenger route) and assume that anti-trust laws forbid mergers between rival firms. Also assume that, initially, a reasonably large number of firms compete in the market. By what mechanisms can advertising by firms increase concentration and possibly price? Mann (1974) has suggested two related possibilities, both of which rely heavily on the law of proportionate effect discussed in chapter 2 above. First, he argues that advertising is very much a hit-and-miss affair with some advertising campaigns being successful and others not. When all firms engage in advertising expenditure there will be greater volatility in market shares than would otherwise be the case. In terms of the analysis in chapter 2, advertising will increase the variance in the distribution of each firm's proportionate growth rate, thereby tending to increase the rate at which market concentration increases. Hence, some successful firms will quickly dominate the market as a result of successful advertising campaigns, while other firms lose customers or leave the market. The resulting increase in concentration may enable firms to coordinate their price policies and raise profits towards monopoly levels.[7]

Several points should be noted about this argument. First, it suggests that advertising, by increasing the variance of proportionate growth rates, enhances rather than creates an existing possible concentrating effect. The importance of this effect, if indeed it is important, will depend on the extent to which advertising can affect probabilities of proportionate growth. Second, the effect would be enhanced further if economies of scale exist in advertising, such that larger firms can win customers at a lower per-unit advertising cost than smaller firms. Such an effect might operate if larger firms were able to use more cost-effective media (e.g. television advertising), for example. On the other hand, even if economies of scale exist in advertising, it is not necessarily the case that large firms in any particular industry need benefit from them. That is, it is size of firm relative to the advertising industry which is relevant here rather than the size of firm in a particular market. The possibility of economies of scale in advertising is further discussed below.

Mann's second argument brings in an interaction between advertising and concentration. As concentration increases, oligopolistic interdependence is recognized and price increases. Firms switch attention from competition in price to competition in advertising, and very high advertising levels are associated with medium concentration levels (see section 6.1.3). This, in turn, enhances the concentrating effect previously discussed. Since we have already noted this two-way relationship between advertising and concentration, with its consequent problems for empirical estimation, we need discuss it no further here. A brief examination of empirical evidence on advertising as a determinant of concentration is given in section 6.2.2 below.

A further case for advertising enhancing market power centres on its effect on price elasticities of demand. Comanor and Wilson (1974) have argued, for example, that firms can use advertising to increase the degree of perceived product differentiation among consumers, thereby lowering the price elasticity of demand for their products. On this argument, advertising will lead to increased market power and higher prices in the market. It is also possible to argue the reverse, however. In a market where consumers are ill-informed as to the nature of products available, advertising can provide valuable information which raises price elasticities of demand and leads to lower prices. On this view, advertising is seen as a useful means of 'widening' the market and breaking up monopoly power based on imperfect information, rather than as a means of increasing product differentiation and price. There is no reason, of course, why one might not accept both views if, for example, one believed that some advertising for information purposes has good effects or that advertising in competitive markets has information advantages. High advertising in oligopolistic markets might, however, be another thing.

Several case studies have provided evidence that some advertising in non-oligopolistic markets can have pro-competitive effects. Most persuasive is the classic study by Benham (1972), which found that prices of eyeglasses were systematically higher in the USA in states which completely restricted advertising compared with states with few or no advertising restrictions. Benham found that, in a sample of 177 individuals in 1963, prices charged for eyeglasses were on average $33 in states with advertising restrictions compared with $26 in states without restrictions. This price differential rose to $37 as against $18 (i.e. a 100 per cent difference) when the most restrictive state (North Carolina) was compared with the most liberal states (Texas and the District of Columbia). In a similar type of study of routine legal services in six US cities, Cox (1982) also reported some evidence of lower prices associated with more advertising. Also, Steiner (1973) suggested that decreases in toy prices in the USA in the 1950s and 1960s were associated with the introduction of television advertising. In this latter case, however, it is not clear whether other developments in retailing (e.g. the growth of discount stores) might have accounted for most of the fall in prices observed.

There are several reasons why the removal of advertising restrictions can lead to lower prices. First, as already noted, the ability of advertising to inform potential customers of the nature of available products can lead to higher price elasticities of demand and, more generally, greater competition, which lowers prices. Second, advertising increases sales, thereby permitting firms to take advantage of economies of scale in production and distribution, which reduces costs and prices. And third, distributors' margins may be reduced (as argued by Steiner in the case of toys), not only because of increased sales but also because of product recognition induced by advertising which forces increased competition on products by retailers. It seems likely that these effects are most likely to be observed in monopolistically com-petitive industries with relatively many sellers, where the information and cost-reducing advantages of advertising may be more pronounced.

Finally, and most importantly, advertising may enhance barriers to entry. We have seen in chapter 4 that Bain believed that product differentiation represented a major barrier to entry in practice. In his view this barrier was closely associated with heavy advertising and other sales promotion expen-ditures by established firms. Bain, however, tended simply to *presume* that advertising created a barrier to entry, and did not give a detailed explanation of why this might be so. His critics have argued that no such barrier in fact exists because new entrants can always provide competing advertising messages to offset those of established firms. Indeed, some authors have suggested that advertising, if anything, facilitates new entry by providing information on new competing products. Clearly, it is necessary to consider the arguments carefully before one can conclude that advertising does necessarily create a barrier to new entry.

A standard argument that advertising creates an entry barrier focuses on the investment nature of advertising. By advertising over a period of time, established firms build up brand loyalty and a stock of goodwill for their products which new entrants must overcome in order to break into the market. Consequently, in an initial period after entry, it is necessary for entrants to incur higher advertising costs and/or lower prices per unit of output in order to compete with established firms. It should be clear, however, that, in so far as this argument relies on the investment character of advertising, it does not support an entry barrier argument. If advertising is an investment, then it is not correct to treat advertising expenditures by new entrants as a current expense to be compared with current advertising expenditures by established firms. Rather, one should compare capital costs, and on this basis there is no reason why the capital nature of advertising in itself should put a new entrant at a disadvantage. In other words, the fact that advertising may have dynamic effects does not in itself mean that it creates a barrier to entry.

It might be argued from this that one really needs to look for asymmetries in demand, etc., between established firms and new entrants in order to discover a basis for barriers to entry. In a recent paper, however, Cubbin (1981) has pointed out that this need not be so. Even where established firms and new entrants have identical cost and demand functions, it is perfectly possible for entrants to expect to make negative profits after entry when an established firm is making a positive profit prior to entry. Cubbin shows that, given (fairly general) assumptions about entrant expectations, established firms can make entry seem unprofitable to new entrants. In its simplest form, when the entrant expects no change in output or advertising after entry, the argument is simply that there is 'no room' for a new entrant in the market given the existing policies of the established firm. The established firm, therefore, may be able to adopt advertising and output policies to prevent entry simply because it is already in the market.

However, the fact that a firm is already in the market can also create asymmetries *vis-à-vis* prospective entrants. Comanor and Wilson (1974), in particular, have argued that established firms have the advantage that consumers have accumulated experience of their products and that this interacts with their advertising to create a barrier to entry. Also, new entrants may find themselves at a disadvantage after entry since their advertising must compete with more market 'noise' from competing advertisements than established firms initially had to contend with. Both arguments might suggest that new entrants cannot compete on equal terms by spending equally on advertising with established firms (adjusting for dynamic advertising effects as necessary) and that, therefore, advertising creates a barrier to entry. Clearly, however, counter-arguments could be put, so that one must turn to empirical evidence to decide this issue.

Second, Comanor and Wilson also argue that scale effects in advertising can create a barrier to entry. Such effects may arise where larger firms can negotiate advertising discounts with the media, or alternatively where larger firms are able to use increasingly effective advertising messages. In this latter category, large firms may be able to benefit from using expert services or from using more cost-effective media (such as television). Also, there may be some benefits from using repetition to reinforce a message in the consumer's consciousness. These arguments lead Comanor and Wilson to suggest that (at least over an initial range) sales revenue will rise disproportionately with the amount of advertising or, alternatively, that a threshold effect might be observed, with a certain level of advertising expenditure necessary to have any marked effect on demand. The presence of such scale effects of whatever form implies an advantage for large established firms.

The argument that it raises entry barriers parallels Bain's classic argument with respect to production scale economies. If firms enter on a small scale, they find that they must bear higher unit advertising costs than their larger established rivals and so operate at a competitive disadvantage. Alternatively, if they enter on a large scale to take advantage of scale in advertising, they must add substantially to production capacity in the industry and hence expect a substantial cut in price. If, therefore, advantages of scale do exist in advertising, they can complement any economies of scale in production to deter entry. In these circumstances large established firms may make significant monopoly profits without attracting entry.[8]

Finally, advertising may be associated with capital requirements barriers to entry, over and above those created by investment in plant and equipment. Since investment in market penetration is a particularly risky use of funds, in that it creates no tangible assets, it is likely to have a high required rate of return. Hence, small firms in particular are likely to suffer a further impediment to entry from this source, the more so the greater is the established goodwill of existing firms in the market and the greater are any scale advantages in advertising. As noted in chapter 4, capital requirements barriers to entry may be less of a problem for existing large firms diversifying into a new industry. Nevertheless, they may have important effects in slowing the rate of entry into profitable industries by reducing the pool of potential new entrants.

6.2.2 Evidence

A great deal of empirical work has been done on various aspects of advertising and competition. In what follows, however, we concentrate mainly on studies linking profitability and advertising, paying particular attention to areas of contention in such studies. A further area of dispute over advertising and concentration is also briefly discussed at the end of this section.

We begin with an important paper by Comanor and Wilson (1967) which set the stage for the subsequent debate on profitability and advertising. Comanor and Wilson argued that advertising was an important source of barriers to entry into an industry, permitting established firms to raise prices above unit costs without attracting entry. They tested this hypothesis using multiple regression techniques in a sample of 41 US consumer goods industries in 1954–7. Using a variety of specifications, they found a strong and substantial positive association between profitability and advertising. Two examples of their results illustrate this point. First, using the advertising/sales ratio, X_1, to proxy advertising barriers, they found that

$$Y = 0.045 + 0.44X_1 + 0.008 \log X_2 + 0.01 \log X_3 + 0.02X_4 \qquad (6.18)$$
$$ (3.1) \qquad (2.4) \qquad\quad (1.3) \qquad\quad (1.4)$$
$$\bar{R}^2 = 0.62$$

where Y is the average rate of return on equity for larger firms in each industry, X_2 is a capital requirements barrier to entry, X_3 is growth of demand and X_4 is a regional market dummy variable (t ratios in parentheses). As can be seen, the advertising/sales ratio has a strong, positive linear effect on rate of return which is statistically significant at better than the 1 per cent level. Second, using a high advertising entry barrier dummy variable (X_1') which reflects absolutely high advertising levels as well as high advertising/sales ratios, they similarly found

$$Y = 0.055 + 0.032X_1' + 0.006 \log X_2 + 0.012 \log X_3 + 0.025X_4 \qquad (6.19)$$
$$ (2.7) \qquad (1.8) \qquad\quad (1.5) \qquad\quad (1.7)$$
$$\bar{R}^2 = 0.59.$$

According to this equation, high advertising barrier industries had a profit rate over 3 percentage points higher than other industries, a differential which was greater than zero at better than the 1 per cent significance level. Comanor and Wilson report that, on average in their sample, this differential represented a 50 per cent increase in profit rates, which is clearly a very substantial differential indeed.

A number of subsequent US studies have also found a strong positive relationship between profitability and advertising in cross-industry regressions. Miller (1969), for example, found that advertising intensity was a very highly significant determinant (with t ratios over 7.5) of profitability in 106 US 'minor industries' in 1958/9–1961/2. He also found, somewhat surprisingly, that the size of the advertising effect was higher in producer as opposed to consumer goods industries. Second, Weiss (1974) also found that advertising intensity was a highly significant determinant of price–cost margins in samples of 227 and 399 US industries in 1963. Results in the UK, however, have been more mixed, with Holtermann (1973), for example, reporting conflicting results for several measures of profitability in 113 three-digit industries in 1963, and Hitiris (1978) reporting negative and insignificant effects on price–cost margins in 40 two-and-a-half-digit industries in 1963 and 1968. Current evidence for the UK (as in the case of the profitability–concentration relationship) is more mixed than for the USA, and we concentrate on studies of the latter country in what follows.

In their original paper, Comanor and Wilson argued that advertising acted as a proxy for product differentiation in creating barriers to entry. In fact, they postulated a two-way relationship between these variables. On the one hand, taking the degree of product differentiation in a market as a datum (determined by basic product characteristics, etc.), they argued that high advertising levels would be associated with greater product differentiation and hence would act as an indicator of the latter. On the other hand, they also recognized that advertising might itself enhance product differentiation in a market in the sense of reducing cross-price elasticities of supply and demand. On both counts they argued that advertising intensity and product differen-tiation would be closely related, and this justified their empirical approach.

Clearly, even in this early formulation, some ambivalence existed as to the structure of the model being tested. This problem is enhanced when it is recognized that reverse causation may also be a feature of the relationship between advertising and profitability. As discussed in section 6.1 above, the Dorfman–Steiner condition for optimal advertising under profit maximization implies that a positive relationship will exist between advertising intensity and the price–cost margin in equilibrium. Put simply, higher price–cost margins, *ceteris paribus*, will tend to increase the marginal value of a unit of advertising leading to higher advertising/sales ratios on average. If we assume that both advertising and price are decision variables under profit maximiza-tion, then advertising and profitability will be jointly determined endogenous variables. Hence, it may be necessary to consider simultaneous equation estimates of the profitability–advertising relationship in order to determine whether an entry barrier effect running from advertising to profitability exists.[9]

Several studies have attempted such a simultaneous-equation estimate. First, Comanor and Wilson (1974) considered a two-equation model in which profit rates and advertising/sales ratios were endogenous variables. Estimating this model on the same data set as employed in their earlier study, they found that the effect of advertising intensity on profitability increased when simultaneous relationships were allowed for, although the standard errors associated with this effect also increased. Specifically, they found, in four alternative specifications of their model, that the effect of advertising on profitability increased in two-stage least squares (2SLS) estimation (almost doubling in magnitude in at least one case), but that in two cases the effect was not statistically significant at the 5 per cent level on a one-tailed test (although it remained significant at the 10 per cent level). They also found that profitability was an important and statistically significant determinant of advertising intensity. Hence, the tenor of these results is that a two-way relationship between advertising and profitability does indeed exist. If anything, their results suggest that allowing for this relationship increases the magnitude of the effect of advertising on profitability, but with somewhat reduced reliability in the results.

Second, Strickland and Weiss (1976) estimated a three-equation model with price–cost margins, advertising intensity and concentration as endogenous variables. Since advertising expenditure was included in their measured price–cost margin, evidence for a positive effect of advertising on profitability was given if the coefficient on advertising exceeded one. In fact, this coefficient turned out to be 1.63 (with a standard error of 0.29) in a sample of 408 US industries in 1963 using 2SLS estimation techniques. Hence, their evidence also supports a positive effect of advertising on profitability using simultaneous-equation techniques. Strickland and Weiss, however, noted that this relationship was no longer statistically significant (notably for consumer goods) when the sample was split into consumer and producer goods industries, and they suggested that this result cast doubt on the importance of the product differentiation barrier. As noted in chapter 5, however, Martin (1979) has criticized their statistical model on technical grounds, and it may be that their results in this respect are thereby suspect. Finally, Pagoulatos and Sorenson (1980/1) also found a significant effect of advertising intensity on price–cost margins in 47 US food processing industries in 1967 in a three-equation, simultaneous-equation model. All in all, these results seem to suggest that, for US industries, a positive effect running from advertising to profitability does exist, even when reverse causality is allowed for.

A second potential problem with the advertising-as-entry-barrier argument concerns the investment nature of advertising. Under conventional accounting procedures, advertising expenditures are treated as a current expense rather than as an investment. Hence, to the extent that current advertising expenditure has effects beyond the current period, measured rates of return will deviate from 'true' rates of return. On the one hand, 'true' rates of return will be overstated in that intangible advertising capital has not been allowed for in the denominator of the measured rate of return. In addition, however, since measured profits are net of current advertising expenditures, 'true' rates of return will be understated (overstated) where current advertising expenditures exceed (fall short of) current depreciation charges on advertising intangibles. While these inaccuracies in measured profit rates might be of little consequence, it could be argued that the errors involved are positively correlated with advertising intensity, giving rise to spurious correlations between measured profitability and advertising. Several authors have argued that such an effect exists *and* that it accounts for all of the observed relationship between advertising and profitability.

Not all studies, however, have come to this conclusion, and we mention first two studies which found the entry barrier argument robust to such considerations. Weiss (1969), in his pioneering study, considered the effects of adjusting rates of return for advertising capital in a sample of 37 US 'minor industries' in 1963–4. Owing to lack of detailed information, he assumed that in each industry advertising investments depreciated over a six-year period with an annual depreciation rate of 33 per cent. This procedure is, of course, essentially crude and could give rise to misleading results. Using it, however, Weiss found that adjusting rates of return produced only marginal changes in the effect of advertising on profitability in multiple regression. In his reported results, advertising effects remained positive and statistically significant at better than the 1 per cent level on a one-tailed test, thereby tending to support the entry barrier hypothesis.

Second, Comanor and Wilson (1974) also tested for advertising capital effects in a sample of 39 US industries in 1954–7. In contrast to Weiss, they estimated the stock of advertising goodwill in each industry and used these estimates to adjust rates of return for advertising capital. Their estimates suggested that a substantial proportion of advertising expenditures should in fact be expensed in the current period in some industries (notably, those producing durable goods) and that depreciation rates of stocks of goodwill were often quite high. Not surprisingly, they then found that adjustments to rates of return were often quite marginal (on average, actually raising the rate of return) and consequently that effects of advertising on rates of return were little affected by these adjustments. In a series of alternative specifications, they found that, while some marginal reductions in t ratios were observed, in all cases the regression coefficient on advertising intensity in multiple regression was statistically significant at at least the 5 per cent level on a one-tailed test.

This apparently strong evidence has been challenged in studies by Bloch and Ayarian, both of whom use firm data in contrast to the industry data used by Weiss, and Comanor and Wilson. Bloch (1974) (see also Bloch, 1980) adjusted profit rates for 40 food manufacturing firms in 1950–3 using a 5 per cent depreciation rate for advertising capital. He found that such adjustments typically lowered rates of return. Moreover, in multiple regression analysis their effect was substantially to reduce the magnitude of the regression coefficient on advertising intensity and make it statistically insignificant. This result was, however, sensitive to the low depreciation rate assumed. Using a 33.3 per cent depreciation rate (following Weiss) increased the advertising coefficient substantially, although it remained statistically insignificant at the 5 per cent level on a one-tailed test.

Ayarian (1975) adjusted profit rates for 39 firms in six product groups in 1968, using an estimate of the advertising stock depreciation rate for each product group. The depreciation rates used were typically quite low (ranging from 5 to 15 per cent, with a 37 per cent rate for food products), and their effect was to reduce profit rates, in some cases quite markedly. Ayarian found that, in simple regression, adjustments for advertising capital markedly lowered the coefficient on advertising intensity in his sample and made it statistically insignificant.

Several weaknesses should be noted in the studies of Bloch and Ayarian. First, in using a 5 per cent depreciation rate for advertising capital, Bloch argued that such a rate was capable of explaining variations in the relationship between the market and book value of his firms. As noted by Comanor and Wilson (1979), however, the market value of a firm is affected not only by the advertising capital but also by the capitalized value of all future monopoly rents, so that Bloch's justification for the depreciation rate used is clearly not appropriate. In this context, the sensitivity of his coefficient estimates to increases in the depreciation rate used is of considerable interest. Second, as again noted by Comanor and Wilson, Ayarian's estimates of the depreciation rate of advertising capital are very crude and, moreover, implausibly low. Independent estimates by Peles (1971), for example, suggest a 100 per cent depreciation rate for automobile advertising, while Ayarian uses a 5 per cent depreciation rate for this product group. Other studies of various nondurable products, while typically suggesting some advertising capital effects, generally put depreciation rates higher than those suggested by Ayarian. Hence, and bearing in mind the apparent sensitivity of the advertising coefficient to depreciation rates used, it would appear that Ayarian's results are due in part to his use of underestimates of depreciation rates.

The balance of evidence currently available probably suggests that entry barrier effects of advertising continue to exist even after adjusting rates of return for the capital effects of advertising. However, this remains hotly contested, with the sensitivity of results to factors such as rivalrous advertising, the use of firm data and appropriate depreciation rates being crucial issues. These problems are primarily factual, and hence capable of empirical determination in principle, although better data and further empirical work may be needed before firm conclusions can be drawn.

Finally, we may briefly mention empirical evidence on advertising as a determinant of market concentration. While a great deal of work has been done on this issue[10] (notably in the late 1960s and early 1970s), its interpretation must be regarded as problematical given the possibility of reverse causality in the relationship (see section 6.1.3). More recent work, however, suggests that some evidence does exist for a positive effect of advertising on concentration. Strickland and Weiss (1976), for example, found that advertising intensity remained as a significant determinant of four-firm concentration in their sample of 408 US industries in 1963 after allowance for reverse causation using 2SLS estimation techniques. Similar results for the USA have been obtained by Pagoulatos and Sorenson (1980/1) in their sample of 47 food processing industries in 1967, but not by Martin (1979) in his sample of 209 industries in 1967.

Second, Mueller and Rogers (1980) have found that advertising intensity was an important determinant of *changes* in market concentration in US industry in 1947–72. Against a background of overall stable concentration levels, concentration in consumer goods industries showed a marked and persistent tendency to increase in this period. Using a sample of 167 four-digit industries, Mueller and Rogers found that advertising intensity was a significant determinant of increasing four-firm concentration, and that advertising intensity on television and radio in fact accounted for the whole (and more) of this effect. Despite the apparent robustness of their results, it should be noted that Asch (1979/80) was unable to obtain positive significant coefficients on advertising intensity using a different data set for the shorter 1963–72 period.

6.3 Summary and Conclusions

The above discussion has suggested that advertising by business firms can create a number of potential problems. Competitive advertising in oligopolistic markets can be excessive and socially wasteful when it leads to mutually self-cancelling messages being foisted on consumers with little or no net effect. Advertising in oligopolistic markets can also increase market concentration and raise barriers to entry, leading to excess prices and profitability. Links between advertising, concentration and profitability, notably in consumer goods industries, therefore suggest a number of avenues for undesirable effects.

It has also been argued that advertising has more general negative welfare effects. In a classic paper, Kaldor (1950) argued that too much advertising tends to take place in a competitive economy because of the practice of subsidizing advertising information to consumers. According to this argument, failure to charge consumers a direct price for the economic cost of advertising (say for television advertising) tends to lead to excess advertising and, more generally, to a misallocation of economic resources. This argument has, however, been challenged by Telser (1966), who argues that resources savings in not having to charge for advertising information may justify its free provision (both from a private and a social point of view).[11] Also, as noted by Kaldor, if consumers tend to undervalue advertising information, then some subsidization of advertising would be socially worthwhile.

In a recent paper, Dixit and Norman (1978) argue that, when advertising increases monopoly power, by reducing the market price elasticity of demand, it tends to be socially excessive. In their model, advertising by a monopolist changes consumer tastes but, regardless of whether one treats pre- or post-advertising tastes as appropriate to economic welfare, socially excessive levels of advertising result. This finding applies *a fortiori* to an oligopolistic market where self-cancelling advertising may take place and to a monopolistically competitive market where free entry further leads to excess advertising. However, Dixit and Norman's results have been criticized by several writers for ignoring possible indirect or informational effects of advertising.[12] Also, in a somewhat different model, Katowitz and Mathewson (1979) show that, where advertising influences consumer quality assessments, welfare losses need not necessarily arise.

There are many other arguments relating to welfare aspects of advertising. On the negative side, it is argued that advertising information is one-sided and biased, and may distort consumer purchasing decisions. Also, in so far as it persuades consumers to purchase products which they really don't want, then again it can be socially harmful. These arguments rely on weaknesses in consumers' abilities to make independent *ex post* judgements on products, which is not to say that such arguments are not important in evaluating advertising from a welfare point of view. On the other side, it is often argued that advertising is socially desirable because it subsidizes the mass communications media (television, radio, newspapers, etc.). Arguments on this, as with arguments on subsidizing advertising information, typically revolve around issues of extra collection costs associated with, for example, metering television and radio usage and arguments that consumers may individually undervalue the social benefits associated with the media.

Clearly, on a general level, the argument that too much advertising takes place, while suggestive, is not proven, given the complex nature of factors involved. It is not clear, therefore, whether general policies (such as a tax on advertising or restrictions on advertising) are desirable. We have seen in this chapter that there are grounds for believing that advertising can be excessive or can have anti-competitive effects in individual industries, however, and some of the industries with particularly high advertising intensity were listed in table 6.1. For such cases, it may be necessary to keep a careful watch on the interrelationships between advertising and other elements of market competition in order to ensure that substantial anti-competitive effects linked to advertising do not arise.

Notes

1 See Waterson, M. J. (1982). About 15 per cent of total advertising expenditure was not spent by private firms, of which 11 per cent was classified advertising and 4 per cent was advertising by government, nationalized industries and charities.

2 The model can also be modified to take account of dynamic effects on demand. See the classic paper of Nerlove and Arrow (1962) and also Schmalensee (1972) and Hay and Morris (1979).

3 For example, of 77 industries for which data are available in 1968 (see table 6.1 above), advertising/sales ratios were on average 2.73 per cent in 29 mainly consumer goods industries compared with only 0.63 per cent on average in mainly producer goods industries.

4 If advertising intensity affects concentration in addition to concentration affecting advertising intensity, then ordinary least squares estimates of the latter relationship will be biased even in large samples; see, for example, Maddala (1977), p. 231. In this case other estimation techniques which take account of simultaneity (such as 2SLS) offer the prospect of more reliable estimates of the underlying relationships.

5 This finding is not accepted by all writers. For a sceptical view, with supporting evidence for the USA, see Ornstein (1977).

6 For a useful survey of the subject, leaning on the anti-competitive side, see Comanor and Wilson (1979). A somewhat extreme defence of the pro-competitive position is given in Brozen (1974).

7 Greater instability in market shares may, of course, lead to difficulties in co-ordinating price policies. This appears to be an issue which has been under-researched in the literature.

8 It should be noted that a body of thought denies the existence of scale economies in advertising. For an exchange of views on the issue see Simon (1980), with a reply by Comanor and Wilson (1980).

9 As noted in section 6.1.3, the possibility of simultaneity 'matters' because in such cases ordinary least squares estimation gives rise to biased estimates of true relationships even in large samples. In such cases, therefore, more complicated techniques are desirable.

10 For a survey see, for example, Mann (1974) or Ornstein (1977).

11 See also the comments of Steiner (1966).

12 See the comments of Fisher and McGowan (1979) and Shapiro (1980).

7 Technical Progress

This chapter is concerned with the dynamic performance of the economy and, in particular, with the contribution of technical progress to economic growth. While it is clearly important to allocate resources efficiently at any point in time, in the long run the economic wellbeing of a community will depend on improvements in the quantity and quality of outputs produced by industry. Such improvements may be brought about by mechanization and increases in the capital stock, or they might occur through the abolition of restrictive practices or improvements in labour skills. In addition, however, the invention and application of new and superior products and processes in industry is likely to make a substantial contribution to economic growth, and it is such technical progress with which we are concerned here.

Several useful distinctions can be made in considering technical progress. A basic distinction is between *process* and *product developments.* Process developments involve the introduction of new processes or techniques, typically embodied in new capital equipment and used in production. Such developments lower the real cost of producing outputs, although they may also give rise to changes in their nature. Product developments, on the other hand, are directly associated with changes in the nature of products offered for sale, and typically such developments (when they are successful) would enhance economic welfare.[1] In practice, it is much easier to measure the contribution of process developments to economic growth, at least in so far as these give rise to increased productivity. Product developments are much more difficult to value and hence are typically ignored in calculations of economic growth. Clearly, product developments have been of major importance in economic change, particularly in recent years, and measured growth rates, therefore, may not adequately reflect changes in economic wellbeing that have taken place.

A second distinction is between the several phases of technical progress. These are often divided in three: invention, innovation and diffusion. The initial stage in product or process development is *invention*, wherein a new idea is developed and possibly a prototype is produced. In some circumstances this phase may involve some basic research into new scientific principles, in addition to the development of an idea towards a particular commercial application. Second comes the *innovation* phase, wherein a company further refines and develops a product for commercial launch. In this phase, technical development is combined with marketing and entrepreneurial expertise as the company strives to produce a successful new product. The culmination of these efforts comes with the introduction of the product on the market by the innovating firm. In the third stage, as other firms come to see that the innovation is worthwhile, they also adopt or imitate the product or process in question; i.e., *diffusion* takes place. From the point of view of economic welfare, it is clearly important that all three stages in technical progress be encouraged, and in this chapter we will be concerned primarily with examining factors which slow or enhance these three phases in technical progress.

Before moving on to these issues, however, it is useful to consider some

Table 7.1 Research and development expenditure as a percentage of sales in selected[a] UK industries, 1978

Industry	Total R & D/sales (%)	Company-funded R & D/sales (%)	Concentration ratio[b] (%)
Aerospace	18.5	5.7	77
Electronic computers	16.1	13.2	70
Electronic components	12.1	4.8	59
Pharmaceutical products	10.4	10.4	40
Misc. electrical goods	2.5	2.0	32
Other chemicals	2.1	2.0	67
Electrical machinery	2.0	1.5	50
Scientific instruments	1.8	1.6	35
Synthetic rubber, etc.	1.8	1.8	45
Textile machinery	1.7	1.6	45
Paint	1.6	1.6	39
Motor vehicles	1.4	1.4	64
Other machinery	1.2	1.2	38
Insulated wires	1.2	1.1	82
Domestic (electrical) appliances	1.0	1.0	57
Pottery, china and glass	1.0	1.0	52
All manufacturing	1.6	1.1	43[c]

Sources: Industrial Research and Development Expenditure and Employment, 1978, Business Monitor MO14 (HMSO, 1980), table 19; *Report of the Census of Production, 1978: Summary Tables,* Business Monitor PA1002 (HMSO, 1981), table 13.

Notes
[a] Industries with a ratio of total R & D expenditure to sales over 1 per cent in 1978.
[b] Five-firm employment concentration ratio; where groups of industries are involved, an employment-weighted average concentration ratio for those industries is given.
[c] Public sector dominated industries are excluded from this figure.

general features of technical progress in practice. For simplicity, we consider data on research and development (hereafter R & D) expenditures in British industry. Taking 1978 as a base, total expenditure on R & D in the UK was estimated at £3.5 billion or 2.4 per cent of the gross national product (GNP). Roughly one-third of this expenditure, however, was non-industrial, being made by government, universities and research associations.[2] An estimated total *industrial* R & D expenditure in 1978 was £2.3 billion, of which £2.2 billion was spent in manufacturing industry. It is this expenditure, representing 1.6 per cent of GNP, which is our principle concern in this chapter.[3]

Several points can be made about this expenditure. First, and particularly in some industries, a substantial portion of industrial R & D spending is funded by government. In 1978, for example, £0.7 billion, or 29 per cent of total industrial R & D spending, was government funded, with a further £0.2 billion coming from overseas funds and £1.4 billion coming from (mainly) private industry. This substantial government funding can be explained in part in terms of the risks of R & D which tend to lead to underinvestment in research by private industry (see section 7.1). In addition, however, it is associated with government involvement in defence spending, and hence with the provision of that particular public good. This point is brought out to some extent in table 7.1, which lists manufacturing industries with important total R & D spending relative to sales. As can be seen, most research activity on this criterion is carried out in the aerospace industry, but the high levels of government funding implied here (and probably also in electronic components) is linked predominantly to defence.

Second, R & D spending varies considerably between industries and between firms, tending to be heavily concentrated in each case. Table 7.1 shows the *industries* in which R & D spending is relatively high. As can be seen, two industries, in addition to aerospace and electronic components, stand out: namely, electronic computers and pharmaceutical products. In both cases, R & D spending is predominantly or wholly company-funded. No other industries listed in table 7.1 have outstandingly high R & D spending, but even these industries undertake more research activity than many others not shown in the table. Traditional, low-technology industries in the textiles, food, metal goods and timber products sectors (not shown) tend to have very low ratios of R & D expenditure to sales.

An analysis of the largest *enterprises* by R & D expenditure in 1978 is shown in table 7.2. As can be seen, 90 per cent of total R & D expenditure was accounted for by the top 100 such enterprises, and these firms employed 88 per cent of R & D employees. Even more surprisingly, just the top five enterprises accounted for 40 per cent of all R & D spending in private industry, although, as can be seen in table 7.2, government funding was of substantial importance here.

Finally, table 7.1 also reports figures for the 1978 five-firm employment concentration ratio for the research-intensive industries listed. On average,

Table 7.2 The 100 largest enterprises by research and development expenditure in the UK, 1978

Largest enterprises	R & D expenditure		R & D employment ('000s)
	Total	Non-govt funded	
	(£ million)		
First 5	857.6	358.9	65.8
First 10	1092.4	552.0	85.6
First 20	1389.1	785.8	105.0
First 50	1726.1	1089.2	131.7
First 100	1902.5	1251.1	147.5
All industry[a]	2117.9	1456.7	168.0

Source: Industrial Research and Development Expenditure and Employment, 1978, table 16.

Note

[a] Estimated total for private industry.

for the 16 industries considered here, this concentration ratio was 51 per cent compared with an average of 43 per cent in all manufacturing industries. This indicates a positive association between proportionate R & D spending and product market concentration which has often been found in empirical work (see section 7.2.2 below). Confirmation of this result is found in the following simple OLS regression (with t ratios in parentheses)

$$Y = -0.15 + 0.03X \qquad r^2 = 0.190 \qquad (7.1)$$
$$(-0.26)\ \ (2.51)$$

In this equation Y is private-company-funded R & D as a proportion of sales and X is five-firm concentration for 29 industries or industry groups (excluding the two outlying observations: computers and pharmaceutical products). As can be seen, R & D activity is positively correlated with concentration and this correlation is statistically significant at the 5 per cent level.[4]

It is necessary to interpret this result with care, however. While it may reflect greater technical progressiveness in more concentrated industries, it might also arise, for example, because industries with greater technological opportunities (and hence greater proportionate R & D spending) tend to be more concentrated. This might occur if high technological opportunity was positively associated on average with high relative scale economies (which favour high concentration). It is clearly necessary to attempt to separate these possible effects, and these matters will be discussed further in section 7.2.2 below.

In what follows we examine three aspects of technical progress. Section 7.1

provides a brief overview of the economics of invention, and in particular examines problems which arise in the production of new ideas and products in a market economy. Section 7.2 then considers links between invention and innovation and market structure, and discusses the Schumpeterian notion that monopoly (and large firm size) may be conducive to technical progress. Finally, section 7.3 looks at the diffusion of new techniques.

7.1 Economics of Research

We begin by briefly considering some basic economics of research or inventive activity. Research is a rather special economic process for at least two reasons: first, because of the high level of uncertainty associated with it, and second, because its output (i.e. information) has characteristics of a public good. It has been argued, in particular by Arrow (1962), that these factors create problems for the provision of research in free market economies, and we consider why this might be so in what follows.

We begin with the problem of uncertainty. In the particular case of investment in inventive activity, uncertainty arises because the output obtained from employing resources in a new research project is not known *a priori*. Inevitably, therefore, there is a risk associated with research and consequently it is necessary for this risk to be borne. As Arrow (1962) points out, an optimal solution in the sense of Pareto would be for risks to be spread over all members of the community such that account be taken of all individuals' resources and preferences with respect to risk. In practice, however, such an outcome is unlikely to be attainable, so it is necessary to rely on imperfect mechanisms for shifting risks.

One way of dealing with the risks of research is for firms to raise money on the capital market, thereby spreading risks over a large number of members of society. Such an approach, in fact, would be socially desirable in so far as it enabled individuals at large to express their preferences towards risky research projects. In practice, however, very little money for R & D projects is raised directly from the capital market, so this link with individual preferences operates only imperfectly. A principle reason for this, according to Arrow, is the problem of *moral hazard*, whereby the incentives to undertake successful research are not independent of the risks borne. In the case of inventive activity, if it were possible to finance R & D completely via the capital market such that a company and its research department bore no risk of failure, then the incentive to produce new products and processes effectively and successfully would be greatly reduced. Consequently, in order to provide incentives for efficient research activity, the firm itself typically bears the risks. But to the extent that it does so, the ability to spread risks over the community at large is reduced. Since firms have limited funds, this implies that insufficient funds are likely to be devoted to research compared with Pareto efficient levels.

This problem might be overcome, however, in a large corporation which undertakes a number of research projects each small in scale relative to the firm's size. In this case, large firms can more easily insure themselves against failure by pooling risks such that successes and failures in research projects are mutually offsetting. In some cases, moreover, independent firms may combine resources to undertake research in an area of common interest, thereby similarly reducing risks. Clearly, such effects can be important in practice, but again they are likely to offer only an imperfect solution: first, because they involve only a partial means of pooling risks, and second, because large firms may have monopolistic motives for retarding invention and innovation (see section 7.2 below). Hence, again, the market system may prove inadequate as a means of encouraging desirable levels of research, and there may therefore be room for positive government action to support inventive activity.

As has been stressed by Demsetz (1969) in his discussion of Arrow's work, the argument that free enterprise tends to underinvest in research need not imply that government intervention is more desirable. Clearly, identifying a potential inefficiency represents only half of the story; in addition, one must show that some real economic alternative (in this case, government finance for research) offers a prospect for improvement. It would take us too far afield to discuss the alternative of government intervention here, despite its crucial importance. Clearly, this would depend on one's faith in government's ability correctly to anticipate and reflect the preferences of individuals with respect to the risks of inventive activity, among other things. No Western country relies solely on the market for its inventive activity, and presumably this does reflect a consensus view that the free market will tend to underinvest in risky research activities.

The second aspect of inventive activity which requires attention is the product itself, i.e. information. It has been argued by Arrow and others that this product, once produced, possesses the characteristics of a *public good*, which again creates problems for a market economy. The characteristics of relevance here are, first, its supposed *non-excludability* or inappropriability and, second, its *non-rivalness* or indivisibility. As far as non-excludability is concerned, Arrow emphasized the difficulties associated with establishing property rights in information, given that once it is available it can be reproduced at little or no cost. A firm may, of course, attempt to keep new product or process inventions secret, but in doing this it may be unable to exploit them to the full. Moreover, industrial secrets are notoriously difficult to maintain given that incentives will exist for industrial espionage and so on, and given that in some circumstances (e.g. with a new chemical product) some information is likely to be embodied in the product itself.

An alternative strategy is to patent the idea or invention, i.e. to establish legal property rights in it. Such a step has the advantage of permitting a firm to license the use of its idea to others in addition to using it itself. It has the disadvantage that, in revealing the idea or invention, patenting may encourage infringement of property rights or outright theft. While it is important to recognize the practical problems in maintaining property rights in ideas via patents, it is also important not to overemphasize them. In one study of the UK patent system, for example, it was argued that, while infringement was likely to be a problem for 'weak' (substantially invalid) patents, this was much less likely to be the case for 'strong' (substantially valid) patents of considerable commercial importance (Taylor and Silberston, 1973, pp. 20–2). To the extent that patent infringements are controlled, therefore, the potential problem of non-excludability will be reduced.

The problem of non-rivalness or indivisibility of information, however, creates different problems. Non-rivalness means that making information available to one person does not reduce the amount available for others. Neglecting (typically small) costs of disseminating information, therefore, the social opportunity cost of providing information is zero, and it would be socially desirable to make new ideas and inventions freely available to all. In a free enterprise system with property rights in invention, however, an inventor is given an incentive to invent precisely because of his ability to restrict the use of his invention in order to earn a monopoly rent. Consequently, to the extent that such a system permits monopolization of a new product or process, it implies a socially suboptimal utilization of that innovation.

Clearly, a patent system which grants a monopoly in the use of an invention for a fixed term (20 years in the UK; raised from 16 years in the 1977 Patents Act) represents a compromise between providing an incentive for invention and allowing full utilization of the invention once the patent's term has expired. Such a system is necessarily arbitrary and crude, offering as it does just a fixed-term monopoly for inventions of widely differing types in widely differing circumstances. Its basic justification in Western countries is that, by providing strong incentives for invention, it fuels technical progress and economic growth, and that such dynamic efficiency overrides the static welfare losses implied in patent rights. This argument is little more than a statement of faith, however, although at the same time few economists have been prepared to suggest that radical changes to the system might be desirable.[5]

7.2 Technical Progress and Competition

We now move on to a more specific examination of technical progress in a market economy. In particular, we examine possible links between invention and innovation and market structure. A crucial issue here concerns the possible influence that monopolistic or competitive market structures may have on innovative activity and consequently on economic welfare. Does a competitive market provide a greater incentive for invention than a monopolistic one? Or are monopolists more willing and able to produce new innovations than competitive firms? Some attempt at answering these questions is made in sections 7.2.1 and 7.2.2 below. Also, technical progress may be affected by firm size and conglomerate diversification in addition to possible market power effects, and a brief consideration of these factors is given in section 7.2.3.

7.2.1 Market Structure and the Incentive to Invent

This section considers the classic analysis of invention due to Arrow (1962). Arrow argued that the incentives to invent (or, more generally, to supply a new innovation)[6] are stronger for competitive as opposed to monopolized industries, so that monopoly was likely to retard technical progress in addition to involving a static welfare loss. Against this, however, Demsetz (1969) argued that monopoly created no additional disincentives for invention and could indeed lead to more invention taking place. Clearly, some differences in analysis are involved here, and we shall examine each argument in turn.

We begin with the analysis of Arrow (1962). Arrow considered a simple case of a process innovation in an industry with constant costs. Also, for simplicity, he ignored possible problems of uncertainty and inappropriability of the invention. In a competitive industry, price equals average cost, and an invention has the effect of shifting down the unit cost curve. The inventor of the new process is assumed to be able to charge all firms in the competitive industry an arbitrary royalty per unit of output for the use of the invention. On the other hand, in the monopoly situation it is assumed that only the monopoly firm itself can invent, and that the monopolist sets marginal

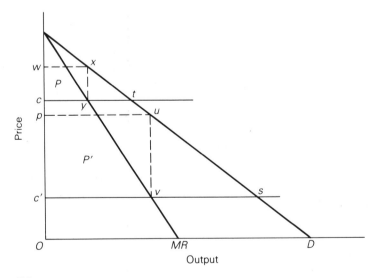

Figure 7.1

revenue equal to marginal cost both pre- and post-invention. The incentive to invent is then defined as the potential profits which can accrue to the inventor or monopolist from the invention.

Arrow considered two cases, the first of which relates to an invention producing a drastic cost reduction. In figure 7.1,[7] if D is a linear market demand curve and c is the pre-invention unit cost curve, then a competitive industry will set price equal to c, while a monopolist will set marginal revenue (MR) equal to c, giving price w and profits equal to area $P = wxyc$. Following the introduction of a drastic cost-reducing innovation, unit costs fall to c'.

(1) In the competitive case, the inventor charges firms a per-unit royalty, r, to maximize his profits. This involves restricting competitive output to where MR is equal to c' giving maximum profits equal to area $P' = puvc'$ from a per-unit royalty, pc'. Thus the competitive industry would set price p and pay a total royalty P' to the inventor. The inventor would then be willing to invest in invention if the cost of the invention to him is less than P'.

(2) In the monopoly case, the monopolist sets MR equal to c', again establishing the price p. His profits are P' but the incentive to invent is $P' - P$, being the extra profits arising from the invention. Since $P' - P$ is less than P', there is less incentive for invention in monopoly than in competition. Given demand and cost conditions, Arrow's argument is thus that the inventor in the competitive situation can extract a total royalty equal to what the monopolist could gain post-invention, and thus the latter has less incentive to invent since he was previously earning some monopoly profits, P.

Before moving on to Arrow's second case, two further results can be illustrated in figure 7.1. First, the incentive to invent under competition, and *a fortiori* under monopoly, will be less than the *realized social benefit* in the case of a drastic cost-saving invention. The argument here is that, with a drastic cost-saving invention, the inventor extracts all the monopoly profits equal to area $P' = puvc'$ from a royalty per unit, pc', and since price has fallen to p, consumers gain a surplus equal to area $ctup$. Since the inventor cannot extract this surplus from consumers by charging producers a royalty, the incentive to invent is less than the total social benefit realized in the competitive case, so that some inventions are forgone which consumers would be willing to pay inventors to undertake. Given a system of royalties per unit of output, therefore, some drastic cost-saving inventions will not be undertaken because of the inventor's inability to extract the whole consumer surplus. This problem does not arise from moderate cost-saving inventions, however, where price does not fall, so there is no consumer surplus that is not extracted by the inventor.

Second, the *potential social benefit* from reducing costs by cc' is equal to area $ctsc'$ in figure 7.1. This benefit would arise only if the invention were made freely available to the competitive industry, so that the competitive

F

price would fall to c'. A system of per-unit royalty payments to an inventor is therefore inefficient in two ways. First, royalty payments lead to an under-utilization of the invention owing to the monopoly incentive for invention provided. This is associated with the deadweight welfare loss area uvs in figure 7.1. Second, since in principle any invention whose research cost is less than area $ctsc'$ is socially worthwhile, some high-cost but desirable inventions will not be undertaken if area $P' = puvc'$ is the maximum royalty obtainable. It should be noted, however, that both of these arguments assume that a simple royalty per unit of output is employed by the inventor. With more complex, non-uniform royalty systems, utilization of the invention and total royalty payments may be enhanced, so that these problems are alleviated. Such solutions, while they do promote more efficient resource allocation, also increase the proportion of benefits obtained by the inventor, and this may give cause for concern on income distribution grounds.

Arrow's second case of a moderate cost-reducing invention is presented in figure 7.2. In this case, costs fall from c to c'.

(1) In the competitive case, the inventor can set a maximum royalty, cc', since a higher royalty makes the invention not worthwhile for the competitive firms. The total royalty is thus equal to area $cabc'$.
(2) The monopolist, in contrast, sets MR equal to c' (as before) after invention, giving profits equal to area $puvc'$. The incentive to invent is $puvc' - wxyc$, as before. The incentive to invent is less under monopoly because
  (a) area $wxyc$ exceeds area $putc$ since the former area is the maximum area under the demand curve given unit cost, c;
  (b) area $cabc'$ exceeds area $ctvc'$ by inspection.

The extra incentive to invent under competition is thus area $tvba + (wxyc - putc)$. Arrow goes on to show that the ratio of the incentive under competition to the incentive under monopoly (which always exceeds 1) is greater the less the invention reduces costs, having an upper limit of approximately the ratio (x_c/x_m) of competitive to monopoly output. Thus, small cost-saving inventions, in particular, are much more worthwhile under competition than monopoly.

Arrow's analysis of the incentive to invent under competition and monopoly has been criticized by Demsetz (1969), who argues, in particular, that Arrow failed to compare like with like in that a valid comparison requires one to put on one side the normally restrictive policies associated with monopoly. In addition, he argued that Arrow dealt with an asymmetrical case in which an outside inventor was assumed to supply a competitive industry but that the monopolist provided its invention itself.[8] Demsetz considered two cases which for simplicity can be illustrated in terms of a drastic cost-reducing innovation.

First, Demsetz postulated a case in which an inventor supplied an invention to both a competitive and a monopolized industry. The inventor is

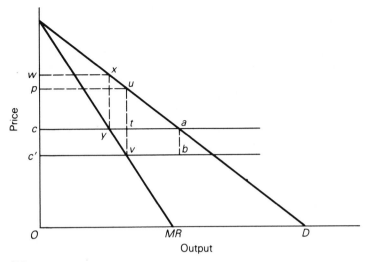

Figure 7.2

assumed to be constrained by regulation or competition from other inventions to charge the same royalty per unit to both industries. If this royalty per unit is pc' in figure 7.3, then in the competitive industry the total royalty payment will be equal to area $P' = puvc'$, while in the monopolized industry it would be only half this since the monopolist expands output only to the intersection of pu and MR. While this implies a greater incentive to invent in a

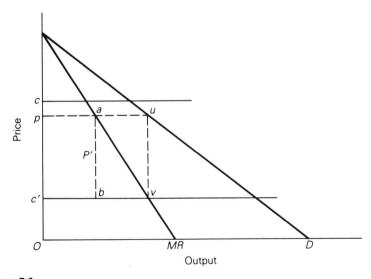

Figure 7.3

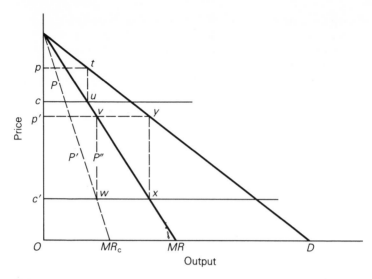

Figure 7.4

competitive industry, Demsetz argued that this is nothing other than the usual monopoly result that the monopolist will hire the input invention, like all inputs, to a limited extent given output limitation. In order to see if there is any special disincentive to invention in a monopolized industry over and above this normal effect, Demsetz argued that one should compare industries of equal size. This can be done by defining D as the demand curve for the monopoly industry and MR as the demand curve for the competitive industry, so that, given unit costs, each industry produces the same output. Doing this with a per-unit royalty pc', both industries will operate where pu intersects MR, and total royalty payments are the same at area $pabc'$. Thus there is no difference in the incentive to invent for the two industries given that they are of equal size.

Second, Demsetz argued that an inventor supplying a monopolized industry will have a greater incentive to invent than if he supplied an equally sized competitive industry if he is not constrained to charge the same per-unit royalty to each. In figure 7.4, as before, MR is the demand curve for the competitive industry while D is the demand curve for the monopoly, so that outputs are the same given unit costs.

(1) Given that competitive demand is MR, the best the inventor can do is to set a per-unit royalty $p'c'$ such that c' equals MR_c, giving a total royalty equal to area $P' = p'vwc'$.
(2) Given that monopoly demand is D, the monopolist earns profits equal to area $P'' = p'yxc'$ post-invention if he is not charged a per-unit royalty, giving an incentive to invent $P'' - P$, where area $P = ptuc$ measures

pre-invention profits. This is the monopolist's incentive if he is the inventor; alternatively, a lump-sum royalty equal to this could be charged by a separate inventor. By inspection, the monopoly incentive exceeds the competitive one if area *vyxw* exceeds area *ptuc*. With linear demand curves this must be so, because the former rectangle has both greater width and greater height. Thus, Demsetz concluded that monopoly offers a greater incentive to invention, given industries of equal size, and this factor can thus be said to offset the usual case against monopoly that it restricts output.

What are we, then, to make of these two conflicting arguments? While Demsetz's analysis is analytically correct, it is not clear that it is practically as useful as Arrow's. According to Arrow, in a given industry a move from monopoly to competition, say (or, more generally, an active policy of deconcentration), will lead not only to static welfare gains in terms of increasing output, but also to greater incentives for invention, since research projects that were not undertaken under monopoly might be undertaken under competition. In this sense, therefore, the greater incentive for invention provides an additional argument in favour of competition policy. According to Demsetz, however, the argument might even be reversed if one compared industries of equal size. On Demsetz's view, one is concerned less with policy action in individual cases than with the general incentives for invention, with market structures taken as data. It is not clear, however, that this represents a reasonable policy position unless one is committed beforehand to not engaging in competition policy. Under these circumstances, and accepting Demsetz's method of comparing industries of equal size, one might conclude that a greater invention incentive exists in monopoly. This, however, does not affect Arrow's argument that a move from monopoly to competition under an active competition policy will increase output *and also* (and thereby) the incentive for invention.[9]

7.2.2 Market Structure and Innovation

The argument over the incentives for invention is only one part of a more general argument over technical progress and market structure. While an inventor may have a greater *incentive* to invent for a competitive industry (if we accept Arrow's argument), this need not mean that competitive industries are *actually* more conducive to technical progress than monopolized industries. Indeed, in a classic book which has been the basis of much research in this area, Schumpeter (1965) asserted the reverse. In his view, monopoly power and large firm size were more likely to stimulate innovation and technical progress than competitive market conditions, and this therefore created a case for defending monopoly and/or large firm size.

In what follows, therefore, we consider the arguments for (and against) monopoly power and large firm size as a basis for technical progress. The monopoly power side of the argument is considered in this section, while other possible effects are considered more briefly in section 7.2.3.

Several reasons why more concentrated market structures may be conducive to more innovation have been suggested in the literature.[10] First, in so far as monopoly profits are associated with market concentration, it is argued that firms in concentrated industries are better able to finance R & D than firms in competitive industries. This argument stresses that research and development is risky and is typically financed with internal funds rather than with funds raised in the capital market. Oligopolistic markets which provide above-normal profits have a ready supply of such funds which may not be available to firms in more competitive markets. Hence one would expect that more competitive industries undertake little or no research on their own behalf, while oligopolistic industries at least have the funds for potential R & D projects. Some recognition that finance for research might be a problem in competitive industries is presumably reflected, for example, in agriculture, where significant government funding of research takes place.

Second (and this is also probably a factor in competitive markets such as in agriculture), there may be economies of scale in research activities which favour relatively large firms. When a minimum efficient scale for research exists it may not be feasible for independent firms in competitive markets to undertake efficient R & D. In some circumstances this problem may be overcome by pooling research efforts, but such a solution may not always be possible given the previously noted financial problems of small, competitive firms and also the large transactions costs implied in organizing a joint research programme. *Ceteris paribus*, a relatively large firm in a more concentrated market is more likely to be able to conduct R & D on an efficient scale. In some circumstances, of course, firms in concentrated industries may need to pool research resources with respect to particularly risky and expensive research projects. And indeed, this may well be socially desirable if wasteful duplication of research is to be avoided. For the moment, however, we merely note the possible research scale advantage that firms in concentrated industries may have relative to firms in competitive industries.

Several other possible advantages of firms in oligopolistic markets may also be noted. First, firms earning monopoly profits may be in a better position to protect their patents than firms in more competitive industries and hence may be more willing to undertake research. Second, rapid process and product innovation is an important competitive strategy not only with respect to existing competitors in some markets, but also with respect to forestalling possible new entry. Firms in more concentrated industries may undertake more research to counter both actual and potential competition. Finally, firms earning monopoly profits in concentrated industries may be able to attract better qualified research personnel and so increase and/or improve their research output per unit of resource. Given a fixed pool of research talent, however, such an effect is likely to be distortionary from a social welfare point of view in that researchers will be attracted to monopoly sectors which may not offer the most socially advantageous research opportunities.[11]

Several arguments against monopoly power being conducive to innovation can also be made. First, firms in monopoly positions may become lax and inefficient and fail to grasp research opportunities and/or to run efficient research programmes compared with firms in more competitive environments. The general notion of slack or X-inefficiency (Leibenstein, 1966) in concentrated markets suggests that less rather than more innovation may be forthcoming in very concentrated markets. Second, firms in concentrated markets may have less incentive to innovate, as already discussed in section 7.2.1. According to Arrow, this effect arises because an innovation produces only limited extra profits for a monopolist. A related argument is that firms in entrenched monopoly positions may also consider the costs of re-equipping their industry to take advantage of potential innovations and so may resist developing major innovations that might require such re-equipment. On this argument, research resources in oligopolistic industries might be diverted into minor innovations and style improvements (as for example in the motor car industry) rather than into more major path-breaking research; or entrenched monopolists might buy and suppress new patents which favour radical production changes for similar reasons. Such effects are, however, likely to be important only where barriers to entry protect established monopoly producers from potential competition.

Broadly speaking, the above arguments suggest that a monopolized industry may have less incentive to innovate than a more competitive industry but that it may be in a better position, in terms of research resources and finance, to undertake research activities. This could mean that some mixture of competition and monopoly is most conducive to innovation; that is, that moderate degrees of concentration in some markets favour R & D and innovation, while too much competition or too much monopoly (particularly where entry barriers are high) leads to less research activity. This hypothesis is only one of several that have been considered in the empirical literature, however, and we shall not confine our attention to it in what follows.

We have seen at the beginning of this chapter that R & D activity tends to be positively linked to market concentration in a cross-section of industries. As noted there, however, this may be due to factors such as technological opportunity tending to favour greater research intensity and greater market concentration. Hence, such a correlation need not reflect a causal relation running from concentration to R & D activity. This has represented an important empirical problem in research in this area, and several attempts at tackling it are considered below.

An early attempt at allowing for differences in technological opportunity between industries was made by Scherer (1967). He looked at employment of scientists and engineers in 56 US industries in 1960 making allowance for four technological opportunity classes.[12] Using a logarithmic multiple regression equation (with t ratios in parentheses), he obtained the following results

$$\ln Y = -0.36 + 0.93 \ln X_1 + 0.80 \ln X_2 + 0.27E$$
$$\qquad (8.45) \qquad (3.33) \qquad (1.12)$$
$$+ 0.51Ch - 0.4T - 0.01D_1 + 0.10D_2 - 0.09D_3 \qquad\qquad (7.2)$$
$$\qquad (3.00) \ (-3.72)(-0.08) \quad (1.00) \quad (-1.00)$$
$$R^2 = 0.805.$$

In this equation Y is an estimate of privately financed research employment of scientists and engineers, X_1 is total employment and X_2 is a (sales-weighted) average four-firm concentration ratio in 1958. In addition, Scherer allowed for electrical (E), chemical (Ch) and traditional (T) technological opportunity classes (omitting a fourth class, general and mechanical industries), plus three further variables D_1–D_3 representing regional markets, durable goods and consumer goods, respectively.[13] Equation (7.2) shows that there was significantly greater research activity in chemical industries and significantly lower research activity in traditional industries, compared with general and mechanical industries, as might be expected. Hence, Scherer's distinction of these industry groups (but not of electrical, and general and mechanical industries) is supported by his data. Even allowing for technological opportunity in this way, however, concentration is positively related to research activity in equation (7.2) and this relationship is statistically significant at better than the 1 per cent level. Hence it would appear that a strong positive association between research effort and market structure was observed.

This conclusion, of course, is conditional on Scherer's method of allowing for technological opportunity. Scherer also reported that the positive association between research activity and concentration was much weaker in ordinary linear multiple regression, where typically the effect was statistically significant at the 10 per cent level or worse. While Scherer's preference for this latter specification might be criticized, it did allow him to test for the possibility of an inverted U-shaped relationship between research activity and concentration. A test for such an effect was conducted in the general and mechanical, and traditional technology groups, but statistically significant evidence at the 5 per cent level was found in only traditional product industries. In both cases, however, relative research employment appeared to fall off somewhat above four-firm concentration levels of 55 per cent. These results may, therefore, offer some support for the view that intermediate levels of oligopoly offer the best prospect for high research activity, but in the general context of Scherer's study they must be regarded as tentative.

A second study was made by Comanor (1967a). He argued that a great deal of research undertaken in industry is for product rather than process development, and that consequently one should consider product differentiation as a crucial factor in research activity. In particular, he argued that industries could be divided into those in which differentiation based on product design was likely to be important (with consequently greater research activity) and those in which it was not. He classified investment goods and consumer durables to the former category, and material inputs and (perhaps more contentiously) consumer nondurables to the latter. Using this distinction, he found that research activity was indeed higher in industries where products were differentiable, but that in these industries there was little evidence that research activity increased with concentration. This result is interesting, since it suggests that in industries where competition in new products is important no advantage in higher concentration appears to exist. On the other hand, in industries where product differentiation was less important, stronger evidence for a positive research activity–concentration relationship was found. As noted by Comanor, however, since technological opportunity was not allowed for in his regressions, and since this tends to be positively correlated with concentration, some caution must be expressed before one argues for a research–concentration relationship in these industries.

Shrieves (1978) has provided a fuller study of research intensity and market concentration allowing for both product market characteristics and technological opportunity factors in his regressions. His study used R & D employment data in 1965 for a sample of 411 firms classified to 56 three-digit US industries. A variety of indicators of product market characteristics and technological opportunity were reduced, using factor analysis, to two product market factors and five technology factors. Allowing for these factors in logarithmic multiple regression analysis, Shrieves found a positive relationship between R & D employment and the four-firm concentration ratio which was statistically significant at the 5 per cent level. In addition, his results showed significantly higher research activity in areas dominated by life science technologies (i.e. firms tending to employ mainly biologists, medical doctors, pharmacists, etc.). Further analysis, according to product market characteristics, showed that a highly significant positive relationship existed between research intensity and concentration in industries producing consumer goods and material inputs, but that no statistically significant relationship existed in industries producing more durable equipment where both R & D intensity and concentration tended to be higher on average. These results are broadly in line with Comanor's study and in fact provide stronger support for the importance of product market characteristics than did Comanor's results. Shrieves argued that the positive research–concentration relationship in industries producing consumer goods and material inputs may reflect easier imitation of innovations in such industries, which reduces the incentive for innovation by small competitive firms compared with oligopolists, who are able to capture more of the benefits of a new product or process.

Several other studies may be mentioned briefly. One problem with the above work is that, in dealing with a cross-section of different industries with different characteristics, one is never sure whether one has sufficiently controlled for variations in technological opportunity, etc., to provide meaningful results linking research activity to market structure. One possible way round this problem is to compare R & D activity and concentration in each industry in several countries. That is, by taking (say) ratios of R & D activity and also concentration in two countries and comparing them, one effectively controls for differences between industries, assuming the industries are closely matched. One study using such an approach, albeit with a limited sample size, has been made by Adams (1970). He matched a sample of 14 industries in the USA and France in the 1960s and found, if anything, that a negative association existed between R & D and concentration in research-intensive industries, with no clear pattern in other industries. Adams did not conduct any statistical tests, however, and his data and analysis were too limited to draw any definite conclusions. Nevertheless, his failure to find any evidence of a positive association between research activity and concentration might suggest grounds for reservations concerning other results.

Second, a study of Rosenberg (1976) considered the effect of market share, in addition to market concentration on research intensity. Using a sample of 100 of the 500 largest US firms in 1964, he regressed the ratio of professional R & D personnel to total employment, Y, on a weighted average of each firm's market share in four-digit industries, X_1, and a variable for operation in above-average concentrated industries, C. Other explanatory variables included were an entry barrier variable, D; a high technological opportunity variable, X_2; a high government R & D funding variable, X_3; and industry growth in 1958–63, X_4.

Rosenberg found (with t ratios in parentheses) that

$$Y = 0.66 - 0.10X_1 + 1.15C + 1.18D + 1.51X_2 + 3.55X_3 + 0.31X_4 \qquad (7.3)$$
$$\quad (1.19) \; (-2.52) \; (2.05) \; (1.82) \; (1.85) \; (3.23) \; (2.78)$$
$$R^2 = 0.447.$$

According to equation (7.3), research intensity increases with market concentration but falls with firm market share, both results being statistically significant at the 5 per cent level. Hence, it would seem that a trade-off of concentration and market share exists with, in particular, very large firms in markets with a given level of market concentration being inimical to research activity. According to Rosenberg, such a result is consistent with leading firms in an industry being prepared to imitate new innovations quickly rather than innovate themselves. It should be noted, however, that (as a broad generalization) firms in Rosenberg's sample with lower average market shares will tend to be diversified over more industries than firms recording high market shares. As explained in section 7.2.3 below, this diversification factor may offer an alternative explanation of Rosenberg's results.

The available evidence on market structure and research intensity tends to support Schumpeter's suggestion that these variables may be positively associated, but the relationship may be complex – and, moreover, variable between different groups of industries. In addition, it should be recognized that in many industries concentration is just as likely to be determined by basic market conditions as is research activity, and that any association between these variables may therefore be neither causal[14] nor manipulable from a public policy point of view. The evidence reported in this section might suggest some grounds for defending concentrated industries in terms of their additional contribution to technical progress, but more work (both theoretical and empirical) is needed before one could firmly support such a view.

7.2.3 Other Hypotheses

The possibility that innovative activity may be linked to market concentration is, of course, not the only hypothesis examined in industrial economics. In this section we briefly review two further hypotheses: that research activity will be positively linked to firm size, and that it will be positively linked to conglomerate diversification.

The argument that corporate size *per se* is conducive to technological innovation derives from the work of Schumpeter (1965) (see also Galbraith, 1963). Several reasons for such a relationship might exist. First, when one considers a spectrum of innovation opportunities, there will obviously be some which require a very large investment in order to be viable. In such cases, innovation may be financially possible only for the largest private companies with access to absolutely large amounts of funds. Second, since R & D is a risky activity, large firms will have an advantage over small firms in being able to diversify their research portfolio and hence reduce the risk of major research failure. This argument, as noted in section 7.1, is one of self-insurance against risks in large corporations, implying that such corporations can undertake proportionately more research while at the same time experiencing less risk. And third, large firms may have advantages in other fields, such as managerial expertise, legal services or marketing, which enable them better to exploit new innovations. These advantages may extend merely to the ability to serve a larger market than a smaller firm, thereby increasing the large firm's ability to extract rents from the innovation. Such an argument might apply in cases where problems of appropriating monopoly rents in the innovation existed and/or where transactions costs of licensing its use were relatively high.

Of course, the above arguments are *a priori*, and it might be just as likely that large firms are sluggish in their response to innovation opportunities, and that research laboratories themselves become bureaucratized and unimaginative in large corporations. A great deal of empirical research has been done on these issues, which cannot, however, be discussed in detail here.[15] Rather, we shall content ourselves with mentioning some conclusions which emerge from this work.

First, if one considers the very largest firms in an economy, then, in terms of *research effort*, such firms engage in a disproportionate amount of innovative activity. In the UK in 1978, enterprises with more than 5000 employees accounted for 89 per cent of R & D employment in firms with over 200 employees but only 58 per cent of total manufacturing employment. Among the very largest UK enterprises, with over 20,000 employees, these figures were 66 and 32 per cent, respectively.[16] Similarly, in the USA (see Scherer, 1980, p. 418) larger US corporations with over 5000 employees in 1972 accounted for 53 per cent of all US manufacturing industry employment but 87 per cent of private-funded R & D expenditure, rising to 89 per cent when government-funded R & D was also included. These figures, therefore, suggest that, from an *a priori* viewpoint, large firms are particularly conducive to new innovation.

Some caution, however, is needed in interpreting these figures. First, since they relate to research inputs rather than outputs, they may not accurately reflect the contribution of large firms to technical progress. This might be so, for example, if smaller firms conduct their R & D activity in a more informal way than larger firms so that R & D statistics tend to understate their research activity. Alternatively, there might be a difference in kind, with smaller firms tending to concentrate on invention and initial development and larger firms tending to concentrate more on expensive development for commercial exploitation. Also, larger firms might be inefficient users of research resources so that their predominant use of R & D inputs might overstate their innovation contribution. All these factors at least suggest some caution before one concludes that large firms are conducive to innovation. Second, aggregate figures give no indication of the importance of firm size *per se* in encouraging innovation. If the largest firms tend on average to operate in industries with greater technological opportunity or with more market power, then these factors might account for part of their greater research effort. Again, if larger firms tend on average to be more diversified (as, in fact, is the case) then their greater research activity may be associated with this. Clearly, therefore, a consideration of crude research–size relationships is insufficient to determine whether size *per se* confers an innovation advantage.

Second, more detailed studies that have been undertaken, mainly in the USA, suggest that within individual sectors there is no general tendency for innovational effort or output to increase with firm size. For example, Comanor (1967a) found, in a sample of 387 firms in 1955 and 1960, that research employment increased less than proportionately with total employment in seven out of 21 industry groups, and that in no case was a statistically significant positive firm size effect observed. Other studies have come .to similar conclusions. However, some studies have singled out the US chemical industry in particular as having more than proportionate research activity among larger firms.[17] Also, a number of authors have discerned a threshold effect, with research intensity rising up to some intermediate firm size but falling or remaining constant thereafter.[18] On balance, however, the available evidence fails to provide general support for a positive innovation–firm size effect.

Finally, we may briefly mention our second hypothesis, that innovation activity may be associated with conglomerate diversification. According to this argument, research activity is uncertain and the outputs generated in research may take the form of 'spin-offs' which have use in unexpected directions. Diversified firms operate in a number of markets and are thus more likely to be able to exploit new innovations in diverse fields. Therefore it is argued that diversified firms will have more incentive to innovate than specialized firms, and that they will correspondingly undertake more research activity.

As noted in section 7.2.2, Rosenberg's work, which associates higher research with firms that, on average, have smaller market shares in particular industries, might reflect such an effect in that such firms will on average be more diversified. Moreover, work by Grabowski (1968) has suggested that diversification had a statistically significant positive effect on R & D spending intensity in the chemicals and drugs industries in the USA in 1959–62 (although not in the petroleum industry). Unfortunately, this relationship may in fact reflect reverse causation, in that more diversification may result from the greater innovative activity of some firms rather than vice versa. As we shall see in chapter 9, a parallel literature exists which uses R & D intensity as a determinant of conglomerate diversification, and further discussion of this issue is reserved for that chapter.

7.3 Diffusion of New Techniques

Finally, we turn to the third stage of technical progress, diffusion. Most of the work in this field has looked at the speed of diffusion of *new techniques* in an industry, and we concentrate our attention therefore on such process innovations. Typically, new processes and techniques are developed by capital goods industries, and are adopted initially by a single firm in some other industry (the innovating firm) in order to reduce production costs. This gives the innovating firm a cost-reducing competitive advantage, which, however, is reduced over time as competing firms themselves adopt the new process and diffusion takes place. The speed of diffusion of new techniques varies widely for different techniques and in different industries, and our primary concern is to consider what factors (including market structure) influence the speed at which diffusion takes place in different industries.

An obvious first step is to consider how to measure the speed of diffusion. Much of the work in this field stems from an important paper by Mansfield (1961) which it is useful to consider in some detail. Mansfield looked at the diffusion of 12 techniques in four industries in the USA: bituminous coal, iron and steel, brewing, and railroads. His work, and indeed much other work since, suggests that, if one measures the proportion of firms that have adopted a technique in an industry plotted against time, then one typically observes a positively sloped S-shaped curve of the type shown in figure 7.5. This

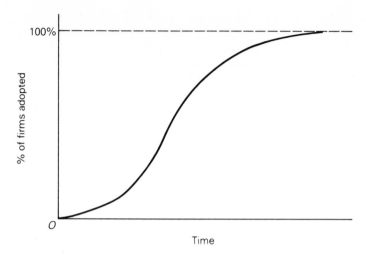

Figure 7.5

diffusion curve must obviously have a positive slope if one considers successful innovations. Its particular S-shape suggests that imitation proceeds relatively slowly at first as most firms are uncertain as to the innovation's worth and view it as a risky investment. After a time, however, as the process proves its worth and 'word gets around', diffusion speeds up. Finally, the speed of diffusion slows down again as the proportion of non-adopters is reduced, and as a few laggard firms eventually decide to make the switch-over.

In his study, Mansfield looked at larger firms in each industry and found a pattern similar to this for all 12 innovations. In particular he noted that:

(1) For the major innovations he examined, in four cases it took over 20 years for all his sample firms to adopt an innovation, and in only three cases was a period of less than ten years involved. Clearly, diffusion often takes a fairly long time to take place.

(2) Second, the variation between innovation's diffusion speeds was large. It took 15 years for 50 per cent adoption of the byproduct coke oven in his sample of large pig-iron producers, but only three years for 50 per cent adoption of continuous mining machinery by major coal producers. On average, 50 per cent adoption in the 12 innovations took 7.8 years with a range of 0.9–15 years.

In the first stage of his analysis, Mansfield developed a theory to explain the shape of the diffusion curve. Consider the jth innovation in the ith industry, and let n_{ij} be the total number of firms being considered. Define $m_{ij}(t)$ as the number of firms having adopted the process at time t, and $m_{ij}(t+1)$ as the number of firms having adopted at time $t+1$. Then the proportion of hold-out firms (i.e. firms who have not adopted) at time t who have adopted at time $t+1$ is

$$\lambda_{ij}(t) = \frac{m_{ij}(t+1) - m_{ij}(t)}{n_{ij} - m_{ij}(t)}. \tag{7.4}$$

Mansfield's basic hypothesis was that this proportion, $\lambda_{ij}(t)$, depends on

(1) the proportion of firms who had already adopted at time t, i.e. $m_{ij}(t)/n_{ij}$;
(2) the profitability of installation, π_{ij};
(3) the size of investment required for installation, S_{ij}; and
(4) other unspecified variables.

These effects will differ in different industries, so we have

$$\lambda_{ij}(t) = f_i\left[\frac{m_{ij}(t)}{n_{ij}}, \pi_{ij}, S_{ij}, \ldots\right]. \tag{7.5}$$

The rationale for this specification is as follows. First, the greater the proportion of firms having adopted, the more information and experience has accumulated on the innovation, and hence the less risky does subsequent adoption seem. Thus we predict that $\lambda_{ij}(t)$ increases with $m_{ij}(t)/n_{ij}$. Second, the more profitable the innovation, the more likely are firms' estimates of the risks of adoption likely to be outweighed, and hence $\lambda_{ij}(t)$ will increase with π_{ij}. Third, ceteris paribus, the larger the investment involved, the greater may be the subjective risks and the more difficult may it be to raise finance, so that $\lambda_{ij}(t)$ should fall as S_{ij} rises. And, finally, other variables will cause $\lambda_{ij}(t)$ to vary between industries. For example, firms in different industries may have different preferences towards risks. Or again, the age of existing capital equipment may influence the adoption decision. Or again, the strength of competitive pressures or their absence may influence adoption policies. We shall return to a consideration of other factors below.

Mansfield next proceeded by a series of mathematical manipulations and approximations to convert (7.5) into a usable form. As a result of these manipulations,[19] he obtained the equation

$$m_{ij}(t) = n_{ij}\{1 + \exp[-(l_{ij} + \phi_{ij}t)]\}^{-1} \tag{7.6}$$

where l_{ij} is a constant of integration, and ϕ_{ij} depends linearly on the variables in f_i of (7.5), excluding $m_{ij}(t)/n_{ij}$.

This result has two implications. First, equation (7.6) is the equation of a symmetrical S-shaped curve frequently used in biology and the social sciences called the *logistic curve*. This curve has been used extensively to model such things as epidemics, the spread of rumours, etc. In this context it suggests that the diffusion of new techniques, like epidemics, spreads slowly at first, then more quickly and then more slowly again, and this tallies well with the observed shape of the diffusion curve.[20] Second, the shape and position of the curve depends on only one parameter, ϕ_{ij}, which determines the rate of imitation. This parameter is a linear function of π_{ij} and S_{ij} if one confines all other variables to the disturbance term, z_{ij}; i.e.,

$$\phi_{ij} = a_{i1} + a_{i2}\pi_{ij} + a_{i3}S_{ij} + z_{ij} \tag{7.7}$$

Mansfield tested this model in two stages. First, he fitted logistic curves to the data on his 12 innovations to estimate ϕ_{ij}. This is done by rearranging (7.6) and taking logarithms (to base e) giving

$$\ln\left[\frac{m_{ij}(t)}{n_{ij} - m_{ij}(t)}\right] = l_{ij} + \phi_{ij}t \tag{7.8}$$

Measuring t in years, he then estimated ϕ_{ij} in each case using least squares regression. These estimates ranged from 0.17 to 0.63, with one outlier (the tin container) having $\hat{\phi}_{ij} = 2.64$, indicating particularly fast diffusion in this case. Mansfield found that the fitted curves gave a good representation of the actual curves in most cases, although he did note some problems with the railroad innovations, of which there were three.

In the second stage of his analysis, he used the estimated parameters $\hat{\phi}_{ij}$ derived from his time series analysis in equation (7.7) on cross-section data. The profitability variable, π_{ij}, was measured as the ratio of the average payback period required by firms to the average payback period for each innovation. The size of investment variable, S_{ij}, was taken as the average initial investment in the relevant period. Mansfield thus had 12 observations corresponding to the number of innovations, and in addition to the two explanatory variables he allowed the intercepts to vary according to industry, presumably using dummy variables. His fitted equation (with t ratios in parentheses) was

$$\hat{\phi}_{ij} = \begin{pmatrix} -0.29 \\ -0.57 \\ -0.52 \\ -0.59 \end{pmatrix} + 0.53\pi_{ij} - 0.027S_{ij} \qquad R^2 = 0.994 \tag{7.9}$$
$$\phantom{\hat{\phi}_{ij} = \begin{pmatrix} -0.29 \\ -0.57 \\ -0.52 \end{pmatrix}} (35.33) \quad (-1.93)$$

where the intercepts refer to brewing, coal, steel and railroads, respectively. The following conclusions emerge.

(1) The model provided a good fit to the data as measured by R^2. This remained true if the extreme observation (tin containers) was omitted.
(2) The coefficients on π_{ij} and S_{ij} had the expected signs and were significantly different from zero on a one-tail test at the 5 per cent level despite having only six degrees of freedom. When tin containers was omitted, however, S_{ij} was no longer significantly different from zero. This evidence supports

the view that the rate of diffusion rises with innovation profitability and falls as the costs of installation rise.

(3) *Ceteris paribus*, the rate of diffusion was particularly fast in brewing, as indicated by the estimates of the intercepts. Mansfield went on to suggest that the pattern of intercepts found was consistent with the view that the rate of imitation was faster in more competitive industries. Clearly, however, observations on more industries are required before one can pass judgement on this issue.

Finally, Mansfield also considered several other variables which might influence the speed of diffusion in different circumstances. Given the limited sample size, he introduced these variables singly into his basic equation (7.9), and while he found some support for them, he was unable to get significant results in any case. Briefly, the variables and results were as follows.

First, to take account of the fact that firms might be loathe to scrap equipment which is durable, Mansfield introduced a variable which measured the typical period that elapsed before the innovation appeared in the industry. This variable had a negative effect on the rate of imitation $\hat{\phi}_{ij}$ when introduced in equation (7.9) with a coefficient of -0.0017 (with t ratio -1.21). The sign is as expected but is not statistically significant.

Second, Mansfield argued that fast market growth will favour diffusion, as in such circumstances new capacity will be installed using the new process. This he measured by the annual rate of growth of industry sales. A positive but non-significant effect was observed with a coefficient of $+0.042$ (1.62).

Third, he considered the possibility that, over time, developments in communications channels and investment appraisal techniques, together with attitudes towards change, may have meant that more recent innovations were diffused more quickly. This effect was measured by the year of innovation and a positive but non-significant effect was observed: $+0.0014$ (1.00).

Finally, he argued that diffusion might be faster if the innovation was introduced in the expansion rather than the contraction phase of the business cycle. This was measured by a dummy variable taking a value 1 for expansion. This variable had the wrong sign but was very close to zero: -0.022 (0.49). Clearly, these hypotheses are of considerable interest from a policy point of view, but Mansfield had insufficient data to test them conclusively.

A number of other studies have followed and extended Mansfield's work, but we shall confine our attention to just two studies here. First, Davies (1979a) examined the diffusion of 22 postwar process innovations in 13 different industries in the UK. Using a more sophisticated theoretical approach than did Mansfield, Davies distinguished between relatively simple (group A) and more complex and expensive (group B) innovations, arguing that an earlier peaking diffusion curve would be appropriate in the former case compared with the latter.[21]

After fitting diffusion curves to each group of innovations, he found that

Table 7.3 Determinants of diffusion speed

Explanatory variable	Type of innovation	Estimated elasticities
π	A	−0.377
	B	−0.725
L	A	0.771
	B	0.876
δ	A	0.006
	B	0.013
N	A	−0.319
	B	−0.198
σ^2	A	−0.215
	B	−0.176

Source: Davies (1979a, table 7.4, p. 137); for explanation see text.

there were five major determinants of diffusion speed in each case. Table 7.3 shows Davies's estimates of the elasticity of the speed of diffusion with respect to each of these variables. They are, in order: the profitability of the innovation (measured inversely as the typical payback period), π; labour intensity in the industry, L; industry growth, δ; firm numbers, N; and the variance of the logarithms of firm size, σ^2. As can be seen, diffusion tended to be quicker for both groups of innovation the more profitable was the innovation, the more labour-intensive it was, the faster was industry growth, the smaller the number of firms and the smaller were firm size differences (as measured by σ^2). Results for both groups of innovation were similar, although complex and expensive (group B) innovations appeared to be much more sensitive to variations in profitability.

Davies's results on market structure and diffusion are of particular interest. As far as firm numbers are concerned, it might be argued that the competitive pressures of many firms tend to speed imitation and the rate of diffusion of new innovations. On the other hand, as Davies pointed out, industries with many firms are likely to suffer from poor communications and slow information flows which tend to retard diffusion. Again, as far as firm size inequality is concerned, Davies argued that inter-firm differences in firms' expectations, goals, etc., associated with differences in firm size tend to imply that diffusion will be slower the less equal in size are firms. The results reported in table 7.3 support this latter hypothesis, and suggest that Davies's argument concerning information problems with more firms is also important. Indeed, this latter effect was one of the stronger statistical results obtained by Davies. Hence, his results suggest that a trade-off exists with respect to market concentration and diffusion, with fewer firms but firms of less unequal size tending to be associated with faster diffusion.

The effect of market structure on diffusion speed has also been examined by Romeo (1977) (see also Romeo, 1975). He looked at the diffusion of a single innovation (the numerically controlled machine tool) in ten US industries in 1951–70. Following Mansfield's approach, he found in logarithmic cross-section regression (with t ratios in parentheses) that

$$\ln \hat{\phi}_i = -3.70 + 0.47 \ln X_{1i} - 0.28 \ln X_{2i} + 0.34 \ln X_{3i} \qquad (7.10)$$
$$\quad (-3.41) \quad (1.74) \qquad (-2.08) \qquad (3.11)$$
$$\quad + 0.18 \ln X_{4i} - 0.47 \ln X_{5i}$$
$$\quad \quad (1.76) \qquad (-7.46)$$
$$\bar{R}^2 = 0.892.$$

where, for industry i, $\hat{\phi}_i$ is the estimated rate of diffusion, X_{1i} is the average rate of return, X_{2i} is the size of investment required for the innovation, X_{3i} is the year the innovation was first adopted in the industry, and X_{4i} and X_{5i} are, respectively, firm numbers and the variance of log firm size. As expected, profitability (X_{1i}) enhanced and the costs of installation (X_{2i}) retarded the speed of diffusion in equation (7.10) while the later the date of first adoption in an industry (X_{3i}) the faster was diffusion (reflecting general learning effects). In contrast to Davies's results, however, larger firm numbers were conducive to faster diffusion in Romeo's sample, tending to support the view that more firms create greater competitive pressure for faster diffusion. This result, combined with the strongly significant negative effect of firm size inequality on diffusion speed in equation (7.10), suggests an unambiguous negative association between diffusion speed and market concentration. It is clearly too early to say, however, whether this effect or the more complex one discovered by Davies applies more generally to the diffusion of new process innovations.

7.4 Summary and Conclusions

In this chapter we have examined the economics of technical progress and considered its possible relationship to economic conditions in the market. In section 7.1 we looked at some basic features of research activity, suggesting in particular that natural and institutional factors can lead to an under-investment in research in a market economy. Then, in section 7.2, we examined the particular role of market structure and, more briefly, firm size and conglomerate diversification in the innovation process. This section suggested that some evidence of a positive relationship between R & D activity and market concentration existed, with less evidence of a positive innovation–firm size effect. Finally, in section 7.3 we examined theory and evidence on the diffusion of new techniques, pointing in particular to the role of profitability and cost of installation as determinants of the speed at which diffusion takes place.

Relationships between research activity, technical progress and market conditions are both dynamic and complex, and it seems unlikely that hard and fast rules can be derived. Available evidence does suggest, however, that some degree of market concentration can be favourable to research activity (but probably not to the diffusion of new techniques). Hence a basis for a Schumpeterian trade-off between static and dynamic efficiency exists, and this may qualify traditional arguments condemning monopoly and high concentration. Such a possibility should clearly be borne in mind in discussion of policy matters, and most particularly with respect to measurement of monopoly welfare losses and monopoly and mergers policy which are discussed in chapters 10 and 12 below.

Notes

1 This statement must, of course, be qualified where, for example, preferences might be distorted by advertising, or, alternatively, if consumers are viewed as not always being the best judge of their own welfare, e.g. in the consumption of cigarettes or drugs. The statement also ignores other possible detrimental effects (e.g. externalities or changes in working conditions) associated with the introduction of a new product.

2 See *Annual Abstract of Statistics* (HMSO), 1982, table 11.11.

3 The basic data source is *Industrial Research and Development Expenditure and Employment, 1978*, Business Monitor MO14 (HMSO), 1980.

4 An even stronger correlation is obtained if Y is measured as (private-company-funded) R & D as a proportion of net output. With the same 29 observations we find

$$Y = -0.94 + 0.08X \qquad r^2 = 0.338$$
$$(-0.93) \quad (3.71)$$

5 Less radical reforms such as compulsory patent licensing have been extensively discussed, however. For a review of the possibilities see Taylor and Silberston (1973).

6 Following Arrow, we refer to the 'incentives for invention' in this section. It is clear, however, that the argument concerns the commercial application of an idea, so that 'incentives for innovation or development' might represent more appropriate terminology.

7 This diagram is originally due to Demsetz (1969, p. 177).

8 Demsetz, in fact, views this asymmetry in terms of an independent inventor being able to choose different royalty payments systems for the two types of industry. In these terms, the inventor can be viewed as using a royalty per unit of output in the competitive industry but a fixed royalty payment in the monopolized industry.

9 Such a benefit may not occur when the invention is embodied in an input which can be used in variable proportions in producing the final output. For an analysis of this more complex case see Waterson (1982a).

10 For a useful survey of the literature see Kamien and Schwartz (1982, chapters 1–3).

11 In an international context, however, with scientists being attracted by high salaries overseas, this effect may offer benefits from a narrower national perspective if it tends to restrict the outflow.

12 In another study Scherer examined links between patenting of leading firms and

concentration in US industry in the early 1950s, but with statistically insignificant results: see Scherer (1965b).

13 Scherer used dummy variables (i.e. variables which take zero or one values) for his technological opportunity classes and also for variables $D1$–$D3$. No statistically significant effects are observed for the latter variables. Note also that by omitting the variable for general and mechanical industries, Scherer measured research employment relative to this class for the other technological opportunity classes. See Wonnacott and Wonnacott (1972), pp. 308–13 for details on dummy variables.

14 For a recent statement of this view, see Dasgupta and Stiglitz (1980).

15 For a survey see Kamien and Schwartz (1982, chapter 3).

16 See *Industrial Research and Development Expenditure and Employment, 1978*, table 13, and *Report of the Census of Production*, 1978, summary table 1. The R & D data are not, in fact, confined to manufacturing industries, but the discrepancy involved is likely to be minor.

17 See, for example, Scherer (1965a).

18 See, for example, Scherer (1965a) and Loeb and Lin (1977).

19 Specifically, he treated $m_{ij}(t)$ as a continuous variable, and used a Taylor's expansion of equation (7.5), dropping third and higher-order terms. In addition, since in his empirical work the coefficient on $[m_{ij}(t)/n_{ij}]^2$ in this expansion was zero, he also suppressed this term. Further, by treating time as continuous, this expansion can be approximated by a differential equation. The solution to this equation (with an initial condition that $m_{ij}(t)$ goes to zero as time goes to minus infinity) gives (7.6).

20 It should be noted, however, that the logistic model implies that the diffusion process is homogeneous both between firms and over time. For further discussion of these weaknesses see Davies (1979a), chapter 2.

21 Davies in fact fitted cumulative lognormal and cumulative normal curves to group A and group B innovations, respectively. For group A innovations, the cumulative lognormal curve has the properties that the increase in adopters peaks earlier and then slows down more markedly, and Davies argued that such a curve fitted the more rapid but less sustained post-innovation improvements found to be more typical of relatively simple (group A) innovations.

8 Vertical Integration

Much of the analysis in previous chapters has been concerned with the structure, conduct and performance of individual markets. In practice, however, many firms, and particularly the largest firms, operate in a number of markets, and this too may affect market conduct and performance. Consequently we examine wider issues of multi-market operation in this and the next chapter.

We begin in this chapter by considering vertical integration, i.e. operation in successive markets, leaving wider issues of conglomerate diversification to chapter 9. In both cases, however, a primary concern will be with possible market power and related effects arising from multi-market operation. We shall see that, in each case, there are some grounds for public policy concern, although the case for general policy action is not clear-cut. This ambivalence is reflected to some extent in current UK policy in these areas, which tends to favour case-by-case investigations rather than general prohibitions (see chapters 11 and 12 below).

In this chapter we shall examine various aspects of vertical integration. We begin in section 8.1 by briefly considering the nature and extent of integration. Sections 8.2 and 8.3 then consider theories of vertical integration, where for convenience we separate general and specifically monopolistic theories between these sections. We shall see that a variety of reasons for integration exist, and possible public policy implications of the various theories are discussed as appropriate as we proceed.

8.1 Nature and Extent of Vertical Integration

The term 'vertical integration' is used in two distinct ways in industrial economics. First, it relates to an existing state or organizational structure. In this sense it refers to the extent to which a single business unit carries on successive stages in the processing and distribution of a product. In addition, however, the term is used to refer to behaviour or conduct. In this sense, it refers to the action of a firm in moving into another processing or distributing stage, either via vertical merger or by setting up new production or distribution facilities. When a firm moves into production of raw materials and inputs, *backward (or upstream) integration* is said to take place; while a move towards final production and distribution is called *forward (or downstream) integration.*

Vertical integration (in the structural sense) can be taken as the converse of specialization. A firm is completely specialized if it undertakes only a single process or function in the production chain. Many small firms, such as small retailers or component makers, might be classified as specialized on this definition. Specialization is likely to be only relative, however, since almost all firms in fact undertake several activities which could be undertaken by separate firms. One only has to think of separate functions such as accounting, marketing, typing, etc., to realize that few (if any) firms are completely specialized. On the other hand, there is a quantitative difference between small firms which undertake their own typing services and so on and firms which engage in many stages of production and distribution, such as car-makers or petroleum producers. In these cases, integration extends beyond ancillary or support services, to take in production of major raw materials and components and/or further production and distribution. It is these more extensive cases of vertical integration with which we are principally concerned in this chapter.

The distinguishing feature of vertical integration is that it involves direction of economic activities within a firm. Following the seminal work of Coase (1937), one can distinguish between market and entrepreneurial coordination in the economy. Many transactions take place in the market and are coordinated by the price mechanism (Adam Smith's *invisible hand*). Within a firm, however, the price mechanism is superseded by entrepreneurial control of economic activity. With regard to vertical integration this means that, instead of buying inputs and selling outputs on an open market, firms undertake to make the input or use the outputs themselves. As we discuss further in section 8.2.1, the decision to integrate vertically is ultimately a decision over whether to use market transactions or not. For a profit-maximizing firm this, by definition, involves an appraisal of the profitability of employing the alternative means of transacting.

It is important to recognize a further distinction which may be relevant in certain circumstances. Not all markets are perfect, and there are relatively few instances in which pure, impersonal transactions are made to buy inputs or sell outputs. In many markets, transactions are coordinated between limited numbers of firms and on a continuing basis. Contracts are drawn up and some degree of cooperation between firms is likely to arise with respect to vertical relationships. This is particularly likely to be the case in successive monopoly (or oligopoly) situations, where (as we shall see in section 8.3.2) firms will have a strong incentive to coordinate policies. More generally, however, there may be incentives for vertical coordination which need not require that vertical integration actually takes place. Hence in some circumstances the distinction between vertical integration and the market may be artificial for purposes of analysis. This argument, of course, parallels the argument over oligopolistic cooperation and monopolization at a single stage of production discussed in chapter 3 above. For present purposes we merely note that undue emphasis on vertical integration as such may not be warranted in some situations.

Very little systematic evidence is available on the extent of vertical integration. In a study of 111 large US corporations in 1954 Gort (1962) attempted to classify firm four-digit product activities into primary and 'auxiliary' categories. Integration was then measured as the ratio of employment in auxiliary activities to total employment for the firm. Taking averages for firms in 13 industry groups, he found that integration (as might be expected) was far and away the highest in the petroleum industry, with a ratio of 67.3 per cent. It was also relatively high in food product industries (30.3 per cent) and machinery industries (30.5 per cent). More specialized industries, on the other hand, were fabricated metal products, electrical machinery and transportation equipment, with ratios of 15.0, 12.8 and 9.7 per cent respectively.

Similar evidence is not available for the UK. However, it is well known that, in addition to the petroleum industry, vertical integration is an important feature of such industries as iron and steel, motor assembly, footwear, brewing, flour milling and baking, and man-made fibres, to name but a few. While in many cases vertical integration has been a long-term feature of economic organization, this is not always the case. For example, a substantial increase in vertical integration in flour milling and baking occurred in the late 1950s/early 1960s owing to forward integration by leading millers Ranks and Spillers (Hart and Clarke, 1980, p. 67). And probably more important quantitatively were the dramatic changes observed in many textile industries in the 1960s and early 1970s occasioned by the forward integration of man-made fibres producer, Courtaulds.[1] As is noted in chapter 9 below, it seems likely that Courtauld's integration policies had a dramatic impact on market structure in this area of UK manufacturing industry.

Clearly, vertical integration can have an important impact on industrial structure and may give rise to policy concern purely from its horizontal effects. In what follows, however, we will be concerned less with such horizontal effects than with the effects of integration itself. Such effects follow most straightforwardly from a consideration of the various theories of integration, and it is to these which we now turn.

8.2 Theories of Vertical Integration

A great number of possible motives for vertical integration exist.[2] Firms may, for example, integrate vertically for tax reasons – to circumvent sales taxes, etc., by replacing taxable market transactions by internal transactions. Or they may integrate vertically to extend their ability to engage in price discrimination or to erect barriers to entry. Again, they may hope to achieve technological cost savings from integration or alternatively to guarantee input supplies or output markets. And they may hope to extend their monopoly power by preventing substitution away from their product or by eliminating wasteful cumulation of markups at successive stages of production or distribution.

In this section and the next we consider some of these hypotheses. In section 8.3 we consider possible 'monopolistic' motives for integration in markets where some degree of monopoly power exists. In contrast, in this section we consider some alternative explanations which do not rely specifically on market power considerations. In section 8.2.1 we consider the market failures framework for analysing vertical integration, while in section 8.2.2 we look at more specific explanations relating to technological interdependence and uncertainty. Finally, in section 8.2.3 we briefly examine a broader 'life-cycle' hypothesis of vertical integration suggested by Stigler.

8.2.1 Market Failures Considerations

As noted in section 8.1, a distinction can be drawn between vertical coordination and vertical integration. Cost savings, uncertainty, monopoly, etc., can all provide incentives for vertical coordination. Such coordination may, however, be achieved by cooperation between independent business units or by integration of activities under single business control.[3] The choice between integration and the market (including cooperation possibilities) is a secondary choice over which organizational form best secures vertical coordination. It is this secondary choice which is the focus of attention of the market failures approach to vertical integration.

The approach derives initially from the work of Coase (1937). In his classic analysis of the firm, Coase distinguished between market coordination and entrepreneurial coordination of economic activity. In his view, the distinguishing characteristic of a firm was that it grouped economic activities under entrepreneurial rather than market control. Consequently, the question arose as to why the market should be superseded; i.e., why do firms exist? Coase's answer to this question was that costs of market transactions could be avoided by coordination of activities within a firm. When market transactions costs are high, the market fails as an efficient means of coordinating economic activity and transactions are therefore internalized within a firm.

This argument has immediate application to vertical integration. Consider a firm operating at one or more stages in a production chain, carrying out some activities internally, while in other cases buying input services and selling outputs on the market. Ultimately, the decision whether to make-or-buy/use-or-sell will turn (for a profit-maximizing firm) on the relative costs of the alternative methods of coordinating activity (or, more generally, on the relative profits of each alternative). Coase argues that the firm will encompass new activities to the point where the cost of coordinating the next activity internally just equals the cost of market coordination. Factors tending to increase integration will be such things as costs of discovering market prices and negotiation costs in arriving at market contracts. On the other hand, factors which tend to limit integration will be diminishing returns to the entrepreneurial function and the increasing likelihood of entrepreneurial mistakes as more activities are encompassed. In Coase's view, an equilibrium degree of vertical integration would arise which would give (under competitive conditions) the most efficient organization of production and distribution.

Coase's work has been developed in particular by Williamson (1971, 1973, 1975).[4] Given that market transactions costs induce firms to integrate vertically, Williamson considers in detail the factors which lead to relatively high market transactions costs and so to vertical integration. In particular, he focuses on the human factors which, together with environmental factors, combine to explain market failure. In contrast to standard economic assumptions, Williamson suggests that certain elementary human attributes, not normally considered, may be of great importance. Of these he singles out opportunism (i.e., the tendency to take advantage of profitable opportunities with guile) and bounded rationality (i.e., human inability to cope with large decision-making problems). These human factors interact with environmental factors, such as uncertainty and small numbers of parties to transactions, to produce market failure and the substitution of internal organization for market coordination.

We can illustrate Williamson's approach by considering the case of the production of a technically complex product for which periodic redesign and/or volume changes are made. Some components for this product are produced with large-scale economies relative to market size dictating small numbers of producers for these components. Three alternative supply arrangements can be considered: long-term contracts, short-term contracts and vertical integration.

The major problem with long-term contracts is that uncertainty of the future combines with bounded rationality to create problems in specifying future contingencies. It is impossible, or at least prohibitively costly, to write a comprehensive contract to cover all contingencies. Hence long-term contracts must be incomplete, and this may create room for opportunistic bargaining should ambiguities arise. Short-term contracts have an advantage over long-term contracts in an uncertain environment in that they permit sequential decision-making to be made which economizes on bounded rationality. They may not be appropriate where component industries must invest in long-life equipment, however. Moreover, if early contract winners acquire specific cost advantages over rivals ('first-mover' advantages) this may give scope for costly haggling between buyers and suppliers at contract renewal times (since such suppliers obtain monopolistic advantages over other suppliers owing to their previous expertise).

Hence it may be desirable, under conditions of uncertainty and small numbers bargaining, to integrate vertically. Internal organization permits adaptive, sequential decision-making and, moreover, is likely to reduce problems of opportunism. Williamson argues that a firm will organize as a complex hierarchy, in which managers as well as workers accept an employment contract. In such an organization, more cooperative behaviour between previously antagonistic parties is likely to be induced as individuals become part of a team and individualistic, self-seeking behaviour is curbed. Also, within an organization disputes can be settled more readily by fiat, hence avoiding costly haggling which might arise with inter-firm disputes. More cooperative attitudes, combined with efficient internal control machinery and sequential decision-making, may make vertical integration an appropriate choice compared with market coordination alternatives.[5]

Clearly, Williamson's analysis is rich in insight into the transactional motives for vertical integration. At the same time, however, it is important to stress again the rather special nature of the approach. By concentrating on the vertical integration *qua* integration, the market failures approach is concerned with the decision to integrate or cooperate given that an incentive to vertical coordination exists. Hence it is consistent with various explanations of an incentive for vertical coordination. For example, if there are technological interdependencies (see section 8.2.2) or, alternatively, successive monopolies in production (see section 8.3.1), then an incentive exists for coordination of successive production stages. Such coordination can, nevertheless, take place through market contracts, and there is no need for integration to internalize transactions. Thus, for example, cost savings associated with integrating several stages of production, as in steel-making, dictate a common location for production but not necessarily integration of the firm. Likewise, decisions to maximize joint profits in the case of successive monopolies can be made with negotiation and need not imply vertical integration. The decision to integrate vertically in each case is taken for transactions cost reasons (to economize on costs of market transactions), and this is ultimately a decision over efficient organizational form.

While the market failures framework incorporates other theories of vertical integration, one can also ask whether it adds new theoretical insights of its own. A basic criticism of Coase's original discussion of the nature of the firm is that it was basically descriptive and that it lacked operational content in the sense of providing additional hypotheses which might be tested against empirical evidence. Williamson's work can be criticized as being largely non-operational in that transactions costs associated with uncertainty and small numbers are very difficult to measure. Some recent work[6] has attempted to develop some testable predictions based on market transactions cost considerations and it may be that more developments along these lines can be made. In our present state of knowledge, however, we have no way of knowing how important transactions cost considerations are in explaining vertical integration. Hence we do not know how far (if at all) they add to other explanations considered in the remainder of this chapter.

8.2.2 Technological Interdependence and Uncertainty

We now consider more specific explanations of vertical integration. While market transactions costs arising from small numbers conditions and bounded rationality induce firms to integrate rather than engage in market transactions, these factors alone do not explain the pattern of integration observed in the economy. In this section we consider more immediate causes relating to technological interdependencies and uncertainty in markets.

Technological interdependence   The simplest explanation of vertical integration is that technological interdependence in production processes provides an incentive for vertical integration. The standard example of this is the case of iron and steel production. Production of steel involves a number of processes which we can classify for simplicity as coking, sintering, iron-making, steel-making and initial rolling. These processes are interdependent in the sense that handling and heating costs are reduced by undertaking them in close proximity. In particular, the need to process iron and steel at very high temperatures means that there are considerable thermal efficiencies derived from integrated production. Such technological economies dictate that steel-making be carried out typically in a single plant. And integration is typically in a single firm as well, for the reasons discussed in section 8.2.1.

There are many examples of vertical integration of production processes for reasons of technological interdependence. Thermal economies are also important in other metal industries. Similarly, pulping and newsprint production are typically integrated to avoid costs of drying and reconstituting materials. More generally, handling and other costs are frequently reduced by integration in many chemical processes, such as petroleum refining. Many of these industries involve flow process operations, and technological economies of integration most often appear in these circumstances.

Uncertainty   A standard explanation of vertical integration employed by businessmen is that it is undertaken in order to obtain a more certain supply of inputs or a more certain market for outputs. This explanation may incorporate monopolistic incentives for integration which we consider further in section 8.3. At the moment, however, we restrict our attention to seemingly competitive markets (i.e. markets with large numbers of buyers and sellers) and consider this proposed motive for integration independently. Under conventional assumptions, it would seem that there is no incentive for vertical integration in competitive markets in the absence of cost savings since all inputs and outputs can be purchased openly at market-determined prices. This argument, however, ignores the problem of uncertainty in otherwise competitive markets, and several writers have suggested that this problem may provide an explanation of vertical integration.

One possibility suggested by Arrow (1975) is that there may be an information asymmetry between upstream and downstream producers which provides an incentive for vertical integration to improve resource allocation in the two stages. In Arrow's analysis, downstream firms have limited information on a raw material price and this hampers their ability to make efficient decisions on the input proportions to use in production. Arrow assumes that upstream producers of the raw material are better informed than the downstream firms. The latter therefore have an obvious incentive to integrate backward to acquire upstream firms in order to get a better forecast of raw material prices. In this model the ability to forecast material prices improves as more raw material producers are acquired, so that a natural tendency to the monopoly acquisition of upstream firms exists. This in turn implies that downstream production will also be monopolized, and so there is an inevitable tendency to unitary supply in the two production stages in this model.

A second possibility, which we consider more thoroughly, has been discussed by Carlton (1979). In his analysis uncertainty combines with rigidities in competitive markets to provide an incentive for vertical integration. This model suggests directly that downstream firms may integrate backward to secure uncertain input supplies. It thus appears to accord with businessmen's explanations of backward integration, and hence justifies detailed examination.

Consider first a single market with uncertain demand. Under conventional assumptions, market price adapts in each period to equate supply and

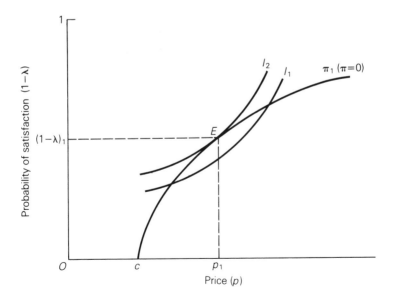

Figure 8.1

demand to clear the market. In many otherwise competitive markets, however, price adjustments are not as instantaneous as the theory assumes, and, moreover, production cannot be adjusted instantaneously to meet demand at the market price. Hence the possibility arises that demand will not equal supply in any market period, i.e. that there will be either under- or overproduction of the product relative to demand. From the point of view of a customer, therefore, there is a chance that he will be unable to obtain a good in the current period, while a seller bears the risk of overproduction and having unsold goods.

These possibilities have important implications. If we assume, for simplicity, that all firms and customers are identical, then we can consider market equilibrium in terms of a typical firm (see figure 8.1). Since, in general, markets will not be cleared, firms compete not only on price but also on reliability of supply.[7] From the point of view of buyers, utility depends on market price, p, and the probability of obtaining the good from the firm, $1 - \lambda$. We can, therefore, draw indifference curves for customers in $(p, 1 - \lambda)$ space. These curves will slope upward such that a higher probability of satisfaction is needed to compensate consumers for higher prices. Two such curves are drawn as I_1 and I_2 in figure 8.1. On the supply side, the firm considers stocking or producing more of the good to better meet consumer demand but notes that as it does so it increases the risk of being left with unsold stocks. Consequently, the price it charges, p, must rise to cover such increased risks, and so we can draw an isoprofit curve for the firm also in $(p, 1 - \lambda)$ space. This too slopes upward in the relevant range, since higher prices are needed to offset a higher probability of consumer satisfaction, $(1 - \lambda)$, in order to leave expected profits unchanged.

Finally, we note that in a competitive market firms will compete till expected profits, π, are zero. The appropriate isoprofit curve is shown as π_1 in figure 8.1. If the product is produced at constant unit cost, c, then for any production at all there is some risk of unsold output, and so π_1 intersects the horizontal axis at c and thereafter slopes upward. Market equilibrium is shown at point E, where the highest consumer indifference curve I_2 is tangential to isoprofit curve π_1. In this equilibrium the trade-offs involved imply that some customers will not be satisfied in the current market period, i.e. that $(1 - \lambda)$ is less than one. Also, and most important, market price will exceed unit cost, c, reflecting the firms' risks of producing unsold goods in addition to the costs of simply producing the product.

We can now apply this analysis to vertical integration. Assume that downstream firms produce an output X using inputs A, B, C, etc., initially produced by upstream firms.[8] The demand for X is uncertain and consequently the derived demand for the inputs is also uncertain. If we focus on input A, the producers of A would initially bear the risk of overproduction of A and hence (as shown in figure 8.1) the price of A will exceed unit production cost; i.e., $p_1 > c$.

The question therefore becomes, Is there an incentive for downstream producers to integrate backward into production of input A? At first sight no such incentive would appear to exist since, while such integration enables downstream firms to produce the input at production cost, c, below market price, p_1, it also implies that they must take on the risk of overproduction of input A themselves. As shown by Carlton, however, an incentive for at least some backward integration may exist because a producer of X will make a *marginal* rather than an *average* decision in deciding to integrate backward. Specifically, it initially considers the expected savings and costs of producing input A corresponding to one unit of output, on the assumption that it uses that input to supply the first customer that it gets. Since the probability of getting at least one customer is likely to be very high, it almost certainly pays the firm to provide input A itself for that first unit of output. Similar marginal decisions are made for successive units of output, and vertical integration proceeds to the point where the expected marginal savings equal the cost of supplying extra quantities of input A. An appealing feature of this model is that downstream firms will use their own production of input A to satisfy their 'high probability' demand, while they may find it desirable to purchase additional requirements of the input from independent producers to meet 'low probability' demand.[9]

This model also has some interesting welfare implications. Carlton notes that one can differentiate firms in terms of their abilities to absorb risk in supplying input A by distinguishing the number of downstream producers, n_1, from the number of upstream producers of A, n_2. If $n_2 > n_1$, then downstream firms are better absorbers of risk (in the sense that they need hold less of the input in order to satisfy a given fraction of the population) and so it is socially efficient for vertical integration to take place. In this case the forces would combine to produce complete integration of downstream and upstream firms. However, if $n_1 > n_2$ such that upstream firms were more efficient risk-absorbers, then vertical integration will be socially inefficient and there will be higher total input costs to satisfy a given fraction of customers, and hence (given our competitive assumptions) lower expected customer utility. In this case vertical integration may be either partial or complete, but in either case the firm's private incentive to integrate in order to 'guarantee' input supply will be socially inefficient.

Welfare conclusions are, however, rarely clear-cut and this is also the case in the present instance. In particular, Carlton shows that vertically integrated firms are more likely to introduce a beneficial new technology than non-integrated firms. This is because integrated firms with control of input production will be able to (and will be forced by competition to) consider and adopt socially beneficial new technologies, while non-integrated firms (both upstream and downstream) may not receive appropriate market signals for a qualitative change of this type. Hence there may be dynamic efficiency advantages of vertical integration which may be set against any static inefficiencies associated with inefficient risk-bearing. This argument should not obscure the point, however, that private incentives to integrate to secure input supplies may exist when such integration is socially inefficient even though markets are essentially competitive.

8.2.3 Stigler's Life-cycle Hypothesis

A somewhat broader integration hypothesis has been suggested by Stigler (1951). Applying Adam Smith's dictum that 'the division of labour is limited by the extent of the market', Stigler suggested that the division of labour within an industry (or, conversely, the extent of vertical integration) will vary with industry size. This led him to the view that the degree of vertical integration in an industry will follow the life cycle of that industry with extensive vertical integration in new industries, followed by disintegration as an industry grows, and reintegration as it passes into decline. Some support for this hypothesis appears to exist in the histories of individual industries in the nineteenth and twentieth centuries, suggesting that it might provide a useful explanation of (long-term) changes in vertical integration.

Stigler's argument appears to turn on the diversity of cost–scale relationships which may exist in a particular industry. Suppose that an output X is produced in an industry from two intermediate inputs, A and B. Assume, for simplicity, that there are fixed input–output proportions and that costs of production of each input are independent of production of the other input. Finally, assume that input A is produced with substantial scale economies while input B is produced with modest scale economies. The situation for a typical firm is shown in figure 8.2, where unit cost curves for production of A and B as functions of output X are shown as AC_1 and AC_2 respectively. We assume that production of X from inputs A and B takes place with constant additional cost shown as AC_3. If a firm carries out all three activities (i.e. if it

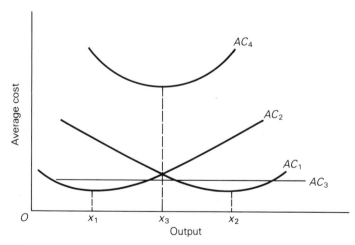

Figure 8.2

is vertically integrated), then the vertical sum of these curves, AC_4, gives the unit costs of an integrated firm on our assumptions.

According to Stigler's argument, a firm will tend to undertake all (or at least some) of the activities described above in the early and late stages of an industry's life cycle, but will tend to hive off activities in the middle stage when the market is large. The basis of Stigler's argument appears to be that input A requires a much larger production scale than input B for cost efficiency, such that technological factors dictate specialized production at different scales for each input. Given a sufficiently large market, activities with such diverse cost–scale relationships can be hived off to specialist producers (who presumably may have other advantages in specialized production compared with an integrated firm). In early and later stages of an industry's development, however, Stigler suggests that the market may be too small to support independent producers of A and B, and in this case integration is forced upon firms in the industry. It may also be the case in a new industry that lack of knowledge and other market imperfections force firms to undertake a number of disparate activities. In these circumstances, firms may not be able to obtain all the cost savings associated with the division of labour and so inefficient production takes place.

Despite the apparent plausibility of Stigler's hypothesis, it should be clear that his argument is not totally convincing. First, if we assume that he is considering basically competitive industries with a number of producers, then the argument of a small market preventing specialized production is not strong. While one firm may not be viable as a producer of input A for one producer of X, it is not clear that specialized production of input A for all producers of X would be so easily ruled out. Indeed, from a technological point of view, even in a small market it would pay to have specialized production of A (e.g. by a joint venture) to gain at least some economies of scale. As Williamson (1975) has suggested, if firms do stick to integrated production in these circumstances, then transactions cost considerations are likely to be at work. Second, and more generally, Stigler's argument relates more to advantages of having *non-integrated production*, with diverse cost–scale relationships, than to *integration within a firm*. Technological factors need not dictate disintegration of the firm in a large market since the firm can coordinate a number of disparate activities in plants of different size producing some outputs for its own needs and some for the open market. It may be, of course, that as the market grows it does become more efficient to buy in previously integrated services, but again this is a matter of relative reductions in market transactions costs rather than technological considerations *per se*.

8.3 'Monopolistic' Motives for Vertical Integration

We now consider possible 'monopolistic' motives for vertical integration. A strong tradition of research, closely associated with Chicago, has argued that vertical integration is not likely to be motivated by monopolistic considerations in many circumstances, and hence should not be the subject of public policy concern.[10] In addition, in cases where monopolistic incentives for integration do exist, it is argued that effects are not necessarily socially harmful. It appears, however, that these conclusions may be too sanguine and that there may be grounds for public concern in certain cases. The 'monopolistic' incentives for vertical integration are an active area of current research, and we consider some provisional results in what follows.

As soon as one drops competitive assumptions, the number of possible vertical integration models multiplies alarmingly. For example, with two production stages and the possibility of monopoly, oligopoly and competition at each production stage, nine possible models can be constructed. This calculation, moreover, ignores other variations, arising from, for example, price discrimination, entry barriers and so on. In what follows we simplify discussion somewhat by setting oligopoly on one side to consider models involving monopoly and competition only. In section 8.3.1 we consider the case of successive monopolies, while in section 8.3.2 we consider the case of an input monopolist and a competitive downstream industry. Finally, in section 8.3.3 we briefly consider possible entry barrier effects.

8.3.1 Successive Monopolies

We begin with the case of successive monopolies at several production stages. Two cases can be distinguished: (1) when there are successive monopolies but the downstream monopolist has no monopsony power in the input market, and (2) when monopsony power is also present so that there is bilateral monopoly in the input market.

Assume that an output X is produced using two inputs, A and B. Input B is produced competitively, but both input A and output X are produced monopolistically. In our first case it is assumed that the use of input A in the production of X is insignificant relative to total production of A. Hence the producer of X has no monopsony buying power over the purchase of input A but rather accepts the price of A as a given cost of production. In this case, therefore, the producer of A sets its price to maximize profits and the producer of X at the next stage likewise sets its price given the price of A.

Consider what happens if both monopolists act independently. We assume for simplicity (and without affecting the basic principle) that the inputs are combined in fixed proportions in the production of X. Figure 8.3 then illustrates the case where there is a constant marginal cost in the production of X, MC_x and a linear demand curve, D_x.[11] Given the assumption of fixed proportions, the input monopolist can raise the price of A to the point where the marginal cost of X shifts up to MC'_x. This policy would enable it to extract maximum monopoly profits equal to area $p_m abc$ from the industry if it were competitively organized such that it set price p_m equal to MC'_x. But production of X is monopolized, and given MC'_x, the producer of X will

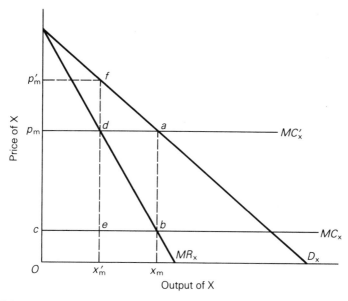

Figure 8.3

restrict output such that marginal revenue, MR_x, equals MC'_x, giving rise to price p'_m. If this outcome were to prevail, then the ultimate consumer would be doubly worse off in the presence of successive monopolies in that price markups are cumulated and prices above simple monopoly levels are set. It goes without saying that this will be the case *a fortiori* if there are more production stages and more monopolists.

As can be seen from figure 8.3, the restrictive policy of the second monopolist by reducing output of X to x'_m reduces the profits of the input monopolist from area $p_m abc$ to area $p_m dec$. Under the assumptions of linear market demand and constant marginal costs, area $p_m dec$ is half area $p_m abc$ (since MR_x falls at twice the rate of D_x). In this case, the monopolist input supplier will maximize its profit, given the policy of the second monopolist, by setting the marginal cost of X at MC'_x, since it thereby receives one-half of the maximum profit obtainable in the market.[12] While this represents a (non-cooperative) equilibrium, therefore, it is clear that, if the final price were set at p_m, then maximum profits would be extracted from the industry. An incentive, therefore, exists for cooperation between the monopolists, and while this may be obtained by negotiation, it may alternatively arise via vertical integration. In this case, vertical integration or cooperation to increase monopoly profits is also socially beneficial. In figure 8.3 the replacement of successive monopolies by a single integrated monopoly lowers output price to p_m giving ultimate consumers a consumer surplus gain of area $p'_m fap_m$. Also, monopoly profits are increased from a total of area $p'_m fec$ to area $p_m abc$. Given that area $p'_m fdp_m$ is a simple transfer from producer to consumer surplus, there is a net welfare gain from vertical integration equal to area *fabe*.

Now consider the second case, in which the producer of output X is also the sole purchaser of input A. In this case the producer of X has monopsony power in the purchase of A, so that in addition to successive monopolies we also have bilateral monopoly in the market for A. As we shall see, this complicates the analysis, although the above result that vertical integration may bring both private and social gains is essentially maintained.[13]

In order to analyse this case we switch attention to the market for input A. In addition, for reasons which will become clear in what follows, we now assume that input A is produced with increasing marginal cost, MC_A (see figure 8.4). Input A is combined as before in fixed proportions with input B to produce output X. It follows, therefore, that one can draw a unique derived demand curve for input A from the marginal revenue curve for output X.[14] This curve is shown as D_A in figure 8.4, with corresponding marginal revenue curve MR_A. Then if, as in the first case above, the input supplier alone had market power, it would set marginal revenue equal to marginal cost and produce output q_1 at price p_1.

Now, however, we assume that there is a single buyer of input A who recognizes that he has monopsony power. If input A was supplied com-

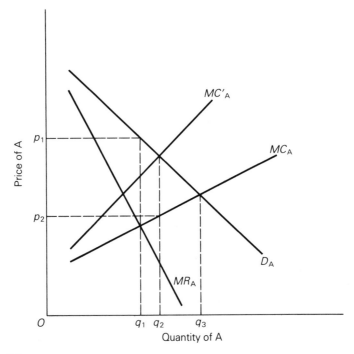

Figure 8.4

petitively according to curve MC_A, then a monopsonistic buyer would regard the curve marginal to this curve, MC'_A, as the marginal cost of buying an additional unit. Curve MC'_A rises faster than MC_A, reflecting the rising supply price (cost per unit of output) of A represented by curve MC_A. The monopsonist buyer would seek to set MC'_A equal to the marginal value of A (as represented by D_A) and buy output q_2 at price p_2.

Clearly, the monopsonistic buyer of A would seek to purchase at a lower price, p_2, than that at which the monopolistic seller would like to sell, p_1. The classic dilemma of bilateral monopoly thus ensues, with the actual price and quantity being determined by negotiation between the parties. In the vertical integration context, the combined interest of the monopolists is to set the industry profit-maximizing price and output for the final good X. Since the monopolist producer of X can alone extract this profit, this requires that production of A be at the competitive level given derived demand curve, D_A. An incentive, therefore, exists to set output q_3 such that D_A intersects MC_A, and this may be attained by negotiation or by vertical integration of the monopolists. In so far as bargaining under bilateral monopoly may tend to reduce output below q_3, both joint profits and economic welfare would be higher if vertical integration took place. Again, therefore, the idea of vertical integration to eradicate the cumulative exercise of monopoly power applies.

It is important to note in this context that vertical integration need not necessarily be required to increase profits and economic welfare. As noted above, vertical coordination rather than integration may produce a satisfactory solution to the successive monopoly problem. In the case illustrated in figure 8.4, for example, negotiation on both price and output is required to maximize joint profits. The parties must agree to transfer q_3 of input A, and a separate negotiation on price will determine the distribution of profits between them. Whether or not such a negotiation can be satisfactorily concluded will depend on market transactions cost considerations discussed in section 8.2.1. The decision to integrate rather than coordinate transactions with successive monopoly ultimately reflects market failure considerations.

8.3.2 Vertical Integration by a Monopolist

In contrast to the previous section, we now take a monopolist at one stage of production who considers vertical integration to another stage. In line with most of the work done on this issue, we assume that the monopolist is an input supplier considering forward integration into a competitive industry. Specifically, output X is initially produced by a competitive industry using two inputs A and B, where A is supplied by the monopolist and B is supplied competitively. The initial question to be answered is, Does the monopolist have an incentive to take over production of X? The answer to this question depends on whether the inputs are used in fixed or variable proportions in the production of X.

Consider first the case in which inputs A and B are combined in fixed

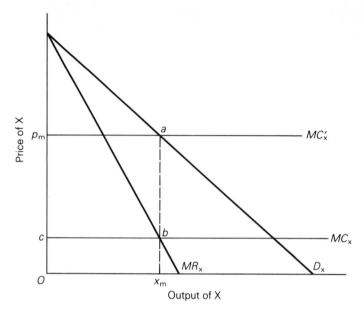

Figure 8.5

proportions to produce X. In this case the monopolist has no incentive to integrate forward since it can extract all monopoly profits from the market from its current position. This result is illustrated in figure 8.5.[15] Assume, as in figure 8.3, that market demand for X is linear (curve D_x) and that marginal costs in the production of X are constant (curve MC_x). This latter curve is in turn the vertical sum of constant marginal cost curves associated with each input, A and B (not drawn). If we take the post-integration situation first, then a monopolist producer of X would set marginal revenue (MR_x) equal to MC_x and produce output x_m at monopoly price p_m. Hence it would extract maximum profits from the industry equal to area $p_m abc$. Prior to integration, however, the monopolist producer of A could likewise extract these same profits (as we have seen) with no need to integrate forward. Specifically, it would raise the price of its input, p_A, above its marginal cost, MC_A, until the marginal cost of production of X was shifted up to MC_x' in figure 8.3. This too would produce an output x_m and price p_m (since price equals the marginal cost for X under competitive conditions). Input B would receive the same total revenue as before, and hence profits of area $p_m abc$ would go to the monopolist.

This is a basic result for fixed-proportions production technologies. When inputs are combined in fixed proportions to produce an output X, then a monopoly of any input is equivalent to a monopoly in production of X. Hence there is no monopolistic incentive for a producer of input A either to integrate forward into X production or, for that matter, to integrate laterally into production of B. Only in the case where the input monopolist is unable to extract full monopoly profits in its own market (e.g. owing to price regulation in that market) would forward or lateral integration be worthwhile. In the absence of such an effect, however, there is no 'monopolistic' incentive for vertical integration. This result, together with others discussed in section 8.3.1, forms the basis of the view discussed above that vertical integration for monopolistic motives is not a matter of public policy concern.

The argument does not apply when inputs are used in variable proportions in the production of X, however. Intuitively, if some substitutability between inputs A and B in the production of X is possible, then a monopolist of input A will find that a falling proportion of its input will be used as it raises its input price. Hence it will not be able to extract full monopoly profits from industry X, and so it has an incentive for vertical integration. This incentive, as we shall see, in part consists of an efficiency gain obtained by the removal of an input price distortion in downstream production. In addition, however, vertical integration may affect the price, and output, of X, further enhancing the incentive for integration.

The argument has been elegantly demonstrated by Vernon and Graham (1971) (see figure 8.6). In contrast to the L-shaped isoquants which would characterize a fixed-proportions technology, we now assume more conventional negatively sloped isoquants with a diminishing marginal rate of

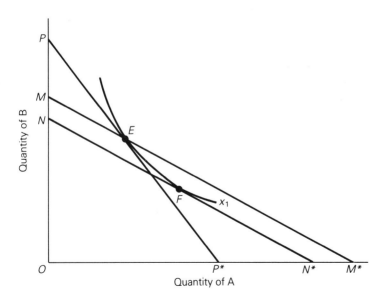

Figure 8.6

technical substitution (MRTS) between inputs. One such curve showing combinations of A and B that could be used to produce output level x_1 is drawn in figure 8.6. Prior to integration the input monopolist sets a price p_A above marginal cost MC_A, giving rise to an isocost line PP^* whose slope reflects the ratio of p_A to the marginal cost of B, MC_B. With this isocost line, the inputs will be used in the proportion E in producing output x_1. If the input A was supplied at marginal cost, however, the isocost lines would be less steeply sloped as MM^* and NN^*. By construction, MM^* is drawn through point E so that (measured in units of B) the input monopolist's profit is PM.[16] Now assume that integration takes place and the input price distortion is removed. Production of x_1 then takes place at point F and the integrated firm increases profit by MN (again in units of B). This increase in profit is always positive with variable proportions. Moreover, it is a minimum bound to the profit that the integrated monopolist may earn since it assumes an unchanged output x_1. If it is also optimal for the integrated monopolist to change the price and output of X, then profits must rise by more than MN.

The argument that a monopolist has an incentive to integrate forward with variable proportions need not imply that economic welfare is reduced. Indeed, in the case where there is no change in the price and output of X following integration, the monopolist merely increases profit by removing an input price distortion which previously applied to input A. Hence there is an improvement in resource allocation arising from vertical integration, the benefits of which flow entirely to the monopolist. Such a benefit is Pareto-efficient, although one may disagree on distributional grounds over how this gain should be shared. When the price of X does change, however, and in particular when it rises, consumer welfare will be affected and the welfare calculation becomes more complicated. It is then crucial to know how the price of X will change and how this relates to the overall welfare effect.

Unfortunately, the effect of vertical integration on the price of X and on economic welfare cannot be signed in general. However, Warren-Boulton (1974)[17] has considered an important special case of demand and production conditions which throws considerable light on these issues. Specifically, he assumes a model with a constant elasticity of substitution (CES) production function for X together with constant input costs and a constant elasticity of demand for X. This model permits considerable variation of parameters and, in particular, allows one to examine the effect of varying the elasticity of substitution between inputs, σ. Using a mixture of analytical and numerical analysis, Warren-Boulton examines, in particular, how increases in substitutability of inputs (with σ rising from zero to infinity) affects the price of X and economic welfare.

In the case when the elasticity of substitution is equal to one and the production function simplifies to the Cobb–Douglas form, vertical integration downstream by an input monopolist can be shown analytically to raise the final product price. On the basis of his numerical analysis, Warren-Boulton also shows that this result appears to hold for all values of the elasticity of substitution above zero. This is as might be expected since, with any substitution between inputs, the non-integrated monopolist is constrained in his ability to raise the input price, p_A, and thus the output price, p_x, would likely be below the full monopoly price.[18]

If vertical integration raises the output price, consumers are definitely made worse off. However, since vertical integration produces an improvement in efficiency, there is in addition a trade-off with respect to the overall welfare effect. Treating consumer and producer surplus equally for simplicity, Warren-Boulton finds (again on the basis of simulations) that, when the monopolist is able to set an unconstrained output price to maximize profits after integration, a low elasticity of substitution results in a welfare gain and a high elasticity of substitution in a welfare loss. In general, in the Cobb–Douglas case ($\sigma = 1$), vertical integration produces an overall welfare loss, and there is some critical value, σ_1, between zero and one (which depends on the values of the other parameters) above which profit-maximizing vertical integration produces an overall welfare loss. In this particular unconstrained case, therefore, it would seem that output price-raising effects of vertical integration are likely to outweigh efficiency gains where the elasticity of input substitution is in the neighbourhood of one or above. This finding, however, may be subject to an important technical proviso.[19]

These results are indicative of the effects of forward integration by an input monopolist; they show that, when inputs can be used in variable proportions, consumer surplus and overall welfare losses can be made. In practice, however, additional complications, such as downstream oligopolistic production and partial acquisition of downstream firms, must also be considered.[20] These problems, combined with the general complexity of the basic problem, mean that simple rules on the welfare effect of vertical integration are difficult to formulate. Roughly speaking, 'noticeable' increases in output prices and 'moderate' substitutability of inputs might suggest cause for policy concern over vertical integration, but it is difficult to be more specific. The analysis does suggest, however, that output price controls will be a sufficient condition to ensure beneficial welfare effects from vertical integration in this case.

The major example of forward integration by a monopolist in recent years in UK industry relates to the case of the rayon producer, Courtaulds. Rayon is a man-made cellulosic fibre which serves as an input, together with natural fibres (wool, cotton, etc.) and synthetic fibres (e.g. nylon), into the textile industry. In many uses, rayon is highly substitutable with other fibres so that its use in textiles is sensitive to its price. The above analysis would suggest an incentive for Courtaulds to integrate forward into textiles, and in fact this is what happened. Cowling *et al.* (1980) show that from 1963 to 1974 Courtaulds took over large portions of various textile industries (spinning, weaving, knitting, etc.) by an active policy of acquisition (although some new investments, e.g. in weaving, were also made). On a prima facie basis, it would seem that the motive for these moves was clear: to extend monopoly power by vertical integration and increase usage of rayon in textile production.

Cowling *et al.*, however, were unable to discover such an effect, although the data they examined were highly aggregative and hence may not have been sufficiently sensitive to enable the effect to be isolated. Consequently we do not at present know if this was an important factor in Courtauld's policy, and *a fortiori* whether the social consequences of the policy were detrimental.

8.3.3 Barriers to Entry

It has been suggested that vertical integration of production may raise barriers to entry, and we briefly consider two possible arguments here.

When vertical integration occurs for efficiency reasons, non-integrated competitors may suffer a cost disadvantage at their stage of production. In addition, when input supplies on the one hand, or downstream production or distribution on the other, are controlled by an integrated firm, non-integrated firms may feel at a disadvantage. They may be subjected to predatory pricing tactics, unsatisfactory service or even refusal of supply. In all cases, there is an added risk of new entry in such a situation, and this may permit the integrated firm to extract larger long-run monopoly profits than might be possible without vertical integration.

One way to avoid these difficulties is for new entrants to enter in an integrated form matching the degree of integration of established firms. The standard argument against this possibility is that vertically integrated entry implies larger capital requirements than non-integrated entry, so that a capital requirements barrier to integrated entry may exist.[21] That is, a rising cost of capital and/or a complete inability of new entrants to be able to raise sufficient capital to enter on an integrated scale may protect the profits of established firms. As noted in chapter 4, however, while capital-raising problems may reduce the pool of potential entrants, they are most likely to affect potential small firm entrants. Larger firms may not be subject to the same capital market disadvantages as small firms, so that it is less clear that established integrated firms can make long-run profits without attracting entry. They may enjoy some slight advantage over all potential entrants, however, in that their established position in the market may in itself confer a cost-of-funds advantage over new entrants by reducing the subjective risks of lenders.

Capital requirements are not the only source of entry barriers to integrated entry. Another possibility arises when some stage of the production process is carried out under licence, and the barriers to entry which this implies are extended to another production stage by vertical integration. An example of this is the tied-house system operated in the brewing trade in the UK (see Monopolies Commission, 1969). In this case a limited number of licensed public houses exist and the majority of these are owned by brewers. By forward integration into these retail outlets the brewers ensure a captive market for their products. In addition, however, by refusing to carry brewing products from other brewers in their 'tied houses' (although with notable exceptions), they create a barrier to the entry of new brewers, thereby keeping up brewing margins. This system works imperfectly since a proportion of public houses are not tied ('free houses') and a new brewer can also produce for the carry-out trade. In addition, some brewing products may be accepted by tied houses, and the purchase of existing public houses (often in disadvantageous situations) may be possible. Nevertheless, established brewers' profits are typically above competitive levels, and there can be no doubt that the tied house system contributes to this result.

8.4 Summary and Conclusions

In this chapter we have considered the economics of vertical integration, whereby a single firm operates in two (or more) successive stages of production. We have seen that a variety of motives for such integration exist, and several of the many possibilities have been discussed. Ultimately, as noted in section 8.2.1, the decision to integrate is a decision to replace market transactions by internal coordination, and (for a profit-maximizing firm) such a decision is taken on the basis of reducing market transactions costs. This argument, therefore, underlies any decision formally to integrate activities within a firm rather than rely on market transactions and/or short- or long-term contracts with other firms.

Given this, however, various factors provide an incentive for vertical coordination and/or integration. Incentives for such integration may exist because of technological interdependencies or market uncertainty, or as a consequence of industry life-cycle considerations. Moreover, market power incentives for integration can also exist. Although such incentives are not necessarily socially harmful, there are some grounds for concern over monopolistic integration, particularly with respect to restraints on input substitution and also possible entry barrier effects.

At the present time, no consensus on the explanation for and effects of vertical integration has been reached. Clearly, vertical integration can be neutral in its effects or even socially beneficial (e.g. when cost savings are involved). In situations where harmful market power effects may arise, moreover, it seems desirable to consider possible problems on a case-by-case basis rather than by means of general rules. Such an approach in fact has been pursued to some extent in the UK (as noted in the introduction to this chapter), and this appears to be the most appropriate policy approach to vertical integration, given the complexity of the issues involved.

Notes

1 For further details see Monopolies Commission (1968) and Cowling *et al.* (1980).
2 For useful surveys see Kaserman (1978) and Casson (1984). See also the earlier work of Oi and Hurter (1973).

3 For further discussion see Richardson (1972).

4 Williamson's work has wider application than simply to vertical integration (see also chapter 9), but we confine our attention to vertical integration here.

5 As noted by Coase, there are also likely to be disadvantages to increased integration; for a discussion of these see Williamson (1975, chapter 7).

6 See, for example, Flaherty (1981).

7 Carlton assumes for simplicity that a buyer approaches a single firm only and that inter-firm sales of the product do not occur. The former assumption could be modified to allow buyers to approach several sellers with appropriate search costs, but this complication would not upset the basic results.

8 We have adapted Carlton's notation here to accord with that used elsewhere in this chapter.

9 Partial integration of this sort is frequently noted in the literature. See for example Carlton (1979, pp. 207–8), and for various examples of partial forward integration into transportation services see Oi and Hurter (1973, pp. 244–7).

10 See, for example, Bork (1954) or McGee and Bassett (1976).

11 The analysis presented here is based on Singer (1968, pp. 206–9). See also Greenhut and Ohta (1976).

12 This result can be generalized to some (but not all) nonlinear demand curves: see Greenhut and Ohta (1976) and Perry (1978). The result does not hold with non-constant costs: see Haring and Kaserman (1978).

13 The standard reference on the bilateral monopoly case is Machlup and Taber (1960).

14 Specifically, if we assume that A and B are combined to produce X, and units are defined such that one unit of A and one unit of B produce one unit of X (i.e. a fixed coefficients production function with unit coefficients), then the marginal cost of X is $MC_X = p_A + p_B$, where p_A and p_B are the input prices. The monopolist producer of X will set marginal revenue, MR_X, equal to MC_X, so that we have $MR_X = p_A + p_B$ and hence $p_A = MR_X - p_B$. Since p_B is the competitive input price and a constant, and $X = A$ by assumption, the equation $p_A = MR_X - p_B$ is the inverse demand curve for A (D_A in figure 8.4).

15 See Singer (1968) and Greenhut and Ohta (1976).

16 Note that the equation of any isocost line is $Y = p_A A + p_B B$ or, on rearrangement, $B = (Y/p_B) - (p_A/p_B)A$ where Y is money cost. Hence the intercept of an isocost line on the vertical axis, Y/p_B, measures cost in terms of B. It follows that PM in figure 8.6 is the extra cost in units of B of producing x_1 at point E with $p_A > MC_A$ compared with $p_A = MC_A$ (i.e. profits attributable to A). Similarly, MN in figure 8.6 measures the cost saving in units of B of forward integration.

17 See also Schmalensee (1973) and Hay (1973).

18 More recent research has shown that, under Warren-Boulton's assumptions, the output price may fall if $0 < \sigma < 1$ but definitely rises if $\sigma \geq 1$. Anomalous cases where the output price falls after vertical integration appear to be associated with a price elasticity of market demand close to its lower limit of one: see Mallela and Nahata (1980).

19 In the case where the elasticity of substitution is greater than one, it is possible to produce output X solely from input B. Hence, after forward integration by the input monopolist, a constraint may be put on the post-integration output price by the price at which an independent producer could produce X solely from input B. When this constraint is effective and the monopolist is unable to raise output price

as high as he would like to, the overall welfare effect may become positive again at some high critical value, σ_u, greater than one. In this case, overall welfare losses will be observed only round about $\sigma = 1$, although the precise range of values depends on the other parameter values in the model.

20 See, for example, Schmalensee (1973) and Waterson (1982b).

21 See, for example, Comanor (1967b) with the accompanying discussion of McGee.

9 Conglomerate Diversification

Recent years have seen a considerable growth in interest in large conglomerate firms and their possible effects on the operation of the economy. Large diversified firms, it is argued, can now be found operating in many UK industries ranging from food products to soap powders, or from hotels to metal goods. Such firms inevitably account for considerable proportions of economic activity which might otherwise be undertaken by separate firms. Inevitably, therefore, question marks arise over possible economic welfare effects associated with diversification, and these and other issues are discussed in this chapter.

While, in principle, any firm which produces more than one product or service may be called 'diversified', it is convenient to narrow the concept somewhat. Thus, a firm producing a number of closely substitutable products (e.g. brands of washing powder) would usually be regarded as *horizontally integrated* rather than diversified, whereas a firm which produces products or services enjoying significant input–output relationships would usually be regarded as *vertically integrated*. Diversification as here defined, therefore, excludes production of highly substitutable or significantly vertically related products.[1]

Even so, a number of categories of diversification can be distinguished. In the USA, for example, the Federal Trade Commission has made a useful three-fold categorization of diversification.[2] *Product extension diversification* involves the production of products related to some extent in their production or demand. When products are related in demand, diversification is referred to as 'marketing concentricity'; while relationships in production are referred to as 'technological concentricity'. *Market extension diversification* relates to the sale of a product in geographically distinct markets. Finally,*'pure' conglomerate diversification* applies where a firm produces products which are seemingly unrelated in production or demand. In this chapter we shall not consider geographic diversification explicitly; it should be recognized that local and regional market distinctions may be important in some industries, however, and that ideas relating to product diversification *per se* may also be applied to market extension diversification.

In section 9.1 we consider measures of diversification together with evidence on its trend in UK industry. In section 9.2 we consider theoretical and empirical work on the determinants of diversification. And finally, in section 9.3 we look at possible competitive effects of diversification together with some limited empirical evidence on diversification and economic performance.

9.1 Diversification: Measures and Evidence

9.1.1 Measures of Diversification

Measures of diversification are formally analogous to measures of concentration (see section 2.1 above). A measure of concentration summarizes the number and relative sizes of firms in a given industry. A measure of diversification, in contrast, summarizes the number and relative sizes of industries operated in by a given firm. Not surprisingly, therefore, the indices suggested as measures of diversification are closely related to conventional concentration indices, and we consider five simple indices in what follows.

It is useful to proceed with reference to what we may call the *diversification curve* analogous to the concentration curve of chapter 2. This plots the cumulative percentage of a firm's employment (or some other measure of firm size) against the cumulative number of industries in which the firm operates, ranked from the most important to the least. Three such curves for firms A, B and C are plotted in figure 9.1.

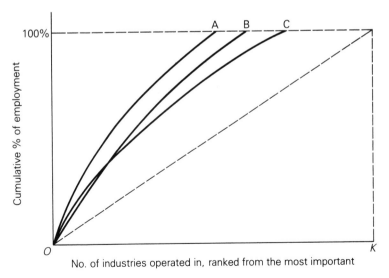

Figure 9.1

Corresponding to our discussion in chapter 2, we may note, first, that the curves in figure 9.1 are concave from below, in the limit being straight lines. This reflects cumulation of employment from the largest industry in which a firm operates, with a straight line applying when a firm operates equally in a number of industries. Hence, relative inequality in a firm's distribution of industrial activities is reflected in the concavity of the curves, and the number of industries in which it operates is reflected in the slope of a line drawn between the endpoints of each curve.

Second, higher curves indicate greater concentration or specialization of a firm's industrial activities. Hence, a firm is more diversified the lower is its diversification curve, and we can say that a firm is more diversified if its diversification curve lies everywhere below that of another firm. In figure 9.1, therefore, firm C is more diversified than firm A, since, for any number of industries operated in (ranked by importance to the firm), firm C has a smaller proportion of its activity committed to those industries. If there are K industries in total, then a completely diversified firm would operate equally in all K industries (shown by the dashed diagonal line in the figure).

Finally, when diversification curves cross, then no unambiguous ranking of firms by diversification exists. In figure 9.1 firm C operates in more markets than firm B but it also has more of its employment concentrated in a limited number of industries. Which firm is regarded as more diversified, therefore, depends on the weight attached to different parts of the diversification curve. As in the case of concentration, different indices give different weights to different parts of the curve, and so may result in different rankings of firms when curves intersect. Since these matters have been discussed thoroughly in the context of concentration indices, we make no further reference to them in what follows.

Consider a typical firm with employment x_j in industry j $(j = 1, \ldots, K)$. The total employment of the firm is $x = \Sigma_{j=1}^{K} x_j$ and its proportion of employment in industry j is $s_j = x_j/x$. When the firm is specialized in one industry (industry 1, say) then $x_1 = x$ and x_j and s_j are zero for $j \neq 1$. More generally, however, a firm will operate in several industries.

As in the case of concentration, such diversification can be measured in a number of alternative ways.

Number of industries   The simplest index is to count the number of industries in which the firm operates. This is analogous to using the reciprocal of firm numbers as an index of concentration. The principal weakness of the index is that it gives no weight at all to the distribution of the firm's employment over those industries.

Specialization ratio   A second index, which because of its simplicity and its ready availability in Census of Production publications is frequently used in empirical work, is the specialization ratio. This index is defined as the ratio of the firm's primary employment to its total employment. Thus, if the firm's activities are ranked by industry from largest to smallest, the specialization ratio is given as $s_1 = x_1/x$. More useful for our purposes is a corresponding diversification index which can be defined as the complement of s_1, giving the ratio of total secondary employment to total employment of a firm; i.e.,

$$DR = 1 - s_1 = \sum_{j=2}^{K} x_j/x. \tag{9.1}$$

This index is zero for a specialized firm and has a maximum value of $(K-1)/K$ for a firm diversified equally over all K industries.

Clearly, the diversification index, DR (which may, for convenience, be referred to as the *diversification ratio*), is analogous to (the complement of) the concentration ratio in chapter 2. As such, it is subject to similar criticisms. In particular, it can be criticized for taking account of only one point on the diversification curve in figure 9.1, thereby suppressing information on the number and distribution of the firm's secondary activities. At the same time, however, its simplicity and its availability operate to make it (or the specialization ratio) the most frequently used diversification index.

Berry's index   A third index, used extensively by Berry (1975), corresponds to the Hirschman–Herfindahl index of concentration. This index is defined as one minus the sum of squared shares of a firm's activities in different industries:

$$D = 1 - \sum_{j=1}^{K} (x_j/x)^2 = 1 - \sum_{j=1}^{K} s_j^2. \tag{9.2}$$

It takes values of zero when a firm is completely specialized in its primary industry and $(K-1)/K$ when a firm operates equally in all K industries. If we make the transformation $K^* = 1/(1-D)$, then we have a *numbers equivalent form* of the diversification index. This shows the number of industries an equally diversified firm would operate in to produce that value of D. Thus a diversification index of 3/4 implies diversification equivalent to operating equally in four separate industries.

The index, by squaring the shares of a firm's activities in different industries, gives particular weight to the firm's principal activities. In the concentration context, this implies that large firm market shares are given particular weight in forming the H index of concentration. In the present context, it means that a firm's secondary activities are given only limited weight in calculating D unless those activities are of considerable importance. Thus, for example, a firm operating in five industries with employment distributed as 0.5, 0.2, 0.1, 0.1 and 0.1 has a diversification index $D = 1 - 0.32 = 0.68$ where only 0.03 of the amount 0.32 is contributed by the firm's last 30 per cent of activity. The index is comparatively insensitive to minor secondary activities, therefore, although it could be argued that this is in fact desirable since it focuses attention on the major activities of the firm.

Entropy index   Just as the Hirschman–Herfindahl concentration index has a corresponding diversification index, so does the entropy concentration index. The entropy diversification index is defined as

$$E = - \sum_{j=1}^{K} s_j \ln s_j. \tag{9.3}$$

This is equivalent to a weighted sum of the s_j where the weights are $\ln(1/s_j)$ (in contrast to weights of s_j in the sum in Berry's index). The index takes values of zero in the case of complete specialization and $\ln K$ in the case of a firm diversified equally over all K industries.

A particular feature of the entropy index which can be useful in studies of diversification is its decomposibility into within- and between-group components. Consider a diversified firm operating in a number of industries in several sectors of manufacturing industry. Then it might be useful to know how much of its total diversification is attributable to diversification within sectors and how much is attributable to diversification between sectors. If there are R sectors ($r = 1, \dots, R$), then it can be shown that[3]

$$E^T = E^B + \sum_{r=1}^{R} s_r E_r^W \tag{9.4}$$

where E^T, E^B and E_r^W are, respectively, entropy diversification indices for total, between-sector and within-sector r diversification and s_r is the share of the firm's employment in sector r. Hence, using an entropy diversification index, one can assess whether a firm tends to diversify mainly within particular areas (as captured by the second term in (9.4)) or on a broader and more conglomerate front (as captured by the first term).

Utton's index   Finally Utton (1979; see also Hart, 1971) has suggested a further index of diversification, following again from work done on measuring concentration. This measure is related to the area above the diversification curve. Specifically, it can be shown that this area is equal to

$$A = s_1 + 2s_2 + 3s_3 + \dots + K s_k - \tfrac{1}{2}$$
$$= \sum_{j=1}^{K} j s_j - \tfrac{1}{2} \tag{9.5}$$

and Utton defines his W index of diversification as twice this area:

$$W = 2 \sum_{j=1}^{K} j s_j - 1. \tag{9.6}$$

This index varies between one for a completely specialized firm and K for a firm equally diversified across all K industries. It also has the property that it is its own numbers equivalent. Thus, in the case considered above of a firm operating in five industries with employment proportions 0.5, 0.2, 0.1, 0.1 and 0.1, $W = 3.2$ and this is equivalent to a firm operating equally in 3.2 industries.

It is clear that this index gives more weight to secondary industries than does the Berry index, for example. In particular, as the above cited example makes clear, activities in industries ranked as quite unimportant in the firm's total operation may receive more weight in calculating W than industries with a higher ranking. At the same time, however, the index does have intuitive appeal derived from its graphical interpretation, and thus provides a useful further index of diversification.

9.1.2 Evidence on Diversification

We now turn to an examination of the descriptive evidence on diversification in UK industry. As we shall see, this evidence relates mainly to diversification in UK manufacturing industry, and hence excludes wider forms of conglomerate activity in non-manufacturing sectors of the economy. In addition, it has not proved possible to distinguish diversification from vertical integration on a systematic basis in currently published work, so that both forms of multi-industry operation are treated as diversification in what follows.

Most data on diversification currently available in the UK are based upon Census of Production industry classifications. As noted in section 2.2.1, however, such classifications do not always tally closely with the economist's idea of a market. In the diversification context, a market should consist of a group of products which are highly substitutable in demand. In practice, however, most analysis must be conducted in terms of three-digit Minimum List Heading (MLH) industries or, alternatively, at even higher levels of aggregation. MLH industries often consist of a number of distinct products and hence may be too aggregated to provide data on a single market. This is a fortiori a problem when higher levels of aggregation are used. Moreover, MLH industries are typically defined in terms of their use of common materials or processes (e.g. plastics products (MLH 496) or timber (MLH 471)) and hence may not accord closely with theoretical notions of a market. These problems imply that evidence on the extent of diversification in particular must be treated with caution, since it is sensitive to the definitions of markets used.[4]

A number of studies have measured the extent of diversification in UK manufacturing industry, the latest being that of Utton (1979).[5] He considered the extent of diversification of the largest 200 manufacturing firms across 120 MLH industries in 1972. These firms accounted for 46 per cent of manufacturing employment in 1972 and are clearly more likely to be diversified than the remaining smaller firms in manufacturing industry.

Table 9.1 Diversification[a] by the 200 largest enterprises in UK manufacturing, 1972

Order	No. of enterprises	Diversification ratio (%)	Utton's W index
III Food, drink and tobacco	31	37.1	3.46
IV Coal and petroleum products V Chemicals	18	64.9	9.12
VI Metal manufacture	10	63.2	5.87[b]
VII Mechanical engineering	31	42.4	3.52
VIII Instrument engineering	3	34.5	1.69
IX Electrical engineering	22	54.7	5.13
X Shipbuilding	6	25.2	2.98
XI Vehicles	17	13.8	1.65
XII Metal goods, n.e.s.	6	57.1	4.65
XIII Textiles	13	61.9	6.69
XV Clothing and footwear	6	28.0	3.34
XVI Bricks, pottery, glass, cement XVII Timber, furniture, etc.	14	40.1	3.71
XVIII Paper, printing, publishing	13	50.9	4.11
XIX Other manufacturing	10	29.9	3.94
Total	200	43.3	4.39

Source: Utton (1979, tables 2.1, 2.2 and 2.5).

Notes
[a] Employment-weighted averages for firms classified to each sector.
[b] Excludes British Steel Corporation.

Hence Utton's data are not representative of all manufacturing firms but rather indicate the extent of diversification by the largest firms.

Table 9.1 presents Utton's results in terms of the diversification ratio and Utton's W index (see section 9.1.1). In order to avoid disclosure of information on individual firms, the reported results are averaged across firms for each Standard Industrial Classification (SIC) two-digit Order, where firms are classified to an Order on the basis of their principal employment. Hence, for example, there were 31 firms classified to food, drink and tobacco and on average they had a diversification ratio of 37 per cent and a W index of 3.5. As noted in section 9.1.1, this means that these firms on average had 37 per cent of their employment outside their primary MLH industry and that (using the W index) they were on average diversified equivalent to operating equally in three-and-a-half MLH industries.

Several interesting points emerge from this table. First, on average, the largest 200 firms were (perhaps surprisingly) rather undiversified in 1972. Thus, they had on average 57 per cent of employment in just one MLH industry, and were diversified equivalent to producing in just over four industries. Given that these firms are likely to be the most diversified firms in UK manufacturing industry, it is clear that the typical UK firm was still comparatively specialized even in 1972. As noted above, however, this conclusion is sensitive to the MLH industry definition used and also ignores diversification outside manufacturing industry. Some firms in the largest 200, moreover, are much more diversified than the average, although Utton reports that only ten firms had a W index over 8, with the most diversified firm having a value of only 16.7. Hence even the most diversified firms are diversified equivalent to operating in only a limited number of manufacturing industries.

Second, considerable variation exists between diversification of firms classified to different manufacturing sectors. Both indices of diversification give a similar picture in this respect. Taking Utton's W index, firms classified to coal and petroleum products and chemicals were by far the most diversified, followed by textiles. A typical large firm classified to coal and petroleum products and chemicals was diversified equivalent to equal operation in just over nine industries. In part, this reflects the many uses of petrochemicals in modern industry, with petroleum companies being particularly prone to multi-industry operation. In addition, Utton suggests that ICI's interests in textiles (particularly through its majority holding in Carrington Viyella) were important, reflecting in this case forward integration into synthetic fibres production. In textiles itself, diversification was on average equivalent to equal operation in 6.7 industries. Part of this, as noted in chapter 8, reflected the forward integration policies of Courtauld's (a monopoly producer of rayon) into clothing and other textile industries in the 1960s and early 1970s.

Diversification was also comparatively high ($W > 5$) in metal manufacture and electrical engineering. In particular, since the British Steel Corporation has been excluded from the W figure, the high diversification recorded for metal manufacture firms probably reflects the activities of non-ferrous metals producers, such as Delta Metal and the Lead Industries Group, in technologically related industries (e.g. engineering, vehicles and metal products). The least diversified enterprises were classified to shipbuilding, instrument engineering and vehicles. An average firm classified to vehicles was diversified equivalent to equal operation in only 1.6 industries, and this contrasts markedly with the average experience of firms classified to coal and petroleum products and chemicals.[6]

Some idea of the nature of diversification activities can be gained by distinguishing diversification into industries within an Order and diversification into industries in other Orders. This breakdown is, of course, necessarily crude since it is sensitive to the classification of industries to Orders in the Census. In particular, it may be argued that engineering and vehicles sectors are closely related technologically so that they are better treated as a single sector. Using such an adjustment, Utton found that, overall for his 200 firms, some 58 per cent of secondary employment was diversified within a firm's primary sector, leaving 42 per cent diversified into industries in other sectors.[7] Part of this latter 'broad spectrum' diversification is also accounted for by vertical integration, in particular between chemicals and textile industries and between textile and clothing industries. Utton therefore suggested that probably two-thirds of diversification occurs into technologically related industries rather than being of a more conglomerate nature, although in some sectors (notably coal and petroleum products and chemicals, and brick etc. and timber etc.) there is apparently substantial 'broad spectrum' diversification of a more conglomerate type. This conclusion must be qualified, however, given the arbitrariness of Census classifications.[8]

Evidence on trends in diversification in UK manufacturing industry is also given by Utton. First, he compared data given by Leak and Maizels (1945) for 1935 with Census of Production data for 1958 and 1963. As he noted, this comparison is not strictly valid owing to definitional changes to industries between 1935 and 1958. Moreover, for the purpose at hand 66 trades were distinguished in 1935 compared with 51 in 1958 and 1963 suggesting, *ceteris paribus*, that any increase in diversification for 1935–58 would tend to be understated. With these reservations in mind, Utton estimated that diversified firms (firms operating in more than one industry) accounted for 34 per cent of manufacturing employment in 1935 rising to 44 per cent in 1958 and 59 per cent in 1963. These results suggest that diversification increased between 1935 and 1958 but probably by less than in the five-year period 1958–63. Given the reservations over the data and the crude diversification index used, however, this conclusion can only be regarded as tentative.

Firmer evidence is available for 1958–68. Using data on manufacturing firms with 100 or more employees, Utton found that employment of firms operating in more than one of 51 two-and-a-half-digit industries was 53 per cent in 1958, rising to 68 per cent in 1963 and 72 per cent in 1968. Thus, on this basis diversification appears to have increased markedly in UK manufacturing industry in the period, and particularly in 1958–63.

Table 9.2 presents data on average diversification ratios of diversified firms in 1958–68 by SIC Orders. In contrast to table 9.1, the data now relate to net output, to all firms with 100 or more employees, and to diversification between 51 (rather than 120) industries. The table also excludes data on firms operating in only one industry, while data from seven industries were excluded because they were incomplete. Table 9.2 reveals that the proportion of secondary employment among these diversified firms rose on average from 23 per cent in 1958 to 27 per cent in 1963 and to 32 per cent in 1968. Hence this measure also suggests that diversification increased in 1958–68, although with similar sized increases in the two sub-periods. Substantial diversification increases on average occurred in metal manufacture, shipbuilding, metal goods, textiles, and timber, furniture, etc. On the other hand, two sectors (food and drink, and vehicles) appear to have experienced slight falls on average in diversification in the period as a whole.

Finally, Utton presents evidence for 1968–72 on diversification trends in

Table 9.2 Average[a] diversification ratios for diversified firms[b] in UK manufacturing, 1958–68

Order	No. of industries	Diversification (%)		
		1958	1963	1968
Food and drink	4	22.5	19.6	21.5
Chemicals	4	31.6	35.1	41.6
Metal manufacture	2	24.6	25.9	45.1[c]
Engineering and electrical goods	12	31.4	33.8	37.8
Shipbuilding	1	12.0	36.8	34.9
Vehicles	3	22.2	12.9	18.5
Metal goods, n.e.s.	1	23.2	36.7	41.2
Textiles	5	22.6	29.6	40.6
Leather, leather goods, fur	1	24.7	28.2	29.5
Clothing and footwear	2	17.9	19.6	19.8
Bricks, pottery, glass, cement	2	17.5	23.4	28.9
Timber, furniture, etc.	2	25.8	31.2	44.6
Paper, printing, publishing	3	19.8	24.6	25.4
Other manufacturing	2	21.7	23.6	30.3
Total	44	22.7	27.2	32.3

Source: Utton (1979, chapter 6, table 6.4).

Notes
[a] Output-weighted averages.
[b] Private sector enterprises employing 100 or more persons, excluding firms operating in a single industry.
[c] Excludes British Steel Corporation.

the largest 200 manufacturing companies. This comparison reveals a weighted average *W* index of diversification of 4.0 in 1968 and of 4.4 in 1972. This increase in the index of diversification must be treated with caution, however, since only 167 firms were common to both years.

Some idea of trends in diversification may also be gained by looking at data on diversification by merger. Evidence presented in the 1978 Green Paper on Monopolies and Mergers Policy, for example, shows that, over the period 1965–77, 21 per cent of mergers (by value of acquired assets) investigated by the government's Merger Panel were classified as conglomerate, with somewhat higher levels recorded post-1970 than before.[9] A second study by Goudie and Meeks (1982) examined evidence for quoted companies (involved principally in manufacturing, distribution and certain other services) for the longer period 1949–73. They classified firms into 22 industry groups, and, defining a diversified merger as a merger between firms classified to different industry groups, they found that, in the whole period, 33 per cent of mergers by value and 39 per cent of mergers by number were diversified. Their results also suggest certain patterns in the time trend of diversified merger. In terms of numbers of mergers, there was a marked upward trend in the proportion of diversifying mergers, rising from 9 per cent of mergers in 1949–53 to 47 per cent of mergers in 1969–73 (although Goudie and Meeks note that this latter period may be somewhat exceptional in historical terms). In terms of value, the picture is less clear, however, with a peak of diversified merger activity in 1954 somewhat obscuring an otherwise rising trend. Nevertheless, their results appear to suggest that diversifying mergers have grown substantially in importance in the postwar period, and that by the early 1970s they may have accounted for 40 to 50 per cent of all mergers.

Some caution must be expressed in interpreting these results, however, since, as Goudie and Meeks admit, their methods of classifying firms and mergers are essentially crude and may give rise to considerable problems of interpretation. In addition, of course, diversification by mergers is not a direct measure of the importance of increased diversification to UK industrial structure.

Such a measure *is* provided in a final study by Clarke and Davies (1983). They considered the extent to which changes in aggregate concentration in the economy can be attributed to changes in concentration in individual markets and changes in firm diversification. Using Hirschman–Herfindahl-based indices of concentration and diversification, they showed that an exact decomposition of aggregate concentration can be made into these components. This decomposition was then applied to Census of Production data for 1963–8 and 1971–7 where Herfindahl concentration indices were estimated from firm size distribution tables.

Their results suggest that for 1963–8, while diversification between MLH industries increased, it accounted for only some 10 per cent of the increase in aggregate concentration observed in this period. The other 90 per cent of the increase was attributable to increases in market concentration, suggesting that increasing diversification was not a major factor at work in this period (at least relatively). A more limited analysis of diversification between Orders in 1971–7 showed a 6 per cent fall in such 'broad spectrum' diversification in the period, which exactly matched a 6 per cent fall in aggregate concentration. There was clearly no evidence here of rising aggregate concentration associated with high levels of conglomerate merger activity. Rather, despite the evidence on conglomerate merger activity for the early 1970s, it appears that 'broad spectrum' diversification decreased in 1971–7 (as it also did slightly in 1963–8). If robust, this result suggests that impressionistic evidence gained from a few spectacular mergers could be seriously misleading as an indicator of overall trends in diversification.

9.2 Determinants of Diversification

In this section we consider reasons why firms diversify. While explanations are many, in what follows we group them together into two categories. In section 9.2.1 we consider the view that a firm diversifies in order to use its assets more effectively. In section 9.2.2 we look at possible financial advantages of diversification associated with the reduction of risks. And finally, in section 9.2.3, we examine some of the empirical evidence currently available on the hypotheses generated by these explanations.

9.2.1 The Asset Utilization Approach

The asset utilization approach considers the firm as a collection of physical, human and intangible assets capable of undertaking a number of separate activities. Some assets may be relatively product-specific, in that they have value in producing only a particular good or service, whereas other assets may have value in producing a number of goods or services. If such assets are insufficiently utilized in the firm's current operations, then it may be worthwhile using them elsewhere. Such use may sometimes take place on a sale or lease basis with other firms, but in other cases the firm will choose to use them itself by diversifying its operations. This latter choice will tend to be made in circumstances of market failure (see chapter 8) when a firm believes that internal organization of production will be more efficient than the sale or lease of the asset in the market.[10]

A simple example of asset utilization relates to the case of an indivisible capital asset or alternatively of a whole plant. If there is excess productive capacity in a firm's current line of activity, then it may attempt to increase asset or plant utilization by selling its services on the market or alternatively by diversifying production. A number of cases can be distinguished. First, an asset may be a fixed factor of production such as a railway track where there are obvious gains from spreading fixed costs over as many products and services as possible (e.g. both freight and passenger services, and private excursions). Second, the demand for a product may be seasonal (e.g. ice-cream), so that plant utilization may be increased by producing a complementary seasonal product (e.g. sausages). Third, the demand for a product may be variable (from month to month, or year to year) such that production of several products is desirable to obtain offsetting reductions in the variability of demand. An instance of this might be production of a number of quite different plastics products to effect high and stable utilization of plastic moulding equipment. Finally, if faced with a secular or cyclical decline in demand, a firm may look to diversification to offset reduced utilization of its productive capacity. In all cases, capacity is not matched completely to demand, and product diversification represents one strategy option for the firm.

The asset utilization argument need not relate merely to physical assets. A second asset which is frequently linked to diversification is managerial experience and expertise. Business skills are clearly an important asset to a firm and some firms will have a manager or managerial team with particular organizational and/or entrepreneurial talents. In these circumstances, the firm may use its managerial assets more effectively by expanding its business. Since business skills, at least at the top management level, are not particularly product-specific, such expansion may take the form of diversification into other products within a sector or even more widely. Popular examples of men with particular managerial skills who head large diversified companies in the UK are Lord Weinstock, managing director of the General Electric Company (GEC) and R. W. (Tiny) Rowland, managing director of Lonrho. Many other large companies, however, have talented and experienced managerial teams, and these may be put to use in producing a diversified range of products and services.[11]

A third asset which is linked closely with diversification in empirical work is technical knowledge. As noted in chapter 7, a basic feature of research and development is that it produces ideas and innovations which may have application beyond the range of a firm's current operations. In some instances the firm may choose to exploit such spin-offs by sale of patent rights to other firms; in other cases, however, it may choose to exploit the idea itself by diversifying its operation. The choice between these alternatives will depend on the firm's assessment of its ability to undertake production in a new industry versus its ability to extract a reasonable royalty from another firm. As noted in chapter 7, the latter will in turn depend partly on the firm's ability successfully to patent the idea or innovation. In some situations successful patenting may not be feasible, in which case the firm may have to exploit the idea itself to preserve secrecy. Where this is an important consideration, firms in research-intensive sectors may gear themselves to diversified operation in order to exploit new ideas and innovations as they arise.

There is some dispute in the industrial economics field as to whether research stimulates diversification or vice versa. One viewpoint is that research and development activities are primarily determined by technological opportunities (as noted in chapter 7) and that diversification takes place in response to the ideas and innovations generated by research. An alternative view, put forward, for example, by Grabowski (1968), is that a diversified firm is better able to make use of new ideas and innovations than a specialized firm, so that greater diversification provides an incentive for greater research and development. Both hypotheses suggest that diversification and R & D activity will be positively correlated, but they differ over the direction of causation. No clear evidence is currently available to disentangle these separate effects.

Several other assets may also be mentioned. For example, a company may accumulate goodwill for itself (in addition to its products), which may be used to advantage in other areas. Several examples of this can be found in retailing – e.g., the diversification of the Boots Company from chemist good retailing into diverse retailing activities; the diversification of Woolworths into DIY retailing. Second, a company may possess particularly able marketing expertise which gives an incentive to diversify its product range. Third, a firm may have an already established distribution system for one product (e.g. milk) which can be used to sell other products (e.g. eggs and chickens). Only limited evidence is available on the general importance of these factors (see section 9.2.3), but they certainly may be important in particular cases.

9.2.2 The Reduction of Financial Risk

A second group of motives for diversification may be classified as financial. These motives may be associated with large firm size *per se* (e.g. economies of size in raising risk capital) and hence may pertain only indirectly to diversification. In addition, however, if diversification reduces the financial risks associated with a company's operations then this may provide a more direct incentive for diversification to take place. Unfortunately, the arguments in support of this contention are not straightforward, and we consider only a simplified account of the issues in what follows.

It is useful to begin by examining the intuitive argument that diversification reduces financial risks. This argument accords with the familiar notion of spreading risks by not having 'all one's eggs in one basket'. Thus a group of activities will be less risky than its constituent parts since bad fortune in one line of activity can be offset by good luck elsewhere, so that the overall chance of a good or a very poor result is reduced. With firm diversification, a company which undertakes several distinct lines of activity will expect that such offsetting effects will be at work tending to stabilize its rate of return (as measured, for example, by its return on capital). In the case where the rate of return in two lines of activity are perfectly negatively correlated, then the rate of return of the group will be completely stable from period to period. In less extreme cases, however, some variability in rate of return will be observed following diversification, although this may be substantially less than that observed in the absence of diversification. Hence, even when firm diversification does not directly affect the expected rate of return of the group, it is likely to reduce the variability in the rate of return.

This can be demonstrated more explicitly with the use of some elementary statistical theory.[12] Assume for simplicity that a firm undertakes two activities which are of similar size with a similar expected return and variability of return. Specifically, let capital K be employed in each activity and let the rate of return in activity i be $r_i = \pi_i/K$ where π_i is the profit in activity i. We assume that r_i is a random variable with the same mean, μ, and variance, σ^2, for each activity. Then the rate of return for the group is

$$r = \frac{\pi_1 + \pi_2}{2K} = \tfrac{1}{2}(r_1 + r_2). \tag{9.7}$$

If ρ is the correlation coefficient between r_1 and r_2, then it can be shown[13] that the standard deviation of the group rate of return is

$$\sigma_r = \sigma\sqrt{[(1+\rho)/2]}. \tag{9.8}$$

It follows that, when r_1 and r_2 are independent ($\rho = 0$), $\sigma_r = \sigma/\sqrt{2}$, while for perfect positive correlation ($\rho = 1$), $\sigma_r = \sigma$ and with perfect negative correlation ($\rho = -1$), $\sigma_r = 0$. The standard deviation of the rate of return of the group falls monotonically as the correlation coefficient, ρ, falls from $+1$ to -1, i.e. as the rates of return for the two activities are less positively correlated.

Clearly, the magnitude of the correlation coefficient, ρ, is crucial to the degree of reduced risk obtained. In the case of $\rho = 0$, for example (i.e. when the rates of return in the separate activities are not correlated), the standard deviation of the group rate of return falls to the square root of one half (i.e. 0.71) of σ. As previously noted, a negative correlation between the rates of return of two activities will reduce the variability in the group rate of return even further. As noted by Prais (1976, p. 93), however, it seems likely that positive correlations between rates of return will occur more often than zero or negative correlations. This is partly because the constituent parts of the firm will face the same general economic climate and partly because they will be subject (to some extent) to the same managerial influences. Hence, in many cases one would expect that the reduction in risks produced by diversification would be less than indicated by the 'square root rule'. Nevertheless, significant reductions of risk may be forthcoming even in such cases, providing the basis for a risk reduction explanation of diversification.[14]

It would appear that, since risk reduction can (and usually does) accompany diversification, it would present a gain to shareholders even in the absence of any other diversification effects. This argument indeed was used as an explanation of conglomerate diversification in several early studies.[15] As pointed out by Levy and Sarnat (1970), however, no such gain in fact exists, at least in the case of a perfect capital market in full equilibrium. The reason for this is obvious, since investors can secure all the diversification they require by diversifying their portfolio of shares in specialized companies. Hence there is no advantage to them of having diversified companies if the expected rate of return is unaffected. Of course, if it were the case that transactions costs of share portfolio diversification were substantial (as they might be for a small investor, for example), then investment in a ready diversified company might be attractive. Small investors can, however, obtain a diversified portfolio with low transactions costs by investing in a unit trust. It is not clear, therefore, that a diversified company is likely to provide a significant benefit to investors when compared with other available institutions for spreading risks.

One must, therefore, consider other, less direct, reasons why risk reduction may be a motive for diversification. Two possibilities are considered in what follows. The first, initially suggested by Lewellen (1971), centres on the debt characteristics of a firm. Consider, for example, the typical case where a firm raises external finance partly in the form of fixed interest obligations (debt, such as debenture finance) and partly in the form of shares or equity. Since a diversified company offers a lower variability of return when compared with equivalent specialized firms, it also offers a reduced risk of default for holders of debt. Consequently a diversified company will be able to raise a greater proportion of its capital as debt (what is known technically as its 'gearing'). In a perfect capital market in equilibrium this effect is unlikely to confer special advantages. However, if in practice there are particular advantages in using debt as opposed to equity finance, then shareholders may gain from an increase in gearing occasioned by increased diversification.

Two types of possibility have been suggested in the literature. First, there may be tax advantages from higher gearing, conferred, for example, by the fact that debenture interest is (by accounting convention) a charge before calculating profit and hence not subject to company taxes.[16] Of course, the market is likely to adjust to take account of differential taxes and any changes in those taxes, and it may do so in the absence of any increased diversification.[17] It is possible, however, that tax gains can be made from increasing diversification and gearing following a rise in corporation tax, say, although direct evidence for this effect does not appear to be available. Second, it has been argued by Prais (1976, pp. 103–5) that failure of investors to anticipate inflation fully can give rise to unrealistically cheap debenture finance and hence an incentive for diversification. Prais points to the fact that the *ex post* real net cost of debentures to companies in the period 1951–70 was close to zero, suggesting that investors agreed to accept nominal interest rates on debentures which consistently failed to anticipate inflation rates in the period. In the period 1970–4, moreover, when the inflation rate accelerated, the real net cost of debentures to companies became negative. This would seem to have offered a dramatic incentive to firms to increase their proportion of debt finance (if they more correctly anticipated inflation) and may have been an important factor in explaining some large conglomerate mergers which took place, particularly in the early 1970s.

A second, somewhat simpler, explanation of diversification to take advantage of risk reduction makes use of the distinction between owner and manager control of firms.[18] Firms are typically controlled by managers, who may or may not have an equity interest in the firm. In some instances, it is argued, managers will follow policies which advance their own interests rather than those of the shareholders. Managers are concerned with their incomes and security of employment, both of which will be related to firm performance. Unlike shareholders, who can diversify their share portfolios to stabilize their incomes, managers are unable to diversify their employment. In particular, they stand to lose heavily if they become unemployed either through poor firm performance or bankruptcy. It is in their interests, therefore, to reduce such employment risk, and this may induce them to engage in diversification purely to reduce the variability in firm performance.

In the case where diversification has only a risk reduction effect, but no effect on expected return, shareholders will be indifferent to managers' diversification policies. In other cases, however, managers may attempt to secure risk reduction at the cost of a reduction in expected return. In these cases shareholders have an incentive to react to stop managers' displacement of their goals. However, it is likely that shareholder monitoring of managers' activities will be less than perfect, so that some goal displacement will be possible. As we shall see in the next section, the evidence that diversification is linked to managerial control of firms is fairly strong.

9.2.3 Empirical Evidence

In this section we briefly review the empirical evidence currently available on determinants of diversification. We shall mainly consider evidence on hypotheses generated by the asset utilization approach discussed in section 9.2.1, although we end with a brief look at some evidence relating to managerial control of firms.

Evidence currently available suggests that there is a robust positive association between diversification and technical activity within a firm or industry, but that other relationships are more problematical.[19] In an early study Gort (1962) examined the effect of technical activity and market concentration on the diversification of firms in US manufacturing industry in 1954. He argued that firms classified to a primary industry with high technical activity and high concentration would tend to be more diversified as they made use of ideas generated by research in other industries and as they sought to grow without encroaching on the outputs of large rival producers. Using ordinary least squares (OLS) multiple regression for 56 US industries, he found that

$$Y = -0.39 + 0.35X_1 + 0.03X_2 \qquad R^2 = 0.377 \qquad (9.9)$$
$$(3.50) \quad\;\; (3.18)$$

where Y is the ratio of non-primary to primary employment of firms classified to a primary industry in 1954, X_1 is an estimate of the primary industry four-firm concentration ratio in 1947 and X_2 is the number of technical personnel per 10,000 employees in the primary industry in 1950. As can be seen (with t ratios in parentheses), both explanatory variables have the expected positive sign and are statistically significant at better than the 1 per cent level. Hence Gort's results strongly support his hypotheses in US industry in 1954.[20]

Amey (1964) also found a strong positive association between diversification and technical activity in his early UK study. He used a logarithmic OLS regression of diversification on research activity in 25 UK manufacturing industry groups. Thus,

$$\log Y = 0.29 + 0.29 \log X \qquad \bar{R}^2 = 0.656 \qquad (9.10)$$
$$(2.64) \quad\;\; (6.83)$$

where Y is the weighted average ratio of non-primary to total employment of firms classified to an industry group in 1958 and X is employment of qualified scientists and engineers in that group in 1960. Note that Amey appears to use the absolute number of scientists and engineers in an industry group as his independent variable. Nevertheless, his results are highly significant (t ratios in parentheses), and suggest that a doubling of research activity (as proxied here) is associated with a 29 per cent increase in diversification.

Gorecki (1975) examined the determinants of diversification in UK manufacturing industry in 1963. Using OLS regression for a sample of 44 two-and-a-half digit manufacturing industries, he obtained the following equation:

$$Y = 0.22 + 0.04D - 5.43X_1 + 3.18X_1D + 0.37X_2$$
$$ (4.82) \quad (0.84) \quad (-2.10) \quad (0.87) \quad (2.34)$$
$$ - 0.36X_2D + 0.08X_3 + 0.002X_4 \tag{9.11}$$
$$ (-2.16) \quad (1.22) \quad (1.25)$$
$$\bar{R}^2 = 0.2435.$$

In this regression Y is the weighted average diversification ratio of firms classified to an industry in 1963, D is a dummy variable for consumer and non-consumer goods industries ($D = 1$ for the latter),[21] and the other explanatory variables are, consecutively, proxies for marketing intensity, research intensity, industry growth and industry concentration. As can be seen (with t ratios in parentheses), research intensity (X_2) (proxied here as the number of qualified scientists and engineers per 100 persons employed in 1959–60) is again positively associated with diversification, and this result is statistically significant at the 1 per cent level (on a one-tail test). It appears, moreover, that this effect was attributable mainly to research activity in consumer goods industries as indicated by the negative and significant coefficient on the interaction variable of research intensity and D.[22]

Other hypotheses fair less well, however. There was no statistically significant evidence that either market growth (X_3) or market concentration (X_4) affected the degree of diversification in UK manufacturing industries in 1963, the latter result in particular conflicting with Gort's US findings for 1954. The negative (and statistically significant) effect of marketing intensity (X_1) (measured here as the 1963 advertising/sales ratio) is, moreover, contrary to theoretical expectations as outlined in section 9.2.1 above. There we argued that a firm's marketing expertise and its accumulated stock of goodwill might provide it with increased opportunities for diversification, and one might think that these factors would be captured in a positive association of diversification and advertising intensity in a primary industry. In fact, a reverse negative association is found in equation (9.11). Gorecki argues that this may be because high advertising intensity is associated particularly with consumer goods industries, and that firms in such industries tend to diversify (or, more correctly, integrate forward) into distribution rather than into other manufacturing industries. Such integration is not captured by the diversification index used by Gorecki, which relates only to manufacturing employment. While this explanation is a possibility, no direct evidence on it is currently available.

Two other studies may be briefly mentioned. First, Grant (1977) examined changes in diversification in UK manufacturing industry in 1963–8. In his study, diversification was measured in terms of changes in proportion of firms classified to one industry operating in a *specified* alternative industry where industries were defined at the two-digit (Order) level. He found, among other things, that such broad spectrum diversification took place from industries with high R & D activity, between industries with similar R & D activity levels and into high-growth industries. Conversely, marketing intensity in the primary industry had no significant effect on diversification.

Second, Wolf (1977) examined the effect of technical activity and average firm size on domestic diversification, exporting and production abroad for US manufacturing firms in the 1960s. He found that all these activities were positively related to research activity in the primary industry, and that average firm size in the industry was also positively and significantly correlated with these activities (bar exporting).

Finally, some evidence on management control of firms and diversification is presented by Amihud and Lev (1981). They considered two tests of the hypothesis that manager-controlled firms engage in more diversification (see section 9.2.2), both of which are consistent with the hypothesis. We consider their first test only, which relates to the number of conglomerate acquisitions of 309 of the largest US industrial firms in 1961–70. These companies were divided into three groups, represented by dummy variables (i.e. variables which take values zero or one) in the regression as manager-controlled ($D_m = 1$ where no single party held 10 per cent or more of the company's stock); weak owner-controlled ($D_w = 1$ where a single party owned between 10 and 30 per cent of the stock) and owner-controlled otherwise.[23] Using a special regression technique, known as Tobit analysis, they found that (with t ratios in parentheses):

$$Y = -1.56 + 1.93D_m + 1.26D_w - 0.0001X \qquad (9.12)$$
$$(-3.20)\quad (3.72)\quad\ (2.16)\qquad (0.75)$$

where Y is the number of large conglomerate acquisitions in 1961–70 (assets acquired in excess of $10 million) and X is the size of firm in terms of sales in 1961. The coefficient on the variable D_m is positive and statistically significant at better than the 1 per cent level on a one-tail test, indicating that manager-controlled firms engage on average in more conglomerate acquisitions than other firms. The significant positive coefficient on D_w shows this is also the case for weak owner-controlled firms, but to a lesser extent than for manager-controlled firms. These results contrast with those for horizontal and vertical mergers, also obtained by Amihud and Lev, which show no significant or consistent pattern by type of firm control. Hence the results suggest strongly that management control is positively associated with conglomerate acquisition, and this result is consistent with the view that managers pursue diversification policies to reduce employment risk.

In sum, evidence on the determinants of diversification shows a link between diversification and research intensity and management control, but other possible links are at present unproven. Only limited empirical evidence is currently available, however, and further work is required at both a theoretical and an empirical level before the diversification phenomenon can be more fully understood.

9.3 Consequences of Diversification

Considerable disquiet has been expressed in the industrial economics literature as to possible 'monopolistic' effects of diversification. However, such effects have been difficult to pin down in either theory or practice. In section 9.3.1 we review some of the possible effects that have been suggested, while in section 9.3.2 we consider the limited evidence currently available on diversification and economic performance.

9.3.1 Diversification and Competition

We begin by considering interrelationships which may exist between diversification and competition. Some of these effects are likely to be socially beneficial as, for example, when diversified new entry leads to increased competition and lower price–cost margins in an industry. In other cases, however, it is suggested that diversification may have ambiguous or socially harmful effects, warranting the consideration of public policy intervention. In what follows we consider the principal hypotheses that have been advanced relating diversification and competition, and indicate (where appropriate) possible grounds for public policy concern.

Diversified entry   As noted in chapters 4 and 6, diversified firms may have particular advantages over specialized firms when it comes to entry into a new market. A diversified firm is likely to be able to raise capital on terms more nearly comparable to existing firms, either from the capital market or from its own sources. In addition, a diversified firm (with alternative profit sources) can more readily stand an initial period of loss-making in a new market until it establishes itself sufficiently to move into profit. On both counts, therefore, diversified entry is likely to provide an important supplementary force tending to promote competition in situations where entry by a new specialist firm would be difficult. *Ceteris paribus*, such entry (provided it was entry by new building, and provided that it did not itself increase monopolization in the industry) would tend to increase competition and lead to lower price–cost margins. Hence, while, as discussed below, there

H

may be other offsetting effects of diversification, diversified entry in itself is likely to be socially beneficial.

Cost savings   Similarly, diversification will tend to be socially beneficial, *ceteris paribus*, when a diversified firm is able to produce in a market at a lower cost than an equivalent specialized firm. If such lower costs exist, then, as noted in chapter 5, the firm may be able to attain a high market share and a high price–cost margin. Nevertheless, the social benefits obtained may be greater than the alternative of specialized production if the latter would mean a loss in efficiency. This might be the case, for example, if the diversified firm had access to superior (and indivisible) management which would not be available to an equivalent specialized firm. As discussed in chapter 5, both market power and cost saving effects may coexist in a concentrated market where superior efficiency is a feature of certain firms. Since the fact that these firms may be diversified adds nothing new in principle to this discussion, we shall pass on to other matters here.

Group interdependence   A third possibility which has not been discussed previously is that a diversified firm will take group decisions which will result in different prices, etc., for its subsidiaries compared with specialized firms. Two possible reasons for this (which are discussed in turn) are that inter-relationships may exist between the diversified firm's products and that, in a situation of uncertainty, firms may be risk-averse.

First, a diversified firm seeking to maximize group profits will in general adopt different prices, etc., compared with equivalent specialized firms when demand and production interrelationships exist between products. On the demand side, substitutability (complementarity) between products will tend to lead to higher (lower) prices in diversified firms compared with equivalent profit-maximizing specialist firms. Thus, for example, specialist producers of paper and plastic bags who act *independently* will not explicitly take account of the fact that a rise in the price of one product raises the consumption of the other in setting prices. A single producer of both products would (in maximizing group profits) take this effect into account, and this would *tend* to raise prices and profits to the detriment of consumers.[24] Conversely, a diversified firm producing complements, e.g. beer and bar snacks, would tend to reduce their prices. On the production side, if the marginal costs of one product were lowered (raised) by an increase in production of the other, or alternatively if costs of diversified production were lower (higher) than for specialized production at a given output rate, then a diversified firm would tend to produce more (less) than equivalent specialized firms. The case in which costs are lower in multi-product production subsumes the traditional case of joint products, e.g. wool and mutton, but is more generally referred to as an economy of scope.[25]

A second possibility, suggested by Bradburd (1980b; see also 1980a), is that a risk-averse diversified firm will adopt different prices from equivalent risk-averse specialized firms. Bradburd assumes that markets are subject to demand uncertainty (with respect to market output) and that firms are risk-averse in attempting to maximize the expected utility of their income. Then, even though firms are identical in all relevant respects, including their degree of risk aversion, they will adopt different price policies when profit streams derived from different markets are correlated. As noted by Bradburd, moreover, such correlations may occur even though products are completely unrelated with respect to demand and cost conditions – as, for example, when both are subject to the common influence of the business cycle. In the case where profits are positively (negatively) correlated, the diversified risk-averse firm will set lower (higher) prices for its products than its specialized equivalent firms. This reflects greater (smaller) risk reduction for the group as a whole as price is lowered from the profit-maximizing level when profits are positively (negatively) correlated. It remains an open question, however, whether diversified and specialized firms are similarly risk-averse in practice, and *a fortiori* whether this line of argument is likely to give rise to appreciable differences in price policies.

While group considerations may dictate modifications in price (etc.) policies for the reasons given above, these effects may be attenuated in practice by problems of coordinating group activities. As Williamson (1975) in particular has stressed, large diversified firms may suffer from acute coordination problems which favour the adoption of decentralized multi-divisional organizational forms (M forms). Such M-form firms obtain efficiency advantages in coordination by decentralizing decision-making to largely autonomous product divisions. To the extent that efficiency gains are obtained in this way, however, it seems likely that some opportunities to obtain market gains from group decision-making will be lost. In practice, some compromise will be made such that important market opportunities (e.g. where products are closely related in demand) are taken into account. In other cases, however, efficient coordination may be judged to be more important, so that group subsidiaries operate largely independently. To the extent that the latter is the case, we would expect to find no substantial modification in diversified firm policies arising from group interdependence effects.

Predatory pricing   A fourth possibility is that diversification in conjunction with market dominance may give rise to predatory pricing and other aggressive business practices. Predatory pricing occurs when a dominant firm or firms cut price to drive out or discipline competitors in the short run in order to raise prices towards monopoly levels in the longer run. Among other things, it requires that 'predator' firms be in a financially strong position relative to their competitors. This, it is argued, will be the case if dominant 'predator' firms are diversified and hence able to cross-subsidize temporary losses in a particular market with profits earned elsewhere. Such cross-subsidization may also support other predatory tactics, such as aggressive advertising campaigns, similarly designed to discipline or eliminate rivals. In addition, diversified firms may also gain from a *demonstration effect* in that their predatory action in one market may discourage actual and potential competitors from competing in other markets. Hence there are potential gains to predatory action by a diversified firm dominant in a number of markets which go far beyond any single market.

Evidence on predatory pricing is rather fragmentary and contentious (not least because of disagreements between economists over how to identify the practice – see section 11.2 below for further details). In the USA a number of early examples, including the cases of Standard Oil and the tobacco and gunpowder monopolies, have been suggested, although some economists dispute that predatory tactics were in fact used in these cases.[26] In the UK several other possible examples have emerged in the reports of the Monopolies Commission.[27] Thus, for example, both the British Match Company and the British Oxygen Company, with virtual monopoly positions in their respective UK markets, used so-called 'fighting companies' to meet new competition in local and regional markets. Other possible instances arose in the cases of metal containers and electrical equipment for mechanically propelled land vehicles. Because of the nature of Monopolies Commission references, however, which until recently were typically restricted to rather narrow product areas, very little evidence on diversification and predatory pricing is available from this source.

Spheres of influence (mutual forbearance)   When diversified companies face each other in a number of markets, it is sometimes suggested that they will adopt a less competitive stance than would equivalent specialist firms. The rationale for this argument is that diversified firms will avoid taking competitive action in any one market if this risks retaliatory action by diversified rivals in other markets. Rather, it is argued that diversified firms will develop 'spheres of influence' and that their rivals will adopt live-and-let-live policies in these areas. The result would be a general stability and lack of vigorous competition in such markets, implying higher prices (and possibly higher costs) to the detriment of consumers.

There is no doubt that, particularly in international markets, firms adopt geographic spheres of influence. Evidence on spheres of influence between products, however, is particularly sparse, and only fragmentary evidence (e.g. in occasional Monopolies Commission reports) exists as to the general importance of this hypothesis.

Other hypotheses   Several other links between diversification and competition may be mentioned in conclusion. First, a diversified firm which produces several products may adopt a policy of tying the sale of one product to that of another. Typical examples are the supply of a machine (e.g. a photocopier) with its consumables (e.g. paper, maintenance, etc.), or the supply of replacement units rather than individual components. Such tie-in sales, while they restrict consumer choice, do not necessarily lead to an additional welfare loss, and these matters are noted further in section 11.2 below. Second, diversified firms operating in a number of markets may gain advantages of a political nature related to their aggregate size rather than their power in individual markets. Courtaulds, for example, claimed that a primary motive for diversifying its activities in UK textile industries in the 1960s was to exert political pressure to protect the declining textile sector.[28] Similar political pressure may be exerted in other fields (e.g. coal and petroleum products) in which a few large, diversified companies are dominant, and such pressure may be of considerable public concern in an economic and also in a wider political sense.

9.3.2 Empirical Evidence

Since many hypotheses surround diversification and economic performance, available empirical evidence does not enable us to determine whether market power or other effects (if any) are significant in determining links between diversification and profitability. It does, however, provide some idea of the net effects that exist and hence may provide a basis for more carefully specified empirical work in the future.

Several studies have suggested that industry profitability is higher when participant firms are more diversified. Miller (1969), for example, examined the effect of corporate diversity on profitability in US manufacturing industries in 1958–62. Using OLS multiple regression techniques for a sample of 106 minor (approximately three-digit) US manufacturing industries, he found that

$$Y = 9.70 + 0.05X_1 - 0.26X_2 + 0.89X_3 - 0.04X_4 \qquad \bar{R}^2 = 0.494 \qquad (9.13)$$
$$ (3.67) \quad (-5.17) \quad (8.76) \quad (3.17)$$

where Y is the annual rate of return on net worth averaged for 1958–9 to 1961–2; X_1 is the four-firm concentration ratio in 1958; X_2 is the marginal eight-firm concentration ratio in 1958;[29] X_3 is the average advertising/sales ratio in 1958–60 and X_4 is the ratio of primary to total employment (specialization ratio) of firms classified to the industry in 1958. All variables have a statistically significant effect on profitability at better than the 1 per cent significance level (t ratios in parentheses). In particular, the negative coefficient on the specialization ratio indicates that profit rates and diversification are positively correlated, and this would support the view, for example, that monopoly power effects are associated with diversification, e.g. through predatory pricing or 'spheres of influence' effects. Miller, however, was not prepared to speculate over the interpretation of his findings in the absence of a general theoretical framework of analysis.

Similar results were obtained by Rhoades (1973) using a sample of 241 four-digit US manufacturing industries in 1963. Using OLS regression, he found that

$$Y = 15.64 + 0.11X_1 - 0.08X_2 + 0.06X_3 + 0.11X_4 + 7.08D - 0.08X_5$$
$$\quad\quad\quad (3.32)\quad (3.35)\quad (3.02)\quad (4.86)\quad (6.12)\quad (2.59)$$
$$\bar{R}^2 = 0.32. \quad\quad\quad\quad\quad\quad\quad\quad\quad\quad\quad\quad (9.14)$$

where Y is the industry price–cost margin; X_1 is four-firm concentration; X_2 is the ratio of primary to total employment of firms classified to the industry, and the other variables reflect market growth, the capital/output ratio, a producer–consumer goods dummy variable (consumer goods = 1) and an index of the geographic concentration of markets, respectively. The negative coefficient on the specialization ratio (X_2) is statistically significant at the 1 per cent level, again indicating a positive relationship between profitability and diversification. Rhoades attributes this to the potential for predatory pricing and for concealment of profits in consolidated accounts by diversified firms. An alternative diversification index, designed to capture the extent to which the secondary activities of diversified companies comprised a leading market share in the industry, failed to attain statistical significance at the 5 per cent level on a one-tail test, however.

While Rhoades's study for US industries in 1963 suggested a positive link between industry performance and diversification, he obtained a reverse result in a follow-up study for 1967 (Rhoades, 1974). This study was based on a sample of 117 two-and-a-half to three-digit US manufacturing industries, in comparison with the 241 four-digit industries used in his study for 1963. Using four alternative measures of diversification, he found a statistically significant *negative* effect of diversification on price–cost margins in each case. In view of the different levels of aggregation employed, Rhoades suggested that the difference in his results might be attributed to the broadness of the concept of diversification involved. Specifically, while narrow spectrum diversification (more readily captured in his 1963 study) into closely related products was associated with higher price–cost margins, diversification over a broader range (captured more in his 1967 study) was dominated by production, distribution and management inefficiencies which contributed to lower margins in firms' primary industries.

This argument is plausible, although not wholly consistent with Rhoades's own explanations of his 1963 results (see above). An alternative suggestion by Scherer (1980) is that the 1967 results may have been unrepresentative, as diversified firms entered a possibly temporary period of readjustment following substantial merger activity in the 1960s. No tests of these competing hypotheses for 1967 are apparently available.

The available evidence for US industry suggests that there may be a positive association between profitability and the diversification of firms in an industry, at least when sufficiently disaggregated data are used. This result may be attributable to a variety of monopoly power or cost-reducing effects, however. Moreover, since diversification is itself likely to be an endogenous variable, it is possible that reverse causation is also at work, e.g. if greater profits in primary industries encourage firms to diversify more. These matters cannot be satisfactorily decided given the limited nature of the empirical evidence currently available.

9.4 Summary and Conclusions

This chapter has examined some of the theoretical and empirical work currently available on the nature and significance of conglomerate diversification. In section 9.1 we examined measurement and trends in diversification, with particular reference (in the latter context) to UK manufacturing industry. In section 9.2 we considered possible determinants of conglomerate diversification, emphasizing asset utilization and risk reduction motives for diversification to take place. Finally, in section 9.3 we considered possible competitive effects of diversification and some of the (limited) empirical evidence currently available on profitability and diversification.

Two issues arise naturally from this discussion. First, is conglomerate diversification an important and growing phenomenon in UK industry? Second, what are the competitive consequences of diversification? On the first question, the evidence presented in section 9.1.2 suggested that, contrary perhaps to impressionistic evidence, many of the largest firms in UK industry remain relatively specialized even today. Nevertheless, diversification is clearly important for some firms and in some sectors, and, moreover, there is some evidence that its growth has played a (limited) part in increasing aggregate concentration. On the second question, conglomerate diversification offers scope for anti-competitive practices such as predatory pricing and mutual forbearance, as well as having possibly wider pricing and political consequences. The concentration of power in large diversified firms inevitably raises questions of possible abuse of such power, and hence warrants public policy attention. At the least, therefore, it seems desirable that provision be made for public investigation of the behaviour of individual conglomerate firms, although limited scope for this exists (as we shall see in chapters 11 and 12) in current UK competition policy.

Notes

1 As explained in section 9.1.2 below, problems exist in putting these distinctions into practice. This arises in part from the essential arbitrariness of the concepts here defined and in part from additional measurement problems created by data availability.

2 See the Federal Trade Commission (FTC) annual *Statistical Report on Mergers and Acquisitions*. The FTC's classification in fact relates to mergers, all three categories being referred to as 'conglomerate mergers'. The categorization, however, applies more generally to diversification. See also Weston (1970).

3 A derivation is given, for example, in Jacquemin and Berry (1979).

4 Note also that the Census practice of classifying an entire plant or establishment to a particular MLH industry on the basis of its principal product(s) means that any diversification within plants is ignored by Census data.

5 Earlier studies include Amey (1964), Gorecki (1975) and Hassid (1975). These studies examine data respectively for 1958, 1963 and 1968.

6 It is important to remember, however, that definitions of industries are important in assessing diversification, and vehicle industries, in particular, may be defined quite broadly. Indeed, the fact that no markets exist in many activities undertaken in a typical car firm is likely to influence the definition of the industry and hence, paradoxically, may lead to an overstatement of car firm specialization. Thanks to Paul Geroski for this point.

7 These figures are based on the amalgamation of Orders VII, IX, XI and XII. In the absence of such an amalgamation, 'narrow spectrum' diversification into industries within a firm's primary Order falls to 45 per cent: see Utton (1979, pp. 24–8).

8 In particular, Census classifications take limited account of possible demand relationships between products, and hence must be treated with care.

9 For further discussion of these data, see chapter 12.

10 Similar arguments are used to explain multinational operation, which is, of course, merely market extension diversification on an international scale. We do not consider multinationals explicitly in this chapter, but the interested reader should consult, for example, Caves (1982).

11 Large diversified firms, of course, are also likely to attract and employ top managers. Hence a chicken-and-egg situation is likely to exist between top managers and conglomerate firms.

12 Only a very simple case is considered here; for a more general formulation see Prais (1976).

13 Since r as given in (9.7) is the weighted sum of two random variables, it follows that its variance is

$$V(r) = (\tfrac{1}{2})^2 V(r_1) + (\tfrac{1}{2})^2 V(r_2) + 2(\tfrac{1}{2})^2 C(r_1, r_2)$$

where $C(\cdot)$ is the covariance of r_1 and r_2 (see, for example, Wonnacott and Wonnacott, 1972, p. 105). Given that

$$C(\cdot) = \rho \sqrt{V(r_1)} \sqrt{V(r_2)},$$

equation (9.8) is obtained by substitution and then taking the square root of $V(r)$.

14 Adding a new activity to a diversified firm in a generalization of equation (9.8) will reduce risk for $0 < \rho < 1$, but, as shown by Prais (1976, pp. 95–8) continued diversification may soon bring rather small risk reduction gains in cases where ρ is positive.

15 See, for example, Adelman (1961).

16 The influence of taxation is in fact complex: see, for example, Sherman (1972).

17 See, for example, Miller (1977). This is a contentious area in financial theory, although it would seem almost inevitable that disequilibrium adjustments to eradicate tax differentials would occur. The important issue may be the speed of such adjustments as taxes change and hence the scope for diversification gains in disequilibrium situations. As noted by Prais (1976, p. 105), capital restructuring to yield a tax gain is prohibited in the UK, although this ban (perhaps significantly)

does not extend to restructuring in a merger where acquisition is partly financed by the issue of debentures.

18 For an excellent discussion of this issue see Amihud and Lev (1981).

19 As noted above, however, links between diversification and technical activity may also be regarded as problematical owing to the possibility of two-way causation.

20 Gort also argued that diversification would be positively associated with average firm size in the primary industry and negatively associated with primary industry growth. He found some support for both hypotheses but apparently not when all variables were included together (although full results were not reported).

21 The variable D takes values zero for consumer goods industries and one for producer goods industries. Hence, when it appears in equation (9.11), *additional* effects in producer goods industries are reported. For further discussion of dummy variables, see Wonnacott and Wonnacott (1972), pp. 308–13.

22 Since this coefficient measures the additional effect of research intensity on diversification in non-consumer goods industries (see previous footnote), the total effect in such industries is estimated to be practically zero (i.e. $0.37 - 0.36$).

23 The owner-controlled variable is excluded from the regression and acts as the 'base line' for the estimates when D_m and D_w are both zero.

24 This is most easily demonstrated by considering products produced under constant costs with constant elasticity demand curves. Independent monopolists of two products, 1 and 2, would set price–cost margins equal to the reciprocal of the own-price elasticity of demand (defined as positive); i.e.,

$$\frac{p_i - MC_i}{p_i} = \frac{1}{\eta_{ii}} \qquad (i = 1, 2).$$

A monopolist producing both products would, as an approximation, set

$$\frac{p_i - MC_i}{p_i} = \frac{1}{\eta_{ii}} \left(1 + \frac{p_j x_j}{p_i x_i} \cdot \frac{\eta_{ji}}{\eta_{jj}} \right) \qquad (i, j = 1, 2; j \neq i)$$

with $\eta_{ji} = (dx_j/dp_i)(p_i/x_j)$ and $\eta_{jj} = -(dx_j/dp_j)(p_j/x_j)$. Since the cross-price elasticity of demand, η_{ji}, is positive for substitutes, the prices of both products will be higher in this case.

25 See, for example, Bailey and Friedlaender (1982) or, more comprehensively, Baumol, Panzar and Willig (1982).

26 See, for example, McGee (1958) on the Standard Oil case.

27 For a detailed survey, see Utton (1979, chapter 5).

28 See, for example, Cowling et al. (1980, pp. 300–2).

29 The marginal eight-firm concentration ratio is the share of firms ranked 5 to 8 in industry output. Miller includes this variable to capture (with negative sign) the effect of competitive pressure of the second group of four firms on the leading four firms. The negative coefficient reported in equation (9.13) may be attributable to statistical bias, however, and hence must be treated with care: see Collins and Preston (1969) and, for a reply, Miller (1971).

10 Social Costs of Monopoly

This chapter is concerned with the social costs of monopoly and attempts which have been made to estimate such costs. In particular, we consider the pioneering work of Harberger (1954) on monopoly and resource allocation, together with subsequent studies which have sought to develop and extend his work. We shall see that, on both general and more specific grounds, one should treat available estimates with care. Nevertheless, the studies that are reviewed provide a useful way of discussing issues in the welfare analysis of monopoly, and as such are of considerable interest.

In what follows, we begin with a brief overview of the problem, outlining some general considerations which should be borne in mind in considering the available evidence. This is followed, in section 10.2, by a review of Harberger's work together with certain other early studies. Finally, in section 10.3 we consider some more recent developments in the field, and how they affect the earlier conclusions of Harberger and others.

10.1 General Issues

The traditional argument against monopoly or less than perfect competition is that it restricts output below competitive levels, implying a misallocation of resources in the economy. In its most general form, the problem arises from price being above marginal cost in the presence of market power, which implies that a Pareto-optimal allocation of resources does not apply. That is, it is possible to obtain a more efficient allocation of resources such that one or some individuals could be made better off without any single individual being made worse off. This gain could be made since high monopoly prices imply that the social value of monopolized goods relative to competitive goods exceeds the relative social costs of their production. Hence, by lowering prices and raising outputs of monopolized goods, incremental gains in net social benefit can be obtained in moving to a socially optimal composition of national output. Such an output configuration (setting aside externalities, etc.) is obtained where prices equal marginal costs in each industry.

In this chapter we are concerned with *measuring* the social costs of monopoly. Almost all studies that have been made have attempted to do this in terms of the partial equilibrium consumer surplus analysis we have used at several places already in this book. That is, it is argued that a measure of *deadweight* welfare loss can be constructed for any particular industry equal to consumer surplus losses (net of producer surplus gains) in deviating from the competitive price. This approach has the advantages of intuitive appeal and simplicity but it also has several weaknesses. This may be particularly true where, as in the present chapter, we are concerned with measuring welfare losses in the economy as a whole (see below).

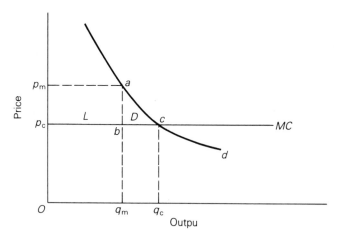

Figure 10.1

Various general criticisms of the various studies that have been conducted can be made. First, and most obviously, by focusing attention on the price-raising effects of monopoly rather than on other possible effects, these studies consider only part of the issue and may, therefore, give a biased view of monopoly welfare loss. Consider figure 10.1, for example. This represents an industry with constant marginal costs, MC, and a normal market demand curve, d. If firms exert monopoly power in the industry then they set a price (say p_m) above competitive levels.[1] If the competitive price is p_c (equal to MC), then monopolization implies a gross loss of consumer surplus equal to area $p_m a c p_c$, of which the area $p_m a b p_c$ is a gain in producer surplus. Hence, the *deadweight loss to monopoly* is area abc. The standard (Harberger-type) method of measuring monopoly welfare loss involves summing areas like abc for each industry to arrive at an aggregate estimate of welfare loss.

Such an approach, however, ignores other possible effects of monopolization. For example, costs as well as prices may differ between competition and monopoly. In some industries, for example, concentration of production is associated with the existence of economies of scale which provide real cost savings for the economy. In such cases a trade-off may exist between monopoly power and real cost savings which should also be considered (see chapter 12). Conversely, if monopolization of an industry gives rise to slack and inefficiency in production, then monopoly welfare losses will exceed areas such as *abc* in the figure. This issue of slack or inefficiency associated with monopoly has been discussed under the generic name of X-inefficiency (see Leibenstein, 1966) and we discuss it further (in relation to mergers) in chapter 12.

We have seen in chapter 5 that differential efficiency between firms can have an effect in tending to increase profits and concentration in an industry. This creates problems of interpretation when one considers monopoly welfare losses. In a competitive industry firms with superior resources, etc., will earn rents associated with those resources in competitive equilibrium. Hence, it would seem that, by including such rents in the measurement of monopoly welfare loss, an overstatement will be made. Subtle problems of interpretation may, however, be involved here (see Demsetz, 1973b), and the actual adjustments needed may be complex.

In addition to affecting costs, monopoly may also have effects of a much broader kind. As noted in chapter 7, a central argument in defence of monopoly is that some degree of monopoly power is conducive to innovation and technical progress. In so far as such an effect operates, dynamic efficiency gains from monopoly must also be considered. No attempts have so far been made, however, to measure the trade-off (if any) between static and dynamic efficiency.

Monopoly can also have effects in other directions. For example, as we noted in chapter 6, it can lead to possibly excessive and wasteful levels of advertising in moderate- to high-concentration industries as oligopolistic firms engage in mutually offsetting advertising. Also, it can lead to excessive brand proliferation or patenting, or alternatively to predatory and other anti-competitive tactics designed to restrict entry and/or discipline rivals. Such effects have mainly been ignored as far as measurement of monopoly welfare losses is concerned. However, some recent studies have looked at costs of attempting to gain or maintain a monopoly position, and we consider this work further in section 10.3 below.

On a somewhat different tack, monopoly welfare loss estimates have recently been criticized at a more general level by Littlechild (1981). Writing from the viewpoint of the new Austrian school of economics, he argues that the monopoly loss estimates of Harberger and others are based on a misconceived methodology. According to the Austrian school of thought, competition should be viewed as a process rather than an equilibrium concept, and, correspondingly, profits should be regarded as an integral feature of this process rather than merely as monopolistic deviations from competitive levels. In Littlechild's view, most profits observed arise from windfall gains or losses arising from uncertainty in the market or because creative and alert entrepreneurs have been able to take advantage of market opportunities. Such profits are a vital feature of a successfully operating dynamic economy and hence should not be looked on as signals of welfare loss. Indeed, in Littlechild's view, any attempt to remove such 'monopoly' profits from an economy, far from improving economic welfare, would be likely to do great harm.

Clearly, this argument relies strongly on a belief in the beneficial operation of the free market economy. Whether Littlechild believes that no monopoly power can exist in private firms (as opposed to government-backed monopolies), or whether he believes that dynamic considerations outweigh any static welfare losses is not entirely clear. Clearly it would be inadmissible to make the first argument, however, since this would be tantamount to defining the monopoly problem away *a priori* without reference to the evidence. On the other hand, if private monopoly power can exist (as it surely can), then Littlechild's argument against its measurement loses its force. In short, therefore, the argument that the equilibrium basis for monopoly welfare loss estimates is misconceived does not itself appear to hold water.

One final general issue relating to monopoly welfare loss estimates may be briefly mentioned. This concerns the use of partial equilibrium measures to estimate monopoly welfare loss. As is well known, consumer surplus can be criticized as a measure of economic welfare for several reasons (see, for example, Gravelle and Rees, 1981, chapter 4). Such measures have an unambiguous interpretation in standard consumer theory only when income effects of price changes are zero, which, of course, is unlikely to be the case for many products. Also, and probably more important, aggregation of such measures across individuals simply ignores questions of *equity* in arriving at a welfare loss estimate. While one could imagine that equity matters could be dealt with separately (e.g. by optimal lump-sum transfers), such an assumption is hardly acceptable in practice. Hence, it is not possible simply to ignore the equity issue, and this should also be borne in mind in considering the studies discussed below.

More fundamentally, however, when one considers the *aggregate* social cost of monopoly in the economy, important reservations exist over the use of *partial equilibrium* methods. In an economy in which monopolistic deviations exist in a number of industries, second-best considerations (Lipsey and Lancaster, 1956/7) suggest that measurement of welfare losses need not be straightforward. The classic case, of course, is where increasing monopolization of one industry can offset distortions arising in an industry producing a substitute product (e.g. gas and electricity). In such cases use of partial equilibrium welfare loss measures can be seriously misleading. Several simulation studies (Bergson, 1973, and more recently Kay, 1983) have suggested that serious errors can arise in using partial equilibrium methods (in particular, leading to underestimates of welfare loss), and this too must lead to reservations concerning the estimates discussed below.

10.2 Some Early Estimates

We now turn our attention to attempts which have been made to quantify the social costs of monopoly. The pioneering work in this field was done by Harberger and we begin by looking at his work. We then consider some subsequent criticisms and extensions which have been made to his work.

In his study, Harberger (1954) considered an ideal economy in equilibrium such that all firms operated on long-run cost curves, all markets were cleared and all firms earned a normal rate of return on invested capital. In the real world, of course, none of these conditions need be observed. However, if one assumes that long-run costs are constant and that one observes a market-clearing equilibrium in the economy, then variations in rates of return between industries can be taken as indicators of resource misallocations. Specifically, Harberger argued that high rates of return could be used to indicate restrictions on output and hence industries with too few resources employed; and conversely, low rates of return would be associated with industries in which resources were overemployed. By looking at deviations in rates of return from the competitive norm, therefore, monopoly welfare losses could be assessed.

Harberger used this perspective to show that monopoly welfare losses in the US were typically very small in relation to US national income. Consider figure 10.1 as representing a typical industry in the US economy. In this industry, with constant marginal costs, MC, the deadweight welfare loss to monopoly is area abc (area D). Harberger argued that, as an approximation, this area can be written as

$$D = -\tfrac{1}{2}\Delta p \Delta q \tag{10.1}$$

where Δp is the rise in price above competitive levels and Δq is the corresponding fall in output. If we define the market price elasticity of demand as $\eta = -(\Delta q/\Delta p)(p_m/q_m)$ and the price–cost margin as $M = \Delta p/p_m$, then it is readily seen that Δp in (10.1) is equal to Mp_m while $\Delta q = -M\eta q_m$. Hence, on substitution into (10.1),

$$D = \tfrac{1}{2}M^2\eta(p_m q_m). \tag{10.2}$$

As an approximation, therefore, one can estimate the deadweight loss D from (10.2) by using the price–cost margin, M, the market price elasticity of demand, η and market sales revenue, $p_m q_m$.

In order to do this Harberger made some special assumptions. First, in the absence of specific information on price elasticities of demand, he assumed that all such elasticities were equal to one. In his view, such an assumption erred on the high side when one considers the general movement of resources required to eradicate monopoly. Second, he assumed that competitive rates of return were given by the average rate of return in his sample, taken as an estimate of the rate of return that would apply if resources were reallocated optimally. (This assumption is particularly open to question, as we discuss further below.) Finally, and building from this, he assumed that welfare losses arose in industries with above-competitive rates of return (as shown in figure 10.1) and correspondingly in industries with below-competitive profits. These assumptions were then employed with data collected by Epstein for 2046 firms in 73 US industries to estimate welfare losses in US industries in 1924–8.

Given these data and assumptions, Harberger estimated the amount of resource misallocation and its consequent welfare effects in US industry. First, assuming the demand curve has unit elasticity over the relevant range, the amount of misallocated resources (area $q_m bcq_c$ in figure 10.1) will be exactly equal to excess profits (area $p_m abp_c$).[2] This simplification allowed Harberger to answer the question, What value of resources must be transferred from low- to high-profit industries to equalize rates of return? The answer for the 73 industries (found by adding up all the deficient profits in worse-than-average industries) was $550 million. Increasing this figure to cover all manufacturing (of which 55 per cent was not represented by his sample) gave $1.2 billion of resources misallocated in manufacturing as a whole. This represented 4 per cent of manufacturing resources or 1.5 per cent of GNP in the USA in the second half of the 1920s.

The welfare gains associated with such a transfer of resources can be computed by equation (10.2) for each industry with $\eta = 1$. This gives an estimate of the deadweight loss triangle *abc* in figure 10.1 for cases of underproduction, and a corresponding triangle for overproduction. Since gains to the economy occur in both types of industry when resources are reallocated, Harberger argued that the total welfare gain consisted of the sum of all the gains in all industries. For the 73-industry sample this sum turned out to be $26.5 million, which, scaled up to all manufacturing, was $59 million. This figure was less than 0.1 per cent of US GNP in the 1920s, and amounted to only $1.50 per capita in the USA at the time Harberger wrote.

Various attempts made by Harberger to use alternative assumptions in his analysis failed materially to affect this basic finding that the welfare gains to be made from eradicating monopolistic resource misallocations in US industry were likely to be negligible. This led him to conclude:

Our economy emphatically does not seem to be monopoly capitalism in big red letters. We can neglect monopoly elements and still gain a very good understanding of how our economic process works and how our resources are allocated. When we are interested in the big picture of our manufacturing economy, we need not apologise for treating it as competitive, for in fact it is awfully close to being so. On the other hand, when we are interested in the doings of particular industries, it may often be wise to take monopoly elements into account. Even though monopoly elements in cosmetics are a drop in the bucket in the big picture of American manufacturing, they still mean a lot when we are studying the behaviour of this particular industry. (Harberger, 1954, p. 87)

Not surprisingly, these strong conclusions attracted a great deal of interest, and a number of criticisms and extensions of Harberger's work have been attempted.

Several criticisms of Harberger's estimates were made in an early paper by Stigler (1956). First, and most obviously, Stigler criticized Harberger's arbitrary assumption that the price elasticity of market demand was unity. Clearly, from equation (10.2) higher values of η give rise to greater welfare loss estimates, and in Stigler's view oligopolistic coordination would restrict output to more elastic parts of the demand curve. Second, Stigler argued that Harberger's use of accounting rates of return might downward-bias his monopoly welfare loss estimates. This was because some part of monopoly profits are likely to be capitalized in asset values, giving rise to an understatement of the true monopoly profit rate. Third, some part of monopoly profits might in fact be absorbed by non-capital inputs showing up as costs rather than profits in the accounts. Monopoly elements in factor payments such as wages, managerial salaries, royalties and rents should also be taken into account. Finally, the average rate of return in Harberger's manufacturing sample might overstate the competitive rate of return, and hence lead to underestimation of welfare losses. On the other hand, if monopoly were more prevalent in manufacturing than other sectors of the economy, then the overall loss in the economy might tend to be overstated by figures for manufacturing alone.

Harberger's use of average rates of return in his sample as the standard by which to judge monopoly welfare losses deserves particular attention. In effect, by doing this he measured gains to be made (both positive and negative) from equalizing profit rates in industry. In so far as monopoly factors were present in his sample, however, the use of average profitability would overstate the competitive rate of return. This would not be the case only when no monopoly elements were present. Hence it would seem that Harberger's method contains a presumption that industry is competitive which downwards biases his estimates. Second, and on the other hand, some part of the deviations in profit rates from the average (in Harberger's view, probably as much as two-thirds) is likely to be due to chance and/or disequilibrium effects rather than monopoly. In so far as this is the case, then monopoly welfare losses are likely to be overstated.

Clearly, all of these arguments have some force and the question arises as to whether Harberger's results are robust. Several early studies sought to answer this question, and typically found similar results to those of Harberger. Schwartzman (1960), for example, found welfare losses to be less than 0.1 per cent of US GNP in 1954, despite using data directly on price–cost margins and allowing elasticities of demand up to 2. Worcester (1973) found that, by introducing strong assumptions into his analysis in order to obtain 'maximum defensible' estimates, monopoly welfare losses typically ranged between 0.43 and 0.73 per cent of US national income in the period 1956–69. This study was novel in that Worcester considered data on individual firms (the largest 500 industrials) rather than industries in an attempt to avoid downward-biased estimation arising from 'averaging' in industry data. Even so, his 'maximum' welfare loss estimates were very small, and in his view probably much too high.

One early study by Kamerschen (1966), however, came to somewhat different conclusions. Kamerschen considered welfare losses owing to monopoly in US industry in 1956/7–1960/1. Using a methodology similar to that of Harberger, he found that monopoly welfare losses were as high as 1.9 per cent of national income in this period: very much higher than those suggested by Harberger. This he attributed to the better quality of his data and to the inclusion of other non-manufacturing and non-corporate sectors in the analysis (as well as possibly to the different time period employed). Modifying the assumption that the price elasticity of demand was unity, moreover, he further assumed monopoly profit-maximizing conditions in each industry (i.e. $M = 1/\eta$ in equation (10.2)). This assumption increased welfare losses to roughly 6 per cent of national income. Clearly, these figures are very much higher than those found by Harberger and others.[3]

With the exception of Kamerschen's study, however, all the early estimates of monopoly welfare loss suggested that these were insubstantial relative to US national income. Hence, it would seem that monopoly was not a general problem in the US economy.[4] This conclusion has, however, been challenged to some extent in more recent studies, and we consider this work in section 10.3.

10.3 More Recent Studies

The studies of Harberger and others considered so far restrict attention to resource misallocation arising from output restrictions. Thus, in terms of the standard analysis of welfare loss (figure 10.1) they consider only magnitudes of deadweight loss areas, D. Several economists, and notably Posner (1975) (see also Tullock, 1967), have argued, however, that when monopoly profits exist they will attract resources into competing for those profits and this in itself may lead to an inefficient use of resources. We consider this argument (as developed by Posner) in greater detail below, and then move on to consider other recent studies of welfare loss.

Competition to *acquire* or *maintain* monopoly profits can take a variety of forms. One example might be non-price competition on advertising, product styling, packaging and so on, whereby firms seek to attract or maintain monopoly profits. In so far as such expenditures would not exist in competitive conditions, they can be regarded as socially wasteful. Again, expenditures designed to erect barriers to entry such as building excess capacity, product proliferation or pre-emptive patenting (see chapter 4) are also designed to maintain monopoly profits. On the other hand, firms may engage in expenditures to break down barriers to entry, by advertising, for example, and these represent an attempt to compete for monopoly profits. Bribing or otherwise lobbying governments and officials are yet other ways of seeking to acquire or maintain profits. All such expenditures which would not arise in competitive conditions are (according to Posner) a potential source of waste arising from monopoly.

In order to measure the magnitude of such wasteful expenditures, Posner made some heroic assumptions. Specifically, he assumed that competition to acquire or maintain a monopoly was essentially like any other competitive activity. Hence, on the specific assumption that resources are in perfectly elastic supply to this activity, resources committed will equal revenues obtainable (i.e. monopoly profits). Moreover, if one adds the assumption that such resources are totally wasted (which is clearly a strong assumption), then social costs also equal monopoly profits. On these assumptions, therefore, the social cost of monopoly in figure 10.1 is area D *plus* area L, where the latter area represents the equilibrium resource waste of competition to acquire and maintain monopoly profits.

Given that area D is approximately equal to $-\frac{1}{2}\Delta p \Delta q$ while $L = \Delta p(q_c + \Delta q)$, the relative sizes of D and L are given as

$$\frac{D}{L} = \frac{-\Delta q}{2(q_c + \Delta q)}. \tag{10.3}$$

In terms of the price elasticity of market demand (at the competitive price), η_c, and the relative markup over the competitive price, $M_c = \Delta p/p_c$, therefore, this becomes

$$\frac{D}{L} = \frac{M_c}{2(1/\eta_c - M_c)}. \tag{10.4}$$

Equation (10.4) shows that area L is large relative to D when M_c is small and η_c is small; for example, with an elasticity of demand of one and a markup of 10 per cent, the ratio of D to L is 1 to 18. Clearly, therefore, Posner's methodology provides scope for substantial increases in monopoly social costs once competition to acquire or maintain monopoly profits is brought into account.

This is, in fact, borne out in the estimates he presents. Using Harberger's data, for example, he finds that, while D is 0.1 per cent of GNP, L is 3.3 per cent, so that the total welfare loss estimated from Harberger's data is 3.4 per cent.[5] More generally, assuming that the average price markup in manufacturing and mining was 2 per cent (with an average price elasticity of market demand fixed at just over one), he calculates that the social cost of monopoly in this sector would be 0.6 per cent of GNP rising to 1.2 per cent if a 4 per cent average markup were used. Such figures are much higher than would be obtained if only area D were counted. In Posner's view, however, even higher social costs were incurred in the regulated sector of the US economy, where typically much higher markups were likely to be found.[6]

Posner's estimates clearly show the potential for increasing the social cost of monopoly by considering wasteful expenditures on competition to obtain monopoly profits. Important reservations exist, however, over his use of monopoly profits to measure such expenditures. On the one hand, wasteful expenditures are likely to be less than monopoly profits, both because such expenditures can have socially beneficial effects and because competition for monopoly profits may not be as strong as Posner assumes. Thus, for example, forms of non-price competition such as advertising or product innovation, while they can be carried to extremes, are likely to offer important benefits to society in the form of improved information and better products. Any social costs of competing for monopoly positions should therefore be considered net of such effects. Also, firms in monopoly positions may be able to collude tacitly (or explicitly) to avoid competition for monopoly profits. In an economy in which monopoly or high concentration is a pervasive feature, moreover, it seems likely that competition over potential profits will be weaker than Posner assumes.

On the other hand, arguments exist for profits to understate the social costs involved. Most obviously, where such expenditures have been incurred by firms actually operating in an industry, part of potential monopoly profits actually appear as costs to the firms. Ideally, one would like to measure full monopoly profits including such expenditures to obtain a correct comparison with competitive conditions. Second, attempts by governments to control monopoly abuses (via monopolies and mergers policies, etc.) will themselves involve social costs, which should also be included in the calculations. Such costs need not be related closely to actual monopoly profits, as is shown for example in an effective (but costly) policy which eliminates monopoly profits from an industry. While it is difficult to weigh these arguments against those for an overstatement of social cost in monopoly profits, it is clear that the link between these factors is unlikely to be very strong so that Posner's estimates must be correspondingly treated with care.

Nevertheless, his work does point to a wider conception of monopoly social cost than considered by Harberger and previous writers, and, in principle, these issues should be considered. In particular, these ideas have been incorporated into welfare loss estimates by Cowling and Mueller (1978), and we now turn to consider their work.

In fact, Cowling and Mueller seek to take account of a number of criticisms of the earlier work of Harberger and others. Their study is novel both in that it provides UK estimates for the first time and because, in contrast to most previous studies, it finds that losses may be quite large. In so far as it retains a partial equilibrium approach, however, it remains open to the criticism that it ignores interdependencies between industries and firms as do earlier studies. It also makes some quite strong assumptions of its own which we discuss further below.

Cowling and Mueller base their analysis on four criticisms of the Harberger approach. First, they argue that, by using separate estimates of the price markup and the demand elasticity in equation (10.2) above, Harberger ignored the interdependence between the price distortion and the output restriction owing to monopoly. At the firm level at which they operate, Cowling and Mueller argue that a firm i will maximize profit by setting

$$\frac{p_i - MC_i}{p_i} = \frac{1}{\eta_i} \tag{10.5}$$

where p_i and MC_i are firm i's price and marginal cost, and η_i is its price elasticity of demand. On the simplifying assumption that costs are constant and demand is linear, therefore, the deadweight welfare loss is

$$\begin{aligned} D_i &= -\tfrac{1}{2}\Delta p_i \Delta q_i \\ &= \tfrac{1}{2}q_i^{\mathrm{m}} \Delta p_i \\ &= \tfrac{1}{2}\pi_i \end{aligned} \tag{10.6}$$

where π_i is monopoly profit. This follows, of course, because, with linear demand, monopoly output is one-half of competitive output; i.e., $-\Delta q_i = q_i^{\mathrm{m}}$. Hence, the deadweight welfare loss can (on these assumptions) be taken as one-half of firm i's monopoly profit (after allowance for the competitive rate of return on capital).

Second, Cowling and Mueller criticize Harberger for measuring competitive rates of return as mean profit rates in the sample. Two criticisms are involved here. First, since possible monopoly rents are included in the calculation of the mean profit rate, these will tend to overestimate the competitive rate of return. Second, as previously noted, by examining deviations in profits from the mean profit rate, Harberger effectively measured gains to be made from equalizing rates of return rather than from moving to a competitive rate of return. Cowling and Mueller avoid these problems by using an independent estimate of the competitive rate of return. Also unlike Harberger, they count only positive deviations from this rate as arising from monopoly, arguing that negative deviations reflect temporary losses rather than long-term monopoly distortions. Inevitably, of course, some temporary positive deviations are also likely to be recorded in their figures.

Third, Cowling and Mueller criticize earlier studies (with the exception of that by Worcester, 1973) for using industry-level data. Such data are likely to lead to downward-biased estimates of monopoly social costs for two reasons. First, since industry profits are aggregates of firm profits, they will include below-competitive-level profits earned by some firms. Since such profits are treated by Cowling and Mueller as temporary, they should be excluded from the analysis. Second, since price–cost margins are squared to estimate the deadweight welfare loss, the above problem is aggravated further. Cowling and Mueller argue that, by looking (in their study) at firm-level monopoly profits, these problems are avoided.

Finally, like Posner, they include estimates of the resource costs of attempts to gain and retain monopoly power. Allowance for such costs involves both a redefinition of monopoly profits such that such expenditures are not treated as costs, and the measurement of wasteful expenditures in terms of full monopoly profits. In the event, Cowling and Mueller make three fairly crude adjustments. First, they adjust monopoly profits upwards by the amount of advertising expenditure, treating this as extra expenditure relative to competitive operation. Second, they assume that all advertising expenditures are designed for monopolization and are socially wasteful. And third, following Posner, they argue that (after-tax) monopoly profits may be used to measure the resources wasted in competing for those profits. The tenuous nature of these kinds of argument in measuring wasteful expenditures has already been noted, and will not be pursued further here.

Cowling and Mueller provide welfare loss estimates for both the USA and UK. Data for the USA relate to 734 large firms in 1963–6, while for the UK data for the largest 103 corporations in 1968/9 were used. In each case, four estimates of monopoly welfare loss were made, corresponding to the above discussion (see table 10.1). Harberger-type estimates corresponding to each of these categories were also reported.

The following points should be noted concerning their results.

(1) First, considering measure (1), we can see that estimates using the Cowling–Mueller method were very much higher than those using the Harberger-type measure. Thus it matters very much whether one adopts the arbitrary assumption that η is unity following Harberger, or allows for a profit-maximizing relationship between price–cost margins and elasticities of demand. While it seems likely that Cowling and Mueller have very much overstated the effect by assuming full monopoly pricing,

Table 10.1 Monopoly welfare loss estimates for the UK in 1968/9 and USA in 1963–6

Cowling–Mueller measure[a]	UK 1968/9 (%)		US 1963–8 (%)	
	CM[b]	H[c]	CM[b]	H[c]
(1) $\pi/2$	3.86	0.21	3.96	0.40
(2) $(\pi+A)/2$	4.36	0.24	6.52	0.79
(3) $A+(\pi+A)/2$	5.39	1.19	12.27	6.52
(4) $\pi'+A+(\pi+A)/2$	7.20	3.05	13.14	7.39

Source: Cowling and Mueller (1978).

Notes
[a] All estimates are expressed as a percentage of gross corporate product (GCP). In the Cowling–Mueller measure, A is advertising and π and π' are pre- and post-tax profits, respectively. Formulae for Harberger-type estimates build on (measure (1)) $(R/2)(\pi/R)^2$ where R is total revenue.
[b] Cowling–Mueller estimates.
[c] Harberger-type estimates.

their results do suggest that Harberger-type estimates may err on the low side by ignoring this possible relationship.

(2) Second, Cowling and Mueller's estimates put monopoly welfare losses as high as 7.2 per cent of gross corporate product in the UK and 13.1 per cent of gross corporate product in the USA. These estimates, however, should be regarded very much as upper bounds, given the assumptions that the authors make.

(3) Third, comparing the UK and the USA, one finds almost twice the welfare loss (on measure (4)) in the USA. This difference primarily reflects the higher levels of advertising found in the USA compared with the UK.

(4) Finally, for individual companies they find for the UK, for example, that their measure (4) singles out BP, Shell and British American Tobacco as companies generating the largest welfare losses. According to Cowling and Mueller's estimates, BP alone accounted for a welfare loss of 0.25 per cent of UK GNP in 1968/9, a figure which well exceeds the total monopoly welfare loss discovered initially by Harberger in the USA.

Cowling and Mueller's estimates can be criticized on a number of grounds. First, as noted previously, estimates of wasteful expenditures used in mono-polizing are particularly difficult to pin down so that Cowling and Mueller's measures (2)–(4) can only be regarded as tentative. In particular, their assumption that advertising expenditures are totally wasteful can be criticized for ignoring the information benefits of advertising. Second, their assumption that firms set profit-maximizing price and output can also be criticized (see discussion of Kamerschen, 1966 in section 10.2 above). Firms may alternatively set a limit price through fear of new competition or government regulation, or they may pursue non-profit goals, or they may coordinate their actions but to a limited degree. The assumption of profit-maximizing monopoly behaviour is clearly an extreme assumption which is likely to set an upper bound to monopoly welfare loss (Cowling and Mueller, 1981) rather than being representative of all cases.

Various other points can also be made.[7] First, in using a single competitive rate of return in each country, Cowling and Mueller made no allowance for differences in risk faced by different firms. This may be an important factor, for example, for the several oil companies analysed, which according to their analysis earned substantially above competitive rates of return. Such companies, however, may well face above-average degrees of risk in their operations, accounting for some part of their higher profits. Second, as noted above, Cowling and Mueller include all profits above competitive levels as monopoly profits when some part of these at least are likely to be due to transitory factors. This is probably less of a problem for their US data, wherein an average of several years' profits was taken, but it may be more important for the UK, where a single year was used. Third, Cowling and Mueller make no allowance for rents earned by superior resources or, more generally, for superior efficiency in the market. In so far as such rents may persist in competitive equilibrium, however, this is again likely to imply an overstatement of monopoly profits.

These reservations clearly imply that Cowling and Mueller's estimates must be treated with care. At the same time, however, their work does indicate that the assumptions one makes over interdependencies of price and output and over resource costs of attempts to monopolize can have important effects on estimates obtained. Viewed in this way, therefore, their study at least suggests that the very low estimates of welfare loss obtained by Harberger and others may be somewhat misleading.

Finally, we may briefly mention a recent study by Masson and Shaanan (1984). This study seeks to distinguish actual as opposed to full monopoly profit-maximizing social costs of monopoly. Masson and Shaanan argue that expected or full social costs of monopoly would be incurred in the absence of both actual and potential competition in a market. In practice, however, most markets are characterized by some degree of competition, and consequently social welfare losses are correspondingly reduced. By using a model of limit pricing together with several other assumptions, Masson and Shaanan are able to derive estimates of deadweight welfare losses both in terms of actual and full monopoly market conditions. These, in turn, were used to assess the value of competition (both actual and potential) relative to a full monopoly position.

They used this approach to estimate welfare losses for a sample of 37 four-digit US industries in 1950–66. On average, for these industries they found that actual welfare losses were 2.9 per cent of the value of shipments, which is considerably higher than found by Harberger. They also found that the average full monopoly welfare loss for their sample was 11.6 per cent of shipments. The difference of 8.7 per cent represents the beneficial effects of competition in the market, of which they attribute 4.9 per cent to potential competition and 3.8 per cent to actual competition. These results, therefore, suggest that, while significant monopoly welfare losses exist (concentrating here on only deadweight losses), the existence of competition in actual markets is also a major force in offsetting the potential for full monopoly welfare losses in the market.

10.4 Summary and Conclusions

This chapter has considered a number of studies of the social cost of monopoly together with some of the problems and limitations of such studies. After an initial discussion of general issues in section 10.1, we considered estimates obtained by Harberger and others in section 10.2 which typically pointed to very small aggregate social costs of monopoly. These studies suggested that as little as 0.1 per cent of GNP was accounted for by monopoly resource misallocation in US industry, implying that as a general rule competitive conditions can be thought to apply quite widely. This conclusion has, however, been challenged by more recent studies (discussed in section 10.3), which put welfare losses considerably higher. While such studies are themselves not without problems, they do indicate grounds (notably in respect of price and output interdependencies, and costs of acquiring and maintaining monopolies) for believing that costs of monopoly are more substantial.

While, as noted in section 10.1, these studies cannot be regarded as providing definitive estimates of monopoly social cost, they do offer useful insights into the problem. At the very least they suggest that grounds for social concern exist in some sectors of the economy, and hence that some public policy intervention is required. More generally, however, they offer a less clear picture on overall welfare losses. More research (both theoretical and applied) is needed, therefore, before one can draw any firm conclusions in this obviously important area of analysis.

Notes

1 A full (profit-maximizing) monopolist would, of course, set price and output such that marginal revenue equals marginal cost. In this chapter, however, we consider monopolization in the broader sense of some or any price-raising above marginal cost.
2 This follows because a unit elastic demand curve is a rectangular hyperbola with an equation $pq = $ a constant. Hence, in figure 10.1, area $Op_m aq_m$ equals area $Op_c cq_c$, and subtracting the common area $Op_c bq_m$ gives the result reported in the text.
3 The assumption of full monopoly pricing is, however, rather extreme. This is discussed further in connection with Cowling and Mueller's (1978) study in section 10.3 below.
4 In a famous statement, Stigler (1956) suggested that the results implied that economists might do better to fight termites than monopoly, in terms of their relative quantitative effect on the economy. It should be noted, however, that Harberger's results do not preclude important monopoly losses in some industries. Also, of course, the estimates give no guide to the effect of abolishing anti-trust enforcement in the USA.
5 Posner notes, however, that, since above-average profit rates were used by Harberger to estimate the monopoly price distortion, no allowance is made for expenditures in obtaining (or maintaining) a monopoly in identifying 'true' monopoly profits. For discussion of this point see below.
6 Posner estimated (on the basis of some sample data) that the social costs of regulation might be as high as 1.7 per cent of GNP compared with his preferred estimate of private monopoly social costs in manufacturing of 0.6 per cent of GNP. In his view, the much higher price increases in the regulated sector mean that more welfare losses arise in this sector despite its smaller size.
7 See, in particular, Littlechild (1981), together with Cowling and Mueller's reply (Cowling and Mueller, 1981). As noted in section 10.1, Littlechild also adopts a more general criticism of the equilibrium approach adopted by Cowling and Mueller and all other writers in the field.

11 Restrictive Trade Practices Policy

In the remaining two chapters of the book we turn our attention away from general issues of social welfare and public policy in order to consider the actual operation of competition policy in the UK. This policy has been developed gradually over a number of years since the Second World War and now encompasses various aspects of market structure and business conduct. In particular, it deals with monopoly and merger policy on the one hand, and with restrictive trade practices policy on the other. In what follows, we deal with the more structurally based monopolies and mergers policies in chapter 12, focusing here on policies relating more exclusively to business conduct.

Policies on restrictive trade practices can be divided into those which relate to agreements between firms and those which deal with single-firm practices. Historically, UK policy has focused mainly on restrictive agreements with regard to prices, terms and conditions, market shares, etc., and we discuss this policy in section 11.1. More recently, however, there has been a growing interest in anti-competitive practices pursued by single firms, and indeed a wide range of such practices have been brought within the scope of government policy with the passing of the 1980 Competition Act. We consider some aspects of such practices in section 11.2.[1]

11.1 Restrictive Trading Agreements

As noted in chapter 3, collusion between firms represents a constant threat or potential threat in oligopolistic markets. In this section, we examine the steps which have been taken in the UK to reduce such collusion by controlling restrictive agreements. We begin by outlining the basic history and provisions of the UK legislation in section 11.1.1. Then we consider the available evidence on the economic impact of the legislation in section 11.1.2, and end with a brief discussion of possible modifications to the law in section 11.1.3.

11.1.1 UK Legislation[2]

UK policy on restrictive agreements dates initially from the 1948 Monopolies and Restrictive Practices (Inquiry and Control) Act. This act established the Monopolies and Restrictive Practices Commission to undertake case-by-case investigations of markets in which at least one-third of goods (supplied, processed or exported) was under monopoly control or subject to restrictive agreement. The Commission was empowered to investigate such situations and to assess them *vis-à-vis* the public interest, recommending remedial action if required. Between 1948 and 1956 it produced 17 reports, of which 15 were concerned mainly with trade association activities; in almost all cases, collective restrictions were found to operate against the public interest. In 1955 it also produced a more general report on *Collective Discrimination*,[3] which in turn was influential in producing the 1956 Restrictive Trade Practices Act which laid the framework of current UK policy.

The 1956 Act has several features of note. In the first place, it replaced the Monopolies and Restrictive Practices Commission system of investigation of restrictive agreements by a judicial system. A newly created Restrictive Practices Court was set up to adjudicate the public interest, consisting of both High Court judges and qualified lay people. This change in the law obviously had the advantage of making the system less arbitrary and more formal by introducing normal judicial procedures. Second, the act required the registration of relevant agreements with a Registrar of Restrictive Trading Agreements, who was also to refer cases to, and present the Crown case in, the Court. Provision was made for the public inspection of the Register, and this provided valuable information on the nature and extent of registrable agreements.

Finally, and most important, registered agreements were presumed to be against the public interest unless proved otherwise. Moreover, parties to an agreement were permitted to defend it in the Court only in terms of seven specified benefits, known as 'gateways'. These relate to such things as protection of the public from injury, protection of employment in an area and the use of an agreement as a counterbalance to monopoly or monopsony power. Gateway (b), however, is more general than the others, referring to the provision of 'specific and substantial benefits' for the public. Firms were required to show that an agreement not only produced one or more of the seven benefits but also on balance was in the public interest: a provision which is known as the 'tailpiece'. Hence, the law offered a number of hurdles for an agreement to surmount if it was not to be declared illegal.

The adoption of a judicial system to regulate restrictive trade agreements in the UK has given rise to considerable debate at the time and since. In contrast to the US system, wherein the ordinary courts are required to determine only whether an agreement exists and is hence illegal, in the UK the Restrictive Practices Court is expected to examine possibly complex economic issues in evaluating agreements. This requirement led several commentators to ask whether a court is best suited for such a task: the so-called question of justiciability.[4] Of course, the reason for establishing a *new* court was to attempt to meet such criticisms, in that the Court is usually composed of a judge and two qualified lay people, and that economic judgements are taken on the basis of majority vote. Also it was felt that, by specifying the gateways, the scope for economic argument would be reduced, although, as noted above, gateway (b) is far from specific. Fears as to the Court's ability to deal with economic issues have to some extent been justified in a number of questionable decisions. On the other hand, the principal effect of the legislation has been to produce the voluntary termination or variation of agreements in the majority of cases. Hence, the issue of justiciability has not been a major issue in practice.

Before we look at the impact of the 1956 Act, let us briefly examine some of the subsequent legislation in this field. The 1956 Act related to restrictive agreements between firms on goods where agreements covered such things as restrictions on price, terms and conditions, quantities supplied, processes used and persons and areas supplied. It soon became clear, however, that the list of registrable agreements was too restricted in that, in particular, an agreement between firms simply to supply information to each other about such things was not registrable (as long as the agreement did not contain provision for action on such information). Obviously, such 'information agreements' create a potential for tacit collusion and possibly also a basis for more explicit restrictive agreements. Consequently in 1968 another Restrictive Trade Practices Act was introduced to provide for the registration of such agreements.[5] This Act also weakened the law slightly, in that

(1) it provided for certain exemptions from registration on advice from the Department of Trade and Industry that an agreement was of importance to the national interest; and
(2) it introduced an eighth 'gateway', with explicit reference to information agreements, that an agreement does not and is not likely to restrict competition to any 'material degree'.

In the 1970s there were three further relevant pieces of legislation. The 1973 Fair Trading Act reorganized UK competition policy in general, setting up the Office of Fair Trading to oversee UK policy. With respect to restrictive agreements, this meant that the Director General of Fair Trading (DGFT) took over the functions of the Registrar, in addition to his newly created powers with respect to monopolies and mergers. Also, and more important, the 1973 Act provided for registration of agreements relating to services, and these were in fact called up for registration in 1976 in the Restrictive Trade Practices (Services) Order. Also in 1976, the Restrictive Trade Practices Act codified previous legislation on restrictive agreements. Finally, the 1977 Restrictive Trade Practices Act exempted certain loan financing agreements from registration. Currently, agreements relating to goods and services (with certain exceptions) are registrable, as are goods information agreements relating to prices and terms of supply. Other goods information agreements and information agreements for services have not yet been called up, however.

Several features of the current legislation may usefully be mentioned in conclusion. First, not all registered agreements are necessarily taken to the Court; in particular, the Secretary of State (on the advice of the DGFT) can discharge the DGFT from taking an agreement to the Court on the grounds that the restrictions involved are not of such significance as to warrant Court proceedings. This is known as a section 21(2) procedure under the 1976 Restrictive Trade Practices Act and it introduces some flexibility into the legislation with respect to inconsequential agreements. Second, if an agreement is referred to the Court and restrictions are found to be against the public interest, then the Court can make an order restraining the parties from giving effect to the restrictions or any others to like effect. Failure to comply with this ruling can lead to prosecution for contempt of Court, with consequent fines and (conceivably) prison sentences for responsible directors. Finally, while failure to register a registrable agreement renders its restrictions void (in law), there are no criminal penalties for such failure (although civil remedies may be sought by injured parties). This represents a peculiar weakness of the UK legislation which is discussed further in section 11.1.3 below.

11.1.2 Economic Impact

In order to appraise the economic impact of UK legislation it is useful to put it in context. Prior to 1956, cartelization of UK industry was widespread, with many agreements stemming from the depressed years of the 1930s.[6] Many sectors of UK manufacturing, in particular, were subject to restrictive agreements, most notably on prices, but also on terms and conditions, market areas, customers and suppliers and so on. Such agreements, according to one estimate, accounted for between 50 and 60 per cent of manufacturing output by 1956.[7] Prima facie, therefore, regulation of industry by restrictive agreement was a pervasive factor in the manufacturing sector at this time.

This picture is reflected in the figures for registration of agreements under the 1956 Act. By 1959, for example, 2240 agreements had been registered covering most areas of manufacturing industry. (This figure had risen to 4978 agreements (846 of which were related to services) by 1983.) Most of these agreements related to prices. For example, of 970 agreements identified as important by the Registrar in 1959, 81 per cent contained restrictions on prices, many also specifying terms and conditions of sale in order thereby to tighten the restrictive effect of the agreement.[8]

Clearly, therefore, agreements on prices, etc., were widespread in 1956. Ten years later, however, most of these agreements had been either varied (to take them outside the registration requirements) or terminated. Thus, in 1966 83 per cent of 2550 registered agreements had been varied or discontinued. The main reason for this was undoubtedly the hard line taken by the Court, particularly in its initial judgements. Seven of the first eight contested agreements were struck down, the most important being the second case (the Yarn Spinners Agreement),[9] in which the Court ruled that the benefit of protecting employment in a region was insufficient on balance to justify the agreement. The failure of this agreement led many firms to abandon or vary their agreements voluntarily rather than incur the costs of a court case with little hope of a successful defence. By 1978, only 39 goods agreements had been terminated by court order, the rest being voluntarily terminated or varied without defence; 487 goods agreements had been referred to the Court by 1978 and only 12 had been upheld (436 were not defended) (Green Paper, 1979, p. 20).

In terms of removing explicit agreements, therefore, the 1956 (and subsequent) Act(s) were very successful. Prior to 1968, many registrable agreements had been replaced by information agreements, although this loophole was removed in the 1968 Restrictive Practices Act. It is one thing to remove registered agreements, however, and another thereby to increase competition. Several studies have considered whether the effects of the Act(s) were significant in this respect, and we consider three such studies below. Unfortunately, none of these studies is free of methodological problems, so that our knowledge of the impact of the legislation remains uncertain.

First, in an early study, Heath (1961) conducted a questionnaire survey of the short-term effects of the termination of price agreements in a sample of 159 agreements. He found that for only a third of agreements did respondents feel that competition had increased after termination. Similarly, for roughly a third of agreements prices were reported as having fallen. Thus, while in these cases it appeared that the Act had had a beneficial short-term effect, in the other cases there was no such evidence. While this might have been due to biased response or alternatively to the short time period allowed (up to mid-1959), Heath also uncovered evidence of switching to non-registrable practices. Thus, for example, for 41 per cent of the responses analysed by agreement firms admitted to recognizing a price leader, while in over half of the responses analysed by agreement the price agreement was replaced by an information agreement. These results suggested that a good proportion of industries had attempted to continue restrictive policies by other means after 1956, although Heath was not able to predict whether such attempts were likely to be successful in the medium/long term.

These issues were tackled more thoroughly by Swann et al. (1974). They looked at a sample of 40 industries of which 18 were investigated in depth (comprising four cases where an agreement was upheld, six cases where it was struck down, and eight abandoned agreements). Their study went up to 1971 and examined both shorter- and longer-run experience. On the competitive front they found that, out of 34 terminated agreements, between 50 and 60 per cent of the industries experienced greater competition after termination. Competition occurred primarily on prices and discounts, but there was also evidence of increased competition on product and service. In six cases

(18 per cent) price falls of around 20 per cent were observed but other price falls were more modest. Swann *et al.* also reported evidence of falls in profit margins, improvements in efficiency and the shake-out of excess capacity and inefficient producers. Such shorter-run competitive gains also appeared to extend into the longer run in a number of industries, with evidence in some cases of greater cost-consciousness, product rationalization and innovation.

On the other hand, restrictive forces were also in evidence. In 50 per cent of the 34 cases of termination, an information agreement was introduced, frequently involving pre-notification of price changes. These agreements were found by Swann *et al.* to be broadly successful in staving off competition, although one or two instances were cited where they failed in the presence of rapidly changing market conditions (e.g. transformers and heavy electric motors). In the longer run, however, Swann *et al.* were optimistic that the calling up of goods information agreements on prices and terms and conditions would produce more competition. Other means of avoiding competition were price leadership, possible illegal collusion and mergers. In particular, Swann *et al.* reported a great deal of merger activity in their sample in the 1960s but they were unable to suggest how much (if any) was attributable to the 1956 Act.

The major problem with the study of Swann *et al.* arises from the difficulty of attributing post-1956 behaviour and performance to the effects of the 1956 Act (rather than to something else). A subsidiary problem arises from their adoption of a basically non-quantitative, case study approach which necessarily relies on impressionistic evidence. A more recent attempt at overcoming these weaknesses has been made by O'Brien *et al.* (1979). They considered a sample of firms in 27 industries over the period 1951–72, where the sample was divided into four groups: upheld agreements (six cases); struck-down agreements (eight cases); abandoned agreements (seven cases) and 'control' industries (six cases). The latter group comprised industries which had not been directly affected by competition policy and were used as a reference group for the study. O'Brien *et al.* also divided their data into sub-periods: a pre-Act stage, 1951–8; the main period, for which an effect of the 1956 Act would be expected, 1959–67; and a final period, 1968–72, in which a great deal of regrouping of industries occurred following the merger boom of the 1960s. This sub-division allowed them to control for trends in economic performance which were occurring independently of the 1956 Act.

It should be noted that there were various problems with their study, such as their use of (possibly misleading) accounting data, the question of sample selection and, in particular, the problems involved in comparing firms in a small number of diverse industries. These problems may account for the rather weak statistical results observed. Among other things, the following were reported.

(1) While all industry groups experienced a fall in return on capital in 1959–67 compared with 1951–8, this fall was lowest in the control group.

However, the greatest fall in return was in group I (upheld agreements), so that the interpretation of this result is difficult.

(2) Group I was also distinguished by a decline in the growth of assets over time in 1959–67 once allowance is made for the general UK experience. There was some evidence that group II industries (struck-down agreements) grew faster in 1959–67 in contrast to their rather poor growth performance in 1951–8, however.

(3) Finally, O'Brien *et al.* considered the hypothesis that the effect of the 1956 Act may have been to induce more merger activity in place of restrictive agreements. They found, however, that, while merger activity increased in the 1960s, this increase was across the board and in no way related to the 1956 Act.

In appraising the evidence on the economic impact of the 1956 Act, the 1979 Green Paper on Restrictive Trade Practices Policy concluded that there was evidence of improved economic efficiency. The attempts which have been made at measuring this gain, however, have not yielded very reliable evidence. In addition, the extent to which the purpose of the law has been circumvented, for example by tacit collusion, price leadership or merger, is uncertain, as is the extent of illegal non-registration of agreements.

These uncertainties, of course, are partly of the nature of collusive agreements, and it might be too much to expect that reliable information of a general kind might be obtainable. In its absence, however, proper evaluation of public policy is difficult and there is clearly a need for further work on these important issues.

11.1.3 Policy Issues

On the face of it, UK law has been successful in reducing the formal cartelization of industry, but the economic effects have been more uncertain. Given the fact that only 12 agreements had been upheld by the Court by 1978, some commentators have suggested that it might be desirable simply to outlaw price-fixing and other agreements *per se*.[10] Such an approach (with exemptions) already applies to interstate trade under EEC law, and also in other countries (such as in the USA). Certainly, there would seem to be a strong case for such a policy within the UK. In its 1979 review of Restrictive Trade Practices, however, the government Green Paper came down in support of the flexibility of the current system rather than for a move towards a *per se* type of approach.[11]

The real issues on restrictive agreements, however, relate to avoidance of the law. While the *intent* of the legislation is to prevent restrictive coordination between firms, serious doubts must exist as to the law's effectiveness. Clearly, the hard line taken by the Court has operated as a major disincentive for firms formally to defend agreements in court. Hence, firms have an obvious incentive to coordinate their activities in ways which are not registrable, e.g.

by non-registrable forms of agreement, or by tacit coordination, price leadership and so on. In the UK such arrangements are dealt with only in so far as they encompass a statutory monopoly situation (see chapter 12) and hence may be subject to possible Monopolies and Mergers Commission investigation. While, in principle, this approach could offer a way of dealing with the worst abuses that might be found, it is (as we shall see in chapter 12) relatively ineffective in practice. Hence, an important grey area exists in the UK law relating to non-registrable forms of coordination, which could be of major importance.

A second weakness of the UK legislation relates to the penalties for illegal non-registration. While failure to register an agreement makes it void in law, there is no provision for criminal proceedings or other penalties for those involved (although the DGFT may apply for a restraining order if an illegally unregistered agreement is discovered). Injured parties may sue participants to an unregistered agreement for damages, although this provision has rarely been used. Hence, it would seem that significant incentives exist for illegal non-registration (or de-registration) of agreements, and indeed growing evidence of such non-registration has been noted in recent years.[12]

These weaknesses provide a prima facie case for believing that control of restrictive arrangements in the UK is not as strong as it at first might appear. One possible reform would be to strengthen penalties for non-registration of agreements, either by introducing fines in the Court (as recommended by the 1979 Green Paper) or by giving injured parties greater incentives to sue for damages. This latter policy has proved quite effective in the USA, for example, where injured parties can sue firms involved in an illegal agreement for triple the damages incurred.[13] Such an approach obviously gives a strong incentive for firms to take court action if they have been injured by an illegal agreement.

A more fundamental reform, however, would be to increase the powers of the Court to challenge more informal agreements and arrangements between firms. Such a reform would require substantial revision of the current registration system to allow the DGFT to challenge less formal coordination between firms. In addition, since it would be likely to lead to an increase in cases going to Court, it would again raise the justiciability issue, i.e. whether the Court could evaluate the economic arguments satisfactorily. At the present time, however (at least as judged by the conclusions of the 1979 Green Paper), no strong support for such a major strengthening of the law appears to exist.

11.2 Single-firm Practices

A further area of restrictive or anti-competitive practice is the single-firm practice. In this case a firm, not necessarily in agreement with other firms, pursues a policy which may have the effect of restricting or distorting competition. For example, a firm may use price as a weapon for eliminating specific competitors from the market (predatory pricing); or it may insist that a customer purchase a good B if it also purchases a good A from it (tie-in sale); or it may fix a minimum price at which a retailer may resell a good (resale price maintenance). These and other practices are frequently observed in reality, and often they are associated with the existence of some degree of market power.

We shall examine the economic arguments surrounding some of these practices in section 11.2.2. We preface this discussion, however, by looking at the legislative background to the subject in the UK.

11.2.1 Legislative Background

UK policy on single-firm restrictive practices can be divided into two: the specific legislation, which deals with resale price maintenance (RPM), and the more general provisions of the 1980 Competition Act.

Before 1964, UK policy on RPM was ambivalent. The 1956 Restrictive Trade Practices Act provided for the prohibition of the *collective* enforcement of RPM, but on the other hand strengthened *individual* enforcement of the practice. In 1964, however, the policy on individual enforcement of RPM was reversed in the Resale Prices Act, which prohibited the practice unless an exemption were granted by order of the Restrictive Practices Court. The legislation was consolidated without substantive change in the Resale Prices Act 1976. Under this Act,

(1) collective enforcement of RPM *per se* is prohibited;
(2) individual enforcement of RPM is prohibited, but subject to exemptions granted by the Restrictive Practices Court;
(3) refusal to supply and supplying on unfavourable terms are also prohibited if used as a means to establish or enforce RPM.

The Court was empowered under section 14 of the 1976 Act to consider five gateways for the maintenance of RPM, and, as with the restrictive agreements legislation, a 'tailpiece' exists in which retention of RPM should be considered on balance to be beneficial. The RPM gateways relate to cases in which the abolition of RPM would cause a reduction in the quality or variety of goods, or the number of retailers, or the services provided with goods, or would cause a rise in retail prices or a danger to health.

Clearly, current legislation on RPM goes beyond other restrictive practices legislation in that both collective and individual RPM enforcement are illegal, although there is provision for exemption in the latter case. In practice only four applications for exemption have been made, of which two were not successful (confectionery in 1967 and footwear in 1968). The successful cases were books in 1968 and medicaments in 1970, and these represent less than 2 per cent of consumers' expenditure. This compares with an estimated 20–25 per cent of consumers' expenditure that was subject to RPM prior to 1964. It thus appears that the *enforcement* of minimum resale prices has largely been eradicated in the UK. The Green Paper on Restrictive Trade Practices Policy pointed out that several loopholes in the law exist, such as refusal to supply discount sellers, but it suggested that these might be dealt with by selective investigation.[14]

A more general policy on single-firm practices has been introduced in the 1980 Competition Act. This Act arose out of the recommendations of the government Green Papers on Monopolies and Mergers Policy in 1978 and Restrictive Trade Practices Policy in 1979. The former Green Paper argued that, while single-firm practices often arose in the context of market dominance, the existing monopolies legislation was not always a suitable means of effecting control. As discussed in chapter 12 below, this legislation allows for lengthy inquiries into whole industries in which a statutory monopoly (at present a 25 per cent market share) is found to exist, and does not permit fast and specific investigation of particular firms' practices. While the 1978 Green Paper felt that certain practices were generally undesirable and might be dealt with harshly (for example, by introducing prohibition along the lines of that for RPM), it called for further study on the matter. Such further study was made in the 1979 Green Paper, which, however, argued that a general policy of prohibiting specified practices was not warranted since practices were often difficult to define adequately and insufficient evidence existed as to their general harmful effects. Rather, the 1979 Green Paper advocated case-by-case investigation of single-firm practices by the Office of Fair Trading and the Monopolies and Mergers Commission (MMC), but unrelated to the statutory monopoly requirements of normal monopoly investigations.[15]

The recommendations of the 1979 Green Paper form the basis for the 1980 Competition Act. This creates wide-ranging powers for the investigation of anti-competitive practices, where these are defined as a course of conduct pursued by a person which has (or is intended or likely to have) the effect of 'restricting, distorting or preventing competition'. Two stages of investigation are provided for. In the first stage the Director General of Fair Trading can undertake a formal *preliminary investigation*, the purpose of which is to establish the facts and to determine whether the practice engaged in is anti-competitive. The DGFT is required to publish his report and may at this stage accept an undertaking from the person involved to desist from the practice. If an undertaking is not offered or accepted, he may then make a *competition reference* to the MMC. The Commission then undertakes its own investigation and, in particular, assesses the practice in terms of the public interest. It is the public interest rather than the existence of an anti-competitive practice which is therefore the deciding factor. In the light of an adverse report, the Secretary of State has wide order-making powers to prohibit the practice in line with the provisions for monopoly investigations (see chapter 12).

It is clear that the provisions of the Competition Act, while wide-ranging, are neutral with respect to anti-competitive practices. Ultimately, the act

Table 11.1 Anti-competitive practice investigations under the 1980 Competition Act, 1980–3

Case	OFT procedure				MMC investigation			Principal practice
	Anti-competitive practice?	Reference to MMC?	Under-taking accepted?	Insub-stantial practice?	Anti-competitive practice?	Against public interest?	Under-taking accepted?	
T. I. Raleigh	✓	✓			✓	✓	✓	Refusal to supply
Petter Refrigeration Ltd	✓		✓					Dealer restrictions
Arthur Sanderson & Sons Ltd	✗							Refusal to supply
Sheffield Newspapers Ltd	✓	✓			✓	✓	✓	Dealer restrictions
London Electricity Board	✓	✓			✓	✗		Cross-subsidization
W. M. Still & Sons Ltd and W. M. Still Service Ltd	✓		✓					Refusal to supply
British Railways Board (hackney carriages)	✓		✓					Restriction of supply
Scottish and Universal Newspapers Ltd	✓		✓					Predatory tactics
British Railways Board (motorail)	✓			✓				Refusal to supply
British Railways Board (car hire)	✓			✓				Exclusive dealing
Essex County Newspapers Ltd	✓		✓					Refusal to supply

Source: Annual Reports of the DGFT, 1980–3.

provides for a detailed cost–benefit analysis of each individual case by the MMC, with no presumption that an anti-competitive practice is against the public interest. At the same time, however, it should be noted that the explicit provisions for a preliminary investigation and the acceptance of undertakings at this stage may in practice operate to produce modifications of anti-competitive practices without reference to costs and benefits, particularly if firms might wish to avoid the publicity, trouble and expense of an MMC investigation. Hence, in so far as undertakings are accepted after preliminary investigation, the policy may well be much tougher on anti-competitive practices than at first sight seems to be the case.

Some evidence on this is presented in table 11.1, which summarizes details of the first 11 cases dealt with under the Act in 1980–3. As can be seen, of these 11 cases, undertakings were accepted after preliminary investigation in six cases, with only three cases going on to MMC investigation. *De facto*, therefore, for the majority of cases a decision was made on the basis of the existence of an anti-competitive practice rather than on its possible cost and benefits. While this, therefore, reflects some ambivalence as to the principles underlying the legislation, it does suggest that the law has (and probably in the future will) take a fairly strong line on anti-competitive practices.

The early cases, moreover, indicate some flexibility in the practices that can be caught by the law (see final column of table 11.1). So far, practices such as refusal to supply discount stores (Raleigh bicycles), restrictions on retailers' rights to handle rival products (Sheffield Newspapers), effective tying of service contracts (W. M. Still) and explicit predatory tactics (Scottish and Universal Newspapers) have all been found (among others) to be anti-competitive. (The first two were also found against the public interest in MMC investigations.) The variety of cases considered suggests that the Act will provide some wide-ranging protection against anti-competitive practices. Whether or not this will provide substantial benefits for the public, however, remains to be seen.

11.2.2 Economic Arguments

The scope for single-firm anti-competitive practices is limited only by human ingenuity. While all such practices are designed to gain private benefits for the firm involved, typically in the form of increased profits, this need not mean that corresponding welfare losses for the community are involved. Rather, in some cases a trade-off of costs and benefits may exist, while in other cases it is conceivable that substantial benefits may typically arise. The issues are often complex, and in this section we can do no more than indicate some of the relevant arguments for particular practices. We look briefly at three such practices: resale price maintenance, tie-in sales and predatory pricing.

Resale price maintenance   The economic case against resale price main-tenance centres on the restrictions on competition that it implies in retailing, and possibly also in manufacturing. At the retail level, it is argued that RPM will lead to higher prices and margins for distributors, less efficient operation of the competitive mechanism, and excessive use of resources in non-price retail competition. If one assumes that there is effective competition in retailing (which need not, of course, be appropriate in all cases), then in the absence of RPM one would expect that competition would lead to direct price reductions – and, moreover, to price and cost reductions in the longer run as less efficient retailers are eliminated and business is concentrated in the hands of the more efficient firms. In contrast, in the presence of RPM prices are likely to be higher on average, directly affecting the consumer and also providing an umbrella for the protection of inefficient firms. Moreover, RPM is also likely to be distortionary, in that it may increase retail competition in non-price areas such as attention from sales staff, delivery speed, after-sales service, etc. To the extent that this involves a different combination of service and price to that which consumers might choose in the absence of restriction, then RPM might be thought to be undesirable.[16]

Added to these arguments is the slightly less well attested argument that the existence of RPM may also restrict the competition of manufacturers. The main argument here is that, by setting minimum resale prices for their products, manufacturers are able to reduce uncertainty in the market, thereby facilitating collusion.[17] In the absence of RPM manufacturers have the opportunity of chiselling on their prices to retailers since their competitors will be uncertain as to whether lower retail prices reflect the policy of manufacturer or the retailer. In a situation such as this it is unlikely that producers will be able to set prices close to joint profit-maximizing levels, since the incentives for individual producers to reduce prices will be great. In a regime of RPM, however, retail prices are fixed and the incentive to offer discounts to retailers exists only in so far as preferential treatment on non-price competition may be secured. Hence, we would expect much closer adherence to joint profit-maximizing prices in this context. Obviously, this argument is most likely to apply in tight oligopoly situations where collusive behaviour may occur, although no systematic evidence exists as to its general significance in restricting manufacturers' competition.

Several arguments exist in favour of RPM. First, it may be argued that, even though RPM protects inefficient (and usually small) retailers from competition from more efficient stores and supermarkets, such protection may be warranted on either political or distributional grounds. The political argument for protecting small businesses held particular sway in the USA at least up to the 1950s, although it has played a less important role in the UK.[18] The distributional argument is that the interests of particular groups of the population, such as the old and the relatively immobile, are protected by RPM at the cost of some general economic inefficiency. This argument has some merit in the absence of adequate compensation for such disadvantaged groups for the abolition of RPM. Finally, in certain circumstances, such as the sale of technical goods like hi-fi equipment. RPM may be justified to prevent discount stores being able to free-ride on pre-sales service provided by specialist shops. This problem arises from the fact that such service is not necessarily tied to a sale, and from the difficulty of extracting payment for information.

As with most policy matters, the arguments for and against RPM are not clear-cut, and this has been reflected in the legislation in the UK in the past. Nevertheless, the efficiency arguments against RPM have gained the ascendancy since 1964, and this state of affairs seems likely to be maintained.

Tie-in sales   Tie-in sales relate to the practice of tying the sale of one or more goods to the sale of another good. Thus, for example, a seller may supply a good A (the tying good) only on condition that the buyer also purchases good B (the tied good). A related but separate practice is line or full-line forcing, whereby the customer is required to accept part or all of a supplier's range of products if he purchases any one. Line forcing differs from tying in that no specific good can be identified as the tying good.

The classic argument against tie-in sales is the so-called *leverage argument*. This suggests that a tie-in is a device for extending monopolistic power beyond the range of the tying good. Thus, it is argued that if the tying good, A, is monopolized but the tied good, B, is produced competitively, then by introducing the tie the producer of A is able to extract *additional* monopoly profits from the sale of B.

This argument, however, at least in its simple form, need not be valid. Writers of the Chicago school, in particular, have stressed the point that a tie-in may provide no leverage at all for the firm involved.[19] Formally, the argument is the same as that for vertical integration where an input monopolist integrates forward into a competitive industry.[20] If two goods A and B are sold to an industry producing a good X, then (as noted in section 8.3) there can be no monopolistic incentive for a monopolist of A to integrate forward into industry X as long as A and B are used in fixed proportions. Similarly, a producer of A has no incentive to tie sales of B to A as long as A and B are used in fixed proportions. In both cases, the producer of A can extract monopoly profits from the pricing of A alone, and hence vertical integration or a tie-in sale cannot add to these profits. This argument does not apply, however, if A and B can be used in variable proportions, in which case a monopolistic incentive for integration or tying does exist. As noted in chapter 8, however, the welfare consequences of such a possibility are not clear-cut.

For many practical cases (e.g. cups and saucers, or machines and their consumables) the assumption of fixed proportions may be valid. For example, a firm which leases photocopying equipment and ties the sale of paper to its lease may not obtain any extra profits from this practice if it can successfully charge for the use of its machine independently of the use of paper. In cases where metering of machine use is difficult, however, the tie may provide a useful metering device which enables it to extract full monopoly profits. Also, tie-in sales may enable firms to adopt more profitable two-part tariff systems (e.g. a monthly machine rental in addition to a charge on use). However, such tariff systems are not necessarily socially inefficient, in that they can lead to increased use of machines offsetting the monopolist restriction of output (Schmalensee, 1981). Hence, it is not clear even in this case that the leverage effected would be socially harmful.

Several other reasons for tie-in sales can be briefly considered. First, in a number of tie-in cases in the USA the firm involved has sought to defend the tie on the grounds of ensuring adequate quality of the tied product. Thus, for example, IBM argued that it was justified in tying its unpatented tabulating cards into leasing contracts for its mechanical data processing equipment on the grounds that use of poor-quality cards would reduce the efficiency of its machines' operations and damage its reputation.[21] (In other cases similar reasoning has been applied to maintenance contracts tied to the sale or lease of equipment.) It goes without saying that such arguments are highly tenuous, in that a manufacturer can protect his reputation by simply specifying standards for tabulating cards (or maintenance personnel) in his contract of equipment sale, with no need to resort to the tie. This point has been recognized in the US courts, in particular in the IBM case.

A second argument is that cost savings may be associated with the tie. This argument is sometimes made with respect to full line forcing, whereby delivery cost savings are made which partly benefit the customer in the form of lower prices. There seems no reason, however, why the customer should not be allowed to choose whether to benefit from such cost and price reductions as opposed to taking a single product at a higher delivered price. Both arguments therefore are unlikely to hold much water.

Despite the ambiguity which surrounds the welfare effects of tie-in sales in general, until quite recently it was believed that such sales were likely to be harmful.

This viewpoint is recognized in the USA, where tie-in agreements which involve substantial restriction of competition are typically struck down in the courts. It also influenced the 1979 Green Paper on Restrictive Trade Practices Policy, which noted that the practice had been found to be against the public interest in almost all cases where it had been investigated by the Monopolies and Mergers Commission.[22] The Green Paper felt that ties would invariably be found to be against the public interest, and recommended a general reference of the practice to the Commission with a view to prohibition. In the event, the Commission's report published in 1981[23] adopted a much more eclectic view of the practice than the Green Paper had and argued against any general prohibition. Rather, it favoured a case-by-case approach within the ambit of the 1980 Competition Act to assess the practice in individual circumstances. While the Commission's report can be criticized for its rather poor analytical content, it may well be that such an approach is sensible, at least until further work has been done on the problem of tie-in sales and social welfare.

Predatory pricing   Finally, we may briefly mention predatory pricing. This arises when a firm or firms reduce price in an attempt to drive out or discipline competitors. In contrast to ordinary price competition, which typically benefits consumers, predatory pricing involves the intent on the part of the predator(s) to drive their rivals out of the market (or at least to discipline them) so that prices can be raised towards monopoly levels. Consequently predatory pricing has very different welfare consequences to ordinary price competition in that, while in the short run consumers benefit from the predatory price cuts, in the long run higher prices mean consumer welfare losses and resource misallocation.

The main problem with predatory pricing is how to identify it. Consider for example, the case of the entry of Laker Airways into the transatlantic passenger air travel market offering low-cost passenger fares. The reaction of established firms to this new competition was to cut fares in response to match or, indeed, undercut Laker, with the eventual result that Laker was bankrupted. Now, the question here is, Was the response of the incumbent firms and the eventual outcome simply the result of the normal workings of the competitive economy, or did the incumbent firms engage in predatory pricing to remove Laker from the market? More generally, how does one identify predatory pricing?[24]

In an influential paper in the USA, Areeda and Turner (1974/5) have suggested that one should examine the relationship between prices and costs to determine whether predation has occurred. Arguing that marginal cost pricing produces an efficient allocation of resources and that protection of inefficient competitors is undesirable, they suggest that a marginal cost pricing standard be adopted as an indicator of predation. Thus, if alleged predators cut prices below marginal cost (which may be proxied by average variable cost), then this involves resource misallocation and may drive out equally efficient rivals; such behaviour is undesirable and may be classified as predatory. Setting aside technical problems associated with this rule, however, its major weakness, as noted by Williamson (1977/8), is that it ignores the essential strategic nature of predatory pricing (the intent to eliminate rivals) and simply focuses on the short-run relationship between price and marginal cost. Temporary marginal cost pricing is not socially optimal if it is part of a predatory pricing strategy, which implies that such pricing will not proceed on a continuing basis. Hence, it may not be an appropriate standard for judging whether price competition is predatory or undesirable.

The Areeda–Turner paper has given rise to a major debate among US economists on how to identify predatory pricing, which we cannot go into here.[25] Suffice it to say that at present no simple rules for its identification are generally accepted. Interestingly, in the one case (in table 11.1) in which predatory tactics have been considered under the new UK legislation (viz. Scottish and Universal Newspapers Ltd (SUNL)), no problems of definition arose. In this case, the Office of Fair Trading (OFT) felt that the actions of SUNL in trying to prevent the establishment of a rival (free) newspaper (including putting pressure on their printer, setting up a rival paper with below-marginal-cost advertising rates, etc.) could clearly be regarded as predatory. This finding may well have important demonstration effects for other firms (notably in the newspaper industry) on competitive tactics likely to be viewed as predatory under the new legislation.

11.3 Summary and Conclusions

This chapter has reviewed the operation of UK competition policy in the fields of restrictive agreements between firms and single-firm anti-competitive practices. On the former, it was noted that UK policy since 1956 has been largely successful in removing many *formal* restrictive agreements between firms. Only limited evidence of pro-competitive effects of this legislation is currently available, however, and this is matched by some evidence that firms have sought to circumvent the law by adopting non-registrable means of coordinating their activities (and even illegal agreements). Grounds may, therefore, exist for strengthening the law in this area, and it was suggested that stiffer penalties for operating illegal agreements and, more fundamentally, an increase in the scope of the law *vis-à-vis* agreements and arrangements between firms, might be desirable.

UK legislation on single-firm practices, which is of more recent origin, was also discussed. With the exception of resale price maintenance (which is largely prohibited), other single-firm practices are subject to case-by-case investigation under the 1980 Competition Act. Early cases (see table 11.1) suggest that this law may take a fairly firm line against such practices, notwithstanding its ostensibly neutral approach to them. Whether or not this will turn out to provide the right balance of policy in this area, however, remains to be seen.

Notes

1 Single-firm practices, particularly in so far as they employ Monopoly and Merger Commission procedures, can be regarded as adjuncts to the monopoly legislation discussed in chapter 12. Whether they are best linked to monopolies or restrictive practices legislation, however, is really a matter of taste, and they are discussed in this chapter mainly for logistical reasons.

2 For detailed discussion of the UK legislation see the 1979 Green Paper on Restrictive Trade Practices Policy. For details of the EEC legislation (not considered here) see Swann (1983).

3 *Collective Discrimination: A Report on Exclusive Dealing, Collective Boycotts, Aggregated Rebates and other Discriminatory Trade Practices,* Cmnd 9504, June 1955.

4 See, for example, Stevens and Yamey (1965).

5 Goods information agreements relating to prices and terms of supply were called

up for registration in the Restrictive Trade Practices (Information Agreements) Order 1969. Few information agreements were in fact registered after this Order despite the known prevalence of such agreements prior to 1968.

6 See, for example, Swann et al. (1974).

7 See Elliott and Gribbin (1977).

8 See Pickering (1974, chapter 15). Useful information on registration of agreements, etc., is given in the Annual Reports of the Director General of Fair Trading.

9 In re Yarn Spinners' Agreement, L.R., I.R.P. 118 (1959).

10 This was suggested, for example, by a group of lawyers in evidence to the 1979 Green Paper (p. 100).

11 It did, however, advocate the prohibition of collusive tendering with criminal penalties (Green Paper, 1979, pp. 49–50).

12 The 1979 Green Paper reported evidence of failure to register, citing a number of cases which had recently come to light, namely cables, road surfacing materials, Diazo copying materials, ready-mixed concrete, baking, animal feeding stuffs and the supply of house coal (p. 48).

13 For details of US law see Scherer (1980) or Neale and Goyder (1980). Analysis and evidence on the deterrent effect of large damage awards is given in an interesting paper by Block, Nold and Sidak (1981).

14 Manufacturers can, of course, still indicate appropriate prices to retailers by use of 'recommended' resale prices. Such prices, however, are not enforceable in law, and hence firms cannot be prevented from competing on price if they want to.

15 In the case of full line forcing and tie-in sales, the 1979 Green Paper argued that there might be grounds for a general prohibition. An MMC report of 1981, however, argued against this (see below for discussion).

16 There appear to be no general grounds, however, for believing that an optimal provision of service will be made under unrestricted (monopolistic) competition: see Lancaster (1979) for details.

17 Note the related arguments of Stigler (1964) discussed in chapter 3.

18 See, for example, Scherer (1980, chapter 21). In recent years US policy has moved againt RPM, however.

19 See, in particular, Bowman (1957).

20 For an explicit discussion of this see Blair and Kaserman (1978).

21 International Business Machines Corp. v. U.S. (1936), cited by Scherer (1980, p. 584).

22 The 1978 Green Paper on Monopolies and Mergers Policy took a similar line. In fact, only five MMC reports are listed as relevant in the 1978 Green Paper, and tie-in sales and full line forcing were not wholly condemned in all cases.

23 See Monopolies and Mergers Commission (1981a). The MMC also reported on discounts to retailers in 1981 (MMC, 1981b) but again found no general public interest problem involved. In this case, countervailing power of large multiple retailers (see Galbraith, 1963) was found to provide important benefits for consumers even though such retailers exercised monopsonistic power.

24 In the Laker case, at time of writing this still has to be decided in practice in the US courts.

25 Important references include Scherer (1976), Williamson (1977/8) and Baumol (1979/80); see also McGee (1980, also 1958).

12 Monopolies and Mergers Policy

This final chapter examines UK competition policy on monopolies and mergers. Section 12.1 focuses attention on monopoly and examines some of the issues raised on the operation and effectiveness of UK monopoly policy. Section 12.2 then takes a more extensive look at merger policy which has been the subject of intense debate in recent years. In particular, we consider whether policy has been too permissive with respect to mergers in the UK.

12.1 Monopoly Policy

Monopoly policy is concerned with the possibility that dominant firms in individual markets may exercise market power. As will become clear in what follows, the policy is designed to cover both dominant firm and oligopolistic situations, and for simplicity in this section we will use the term 'monopoly' in this broad sense. Section 12.1.1 outlines current UK policy on monopoly, while in section 12.1.2 we consider the operation and effectiveness of that policy.[1]

12.1.1 UK Legislation

The framework of UK monopoly policy derives from the 1948 Monopolies and Restrictive Practices (Inquiry and Control) Act. This act established the Monopolies and Restrictive Practices Commission to carry out case-by-case investigations into monopolies and, as noted in chapter 11 (prior to 1956), collective restrictive practices also. As far as monopolies were concerned, the Act required the Commission, first, to establish whether a monopoly existed as defined by the Act, and, second, to evaluate the performance of the monopoly relative to the public interest. A statutory monopoly was defined as a situation in which *one-third* of the UK supply of a good was monopolized. In evaluating a monopoly in terms of the public interest, the Commission was required to take all relevant circumstances into account, particular reference being made to efficiency, productivity, full employment and technical progress. Thus, the Commission was given a wide remit for its investigations, and was basically required to examine all aspects of a monopoly's behaviour and performance which might be of relevance. Then, as now, the Commission was given only an investigatory role, at that time undertaking investigations at the request of the Board of Trade.

The Monopolies and Restrictive Practices Commission was renamed the Monopolies Commission under the 1956 Restrictive Trade Practices Act and the Monopolies and Mergers Commission under the 1973 Fair Trading Act. The 1965 Monopolies and Mergers Act, as discussed in section 12.2.3 below, extended the Commission's investigatory powers to mergers. In addition, it strengthened monopoly legislation in two ways: by extending the legislation to cover services as well as goods, and by increasing the powers of the government to take remedial action, in particular by ordering the division of companies. This latter power has rarely been used, however.

Current monopoly policy stems from the 1973 Fair Trading Act, which established the Office of Fair Trading and its Director General to oversee UK competition policy. Under this Act the Secretary of State and the Director General of Fair Trading (DGFT) make references to the Monopolies and Mergers Commission (MMC). The Act redefined a statutory monopoly as involving supply of *one-quarter* of a market by a single firm. In addition, it permitted the investigation of *complex monopolies*, where several firms have a combined 25 per cent market share and restriction of competition is involved.[2] As in the 1948 Act, the Commission is required to consider all matters of relevance to the public interest in its investigation. In contrast to the particular factors mentioned in the 1948 Act, however, the 1973 Act specifies the importance of maintaining competition and promoting the interests of consumers as being of particular importance to the public interest. This represents a limited attempt to adopt a more specifically pro-competitive line in UK monopoly policy.

Finally, under the 1980 Competition Act, powers to undertake monopoly investigations of public bodies (such as nationalized industries, water authorities and providers of bus services) were increased.[3] Such powers permit MMC investigations of efficiency, service provided and abuse of monopoly power, but do not extend to financial targets set by ministers or under statute.

Several features of the current legislation should be stressed. First, under the 1973 Fair Trading Act, the DGFT (and hence the Office of Fair Trading (OFT)) plays an important role in screening possible monopoly situations. The 1973 Act provides a statutory obligation for the DGFT to keep UK markets under review, and this represents an important means of keeping abreast of possible monopoly abuse and of establishing priorities for MMC investigations. Second, despite explicit reference to 'maintaining and promoting effective competition' in the 1973 Act, MMC reports have continued to consider all aspects of conduct and performance thought to be relevant in evaluating the public interest in a monopoly investigation. This is in line with the general requirements of the 1973 Act, and indeed competition *per se* has not figured large in the question of social welfare (as opposed to establishing whether a statutory monopoly exists). Third, and finally, while the Secretary of State has wide order-making powers to regulate prices, forbid certain practices or divide companies, these are not normally exercised. Rather, undertakings of remedial action are usually sought by negotiation between the DGFT and the firms involved, with an order being used as a last resort. This rather gentlemanly conduct suggests an ambivalence to the abuse of monopoly power in the UK which we refer to further below.

By the end of 1983 the Commission had completed over 90 reports. Eighteen of these prior to 1956 were concerned mainly with the activities of trade associations, and six general reports had also been produced.

12.1.2 Policy Issues

UK policy is based on the pragmatic assumption that there may be costs and benefits associated with monopoly and that consequently a case-by-case investigation of monopolized markets is required to assess the public interest. Hence, while it is recognized (in the use of a criterion of statutory monopoly) that a concentrated market structure creates the potential for the exercise of market power, there is no presumption of actual market power abuse. Indeed, given that the MMC is required to report 'whether any particular matter operates, or may be expected to operate, against the public interest', the burden of proof is left with the Commission to establish adverse consequences of a monopoly situation. Notwithstanding the particular matters mentioned in the 1973 Act, moreover, it considers the public interest by means of a detailed investigation of all the conduct and performance of the firms involved which it deems relevant.

In terms of philosophy, the UK approach stops short of the view that a competitive economy is desirable *per se*: either because it produces socially desirable economic conduct and performance or, *a fortiori*, because it is desirable as an end in itself. The view that a competitive economy might be an end in itself is an important idea in some areas of US policy but has never figured strongly in the UK (see section 12.2 below).[4]

Moreover, on the question of economic benefits, it is argued that competition is not necessarily the only or the best way of attaining economic ends. This latter argument in part reflects a deep division in government between groups which favour strong competition policy and groups which favour reorganization of industry as a means towards increasing international competitiveness. This division is well illustrated in the government's 1978 Green Paper on Monopolies and Mergers Policy where it manifests itself in a discussion of the relationship between the then Labour government's so-called 'industrial strategy' and competition policy. More generally, however, bodies which work closely with industry, such as the National Economic

Development Council (NEDC), often place much less emphasis on the benefits arising from competition than might the Office of Fair Trading, for example.

The economic case for cost–benefit investigations of monopoly situations is quite strong. Given the complexity and variety of real-world markets and the absence of clear evidence from economic theory and empirical studies of general detrimental effects of monopoly (see chapter 5), it would seem desirable to consider each case on its merits. Against this, however, there are several practical criticisms of the policy, which are discussed below. Further, as was stressed in chapter 2, there may be persistent forces at work tending to increase market concentration over time. By adopting a cost–benefit approach, therefore, UK monopoly policy may be operating against a background of the continuing erosion of the competitive economy, which may in itself create problems of a wider economic, social and political kind, e.g. the problem of concerted political pressure. Such wider issues go beyond the bounds of the kind of partial equilibrium, cost–benefit analysis of current UK monopoly policy. While at the present time little consideration has been given to them in the UK policy debate, they may become increasingly important if concentration continues to increase in the long run.

When one considers the practical operation of UK monopoly policy, a number of points can be made. First, the policy can be criticized for the burden it places on the firms investigated, particularly with respect to the time and effort demanded of senior management. Such costs may well be appreciable and must be added to the public costs of operating the policy. Second, since detailed cost–benefit analysis takes time, the process by which monopoly situations are brought under control is inevitably slow. For example, if one considers the major industries which were highly concentrated in 1975 according to table 2.3 above, then only a third of those industries had been investigated in the period 1948–83. Moreover, if one takes the much wider pool of industries which might meet the statutory monopoly criterion, then the 65 or so monopoly investigations made since 1948 have been but a drop in the ocean. Third, there are certain technical problems in dealing with 'complex monopolies' in that the MMC must establish that oligopolists are acting to restrict competition in order to establish that a complex monopoly exists. This contrasts with a statutory monopoly which is defined solely in terms of market share irrespective of market behaviour.

Criticisms have also been levelled at the MMC's reports. In particular, it has been argued that the MMC has been extremely liberal in its treatment of monopoly profits. Sutherland (1970), for example, in a study of monopoly reports in the 1960s, found that a company had to be earning profits within the upper quartile for large manufacturing companies to attract adverse MMC comment. Similar comments can be made about more recent reports. For example, in the Cat and Dog Foods Report in 1977 the MMC found that the dominant firm, Pedigree Petfoods, with a 50 per cent market share, earned a rate of return on capital on an historic cost basis of 47 per cent on average in 1972–5 compared with an average for all manufacturing of 16 per cent in the same period. Pedigree claimed, however, that this return reflected its high level of efficiency, particularly its tight policy of capital and financial control; and in the absence of evidence of anti-competitive practices the MMC was prepared to accept this rate of profit as reasonable. In the Breakfast Cereals Report of 1973, moreover, while the MMC argued that Kellogg's rate of return (again on an historic cost basis) of 70 per cent on average in 1962–6 was excessive, it regarded a lower rate of return of 46 per cent earned on average in 1967–71 as acceptable.

These two cases illustrate the degree to which the MMC is prepared to allow above-average rates of return in monopolized industries. Both Pedigree Petfoods and Kellogg argued among other things that comparison of their profitability with the average for all manufacturing was unfair since profitability on average was unacceptably low, being in Kellogg's view (after tax) below the cost of capital. Comparisons with more profitable companies, however, which themselves might have monopoly power advantages, were also favourable to Kellogg and Pedigree.

Second, the MMC's tacit acceptance that superior efficiency justifies high prices/profits can also be criticized. From a theoretical point of view, while efficiency on the part of firms is to be supported, it is also the case that welfare gains (and, in particular, benefits to consumers) arise if firms are restricted in their ability to exploit their monopoly position by charging high prices (relative to marginal costs). Against this it might be argued that allowing firms to extract monopoly rents from their advantageous positions offers an incentive to increased efficiency. The issue is not clear-cut, but it might be argued that, in not even considering the possibility of moderating prices and profits in such cases, the MMC has excluded a possibly important source of monopoly welfare loss from its purview by default.

Consider, finally, the effectiveness of UK monopoly policy. While the Secretary of State has wide order-making powers, including powers to split up existing companies, in practice the government has typically tried to negotiate voluntary changes in business conduct or reductions in price from the companies concerned. In particular, divestment of shares or assets has rarely been used. This has led some commentators to suggest that UK policy simply amounts to tinkering with the problem without tackling the root cause of the adverse consequences reported, namely the monopolistic structure of the market.[5] Against this (and somewhat surprisingly), the 1978 Green Paper took the view that 'most monopolists behave responsibly' and that the threat of MMC investigation was an important restraining influence on the exercise of monopoly power (Green Paper, 1978, pp. 38–9).

Such a view may well be questioned, however. In the first place, given the limited number of investigations that the MMC can undertake, it does not seem likely that the threat of investigation can represent a major business risk. On the other hand, it might be argued that some moral pressure to moderate the exercise of monopoly power might exist, if it were known that a market was under OFT review for possible monopoly investigation. Second, the view that monopolists and oligopolists typically do not exercise monopoly power, like its converse, cannot be taken as a general presumption. Curiously, the 1978 Green Paper itself cites the 1973 MMC general report on Parallel Pricing (Monopolies Commission, 1973b), which suggested that coordinated pricing behaviour might well be a widespread feature of particularly oligopolistic markets (Green Paper, 1978, p. 72).

Third, there are important practical problems associated with the use of non-structural remedies to adverse MMC findings. Apart from the point that negotiated remedies have in some cases fallen short of MMC recommendations, there is also a problem of monitoring firm conduct and performance to ensure that alternative means are not found to counteract the intention of the MMC. It could be argued that the likelihood of a market being referred a second time to the MMC is slight, so that only moral pressure from the OFT stands in the way of such action. Further, in cases where price reductions have been recommended and accepted, such remedies may confer only short-run benefits and are unlikely to provoke the increased competition which would be desirable from a longer-run point of view. Indeed, as the MMC's Parallel Pricing report stressed, it is very difficult to get oligopolistic firms that are set on a course of coordinated action to compete if they do not want to. In circumstances such as these, and *a fortiori* in dominant firm situations, it would seem that more drastic action designed to break up monopolistic or oligopolistic situations would be required.

It is argued in section 12.2.2 below that, in considering a merger or amalgamation of two firms, one should weigh the efficiency gains from the merger against the market power costs, in order to decide whether the merger should take place. In principle, the converse calculation could be made in deciding whether to break up a monopoly. While dissolution of monopolies has been used to some extent in the USA (notably in the early years of US policy – see Scherer, 1980, chapter 20), it has hardly figured at all in UK policy. Most recently, however, there have been moves in this direction (in the cases of British Gas showrooms in 1980 and British Posters Ltd in 1981).[6] Whether or not this represents a change towards a more openly structural policy, however, remains to be seen.

12.2 Merger Policy

Mergers and takeovers involve the amalgamation of two or more independent firms under common control, and are typically divided into horizontal, vertical and conglomerate mergers. In this section we mainly deal with the first type, whereby two or more firms producing competing products amalgamate. Some brief attention to the other cases, however, is given below.

We begin our discussion by considering the size of the problem as indicated by UK data on merger activity. In section 12.2.2 we then consider a framework for the cost–benefit analysis of horizontal mergers. Finally, we compare and contrast US and UK policy approaches, and consider in particular whether and in what ways UK policy on horizontal mergers might be improved.[7]

12.2.1 Merger Activity in the UK

Evidence on recent merger trends is given in table 12.1. This shows the number of mergers and consideration paid in mergers of industrial and commercial companies in 1963–83. In terms of numbers of mergers, the years

Table 12.1 UK merger trends for commercial and industrial companies, 1963–83

Year	No. of mergers	Consideration for acquired company (£m current prices)	Index[a]
1963	888	352	100
1964	940	505	134
1965	1000	517	146
1966	807	500	140
1967	763	822	216
1968	946	1946	362
1969[b]	907	935	176
1969[b]	846	1069	201
1970	793	1122	238
1971	884	911	164
1972	1210	2532	357
1973	1205	1304	213
1974	504	508	141
1975	315	291	64
1976	353	427	79
1977	482	812	117
1978	567	1140	—
1979	534	1656	—
1980	469	1475	—
1981	452	1144	—
1982	463	2206	—
1983	447	2343	—

Source: Green Paper (1978, Annex D), and Business Statistics Office, *Business Monitor* MQ7, table 1.

Notes
[a] Consideration in current prices deflated by the FT Actuaries 500 Ordinary Share Index, as given in 1979 Green Paper (not available for 1978–83).
[b] Based on company accounts prior to 1970, and on the financial press and other sources since 1969.

1965, 1972 and 1973 stand out, with 1000 or more mergers in a year. In terms of consideration paid in real terms, as indicated by the index computed in the final column, 1968 and 1972 stand out as involving three-and-a-half times the amount of activity of 1963.[8] There is clearly considerable variation in merger activity from year to year, but, with the exception of 1975 and 1976, the figures reveal a great deal of merger activity in the UK commercial and industrial sectors.

Some idea of the breakdown of mergers into different types is provided by table 12.2. Since 1965 proposed mergers have been vetted by the Mergers Panel for possible referral to the Monopolies Commission. Originally such vetting took place where assets worth £5 million or more were transferred or the merged company accounted for one-third of the supply of a good or

Table 12.2 Horizontal, vertical and conglomerate mergers investigated by the Mergers Panel, 1965–83

Type of integration[a]	Horizontal (%)	Vertical (%)	Conglomerate (%)	Total value (£m)
1965	84	9	7	1,125
1966	85	8	7	998
1967	92	4	4	2,273
1968	91	2	7	8,499
1969	91	0	9	3,714
1970	78	0	22	2,596
1971	66	4	30	1,687
1972	40	10	50	3,588
1973	76	2	22	4,878
1974	65	2	33	7,621
1975	77	4	19	5,786
1976	66	7	27	4,123
1977	57	11	32	4,676
1978	67	10	23	11,999
1979	68	4	28	13,140
1980[b]	68	1	31	22,289
1981	71	2	27	43,597
1982	64	4	32	25,939
1983	73	1	26	45,495
1965–83	72	4	23	214,024

Source: Green Paper (1978, Annex D), and *Annual Report* of the Director General of Fair Trading, 1983, pp. 89–91.

Notes
[a] Proportion of proposed mergers by value of acquired assets considered by the Mergers Panel, 1965–83.
[b] Figures for 1980 and after are not strictly comparable with earlier years owing to the increase in the assets criterion in 1980 (see text). The discrepancies involved are very small, however.

service. The former figure was raised to £15 million from 1980, while the latter provision was altered to a 25 per cent market share by the 1973 Fair Trading Act. Table 12.2 shows the breakdown of the percentage of the value of acquired assets classified as horizontal, vertical or conglomerate merger out of all mergers investigated by the Mergers Panel for 1965–83. While this classification is somewhat arbitrary, it suggests that over the whole period nearly three-quarters of all mergers (involving £154 billion of assets acquired) took the form of horizontal mergers. Some evidence exists for a switch towards conglomerate mergers after 1970, but horizontal mergers were by far the most important category even in the 1970s. While these figures are biased towards horizontal mergers (in that market share is a criterion for vetting), it should nevertheless be clear that horizontal mergers are a major factor in ongoing merger activity, and it is these with which we are mainly concerned below.

12.2.2 Horizontal Mergers: A Welfare Framework

The issue of the appropriate public policy to deal with horizontal mergers can be discussed within the framework suggested by Williamson (1968a; see also Williamson, 1977). If a horizontal merger simply has the effect of increasing the market power of the merged firms, enabling them to raise prices and profits, then a prima facie case against the merger exists. In so far as it may produce some social benefits, however, the case is not so clear-cut, and it is necessary to trade-off social costs and benefits of the merger. Williamson in particular focuses attention on economies or real cost savings as a defence of

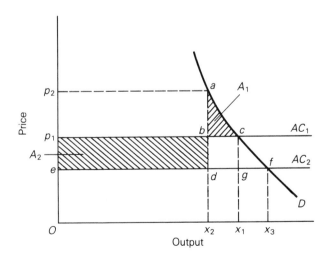

Figure 12.1

horizontal mergers, and we begin by considering his so called 'naive' trade-off model incorporating this effect.

Assume for simplicity a competitive market with constant costs, AC_1, and a market demand curve, D, as shown in figure 12.1. In competitive equilibrium, price is equal to marginal and unit cost, p_1, and competitive output is x_1. Assume that a series of mergers now takes place giving rise to real cost savings which reduce costs to AC_2. Such cost savings may arise, for example, from rationalization of production and the exploitation of economies of scale and/or from the massing of more resources under the control of superior management. If the merged firms continue to charge price p_1 or below then consumers are no worse off and there is a saving in resources in producing output x_1 equal to area $p_1 cge$. The merger is therefore strictly beneficial.

Suppose, however, that the post-merger price rises above p_1 to, say, p_2. Output is restricted to x_2 and consumer surplus is reduced by area $p_2 acp_1$. If we treat the transfer of income (utility) from consumers to producers as neutral, then the net welfare loss is area abc (A_1). Against this, however, cost savings are made on production of output, x_2, equivalent to area $p_1 bde$ (that is, area A_2). Compared with the competitive situation, these savings represent scarce resources freed for alternative uses. Consequently, the overall net social benefit of the merger is the difference between A_2 and A_1. As Williamson points out, this may well be positive for comparatively small cost savings owing to merger. For example, with a market elasticity of demand of 2, a 10 per cent price rise is offset by a 1.2 per cent cost saving while a 20 per cent price rise is offset by a 5.8 per cent cost saving.[9] Hence, even small cost saving benefits may offer an important defence for horizontal mergers.

Several points may be noted concerning this model. First, the argument relies on an assumption that the transfer of income (utility), $p_2 abp_1$, from consumers to producers is treated as neutral. Relaxation of this assumption in the direction of weighting consumer losses more heavily will increase the social cost of merger and hence require greater cost savings to make a merger beneficial. For example, a 2/1 weight in favour of consumers requires cost savings of 5.9 and 14.0 per cent respectively to offset the 10 and 20 per cent rises in the above example.[10] The importance of this factor is clear in figure 12.1 on comparison of the magnitudes of areas $p_2 abp_1$ and abc. It could be argued, however, that questions of distributional equity are really much wider than the inspection of income redistributions in particular markets. Consequently, in assessing a particular merger it may be advisable to set such issues on one side on the grounds that, at least in principle, income redistribution can be obtained by appropriate tax policies.

Second, even if the merger produces positive net social benefits, it does not represent an ideal solution. Consumers could in principle bribe the merged firm to produce output x_3 at a price equal to AC_2 by paying it a sum equal to the monopoly profits area $p_2 ade$. The gross consumer benefit from such a move is area $p_2 afe$, giving a net consumer benefit of area adf. Thus area adf would measure the social costs of a permissive merger policy compared with the first-best optimum of pricing at (lowest) marginal cost. Before we could say that Williamson's trade-off is not relevant, however, we would have to consider the desirability and feasibility of introducing policies such as price regulation or nationalization to secure the first-best optimum. Among other things, it might be suggested that nationalized industries may suffer from political interference and/or the inability to attract top-quality management, so that lowest cost production, AC_2, may not be obtainable. These issues are beyond the scope of this book, and we confine ourselves in this chapter to a consideration of less radical merger policies.

Williamson's argument relies, of course, on the assumption that mergers give rise to cost savings. Several authors, and most notably Leibenstein,[11] have argued that lack of competitive pressures may well cause costs to rise after merger. Leibenstein has coined the term 'X-inefficiency' to denote such an effect and has stressed its importance to economic welfare. The argument is illustrated in figure 12.2, where initially competitive price is p_1 and output is x_1. Following a merger, however, price rises to, say, p_2 and in addition costs rise to AC_2. In the absence of a cost increase, the price effect of the merger is to reduce consumer surplus by area p_2acp_1, of which area p_2abp_1 would be a transfer to producers, leaving area abc (i.e. area A_1) as the net welfare loss. Because of the cost increase, however, producers receive only area p_2ade as profit. On the simplifying assumption (see below) that the increase in costs represents a pure waste of resources, area p_1bde (i.e. area A_2) must be added to the welfare loss. Thus, both the price increase and the cost increase contribute to the reduction in social welfare and the merger is unambiguously bad.

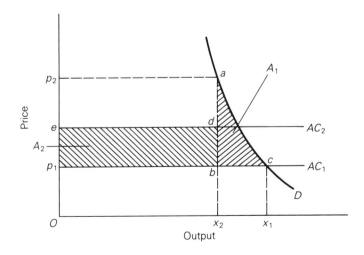

Figure 12.2

The above argument should be qualified, however, if some individuals benefit from the increase in costs (Parish and Ng, 1972). For example, if costs rise owing to a transfer of some monopoly profits to workers in the form of higher wage rates (and there are no consequent price effects), then area A_2 represents not a waste of resources but merely a transfer. Again, if the increase in costs arises from a conscious decision of managers and/or workers to improve working conditions, the value of this benefit should be allowed for. Against this, rises in costs arising from reduced managerial control, slack and technical inefficiency are less likely to produce substantive benefits. In short, it is unlikely that the whole of area A_2 in figure 12.2 should be regarded as a loss, but the proportion so regarded would depend on the circumstances behind the cost increase in each particular case. The argument that a merger which increases costs involves a net social welfare loss is nevertheless maintained.

Williamson's naive model is useful as a pedagogic device, but a number of other factors must be taken into account where practical merger policy is concerned. First, it is necessary in evaluating the costs and benefits of any particular merger to consider what Williamson calls *weighting* and *incipiency* effects. These relate to external effects of the merger within the market concerned. Thus, a merger of two firms within a market may cause other firms as well as the merged firm to raise price. Consequently, in assessing the costs and benefits of the merger, this more general price effect must be appropriately allowed for (weighted).

Incipiency, on the other hand, relates to the possibility that the merger under consideration might be part of a trend of mergers in the industry. In this case a single merger cannot be considered in isolation; rather, the costs and benefits of all the mergers must be assessed. For example, it may be the case that cost savings are obtained in one merger, making it seemingly beneficial, but that other mergers which follow offer no such savings so that in total the mergers are not beneficial. If the costs and benefits of each individual merger are difficult to predict and/or if investigation costs are high (as seems likely), then evaluation of each merger separately is not feasible and an industry cost–benefit analysis should be made.

Second, external effects in other industries should also be considered. We have already noted in chapter 10 that general equilibrium considerations may be important, and this need not detain us further here. Suffice it to say that the effects of the merger on closely related products should be considered where relevant. Also, of course, it is quite likely in practice that horizontal mergers of major companies involve amalgamation of a great deal of other business ancillary to the main product under consideration. Possible costs and benefits involved in relation to this business must also be considered.

Third, it is necessary to consider the treatment of time in assessing a merger. A horizontal merger may be a quick way of bringing about cost savings, but the relevant question is whether such cost savings would eventually be obtained anyway in the absence of mergers, and, if so, whether it is better to obtain them by merger or by competition. Such arguments suggest that one should consider the time stream of costs and benefits arising from a horizontal merger, and this in turn requires one to make assumptions concerning the cost savings and market power effects of internal expansion over time.

Consider a simple example (due to Ross, 1968; see also Williamson, 1968b) in which, by internal expansion in a growing market, firms can progressively reduce costs and price to AC_2 in figure 12.1. In this case, area A_2 minus area A_1 is the *initial* net social benefit from merger, but over time the cost saving area is reduced and the deadweight loss area increases relative to the competitive alternative. Diagrammatically (and abstracting from the growth in market demand), area p_1bde reduces to zero as the competitive firms make cost savings and area abc expands to adf as the output restriction becomes more severe. Formally, if $S(t)$ is the cost saving at time t, $L(O)$ is the fixed initial loss, and $L(t)$ the subsequent additional loss, then the present value of the net social benefit of the merger is

$$V = \int_O^T [S(t) - L(O) - L(t)]e^{-rt}\,\mathrm{d}t \tag{12.1}$$

where r is the social discount rate. In this expression, the cost saving benefit of the merger, $S(t)$, falls over time, while the additional deadweight loss, $L(t)$, rises. Clearly, it is quite possible in these circumstances for V to be negative, implying that it would be better for the merger to be banned and to allow the ordinary competitive process to secure the desired social benefits.

In a more general framework one would have to allow for further complications, such as the fact that the cost savings of the merger are themselves likely to take time to emerge, and that, in the absence of merger, competition and internal expansion may themselves give rise to market power effects. Obviously the first factor is likely to reduce the benefit of the merger while the second is likely to increase it. A full cost–benefit analysis of a merger would thus have to take account of the expected stream of costs and benefits over time relative to the expected pattern of events if the merger were disallowed, and obviously this would be a difficult task. In such an analysis it should also be remembered that, if the merged firm restricts output and raises price, it may attract new entrants to the industry, thereby attenuating the monopoly effects. It would thus be necessary to consider the threat of potential competition and the height of entry barriers in the industry in assessing the likely effects of the merger.

Any practical cost–benefit-based merger policy, constrained by deadlines for decisions and imperfect foresight concerning future events, must inevitably be a second-best compared with Williamson's analysis. In the next section we consider UK merger policy which, in contrast to US policy, attempts to employ an appraisal of costs and benefits in merger control.

12.2.3 UK Merger Policy

UK merger policy is a market-performance-based policy in that it relies on an assessment of potential social costs and benefits rather than on market structure considerations in judging a merger. Current policy stems from the 1965 Monopolies and Mergers Act as codified by the 1973 Fair Trading Act. Prior to 1965, the Monopolies Commission was empowered to investigate statutory monopoly positions at the direction of the appropriate government minister, but not mergers which might create or enhance such monopolies. The 1965 Act rectified this, by permitting Commission investigation of mergers if a statutory monopoly was created or enhanced, or alternatively if assets transferred in the merger were of £5 million value or more (raised to £15 million of assets in 1980). The 1973 Act, which set up the Office of Fair Trading (OFT) to administer UK competition policy, extended the policy by redefining a statutory monopoly as involving control of supply of one-quarter (as opposed to one-third) of a market. Under the policy the Secretary of State can refer a proposed merger to the (renamed) Monopolies and Mergers Commission (MMC), which is required to report (normally within six months) whether the merger can be expected to operate against the public interest, as defined in broad terms in the 1973 Act. An adverse report can lead the Secretary of State to order that a merger should not take place, or that it be reversed if it has already taken place. The policy embodies a *de facto* belief that most mergers are likely to be in the public interest, but provides a mechanism for investigating the (assumed) minority of cases which might not be so. This is revealed in the figures for the period 1965–77, for example (see Green Paper, 1978), which show that of the 1500+ mergers which fulfilled the requirements of the legislation, 43 (less than 3 per cent) were referred to the MMC, although 60 per cent of these were either abandoned or received an adverse MMC report.

US policy offers some interesting contrasts to this. First the policy in the USA, which dates back originally to the 1890 Sherman Act and the 1914 Clayton Act, is based largely on structural rather than performance considerations. This reflects the general approach to anti-trust policy in the USA, which aims to protect the competitive economy (in a structural sense) and prevent the creation of monopoly. The US system is also judicial in that the Justice Department and the Federal Trade Commission prosecute companies under the legislation in the ordinary courts, and decisions and hence the law are *de facto* made in the Supreme Court. On the question of mergers, current US policy stems from the Celler–Kefauver Act of 1950 which amended the Clayton Act and turned US policy from being largely ineffective into probably the strongest policy on mergers of any country.

The strength and nature of the US policy is revealed in the Justice Department's guidelines to prosecutions under the Act issued in 1982. Noting that, in the USA, a market may be defined over a relatively small geographic area, these provide a sliding scale for the structural effects of mergers (based on the Herfindahl concentration index) under which prosecution in the courts would normally follow. The guidelines distinguish unconcentrated post-merger markets (with a Herfindahl index, H, less than 1000), moderately concentrated industries (with H between 1000 and 1800) and highly concentrated industries (with H over 1800).[12] In the latter category, in particular, mergers are likely to be challenged, especially if a Herfindahl increase over 100 is implied, and possibly for one over 50. An increase in H close to 100 might be involved, for example, if a firm with a 10 per cent market share took over a firm with a 5 per cent market share, or if a firm with a 25 per cent market share took over one with a 2 per cent market share. These guidelines are probably weaker than previous (1968) guidelines operated by the Department of Justice, but not by all that much (Tollison, 1983).

US merger policy has at times been notably strict on horizontal mergers. This can be illustrated by a case in the 1960s (cited by Scherer, 1980, p. 550). In 1966 the Supreme Court ruled by a 6–2 majority that Von's Grocery Co., with a 4.7 per cent share of the Los Angeles retail grocery market, would, by taking over Shopping Bag Food Stores, with a 2.8 per cent share, contribute illegally to reducing competition in that market. This ruling and many others since 1950 have meant that, apart from an occasional case, significant US horizontal mergers have largely not taken place. In particular, consistent rulings by the Courts have said that illegality is to be determined on structural grounds and that 'possible economies cannot be used' as an anti-trust defence.[13]

In addition to controlling horizontal mergers, both the UK and US legislation offer scope for controlling vertical and conglomerate mergers. In the UK these can, in particular, be captured by the assets criterion, and a limited number of cases have been investigated.[14] In the USA such mergers would be caught if it could be shown that they significantly lessened competition or tended to create a monopoly. Some early prosecutions involving vertical mergers were successful in the USA in the 1950s and 1960s, but more recent thinking has suggested that vertical integration may often enhance efficiency rather than create monopoly (see chapter 8) so that less need for public policy action exists.[15] Conglomerate mergers have largely escaped prosecution in the USA, and this has been an important factor (see Scherer, 1980, p. 558) in their growth in prominence in recent years.

Clearly, UK and US policies on mergers are substantially different in principle and practice. In the remainder of this section we consider some of the weaknesses and merits of the UK system set against the background of the US approach.

The principal merit of the UK system would appear to be its performance-based approach, wherein mergers are assessed according to probable social costs and benefits. Indeed, Williamson specifically attacked the US policy approach for creating the potential for socially inefficient merger policy. As we have previously seen, however, cost–benefit analyses of individual mergers may well not be straightforward, as factors such as uncertain future cost savings and price movements, market developments in the absence of the merger and possible retaliatory defensive mergers have to be evaluated.

These issues, which are difficult to deal with conceptually, are exacerbated by the time limit which is of necessity imposed on an investigation. The six months normally allowed for an MMC investigation hardly permits a full and satisfactory cost–benefit analysis so that decisions may be impressionistic and arbitrary to some extent. And, of course, the vast majority of mergers vetted each week and passed by the Mergers Panel are likely to be only cursorily appraised. One could well argue that, while cost–benefit analysis is an ideal, in practice it is a costly and arbitrary approach which leaves much to be desired, for a number of reasons.

(1) It can be argued, for example, that it is arbitrary and inequitable, in that a company must regard itself as very unlucky to be referred to the MMC when other mergers which are not necessarily any less against the public interest escape scrutiny.

(2) It can be attacked on cost grounds, in that companies wishing to pursue a merger may be involved in much expense in making a case, providing evidence for the Commission, etc.

(3) It can also be attacked as creating uncertainty as to whether a merger will be referred, and if so what the outcome of the investigation will be. The OFT currently attempts to reduce the former uncertainty by providing 'off-the-record' advice in advance of its likely attitude to a proposed merger.

UK policy contains an implicit presumption that most mergers, by producing cost savings and other benefits, are in the public interest. Indeed, in the years of the Labour government of the 1960s, an Industrial Reorganisation Corporation was set up (in 1966) actively to encourage mergers in order to rationalize production and hence enable firms to compete effectively in international markets. This presumption that mergers are typically socially beneficial, which remains a feature of UK policy today, is not, however, consistent with evidence on the private and social gains from mergers that has been collected. Rather, this evidence suggests that many mergers do not confer private benefits on the merged company, let alone social benefits for the community.

Several examples of this work may be mentioned. First, in an early study, Singh (1971) considered a sample of 77 firms involved in horizontal mergers in the period 1955–60. He found that at least half of these firms suffered a decline in profitability in each of several years following the merger compared with the pre-merger performance of the companies involved. Meeks (1977) did a more comprehensive study along similar lines involving 233 large companies which merged in 1964–72. He made adjustments for industry, year and accounting biases and compared the three-year pre-merger profitability of the companies with post-merger profitability. On average, profitability was lower in each of seven years after the merger, although probably for accounting reasons profitability on average rose in the actual merger year. Between a half and two-thirds of companies had lower profitability in each year after the merger. In some cases the decline in average profitability was small, with statistically significant reductions being found in only the third, fourth and fifth years after merger. Nevertheless, with the exception of the merger year itself, the evidence suggests that on average there was no support for supposed efficiency gains of merger.[16]

A second, somewhat different, approach was adopted by Firth (1979). He looked at stock market evidence on how investors appraised the private benefits of potential mergers using the 'efficient markets' hypothesis that stock market prices will represent best available judgements on the combined company's expected future stream of net income. Evidence on share prices before and after a takeover proposal becomes known then gives the stock market's assessment of the private net benefits of the merger. Using a sample of 224 successful takeover bids in 1972–4, Firth found that the market value of the firms involved fell in 53 per cent of cases on announcement of the merger, with the average decline in value being £9.1 million over the whole sample. In 80 per cent of cases the shares of the acquiring company were written down, with an average decline of £664.7 million over the whole sample compared with an average write-up of £655.6 million in the acquired companies. In other words, the stock market took, on average, a slightly pessimistic view of mergers in this period, with gains and losses fairly evenly balanced but heavily weighted in favour of acquired companies' shareholders. These results conflict with those in the USA, which have found significant gains from mergers which were equally divided between acquiring and acquired firms (Halpern, 1973). In the UK, the stock market on average discounted any supposed benefits of merger, and as Firth points out, this judgement proved correct up to two years after the merger announcement.

Finally, Cowling et al. (1980) have adopted a case study approach to mergers. In particular, they made an in-depth analysis of nine mergers, all but one of which took place in the period 1965–70, and this, together with other evidence, led them to conclude that no general efficiency gains from mergers were forthcoming. One aspect of their study was to measure efficiency in terms of a unit factor requirement index, which estimates total input requirements per unit of output. This (inverse) measure of efficiency revealed four mergers in which a firm bettered a $1\frac{1}{2}$ per cent per annum efficiency growth rate in any of five or six post-merger years. In two of these cases for which further examination was possible, it was found that one firm (Rowntree Mackintosh) roughly matched the efficiency performance of its non-merger competitors while the other (Ransome, Hoffman and Pollard) showed some evidence of under-performance. The limited evidence available from this study is thus consistent with the previous findings. Cowling et al. did find one or two instances of efficiency gains, notably when superior management gained control of more resources, but in their view these were not sufficient to suggest that efficiency gains typically apply.[17]

These and other studies suggest that, while some mergers may produce private benefits to the merged companies, such an effect is by no means universal or indeed typical. The question immediately arises, of course, as to why such mergers take place. Motives for mergers are complex, but as noted by Firth the available evidence is consistent with the hypothesis that such mergers arise from managerial preferences for growth of their companies rather than profits. This hypothesis, if found applicable, would itself have consequences for economic welfare, not least because managers might choose to lower prices below profit-maximizing levels in order to increase firm size. On the other hand, some degree of exploitation of monopoly power might be expected in order to generate funds for future expansion. This latter effect would suggest that both growth-maximizing and profit-maximizing firms would undertake mergers for monopoly power purposes, creating the potential for social welfare losses.

The empirical evidence available on mergers casts serious doubt on the *de facto* presumption of UK merger policy. Such considerations lie behind the most recent government reappraisal of merger policy, which suggests that a shift to a more *neutral presumption* is required, but with a continuance of the existing legislation and institutional framework (Green Paper, 1978). This change it envisaged would possibly quadruple the number of cases referred to the MMC. Further, it suggested that effects on structural competitiveness also be explicitly considered by the MMC.

The obvious problem for UK policy, which implicitly lies behind these recommendations, is that the current institutional framework of MMC investigations could not cope with a strong merger policy without being extremely costly and disruptive of industry. It simply would not be feasible to have large numbers of cost–benefit analyses of individual mergers going on simultaneously. It would appear, therefore, that if a stronger merger policy was thought desirable there would have to be institutional changes and, more importantly, a change in basic principles from a cost–benefit to a structural policy.

There are several arguments for and against such a move to a US-type policy. First, such a policy might be distortionary, diverting activity into non-horizontal (vertical and conglomerate) mergers. Second, while the evidence is against significant forgone benefits in the typical merger case, there may be a few important cases in which substantial social benefits might arise from the restructuring of an industry. On the other side, a US-type policy is relatively simple to run, and may actually provide positive benefits of increasing competitiveness in ruling out the option of merger.

In conclusion, however, one further problem might be mentioned as being pertinent to the UK in contrast to the US: namely, the non-judicial approach to merger policy in the UK. Clearly, a structural merger policy ought to be run through the judicial system so that both companies and the anti-trust authorities can present a case to an independent body. Unlike in the USA, however, there is no tradition of anti-trust cases in the UK courts and it might be difficult to graft one on. It might be necessary to create special merger courts to run the policy as with the Restrictive Practices Court. Institutional changes of this magnitude are obviously not made lightly, and this may be an important reason why major change in UK merger policy is not likely to occur in the near future.

12.3 Summary and Conclusions

This chapter has examined UK public policy on monopolies and mergers, paying particular attention to the problem of horizontal mergers which remain at worryingly high levels in the UK. As far as monopolies are concerned, it was noted that, while in principle cost–benefit analysis of individual cases was desirable, a number of weaknesses of the UK system existed. In particular, it was suggested that the MMC might be encouraged to toughen its stance on monopoly abuse (including high prices and profits) and employ structural remedies more freely in its recommendations.

On the other hand, problems with UK merger policy are perhåps even more acute. Given the sheer number of mergers that take place, the policy leads to only a very small proportion of referrals to the MMC. Serious doubts, moreover, exist as to whether significant social benefits do arise in a typical merger, and whether, indeed, the MMC is able adequately to appraise potential costs and benefits involved in particular cases. A case may exist, therefore, for a major change in UK merger policy, and it was suggested that a more structural approach (along US lines) might be more practical. US experience has shown that tight control of horizontal mergers is likely to divert merger activity in particular along conglomerate lines. The aggregate effects of this (together with possible efficiency costs of a tight merger policy) must also be considered in any final appraisal of possible reforms.

Notes

1 For recent discussion of UK monopoly policy see Swann (1979) and the 1978 Green Paper on monopolies and mergers policy. Details of EEC policy, which is not covered in this chapter, can be found in Swann (1983).

2 This power was also available under the 1948 Act.

3 These powers are in addition to the provisions of the Act dealing with anti-competitive practices discussed in chapter 11.

4 US policy on monopoly derives from section 2 of the 1890 Sherman Act which forbids any attempt to 'monopolize' a trade. The meaning of the term 'monopolize' has varied somewhat in interpretation in the US courts, but, by and large, it has included some conduct aspect (intention to monopolize) as well as a structural aspect (possession of a monopoly position). In practice, therefore, the existence of a monopoly position is not itself illegal in the USA, although it may become so if

the monopolist pursues policies designed to exclude new competition and maintain his position. For further details see, for example, Scherer (1980, pp. 527–44).

5 See, for example, the review of main economic issues by George and Joll (1975).

6 In the case of British Gas showrooms, the Commission found the British Gas monopoly of gas appliance retailing to be against the public interest and recommended either withdrawal from retailing or important weakening of the monopoly position. Similarly, in the British Posters Ltd case, the Commission found the monopoly against the public interest and recommended it be broken up, a recommendation that was put into effect in 1982.

7 For useful discussions of UK merger policy see the 1978 Green Paper, Swann (1979) and Utton (1975).

8 No index is published for 1978–83 (in *Business Monitor* MQ7), but the data available suggest that no further peaks occurred in these years.

9 Williamson (1977). These figures assume a constant elasticity market demand function of the form $x = Ap^{-\eta}$, where x is output, p is price, η is the elasticity of demand and A is a constant. By inspection of figure 12.1,

Net social benefit (*NSB*)

$$= A_2 - A_1 = x_2(p_1 - AC_2) - \int_{p_1}^{p_2} Ap^{-\eta}dp + x_2(p_2 - p_1).$$

It can be shown (see Cowling *et al.* (1980), pp. 34–7) that this implies a trade-off

$$\left(\frac{1}{1-\eta}\right) - \left(\frac{\eta}{1-\eta}\right)\left(\frac{p_2}{p_1}\right)^{1-\eta} - \left(\frac{p_2}{p_1}\right)^{-\eta}\left(\frac{AC_2}{p_1}\right) = 0.$$

10 The trade-off in this case is

$$\left(\frac{1}{1-\eta}\right) + \left(0.5 - \frac{1}{1-\eta}\right)\left(\frac{p_2}{p_1}\right)^{1-\eta} + \left(\frac{p_2}{p_1}\right)^{-\eta}\left(0.5 - \frac{AC_2}{p_1}\right) = 0.$$

11 See Leibenstein (1966) and also Comanor. and Leibenstein (1969). For a critical view, see Parish and Ng (1972).

12 For these purposes, market shares are treated as percentages so H varies from 0 to 10,000. To convert to a numbers equivalent (see chapter 2), divide by 10,000 and take the reciprocal; e.g., $H = 1800$ is equivalent to 5.6 equally sized firms operating in an industry. Further details on the H measure as used in the Department of Justice Guidelines can be found in Fox (1982) and Miller (1982).

13 Similarly, the 1982 Department of Justice Guidelines rule out economies as a defence for horizontal mergers in all but exceptional circumstances. See Fox (1982) for further details.

14 See, for example, Pickering (1974, table 8.4) for details of some early cases.

15 Early US prosecutions, in particular, involved cases in which possible foreclosure of markets was involved. For a similar UK case (in which the merger was in fact allowed) see the BMC–Pressed Steel Co. Ltd merger of 1966. The recent Department of Justice Guidelines have abandoned arguments about foreclosure as possible grounds for challenging vertical mergers and now concentrate squarely on possible price-enhancing monopoly effects: see Fox (1982) for details.

16 In a more recent study of the peak merger years 1967–9, Cosh, Hughes and Singh (1980) found no evidence of falling post-merger profitability, however. Whether this difference in result is due to the different sample used, different methods or something else is not clear.

17 This conclusion does not square altogether with the details of the case studies, which seem to show more evidence of efficiencies than Cowling *et al.* appear to admit.

References

Adams, W. J. (1970) 'Firm size and research activity: France and the United States', *Quarterly Journal of Economics*, **84**, 386–409.

Adelman, M. A. (1961) 'The anti-merger act: 1950–60', *American Economic Review*, Papers and Proceedings, **51**, 236–44.

Aitchison, J. and Brown, J. A. C. (1966) *The Lognormal Distribution*. Cambridge: Cambridge University Press.

Amey, L. R. (1964) 'Diversified manufacturing businesses', *Journal of the Royal Statistical Society*, series A, **127**, 251–90.

Amihud, Y. and Lev, B. (1981) 'Risk reduction as a managerial motive for conglomerate mergers', *Bell Journal of Economics*, **12**, 605–17.

Areeda, P. and Turner, D. F. (1974/5) 'Predatory pricing and related practices under section 2 of the Sherman Act', *Harvard Law Review*, **88**, 697–733.

Arrow, K. J. (1962) 'Economic welfare and the allocation of resources for invention', in National Bureau of Economic Research, *The Rate and Direction of Inventive Activity: Economic and Social Factors*. Princeton: Princeton University Press; reprinted in Lamberton (1971).

Arrow, K. J. (1975) 'Vertical integration and communication', *Bell Journal of Economics*, **6**, 173–83.

Asch, P. (1979/80) 'The role of advertising in changing concentration, 1963–71', *Southern Economic Journal*, **46**, 288–97.

Asch, P. and Seneca, J. J. (1975) 'Characteristics of collusive firms', *Journal of Industrial Economics*, **23**, 223–37.

Ayarian, R. (1975) 'Advertising and rate of return', *Journal of Law and Economics*, **18**, 479–506.

Bacharach, M. (1976) *Economics and the Theory of Games*. London: Macmillan.

Bailey, E. E. and Friedlaender, A. F. (1982) 'Market structure and multiproduct industries', *Journal of Economic Literature*, **20**, 1024–48.

Bain, J. S. (1951) 'Relation of profit rate to industry concentration: American manufacturing, 1936–40', *Quarterly Journal of Economics*, **65**, 293–324 (with corrigendum on p. 602).

Bain, J. S. (1954) 'Conditions of entry and the emergence of monopoly', in E. H. Chamberlin (ed.), *Monopoly and Competition and their Regulation*. London: Macmillan.

Bain, J. S. (1956) *Barriers to New Competition*. Cambridge, Mass.: Harvard University Press.

Bain, J. S. (1968) *Industrial Organisation* (2nd edn). New York: John Wiley.

Baumol, W. J. (1979/80) 'Quasi-permanence of price reductions: a policy for prevention of predatory pricing', *Yale Law Journal*, **89**, 1–26.

Baumol, W. J. (1982) 'Contestable markets: an uprising in the theory of industry structure', *American Economic Review*, **72**, 1–15.

Baumol, W. J., Panzar, J. C. and Willig, R. D. (1982) *Contestable Markets and the Theory of Industry Structure*. New York: Harcourt Brace Jovanovich.

Benham, L. (1972) 'The effect of advertising on the price of eyeglasses', *Journal of Law and Economics*, **15**, 337–52.

Bergson, A. (1973) 'On monopoly welfare losses', *American Economic Review*, **63**, 853–70.

Berry, C. H. (1975) *Corporate Growth and Diversification*. Princeton: Princeton University Press.

Bertrand, J. (1883) 'Book review of Cournot's work', *Journal des Savants*, pp. 499–508.

Bevan, A. (1974) 'The UK potato crisp industry 1960–72: a case study of new entry competition', *Journal of Industrial Economics*, **22**, 281–98.

Bhagwati, J. N. (1970) 'Oligopoly theory, entry prevention and growth', *Oxford Economic Papers*, **22**, 297–310.

Blair, R. D. and Kaserman, D. (1978) 'Vertical integration, tying and antitrust policy', *American Economic Review*, **68**, 397–402.

Bloch, H. (1974) 'Advertising and profitability: a reappraisal', *Journal of Political Economy*, **82**, 267–86.

Bloch, H. (1980) 'The effect of advertising on competition: comments on a survey', *Journal of Economic Literature*, **18**, 1063–6.

Block, M. K., Nold, F. C. and Sidak, J. G. (1981) 'The deterrent effect of antitrust enforcement', *Journal of Political Economy*, **89**, 429–45.

Bond, R. S. and Greenberg, W. (1976) 'Industry structure, market rivalry and public policy: a comment' (with reply by Demsetz), *Journal of Law and Economics*, **19**, 201–9.

Bork, R. H. (1954) 'Vertical integration and the Sherman Act: the legal history of an economic misconception', *University of Chicago Law Review*, **22**, 157–201; partially reprinted in Yamey (1973).

Bowman, W. S. Jr (1957) 'Tying arrangements and the leverage problem', *Yale Law Journal*, **67**, 19–36.

Bradburd, R. M. (1980a) 'Conglomerate power without market power: the effects of conglomeration on a risk-averse quantity-adjusting firm', *American Economic Review*, **70**, 483–7.

Bradburd, R. M. (1980b) 'A model of the effect of conglomeration and risk aversion on pricing', *Journal of Industrial Economics*, **28**, 369–86.

Bresnahan, T. (1981) 'Duopoly models with consistent conjectures', *American Economic Review*, **71**, 934–45.

Brozen, Y. (1971) 'Bain's concentration and rates of return revisited', *Journal of Law and Economics*, **14**, 351–69.

Brozen, Y. (1974) 'Entry barriers: advertising and product differentiation', in Goldschmid *et al.* (1974).

Brozen, Y. (1975) 'Competition, efficiency and antitrust', in Y. Brozen (ed.), *The Competitive Economy: Selected Readings*. Morristown, NJ: General Learning.

Buxton, A. J., Davies, S. W. and Lyons, B. R. (1984) 'Concentration and advertising in consumer and producer markets', *Journal of Industrial Economics*, **32**, 451–64.

Cable, J. (1975) 'Intermarket differences in advertising intensity', in K. Cowling, J. Cable, M. Kelly and A. J. McGuinness, *Advertising and Economic Behaviour.* London: Macmillan.

Cannon, C. M. (1978) 'International trade, concentration and competition in UK consumer goods markets', *Oxford Economic Papers*, **30**, 130–7.

Carlton, D. W. (1979) 'Vertical integration in competitive markets under uncertainty', *Journal of Industrial Economics*, **27**, 189–209.

Carter, J. R. (1978) 'Collusion, efficiency and antitrust', *Journal of Law and Economics*, **21**, 435–44.

Casson, M. (1984) 'The theory of vertical integration: a survey and synthesis', paper presented at the 11th European Industrial Economics (EARIE) Conference, Fontainebleau, France.

Caves, R. E. (1982) *Multinational Enterprise and Economic Analysis.* Cambridge: Cambridge University Press.

Caves, R. E., Porter, M. E. and Spence, A. M. with Scott, J. T. (1980) *Competition in the Open Economy: a Model applied to Canada.* Cambridge, Mass.: Harvard University Press.

Chamberlin, E. H. (1966) *The Theory of Monopolistic Competition* (8th edn). Cambridge, Mass.: Harvard University Press.

Clarke, R. (1983) 'On the specification of structure–performance relationships: a comment', *European Economic Review*, **23**, 253–6.

Clarke, R. (1984) 'Profit margins and market concentration in UK manufacturing industry: 1970–6', *Applied Economics*, **16**, 57–71.

Clarke, R. and Davies, S. W. (1982) 'Market structure and price–cost margins', *Economica*, n.s., **49**, 277–87.

Clarke, R. and Davies, S. W. (1983) 'Aggregate concentration, market concentration and diversification', *Economic Journal*, **93**, 182–92.

Clarke, R., Davies, S. W. and Waterson, M. (1984) 'The profitability–concentration relation: market power or efficiency?' *Journal of Industrial Economics*, **32**, 435–50.

Coase, R. H. (1937) 'The nature of the firm', *Economica*, n.s., **4**, 386–405; reprinted in Stigler and Boulding (1960).

Collins, N. R. and Preston, L. E. (1968) *Concentration and Price–Cost Margins in Manufacturing Industries.* Berkeley: University of California Press.

Collins, N. R. and Preston, L. E. (1969) 'Price–cost margins and industry structure', *Review of Economics and Statistics*, **51**, 271–86.

Comanor, W. S. (1967a) 'Market structure, product differentiation and industrial research', *Quarterly Journal of Economics*, **81**, 639–57.

Comanor, W. S. (1967b) 'Vertical mergers, market power and the antitrust laws', *American Economic Review*, Papers and Proceedings, **57**, 254–65; with discussion by McGee, 269–71.

Comanor, W. S. and Leibenstein, H. (1969) 'Allocative efficiency, *X*-efficiency and the measurement of welfare losses', *Economica*, n.s., **36**, 304–9.

Comanor, W. S. and Wilson, T. A. (1967) 'Advertising, market structure and performance', *Review of Economics and Statistics*, **49**, 423–40.

Comanor, W. S. and Wilson, T. A. (1974) *Advertising and Market Power.* Cambridge, Mass.: Harvard University Press.

Comanor, W. S. and Wilson, T. A. (1979) 'The effect of advertising on competition: a survey', *Journal of Economic Literature*, **17**, 453–76.

Comanor, W. S. and Wilson, T. A. (1980) 'On the economics of advertising: a reply to Bloch and Simon', *Journal of Economic Literature*, **18**, 1075–8.

Cosh, A., Hughes, A. and Singh, A. (1980) 'The causes and effects of takeovers in the United Kingdom', in D. C. Mueller (ed.), *The Determinants and Effects of Mergers.* Cambridge, Mass.: Delgeschlager, Gunn and Hain.

Cournot, A. A. (1960) *Researches into the Mathematical Principles of the Theory of Wealth* (1838), trans. N. T. Bacon. New York: Augustus Kelley.

Cowell, F. A. (1977) *Measuring Inequality.* Oxford: Philip Allan.

Cowling, K. (1978) 'Monopolies and Mergers Policy: a view on the Green Paper', Economic Research Paper no. 139, Warwick University.

Cowling, K. and Mueller, D. C. (1978) 'The social costs of monopoly power', *Economic Journal*, **88**, 727–48.

Cowling, K. and Mueller, D. C. (1981) 'The social costs of monopoly power revisited', *Economic Journal*, **91**, 721–5.

Cowling, K. and Waterson, M. (1976) 'Price–cost margins and market structure', *Economica*, n.s., **43**, 267–74.

Cowling, K. *et al.* (1980) *Mergers and Economic Performance.* Cambridge: Cambridge University Press.

Cox, S. R. (1982) 'Some evidence on the early price effects of attorney advertising in the USA', *Journal of Advertising*, **1**, 321–31.

Cubbin, J. (1981) 'Advertising and the theory of entry barriers', *Economica*, n.s., **48**, 489–98.

Curry, B. and George, K. D. (1983) 'Industrial concentration: a survey', *Journal of Industrial Economics*, **31**, 203–55.

Cyert, R. M. and de Groot, M. H. (1973) 'An analysis of cooperation and learning in a duopoly context', *American Economic Review*, **63**, 24–37.

Dasgupta, P. and Stiglitz, J. (1980) 'Industrial structure and the nature of innovative activity', *Economic Journal*, **90**, 266–93.

Davies, S. W. (1979a) *The Diffusion of Process Innovations.* Cambridge: Cambridge University Press.

Davies, S. W. (1979b) 'Choosing between concentration indices: the iso-concentration curve', *Economica*, **46**, 67–75.

Davies, S. W. (1980a) 'Measuring industrial concentration: an alternative approach', *Review of Economics and Statistics*, **62**, 306–9.

Davies, S. W. (1980b) 'Minimum efficient size and seller concentration: an empirical problem', *Journal of Industrial Economics*, **28**, 287–301.

Davies, S. W. and Lyons, B. R. (1982) 'Seller concentration: the technological explanation and demand uncertainty', *Economic Journal*, **92**, 903–19.

Demsetz, H. (1969) 'Information and efficiency: another viewpoint', *Journal of Law and Economics*, **12**, 1–22; reprinted in Lamberton (1971).

Demsetz, H. (1973a) *The Market Concentration Doctrine.* AEI-Hoover Policy Studies.

Demsetz, H. (1973b) 'Industry structure, market rivalry and public policy', *Journal of Law and Economics*, **16**, 1–9.

Demsetz, H. (1974) 'Two systems of belief about monopoly', in Goldschmid *et al.* (1974).

Demsetz, H. (1982) 'Barriers to entry', *American Economic Review*, **72**, 47–57.

Dixit, A. (1979) 'A model of duopoly suggesting a theory of entry barriers', *Bell Journal of Economics*, **10**, 20–32.

Dixit, A. (1980) 'The role of investment in entry-deterrence', *Economic Journal*, **90**, 95–106.

Dixit, A. (1982) 'Recent developments in oligopoly theory', *American Economic Review*, Papers and Proceedings, **72**, 12–17.

Dixit, A. and Norman, V. (1978) 'Advertising and welfare', *Bell Journal of Economics*, **9**, 1–17.

Dixit, A. and Stern, N. (1982) 'Oligopoly and welfare: a unified presentation with applications to trade and development', *European Economic Review*, **19**, 123–44.

Dolbear, F. T. *et al.* (1968) 'Collusion in oligopoly: an experiment on the effect of numbers and information', *Quarterly Journal of Economics*, **82**, 240–59.

Dorfman, R. and Steiner, P. O. (1954) 'Optimal advertising and optimal quality', *American Economic Review*, **44**, 826–36.

Edgeworth, F. Y. (1925) 'The pure theory of monopoly' (1897); reprinted in F. Y. Edgeworth, *Papers Relating to Political Economy*, vol. 1. London: Macmillan.

Elliott, D. C. and Gribbin, J. D. (1977) 'The abolition of cartels and structural change in the United Kingdom', in Jacquemin and de Jong (1977b).

Firth, M. (1979) 'The profitability of takeovers and mergers', *Economic Journal*, **89**, 316–28.

Fisher, F. M. and McGowan, J. J. (1979) 'Advertising and welfare: comment', *Bell Journal of Economics*, **10**, 726–9 (including reply by Dixit and Norman).

Flaherty, M. T. (1981) 'Prices versus quantities and vertical financial integration', *Bell Journal of Economics*, **12**, 507–25.

Fog, B. (1956) 'How are cartel prices determined?' *Journal of Industrial Economics*, **5**, 16–23.

Fouraker, L. E. and Siegel, S. (1963) *Bargaining Behaviour*. New York: McGraw-Hill.

Fox, E. M. (1982) 'The new merger guidelines – a blueprint for microeconomic analysis', *Antitrust Bulletin*, **27**, 519–91.

Fraas, A. G. and Greer, D. F. (1977) 'Market structure and price collusion: an empirical analysis', *Journal of Industrial Economics*, **26**, 21–44.

Friedman, J. W. (1977) *Oligopoly and the Theory of Games*. Amsterdam: North Holland.

Friedman, J. W. (1983) *Oligopoly Theory*. Cambridge: Cambridge University Press.

Galbraith, J. K. (1963) *American Capitalism*. Harmondsworth: Penguin.

Gale, B. T. and Branch, B. S. (1982) 'Concentration versus market share: which determines performance and why does it matter?' *Antitrust Bulletin*, **27**, 83–105.

Gaskins, D. W. Jr (1971) 'Dynamic limit pricing: optimal pricing under threat of entry', *Journal of Economic Theory*, **3**, 306–22.

George, K. D. and Joll, C. L. (eds) (1975) *Competition Policy in the UK and EEC*. Cambridge: Cambridge University Press.

Geroski, P. (1981) 'Specification and testing the profits–concentration relationship: some experiments for the UK', *Economica*, n.s., **48**, 279–88.

Geroski, P. (1982) 'Simultaneous equations models of the structure–performance paradigm', *European Economic Review*, **19**, 145–58.

Gibrat, R. (1931) *Les Inegalities Economiques*. Paris: Sirey.

Gilbert, R. J. and Newbery, D. M. G. (1982) 'Pre-emptive patenting and the persistence of monopoly', *American Economic Review*, **72**, 514–26.

Goldschmid, H. D., Mann, H. M. and Weston, J. F. (eds) (1974) *Industrial Concentration: the New Learning*. Boston: Little, Brown.

Gorecki, P. K. (1975) 'An inter-industry analysis of diversification in the UK manufacturing sector', *Journal of Industrial Economics*, **24**, 131–46.

Gort, M. (1962) *Diversification and Integration in American Industry*. Princeton: Princeton University Press.

Goudie, A. W. and Meeks, G. (1982) 'Diversification by merger', *Economica*, n.s., **49**, 447–59.

Grabowski, H. G. (1968) 'The determinants of industrial research and development: a study of the chemical, drug and petroleum industries', *Journal of Political Economy*, **76**, 292–306; reprinted in Yamey (1973).

Grant, R. M. (1977) 'The determinants of the inter-industry pattern of diversification by UK manufacturing enterprises', *Bulletin of Economic Research*, **29**, 84–95.

Gravelle, H. and Rees, R. (1981) *Microeconomics*. London: Longman.

Green Paper (1978) *A Review of Monopolies and Mergers Policy*, Cmnd 7198. London: HMSO.

Green Paper (1979) *A Review of Restrictive Trade Practices Policy*, Cmnd 7512. London: HMSO.

Greenhut, M. L. and Ohta, H. (1976) 'Related market conditions and interindustrial mergers', *American Economic Review*, **66**, 267–77.

Grether, E. T. (1970) 'Industrial organisation: past history and future problems', *American Economic Review*, Papers and Proceedings, **60**, 83–9.

Hall, M. and Tideman, N. (1967) 'Measures of concentration', *Journal of the American Statistical Association*, **62**, 162–8.

Hall, R. L. and Hitch, C. J. (1939) 'Price theory and business behaviour', *Oxford Economic Papers*, **2**, 12–45; reprinted in Wilson and Andrews (1951).

Halpern, P. J. (1973) 'Empirical estimates of the amount and distribution of gains to companies in mergers', *Journal of Business*, **46**, 554–75.

Hannah, L. and Kay, J. A. (1977) *Concentration in Modern Industry*. London: Macmillan.

Harberger, A. C. (1954) 'Monopoly and resource allocation', *American Economic Review*, Papers and Proceedings, **44**, 77–87.

Haring, J. R. and Kaserman, D. L. (1978) 'Related market conditions and interindustrial mergers: comment', *American Economic Review*, **68**, 225–7.

Hart, P. E. (1971) 'Entropy and other measures of concentration', *Journal of the Royal Statistical Society*, series A, **134**, 73–85.

Hart, P. E. (1975) 'Moment distributions in economics: an exposition', *Journal of the Royal Statistical Society*, series A, **138**, 423–34.

Hart, P. E. and Clarke, R. (1980) *Concentration in British Industry: 1935–75*. Cambridge: Cambridge University Press.

Hart, P. E. and Morgan, E. (1977) 'Market structure and economic performance in the United Kingdom', *Journal of Industrial Economics*, **25**, 177–93.

Hart, P. E. and Prais, S. J. (1956) 'The analysis of business concentration: a statistical approach', *Journal of the Royal Statistical Society*, series A, **119**, 150–91.

Hassid, J. (1975) 'Recent evidence on conglomerate diversification in UK manufacturing industry', *Manchester School*, **43**, 372–95.

Hay, D. A. (1976) 'Sequential entry and entry-deterring strategies in spatial competition', *Oxford Economic Papers*, **28**, 240–57.

Hay, D. A. and Morris, D. J. (1979) *Industrial Economics: Theory and Evidence*. Oxford: Oxford University Press.

Hay, G. A. (1973) 'An economic analysis of vertical integration', *Industrial Organisation Review*, **1**, 188–98.

Hay, G. A. and Kelley, D. (1974) 'An empirical survey of price fixing conspiracies', *Journal of Law and Economics*, **17**, 13–38.

Heath, J. B. (1961) 'Restrictive practices and after', *Manchester School*, **29**, 173–202.

Herfindahl, O. C. (1950) *Concentration in the US Steel Industry*. PhD thesis, Columbia University.

Hewer, A. (1980) 'Manufacturing industry in the seventies: an assessment of import penetration and export performance', *Economic Trends*, no. 320, pp. 97–109.

Hirschman, A. O. (1945) *National Power and the Structure of Foreign Trade*. Berkeley: University of California Press.

Hirschman, A. O. (1964) 'The paternity of an index', *American Economic Review*, **54**, 761–2.

Hirshleifer, J. (1980) *Price Theory and Applications* (2nd edn). Hemel Hempstead: Prentice-Hall International.

Hitiris, T. (1978) 'Effective protection and economic performance in UK manufacturing industry, 1963 and 1968', *Economic Journal*, **88**, 107–20.

Holtermann, S. E. (1973) 'Market structure and economic performance in UK manufacturing industry', *Journal of Industrial Economics*, **21**, 119–39.

Hotelling, H. (1929) 'Stability in competition', *Economic Journal*, **39**, 41–57.

Ijiri, Y. and Simon, H. A. (1977) *Skew Distributions and the Size of Business Firms*. Amsterdam: North Holland.

Jacquemin, A. P. and Berry, C. H. (1979) 'Entropy measure of diversification and corporate growth', *Journal of Industrial Economics*, **27**, 359–69.

Jacquemin, A. P. and de Jong, H. W. (1977a) *European Industrial Organisation*. London: Macmillan.

Jacquemin, A. P. and de Jong, H. W. (eds) (1977b) *Welfare Aspects of Industrial Markets*. Leiden: Martinus Nijhoff.

Kaldor, N. (1950) 'Economic aspects of advertising', *Review of Economic Studies*, **58**, 1–27.

Kamerschen, D. R. (1966) 'An estimation of the "welfare losses" from monopoly in the American economy', *Western Economic Journal*, **4**, 221–36.

Kamien, M. I. and Schwartz, N. L. (1982) *Market Structure and Innovation*. Cambridge: Cambridge University Press.

Kamien, M. I. and Schwartz, N. L. (1983) 'Conjectural variations', *Canadian Journal of Economics*, **16**, 191–211.

Kaserman, D. L. (1978) 'Theories of vertical integration: implications for antitrust policy', *Antitrust Bulletin*, **23**, 483–510.

Katowitz, Y. and Mathewson, F. (1979) 'Advertising, consumer information and product quality', *Bell Journal of Economics*, **10**, 566–88.

Kay, J. A. (1983) 'A general equilibrium approach to the measurement of monopoly welfare loss', *International Journal of Industrial Organisation*, **1**, 317–31.

Khalilzadeh-Shirazi, J. (1974) 'Market structure and price–cost margins in UK manufacturing industries', *Review of Economics and Statistics*, **54**, 64–76.

Kilpatrick, R. W. (1968) 'Stigler on the relationship between industry profit rates and market concentration', *Journal of Political Economy*, **76**, 479–88.

Koutsoyiannis, A. (1975) *Modern Microeconomics*. London: Macmillan.

Lamberton, D. M. (ed.) (1971) *Economics of Information and Knowledge*. Harmondsworth: Penguin.

Lancaster, K. (1979) *Variety, Equity and Efficiency*. Oxford: Basil Blackwell.

Leak, H. and Maizels, A. (1945) 'The structure of British industry', *Journal of the Royal Statistical Society*, series A, **108**, 142–99.

Leibenstein, H. (1966) 'Allocative efficiency vs. "X-efficiency"', *American Economic Review*, **56**, 392–415.

Lerner, A. P. (1934) 'The concept of monopoly and the measurement of monopoly power', *Review of Economic Studies*, **1**, 157–75.

Levy, H. and Sarnat, M. (1970) 'Diversification, portfolio analysis and the uneasy case for conglomerate mergers', *Journal of Finance*, **25**, 795–802.

Lewellen, W. G. (1971) 'A pure financial rationale for the conglomerate merger', *Journal of Finance*, **26**, 521–37.

Lipsey, R. and Lancaster, K. (1956/7) 'The general theory of the second best', *Review of Economic Studies*, **24**, 11–32.

Littlechild, S. C. (1978) *The Fallacy of the Mixed Economy*, Hobart Paper no. 80. London: Institute of Economic Affairs.

Littlechild, S. C. (1981) 'Misleading calculations of the social costs of monopoly power', *Economic Journal*, **91**, 348–63.

Loeb, P. D. and Lin, V. (1977) 'Research and development in the pharmaceutical industry–a specification error approach', *Journal of Industrial Economics*, **26**, 45–51.

Lowes, B. and Pass, C. L. (1970) 'Price behaviour in asymmetrical duopoly: some experimental observations', *Manchester School of Economic and Social Studies*, **38**, 29–43.

Lustgarten, S. (1979) 'Gains and losses from concentration: a comment', *Journal of Law and Economics*, **22**, 183–90.

Lyons, B. R. (1980) 'A new measure of minimum efficient plant size in UK manufacturing industry', *Economica*, **47**, 19–34.

Lyons, B. R. (1981) 'Price–cost margins, market structure and international trade', in D. Currie, D. Peel and W. Peters (eds), *Microeconomic Analysis*. London: Croom Helm.

Lyons, B. R., Kitchen, P. D. and Hitiris, T. (1979) 'Effective protection and economic performance in UK manufacturing industry, 1963 and 1968: an interchange', *Economic Journal*, **89**, 926–41.

Machlup, F. and Taber, M. (1960) 'Bilateral monopoly, successive monopoly and vertical integration', *Economica*, n.s., **27**, 101–19; reprinted in Yamey (1973).

Maddala, G. S. (1977) *Econometrics*. Tokyo: McGraw-Hill Kogakusha.

Mallela, P. and Nahata, B. (1980) 'Theory of vertical control with variable proportions', *Journal of Political Economy*, **88**, 1009–25.

Mann, H. M. (1966) 'Seller concentration, barriers to entry, and rates of return in thirty industries, 1950–60', *Review of Economics and Statistics*, **48**, 296–307.

Mann, H. M. (1974) 'Advertising, concentration and profitability: the state of knowledge and directions for public policy', in Goldschmid *et al.* (1974).

Mansfield, E. (1961) 'Technical change and the rate of imitation', *Econometrica*, **29**, 741–66; reprinted in E. Mansfield (1968), *Industrial Research and Technological Innovation*. New York: W. W. Norton.

Marfels, C. (1971) 'Absolute and relative measures of concentration reconsidered', *Kyklos*, **24**, 753–66.

Martin, S. (1979) 'Advertising, concentration and profitability: the simultaneity problem', *Bell Journal of Economics*, **10**, 639–47.

Martin, S. (1984) 'Comment on the specification of structure–performance relationships', *European Economic Review*, **24**, 197–201.

Mason, E. S. (1939) 'Price and production policies of large-scale enterprise', *American Economic Review*, supplement, **29**, 61–74.

Mason, E. S. (1957) *Economic Concentration and the Monopoly Problem*. Cambridge, Mass.: Harvard University Press.

Masson, R. T. and Shaanan, J. (1984) 'Social costs of oligopoly and the value of competition', *Economic Journal*, **94**, 520–35.

McGee, J. S. (1958) 'Predatory price cutting: the Standard Oil (NJ) case', *Journal of Law and Economics*, **1**, 137–69.

McGee, J. S. (1980) 'Predatory pricing revisited', *Journal of Law and Economics*, **23**, 289–330.

McGee, J. S. and Bassett, L. R. (1976) 'Vertical integration revisited', *Journal of Law and Economics*, **19**, 17–38.

McKinnon, R. I. (1966) 'Stigler's theory of oligopoly: a comment', *Journal of Political Economy*, **74**, 281–5.

Meeks, G. (1977) *Disappointing Marriage: a Study of the Gains from Merger*. Cambridge: Cambridge University Press.

Miller, M. H. (1977) 'Debt and taxes', *Journal of Finance*, **32**, 261–76.

Miller, R. A. (1969) 'Market structure and industrial performance: relation of profit rate to concentration, advertising intensity, and diversity', *Journal of Industrial Economics*, **17**, 104–18.

Miller, R. A. (1971) 'Marginal concentration ratios as market structure variables', *Review of Economics and Statistics*, **53**, 289–93.

Miller, R. A. (1982) 'The Herfindahl–Hirschman index as a market structure variable: an exposition for antitrust practitioners', *Antitrust Bulletin*, **27**, 593–618.

Modigliani, F. (1958) 'New developments on the oligopoly front', *Journal of Political Economy*, **66**, 215–32.

Monopolies Commission (1966) *A Report on the Supply of Household Detergents*. London: HMSO.

Monopolies Commission (1968) *Man-made Cellulosic Fibres*. London: HMSO.

Monopolies Commission (1969) *Beer*. London: HMSO.

Monopolies Commission (1973a) *A Report on the Supply of Ready Cooked Breakfast Cereal Foods*. London: HMSO.

Monopolies Commission (1973b) *A Report on the General Effect on the Public Interest of the Practice of Parallel Pricing*. London: HMSO.

Monopolies and Mergers Commission (1977) *Cat and Dog Foods*, HC447. London: HMSO.

Monopolies and Mergers Commission (1981a) *Full-line Forcing and Tie-in Sales*. London: HMSO.

Monopolies and Mergers Commission (1981b) *Discounts to Retailers*. London: HMSO.

Mueller, W. F. and Hamm, L. G. (1974) 'Trends in industrial market concentration: 1947 to 1970', *Review of Economics and Statistics*, **56**, 511–20.

Mueller, W. F. and Rogers, R. T. (1980) 'The role of advertising in changing concentration of manufacturing industries', *Review of Economics and Statistics*, **62**, 89–96.

Murphy, J. L. (1966) 'Effects of the threat of losses on duopoly bargaining'. *Quarterly Journal of Economics*, **80**, 296–313.

Neale, A. D. and Goyder, D. G. (1980) *The Antitrust Laws of the USA* (3rd edn). Cambridge: Cambridge University Press.

Nelson, P. (1970) 'Information and consumer behaviour', *Journal of Political Economy*, **78**, 311–29.

Nelson, P. (1974) 'Advertising as information', *Journal of Political Economy*, **82**, 729–54.

Nerlove, M. and Arrow, K. J. (1962) 'Optimal advertising policy under dynamic conditions', *Economica*, **29**, 129–42.

Nickell, S. and Metcalf, D. (1978) 'Monopolistic industries and monopoly profits; or, are Kellogg's cornflakes overpriced? *Economic Journal*, **88**, 254–68.

O'Brien, D. P., Howe, W. S. and Wright, D. M., with O'Brien, R. J. (1979) *Competition Policy, Profitability and Growth*. London: Macmillan.

Oi, W. Y. and Hurter, A. P. Jr (1973) 'A theory of vertical integration in road transport services', in *Economics of Industrial Structure*, edited by B. S. Yamey. Harmondsworth: Penguin.

Ornstein, S. I. (1977) *Industrial Concentration and Advertising Intensity*. Washington, DC: American Enterprise Institute for Public Policy Research.

Pagoulatos, E. and Sorenson, R. (1980/1) 'A simultaneous equation analysis of advertising, concentration and profitability', *Southern Economic Journal*, **47**, 728–41.

Parish, R. M. and Ng, Y. K. (1972) 'Monopoly, X-efficiency and the measurement of welfare loss', *Economica*, n.s., **39**, 301–8.

Pautler, P. A. (1983) 'A review of the economic basis for broad-based horizontal-merger policy', *Antitrust Bulletin*, **28**, 571–651.

Peles, Y. (1971) 'Rates of amortization of advertising expenditures', *Journal of Political Economy*, **79**, 1032–58.

Peltzman, S. (1977) 'The gains and losses from industrial concentration', *Journal of Law and Economics*, **20**, 229–63.

Peltzman, S. (1979) 'The causes and consequences of rising industrial concentration: a reply', *Journal of Law and Economics*, **22**, 209–11.

Perry, M. K. (1978) 'Related market conditions and interindustrial mergers: comment', *American Economic Review*, **68**, 221–4.

Perry, M. K. (1982) 'Oligopoly and consistent conjectural variations', *Bell Journal of Economics*, **13**, 197–202.

Phillips, A. (1972) 'An econometric study of price-fixing, market structure and performance in British industry in the early 1950s', in K. Cowling (ed.), *Market Structure and Corporate Behaviour*. London: Gray-Mills.

Pickering, J. F. (1974) *Industrial Structure and Market Conduct*. Oxford: Martin Robertson.

Porter, M. E. (1974) 'Consumer behaviour, retailer power and market performance in consumer goods industries', *Review of Economics and Statistics*, **56**, 419–36.

Porter, M. E. (1976) *Interbrand Choice, Strategy and Bilateral Market Power*. Cambridge, Mass.: Harvard University Press.

Posner, R. A. (1970) 'A statistical study of antitrust enforcement', *Journal of Law and Economics*, **13**, 365–419.

Posner, R. A. (1975) 'The social costs of monopoly and regulation', *Journal of Political Economy*, **83**, 807–27.

Posner, R. A. (1979) 'The Chicago school of antitrust analysis', *University of Pennsylvania Law Review*, **127**, 925–48.

Prais, S. J. (1976) *The Evolution of Giant Firms in Britain*. Cambridge: Cambridge University Press.

Pratten, C. F. (1971) *Economies of Scale in Manufacturing Industry*. Cambridge: Cambridge University Press.

Primeaux, W. J. and Bomball, M. R. (1974) 'A re-examination of the kinky oligopoly demand curve', *Journal of Political Economy*, **82**, 851–62.

Primeaux, W. J. and Smith, M. C. (1976) 'Pricing patterns and the kinky demand curve', *Journal of Law and Economics*, **19**, 189–99.

Reekie, W. D. (1975) 'Advertising and market structure: another approach', *Economic Journal*, **85**, 156–64.

Reekie, W. D. (1979) *Industry, Prices and Markets*. New York: John Wiley.

Rees, R. D. (1975) 'Advertising, concentration and competition: a comment and further results', *Economic Journal*, **85**, 165–72.

Rhoades, S. A. (1973) 'The effect of diversification on industry profit performance in 241 manufacturing industries: 1963', *Review of Economics and Statistics*, **55**, 146–55.

Rhoades, S. A. (1974) 'A further evaluation of the effect of diversification on industry profit performance', *Review of Economics and Statistics*, **56**, 557–9.

Richardson, G. B. (1972) 'The organisation of industry', *Economic Journal*, **82**, 883–96.

Romeo, A. A. (1975) 'Interindustry and interfirm differences in the rate of diffusion of an innovation', *Review of Economics and Statistics*, **57**, 311–19.

Romeo, A. A. (1977) 'Rate of imitation of a capital-embodied process innovation', *Economica*, n.s., **44**, 63–9.

Rosenberg, J. B. (1976) 'Research and market share: a reappraisal of the Schumpeter hypothesis', *Journal of Industrial Economics*, **25**, 101–12.

Ross, P. (1968) 'Economies as an antitrust defence: comment', *American Economic Review*, **58**, 1371–2.

Saving, T. R. (1970) 'Concentration ratios and the degree of monopoly', *International Economic Review*, **11**, 139–46.

Sawyer, M. C. (1982) 'On the specification of structure–performance relationships', *European Economic Review*, **17**, 295–306.

Sawyer, M. C. (1983) 'On the specification of structure–performance relationships: a reply', *European Economic Review*, **23**, 257–9.

Schelling, T. (1960) *The Strategy of Conflict*. Cambridge, Mass.: Harvard University Press.

Scherer, F. M. (1965a) 'Size of firm, oligopoly and research: a comment', *Canadian Journal of Economics and Political Science*, **31**, 256–66.

Scherer, F. M. (1965b) 'Firm size, market structure, opportunity, and the output of patented inventions', *American Economic Review*, **55**, 1097–1125.

Scherer, F. M. (1967) 'Market structure and the employment of scientists and engineers', *American Economic Review*, **57**, 524–31.

Scherer, F. M. (1976) 'Predatory pricing and the Sherman Act: a comment', *Harvard Law Review*, **89**, 869–90.

Scherer, F. M. (1979a) 'The causes and consequences of rising industrial concentration', *Journal of Law and Economics*, **22**, 191–208.

Scherer, F. M. (1979b) 'The welfare economics of product variety: an application to the ready-to-eat cereals industry', *Journal of Industrial Economics*, **28**, 113–34.

Scherer, F. M. (1980) *Industrial Market Structure and Economic Performance* (2nd edn). Chicago: Rand McNally.

Schmalensee, R. (1972) *The Economics of Advertising*. Amsterdam: North Holland.

Schmalensee, R. (1973) 'A note on the theory of vertical integration', *Journal of Political Economy*, **81**, 442–9.

Schmalensee, R. (1978) 'Entry deterrence in the ready-to-eat breakfast cereal industry', *Bell Journal of Economics*, **9**, 305–27.

Schmalensee, R. (1981) 'Economies of scale and barriers to entry', *Journal of Political Economy*, **89**, 1228–38.

Schumpeter, J. A. (1965) *Capitalism, Socialism and Democracy*. London: George Allen and Unwin.

Schwartzman, D. (1960) 'The burden of monopoly', *Journal of Political Economy*, **68**, 627–30.

Seade, J. (1980) 'On the effects of entry', *Econometrica*, **48**, 479–89

Shapiro, C. (1980) 'Advertising and welfare: comment', *Bell Journal of Economics*, **11**, 749–54 (including reply by Dixit and Norman).

Shepherd, W. G. (1972) 'Structure and behaviour in British industries, with US comparisons', *Journal of Industrial Economics*, **20**, 35–54.

Sherman, R. (1972) 'How tax policy induces conglomerate mergers', *National Tax Journal*, **25**, 521–9.

Shrieves, R. E. (1978) 'Market structure and innovation: a new perspective'. *Journal of Industrial Economics*, **26**, 329–47.

Shubik, M. (1980) *Market Structure and Behaviour*. Cambridge, Mass.: Harvard University Press.

Silberston, A. (1972) 'Economies of scale in theory and practice', *Economic Journal*, supplement, **82**, 369–91.

Simon, H. A. and Bonini, C. P. (1958) 'The size distribution of business firms', *American Economic Review*, **48**, 607–17.

Simon, J. L. (1969) 'A further test of the kinky oligopoly demand curve', *American Economic Review*, **59**, 971–5.

Simon, J. L. (1980) 'On firm size and advertising efficiency: a comment'. *Journal of Economic Literature*, **18**, 1066–75.

Singer, E. M. (1968) *Antitrust Economics*. Englewood Cliffs, NJ: Prentice-Hall.

Singh, A. (1971) *Takeovers*. Cambridge: Cambridge University Press.

Smith, A. (1970) *The Wealth of Nations* (1776). Harmondsworth: Penguin.

Spence, A. M. (1977) 'Entry, capacity, investment and oligopolistic pricing', *Bell Journal of Economics*, **8**, 534–44.

Spence, A. M. (1983) 'Contestable markets and the theory of industry structure: a review article', *Journal of Economic Literature*, **21**, 981–90.

Spulber, D. (1981) 'Capacity, output and sequential entry', *American Economic Review*, **71**, 503–14.

Stackelberg, H. von (1952) *The Theory of the Market Economy* (1934), trans. A. T. Peacock. London: William Hodge.

Steiner, P. O. (1966) 'Comment', *American Economic Review*, Papers and Proceedings, **56**, 472–5.

Steiner, R. L. (1973) 'Does advertising lower consumer prices?', *Journal of Marketing*, **37**, 19–26.

Stevens, R. B. and Yamey, B. S. (1965) *The Restrictive Practices Court: A Study of the Judicial Process and Economic Policy*. London: Weidenfeld and Nicolson.

Stigler, G. J. (1947) 'The kinky oligopoly demand curve and rigid prices', *Journal of Political Economy*, **55**, 432–49; reprinted in Stigler and Boulding (1960).

Stigler, G. J. (1951) 'The division of labour is limited by the extent of the market', *Journal of Political Economy*, **59**, 185–93; reprinted in Stigler (1968).

Stigler, G. J. (1956) 'The statistics of monopoly and merger', *Journal of Political Economy*, **64**, 33–40.

Stigler, G. J. (1961) 'The economics of information', *Journal of Political Economy*, **69**, 213–25.

Stigler, G. J. (1963) *Capital and Rates of Return in Manufacturing Industries*. Princeton: Princeton University Press.

Stigler, G. J. (1964) 'A theory of oligopoly', *Journal of Political Economy*, **72**, 44–61; reprinted in Stigler (1968).

Stigler, G. J. (1968) *The Organisation of Industry*. Homewood, Illinois: Irwin.

Stigler, G. J. (1978) 'The literature of economics: the case of the kinky oligopoly demand curve', *Economic Inquiry*, **16**, 185–204.

Stigler, G. J. and Boulding, K. E. (eds) (1960) *Readings in Price Theory.* London: George Allen and Unwin.

Strickland, A. D. and Weiss, L. W. (1976) 'Advertising, concentration and price–cost margins', *Journal of Political Economy,* **84**, 1109–21.

Sutherland, A. (1970) *The Monopolies Commission in Action.* Cambridge: Cambridge University Press.

Sutton, C. J. (1974) 'Advertising, concentration and competition', *Economic Journal,* **84**, 56–69.

Swann, D. (1979) *Competition and Consumer Protection.* Harmondsworth: Penguin.

Swann, D. (1983) *Competition and Industrial Policy in the European Community.* London: Methuen.

Swann, D., O'Brien, D. P., Maunder, W. P. and Howe, W. S. (1974) *Competition in British Industry.* London: George Allen and Unwin.

Sweezy, P. M. (1939) 'Demand under conditions of oligopoly', *Journal of Political Economy,* **47**, 568–73; reprinted in Stigler and Boulding (1960).

Sylos-Labini, P. (1962) *Oligopoly and Technical Progress.* Cambridge, Mass.: Harvard University Press.

Taylor, C. T. and Silberston, Z. A. (1973) *The Economic Impact of the Patent System: a Study of the British Experience.* Cambridge: Cambridge University Press.

Telser, L. G. (1966) 'Supply and demand for advertising messages', *American Economic Review,* Papers and Proceedings, **56**, 457–66.

Tollison, R. D. (1983) 'Antitrust in the Reagan administration: a report from the belly of the beast', *International Journal of Industrial Organisation,* **1**, 211–21.

Tullock, G. (1967) 'The welfare costs of tariffs, monopolies and theft', *Western Economic Journal,* **5**, 224–32.

Ulph, D. (1983) 'Rational conjectures in oligopoly theory', *International Journal of Industrial Organisation,* **1**, 131–54.

Utton, M. A. (1975) 'British merger policy', in George and Joll (1975).

Utton, M. A. (1979) *Diversification and Competition.* Cambridge: Cambridge University Press.

Utton, M. A. (1982) 'Domestic concentration and international trade', *Oxford Economic Papers,* **34**, 479–97.

Vernon, J. M. and Graham, D. A. (1971) 'Profitability of monopolisation by vertical integration', *Journal of Political Economy,* **79**, 924–5; reprinted in Yamey (1973).

von Neumann, J. and Morgenstern, O. (1944) *The Theory of Games and Economic Behaviour.* Princeton: Princeton University Press.

Warren-Boulton, F. R. (1974) 'Vertical control with variable proportions', *Journal of Political Economy,* **82**, 783–802.

Waterson, M. (1981) 'On the definition and meaning of barriers to entry', *Antitrust Bulletin,* **26**, 521–39.

Waterson, M. (1982a) 'The incentive to invent when a new input is involved', *Economica,* n.s., **49**, 435–45.

Waterson, M. (1982b) 'Vertical integration, variable proportions and oligopoly', *Economic Journal,* **92**, 129–44.

Waterson, M. J. (1982) 'Advertising expenditure in the UK: 1981 survey', *Journal of Advertising,* **1**, 261–72.

Weiss, L. W. (1963) 'Factors in changing concentration', *Review of Economics and Statistics,* **45**, 70–7; reprinted in Yamey (1973).

Weiss, L. W. (1969) 'Advertising, profits and corporate taxes', *Review of Economics and Statistics,* **51**, 421–30.

Weiss, L. W. (1971) 'Quantitative studies of industrial organisation', in M. D. Intriligator (ed.), *Frontiers of Quantitative Economics*. Amsterdam: North Holland.

Weiss, L. W. (1974) 'The concentration–profits relationship and antitrust' in Goldschmid *et al.* (1974).

Weiss, L. W. (1979) 'The structure–conduct–performance paradigm and antitrust', *University of Pennsylvania Law Review*, **127**, 1104–40.

Weston, J. F. (1970) 'The nature and significance of conglomerate firms', *St John's Law Review*, **44**, 66–80; reprinted in Yamey (1973).

Williamson, O. E. (1968a) 'Economies as an antitrust defense: the welfare trade-offs', *American Economic Review*, **58**, 18–31.

Williamson, O. E. (1968b) 'Economies as an antitrust defense: correction and reply', *American Economic Review*, **58**, 1372–6.

Williamson, O. E. (1971) 'The vertical integration of production: market failure considerations', *American Economic Review*, Papers and Proceedings, **61**, 112–23.

Williamson, O. E. (1973) 'Markets and hierarchies: some elementary considerations', *American Economic Review*, Papers and Proceedings, **63**, 316–25.

Williamson, O. E. (1975) *Markets and Hierarchies*. New York: Free Press.

Williamson, O. E. (1977) 'Economies as an antitrust defense revisited', in Jacquemin and de Jong (1977b).

Williamson, O. E. (1977/8) 'Predatory pricing: a strategic and welfare analysis', *Yale Law Journal*, **87**, 284–340.

Wilson, T. and Andrews, P. W. S. (eds) (1951) *Oxford Studies in the Price Mechanism*. Oxford: Clarendon Press.

Wolf, B. M. (1977) 'Industrial diversification and internationalisation: some empirical evidence', *Journal of Industrial Economics*, **26**, 177–91.

Wonnacott, T. H. and Wonnacott, R. J. (1972) *Introductory Statistics* (2nd edn). New York: John Wiley.

Worcester, D. A. Jr (1973) 'New estimates of the welfare loss to monopoly, United States: 1956–69', *Southern Economic Journal*, **40**, 234–45.

Yamey, B. S. (ed.) (1973) *Economics of Industrial Structure*. Harmondsworth: Penguin.

Index